THE WORLD AND MEN AROUND LUTHER

The World and Men Around Luther

By Walter G. Tillmanns

Illustrations by Edmund Kopietz

AUGSBURG PUBLISHING HOUSE

Minneapolis, Minnesota

THE WORLD AND MEN AROUND LUTHER
© 1959 Augsburg Publishing House
Library of Congress Catalog Card No. 59-11763

270.6
T577

Photograph insert pages are from the Schoenfeld Collection
from Three Lions, Inc.

41666

Manufactured in the United States of America

Students please note this is a very prejudiced and non-scholarly of the subject indicated by the title.
Graduates in the field of History would use it for comparison with such works as Grison's <u>father</u>.

To Verna

Preface

The story of the world and men around Luther presents a fascinating picture. In order to understand the Reformer and his work we must know the world in which he lived and the men with whom he had to deal. Thus, while during the last fifty years more Luther biographies have been written than in the preceding four hundred years, and while we have a better understanding of Luther's theology now than before 1900, very few of these volumes have introduced us to the world around Luther and fewer yet to the men in his life: those who influenced him or were influenced by him; those who followed him or opposed him; those who were in the center of the Reformation movement and those who were on the sidelines.

To fill this gap in the rich Luther literature the present volume has been written. It is not another Luther biography or another evaluation of Luther's theology. As a matter of fact, the reader will find very few biographical and theological data in these pages. Rather, it is an effort to bring together under one cover the world and the men around Luther, to show the magnitude of the Reformation in the sixteenth century, and to acquaint the reader with the powers and the personalities who helped shape—as friends or foes—the destinies of Christians not only during the decades of Luther's life, but in the centuries since.

As much as humanly possible an effort has been made to be fair to friend and foe alike. Strong Catholic partisans have been given the same kind treatment as strong Lutheran pillars. On the other hand, weaknesses have been pointed out where they occurred, both among friends and foes.

The work on the present volume was begun eight years ago when I wrote a number of articles on men around Luther for the *Lutheran Standard, The Lutheran,* and the *Concordia Theological Monthly.* After that I continued to collect biographical data wherever I could find them, until the Biographical Index contained over 600 names. The first part, The World Around Luther, may serve as an introduction to the lives of these men too. The twelve chapters of the second part, The Men Around Luther, aim to be as inclusive as possible without trying to give complete biographies and detailed accounts. The emphasis has been to weave all these men, Lutherans, other Protestants, Catholics, Princes and burghers, into the pattern of Luther's life.

My interest in Luther and Reformation research has been of long standing. At Heidelberg I studied under the late Walther Koehler, eminent Reformation scholar. Professor Rueckert was my teacher at Tuebingen. He is well known among Luther scholars. Georg Merz, editor of the Munich Edition of Luther's works, kept the interest alive at Bethel-Bielefeld, and the late Johann Michael Reu, trailblazer of American Luther research, was my professor at Wartburg Seminary, Dubuque, Iowa.

It is a pleasure to express my heartfelt thanks to the Reverend William H. Gentz, Book Editor of Augsburg Publishing House, for the encouragement which he has given to this project. Without his patient help the manuscript would not have been finished.

New Year's Day 1959.

WALTER G. TILLMANNS

Contents

xii CONTENTS

ILLUSTRATIONS

Insert between pages 24 and 25

Wycliffe sends out his translation of the Bible.
John Huss burned at the stake.
Savonarola preaches against luxury.
Pope Julius II and his court.

Insert between pages 48 and 49

Magellan lands in the Philippines.
Victory of Cortes over the Aztecs.
Vasco da Gama in Calcutta, India.
Balboa discovers the Pacific Ocean.
The "world" of Christopher Columbus.

Introduction

"The Reformation," said Wilhelm Scherer, eminent literary critic of the nineteenth century, "was Martin Luther. His will, his spiritual genius decided it. The many important men who had been trained by humanism and were connected with the Reformation, either had to follow Luther or they disappeared behind him."

This is the picture which the world has of Luther. While Zwingli and the numerous other reformers—with the possible exception of Calvin—attained only local importance, Luther's importance was universal. While Zwingli and others were often concerned merely with the externals of Church reform, the Reformation of Martin Luther went deep to the roots of the Christian faith. Beside the practical Swiss moral reformer there stands the uncompromising theologian from Wittenberg. Even Calvin admitted that he owed much to Luther. Luther's works brought him to faith, he celebrated Lutheran Communion in the grotto at Poitiers, he served a Lutheran congregation at Strassburg and signed the Lutheran Confessions. Besides Calvin scores of other great Christian leaders have paid homage to the Great Reformer, notably John Wesley who was converted while reading Luther's Preface to Romans. Thus Gustav Freytag—like Scherer, another outstanding secular scholar of the last century—admiringly said: "His picture has the remarkable quality of becoming bigger and more lovable the closer it is approached."

Yet Luther himself would insist, in the words of Julius Hare, the Anglican divine, that the work of the Reformation did not rest upon the work of Martin Luther, but on the Word of God alone. It was his work to bring this Word again into the center of Christian proclamation. His lasting influence rests on the fact that he was found a faithful servant of his Lord Jesus Christ. The willingness with which the Spanish and Italian martyrs died for their faith, the heroism with which the evangelical Christians in the Netherlands and many other countries fought for their faith, was not due to any loyalty to the man Luther. It was loyalty to the Christ whom Luther preached. The impact which the Lutheran movement made in France was not due to the number of Lutherans in that country—for they were few—but to the power of a faith based on the Gospel. Even today the influence of Luther's theology is strong in countries where there are few or almost no Lutherans, e.g., England.

Thus we see that the influence of Luther's Reformation does not necessarily depend upon the number of people who call themselves Lutherans. True, a strong Lutheran Church has helped to bring the Gospel to others. But apart from the Church there is still the powerful influence of the man Martin Luther. Catholics like Lortz and Adam, Schlegel and Taine, non-Lutheran Protestants like Rupp and Watson, Bainton and Fife, to mention just a few names from among hundreds, were not influenced by the strength of the Lutheran Church, but by the religious genius of the Wittenberg Reformer. In the opinion of many, Lutherans and non-Lutherans alike, Martin Luther stands before us as the greatest Christian thinker and the most powerful ambassador of Christ since the days of Saint Paul.

But this Luther was not a Saint above all saints, i.e., believers. He was a Christian, saved by Christ; a sinner, with all the sins that beset us; a man of strong convictions and weak moments, like us. He was above all a child of his time. Jorgensen, the Danish Luther scholar, pointed out that Luther shared the superstitions of his age. He not only believed in the existence of the devil, as orthodox Christians have done throughout the ages; he heard him and, perhaps, saw him. The story of the throwing of the inkwell at the devil while translating the New Testament at the Wartburg may be apocryphal, but it illustrates the point. He grew up in a home and in a community where people believed in the existence of witches and in the power of the "evil eye." Yet this same Luther cleansed the Church from unchristian ideas and practices which had crept in during the centuries before the Reformation.

Luther was also the product of the education of his times, of humanism and its cousin, the Renaissance. Although his appreciation of the arts and of literature was often limited to the godly use which he saw in them as tools for the proclamation of the Gospel, yet he showed great eagerness to master these tools. Thus the Renaissance which had almost succeeded in de-Christianizing the Western World was given new direction by the monk of Wittenberg who, in the angry words of Friedrich Nietzsche, destroyed the work of unbelieving scholars and led the world back to faith in Christ.

During Luther's lifetime the size of the known world more than doubled. The sun never set on the empire of Charles V. Never before in history, even in the greatest days of the empires of Alexander and Augustus, had this been true. Luther and his contemporaries lived in this world and changed with it. Into this changing world Luther brought the Gospel of Jesus Christ, "a sign that is spoken against . . . that thoughts out of many hearts may be revealed."

Thus the world and men around Luther are inseparable from the work of Martin Luther, which was the Reformation of the Church.

PART ONE

The World

Around Luther

I.

Luther's World

Luther was born in the Middle Ages and died in modern times.

In the year of our Lord 1483 Frederick III was emperor of the Holy Roman Empire, ruling most ineffectually in one of the longest reigns in history. Edward V, child king of England, was sent to the Tower of London by his uncle, the cynical Duke of Gloucester, who later, as Richard III, killed the unfortunate boy and his brother.

In Spain the Moors were defending their last strongholds against Ferdinand and Isabella who forged together Aragon and Castile into what was to become the first great power of modern times, Spain. In Italy, the rebirth of the world, the Renaissance, was in full bloom. In Sicily and Naples there ruled another Ferdinand,[1] one of the most unscrupulous Renaissance princes, a beast in the form of man. Florence was still experiencing its great bloom shortly before the doom under Savonarola. At that time Savonarola was still far away and Lorenzo il Magnifico, builder of edifices, and patron of arts, ruled in magnificent irresponsibility, while in Milan Ludovico Moro, protector of Leonardo da Vinci, was holding on to his precarious position. Sixtus IV was sitting on the throne of St. Peter, an unscrupulous nepotist who helped make the papacy odious to all nations.

3

The Turk and his cohorts were far away. But they were stirring. During this year 1483 the Great Turk, Bayazid II, conquered an unknown province called Herzogowina which was to serve him later as a jumping off place for the conquest of Hungary which ultimately brought the hordes of the infidels to the gates of Vienna. In the east Ivan III, also called The Great, was gobbling up territories for Russia, but no one paid attention to him except a few unhappy eastern potentates, too far away from the center of things to get effective help.

The attention of the world also was not focussed on a poor Italian adventurer, Christopher Columbus, who in this year appealed to King John II of Portugal to finance a proposed voyage to the west. He was considered a vain boaster without any scientific knowledge to back him up and his request was denied. However, Portugal and Spain were interested in conquests. In that year Diogo Cao reached the mouth of the Congo River and Cape St. Augustine.

The attention of the world was centered on France where a king with a strong ambition, but a weak mind, Charles VIII, ascended the throne. His ambition, to gain Italy for the French crown, kept France in turmoil for the next fifty and more years, kept the Empire occupied, too busy to deal with the man who was born in that year 1483, on November 10, shortly before midnight, and who was baptized on the next day in the St. Peter-Paul Church in Eisleben by Pastor Rennebecher, receiving the name Martin Luther. Sixty-four years later a Holy Roman Emperor, who was not even born at this time, had to acknowledge the frustration of his life when he was standing on the grave of the great Reformer and replied to the impatient Duke of Alba who wanted the bones of Luther disinterred and burned: "I fight against the living, but not against the dead!"[2]

In those sixty-four years the face of the world had changed. In 1484 Giovanni Cibo had become pope under the name of Innocent VIII—all but innocent, the first pope who dined with ladies in public and acknowledged his bastards. In 1485 the bloody Richard III had been defeated on Bosworth Field by Henry, Earl of Richmond, who established the dynasty from which Henry VIII, the oft-married English reformer, descended. In 1486 the foxy Ferdi-

nand of Aragon, husband of Isabella, was looking for an opportunity to outwit the witless King of France in Italy. Columbus was
still trying to convince powerful princes that his plan was not
impractical, while Bartolomeu Dias reached the southern tip
of Africa and rounded the Cape of Good Hope, and Covilha
actually reached India and on his return trip followed the African
coast as far south as the mouth of the Zambesi, and another Portuguese expedition reached Timbuktu, the fabulous African city,
overland from the coast. At that time little Martin Luther entered
the town school in Mansfeld.

While Luther studied the *trivia* at the Mansfeld school, the
Venetians acquired Cyprus from the last Christian ruler of the
torn island and unloosened thereby a disastrous war with the
Turk. In 1490 Vladislaw of Bohemia added Hungary to his realm,
after the death of Mathias Corvinus, the greatest of all Hungarian
kings. During the next four hundred years and more Hungary
was never to be free again. The aging Emperor Frederick, becoming more lazy with advancing age, was unable to curb the robber
barons and rapacious ecclesiastics in his Empire. Finally, after he
had kicked open a door with his foot, because he was too lazy
to use his hands, he contracted an infection and died. Maximilian,
the amiable marriage broker, succeeded him.

Meanwhile, in 1491, Girolamo Savonarola, a Dominican and a
dedicated man of God, had become prior of a Dominican
convent in Florence. Here he began his great work which led
to the expulsion of the corrupt Medici and the attempt at Reformation which was quenched only when the intrepid monk was burned
on May 23, 1498, on orders of Alexander VI, the infamous Borgia
pope.

In 1492 Columbus finally succeeded, after gaining support from
Queen Isabella, in his fantastic voyage beyond the western seas.
On October 12, 1492, the Great Admiral set foot on land at Guana-
hani and called it San Salvador, Our Savior's Land. In that same
year the last vestige of Mohammedan rule was wiped out from
the Iberian peninsula with expulsion of the Moors, and Rodrigo
Borgia, father of incestuous children, became pope under the
name of Alexander VI.[3]

At Christmas time 1492 the newly discovered world and the world yet to be discovered was divided between Spain and Portugal by a decree of the new pope. In the meantime the race for new discoveries continued. Columbus undertook his second voyage and soon two more. Vasco da Gama, Cabral, Magellan, Almeida, Albuquerque became famous names. In 1494 Spain and Portugal again divided the world which had been given to them by the generosity of Alexander VI. By this treaty Brazil was brought into the Portuguese empire, the rest of South America and all of North America became theoretically Spanish.

Maximilian I made a valiant attempt to cure the ills of the Empire. He instituted constitutional reforms, modernizing the judicial system and applying stricter controls. He was only partly successful. Being more interested in the advance of his dynasty through marriage deals, Maximilian had to fight a constant battle against the suspicious princes of the Empire, who moreover liked their license more than their responsibilities. In Eastern Europe darkness was falling on the nations, serfdom was introduced in Poland, and Russia was still advancing. In Italy Charles VIII was able to conquer Florence and to continue to Naples, only to be betrayed by his erstwhile ally, Ferdinand of Spain, who forsook him and turned on him, forcing him to flee from Italy ignominiously.

Spain expelled the Jews and Portugal massacred most of hers, when Luther went from Mansfeld to Magdeburg to attend the school of the Lollards, the famous Nullbrueder, who were known for their erudition and piety. In that year Vasco da Gama rounded the Cape of Good Hope and continued to Mozambique and the Malabar coast in spite of the efforts of Arab traders to keep him from attaining his goal. John Cabot, an Italian from Genoa like Columbus, but in the service of the King of England, discovered Newfoundland, believing that he had found the land of the Great Khan. In 1498 the English claimed Canada for themselves. Another Italian, more adventurer than explorer, Amerigo Vespucci, claimed to have reached the main land of America the year before Columbus. His claim was widely believed, and the German geographer Waldseemueller (Hylolacumollarius) named the new world "America" after Amerigo Vespucci, the braggard. The Turks, without meeting effective opposition from the west, continued to devastate Moldavia and to get ready for their conquest of Hungary. Martin Luther, after one year at Magdeburg, transferred to the school at Eisenach.

In France Charles VIII was dead, but his foolhardy policy was continued by Louis XII of Orleans who married Charles' widow and laid claim to the vacant throne and all the projects of his unfortunate predecessor. He invaded Italy, conquered Milan and imprisoned Ludovico Moro, who managed to escape to Germany where he was received as a friend. France which had not learned a lesson in previous dealings with the foxy Ferdinand of Spain made another treaty with him, the Treaty of Granada, in which the Spanish and French kings agreed to cooperate in their Italian ventures. Again Ferdinand forsook his ally, driving him from Italy with the help of other accomplices.

In 1498 the Portuguese under Duarte finally reached South America which had been assigned to them previously. But while the Portuguese were successful Columbus had to face a revolt and was brought back to Spain in chains. From then on, although he was subsequently released and treated with dignity, he was a "has been" and died poor and abandoned a few years later, another victim of Spanish intrigue. John and Sebastian Cabot set out on their second voyage conquering lands for the King of England and penetrating, perhaps, as far as Delaware. But since they found no spices, the English king lost interest in them. After March 1499 they were not heard of again. Vasco da Gama in that year landed in India.

The year of 1499 was one of those disastrous years which were to recur again and again during the next century and a half. While the Western powers were busy in their backyards and while the great voyages of discovery continued—Ojeda discovered the mouth of the Amazon—the Turks conquered large parts of Montenegro and won a decisive victory against the Venetians. Their fleet under the powerful admiral, Kemal Reis, defeated the Venetians off Modon. They thereupon took not only Modon, Lepanto, Koron, but their cavalry advanced as far as Vicenza in the heart of Italy, the first serious threat to Western Christendom since the days of Charles Martel. Fortunately and unexplicably, the Turks did not follow up their victory, but withdrew, and at the beginning of the new century Europe was once more quiet, with a humbled France, a divided Italy, a forgotten Germany, a scheming Spain, and a corrupt Church.

In the year 1501, when Luther enrolled at the University of Erfurt, the French relinquished their claims to Naples, the Russians reached the left bank of the Dnieper and took White Russia and Little Russia, and in Italy cardinals were being poisoned by Cesare and Lucretia Borgia, the bastards of Pope Alexander VI. Finally, Alexander VI died after having imbibed, by mistake, some said, of poisoned wine. Cesare fled and was killed a few years later. Lucretia reformed and became a good woman and princess.

In Germany Maximilian I, tempestuous and proud, had withdrawn into splendid isolation, "pouting," because the princes had not been pliable to his wishes. To offset his defeats he was happy to see a son born to Philip whom he had married a few years previously to the daughter and heiress of Ferdinand and Isabella. This son, born in 1500 to Philip the Handsome and Joanna the Mad, was to become later the Emperor Charles V.[4]

Switzerland, being more and more aware of her independence, used the opportune moment to seize from the French Bellinzona and other territories which increased her power considerably. Otherwise the decade was marked mostly by deaths and accessions. Alexander VI died of poison, and after the short reign of Pius III, Julius II became pope, the greatest pope between Innocent III and Leo XIII, but not the most spiritual. In 1504, Isabella of Castile, faithful co-regent of Ferdinand of Aragon, died leaving her country to her daughter Joanna who, however, at the death of her husband Philip went mad and lived in mental darkness for another fifty years, almost to the end of her famous son, Charles V. In 1505 Ivan the Great left the Muscovite territories to his successor, Basil III, who used his long and quiet reign to consolidate Russian power. In 1506 Columbus died at Valladolid, without knowing that he had discovered a new world. Poland had a new king who continued to enslave his peasants, and Henry VII of England died, leaving his realm to the famous Henry VIII.

In these years the French king kept on plotting, Maximilian continued his useless struggle against German petty princes, and Ferdinand of Spain was busy with dynastic troubles. Portugal took Sofala and Kilva from the Arabs, founded Mozambique, and Francisco de Alemida ruled as first governor of India on the Malabar coast. In 1507 Leo Africanus invaded the Songhoi Empire, and in 1509 the Spanish power extended to the northern coast of Africa. Led by Cardinal Ximenes the Spaniards took Oran, Bougie, and Tripoli, and forced the Moslem rulers to pay tribute. During that decade Ferdinand of Spain knifed the French in the back, for the third time. An unholy Holy League was formed to help the pope, Spain, and the emperor to carve up Italy.

During that decade Martin Luther entered the monastery of the Augustinian Hermits in Erfurt (1505), became a priest and a teacher at Wittenberg, and was sent to Rome. When Luther arrived in Rome, in January 1511, he did not see the pope, because Julius II was busy in Northern Italy revitalizing the faltering Holy League, while the Swiss, who had joined the League, took for themselves Locarno, Lugano, and Ossala.

Luther returned from Rome to Erfurt and soon moved to Wittenberg. The King of France called a council at Pisa to censure the pope. Pope Julius II, in turn, called a rival council to the Lateran which met for the next six years right up to the eve of the Reformation, but accomplished nothing. The new King of England thought that the time was propitious, and combining his forces with those of the Emperor Maximilian, Henry VIII invaded France routing the French army in the bloodless victory of the Battle of the Spurs.[5]

In the meantime the Emperor Maximilian had finally succeeded in bringing more effective rule to Germany. While he was unable to undo the fruits of centuries of misrule of his predecessors, he at least succeeded in eliminating the most glaring abuses through the establishment of ten governmental districts and of the Aulic Council, a supreme imperial court.

In the East there were new stirrings in the Turkish Empire. Selim I, called in history "the Grim," forced his cultured, indecisive father to abdicate, fought against his brother and rival Ahmed, defeated him and had him executed. Since the Persians had supported the claims of Ahmed, Selim now turned against them, halting for the next few years the Turkish march towards the West. He defeated the Persians, conquering Anatolia and Kurdistan. The following year he also turned against Egypt which had been allied with Persia against Turkey. Cairo was sacked and terribly ravaged, and Egypt passed under Turkish rule for the next four hundred years. Selim acquired the Holy Places of the Moslem religion and thus became the acknowledged leader of the Mohammedans. Fortunately he died, before he could turn his hordes once more against the West.

In the West the French once again made peace with their neighbors. Louis XII of France took for his third and final wife, Mary, the sister of Henry VIII. The new pope, Leo X, absolved the repentant Catholic King from his sins and Louis died, leaving his realm to an even more ambitious successor, Francis I.[6]

There was also a new king in Denmark, the unstable and capricious Christian II, who a few years later caused Sweden to secede under Gustavus Vasa and was exiled and found a refuge in Wittenberg. The Swiss had taken advantage of the French troubles to increase their territories. They now numbered thirteen cantons. Their soldiers were the most feared among European mercenaries. Hungary which had a respite from Turkish troubles faced a peasant revolt which was suppressed in a sea of blood by the heartless John Zapolya who later became a willing puppet of the Turks. The new French King began another war against Italy and the pope, this time a successful war, which ended in the victory of Marignano. Elated by this initial victory Francis I drastically curtailed the power of the pope in his realm and began to choose his own bishops.

In Spain, foxy old Ferdinand of Aragon died, leaving his possessions to his grandson, Charles, who soon arrived on the scene with a large retinue of Flemish nobles, causing widespread opposition among the proud Spanish grandes. Under Charles all of Spain was united into one mighty empire.

During these troublous times the quest for adventure had not slackened. In 1512 Ponce de Leon, searching for Eldorado, had discovered Florida. In 1513 Vasco Nunez de Balboa had crossed the Isthmus of Panama and, on September 25, discovered the Pacific Ocean. In Africa the Portuguese had ascended the Zambesi while their missionaries had penetrated the hinterland. Jorge Alvarez had landed near Canton. Later Juan Dias de Solis had explored the coast of South America from Rio de Janeiro to the Rio de la Plata where he was slain. And, finally, Fernando Hernandez de Cordova had discovered Yucatan, finding traces of large cities and great wealth, whetting the appetites of greater conquistadores.

Giovanni dei'Medici, Pope Leo X, unworthy and wastrel successor of the ascetic Julius II, was sitting on the throne of St. Peter, and had just sold another bishopric to a German princeling, Albert of Mainz. Albert, deeply in debt to the rapacious Augsburg bankers, the Fuggers, had appointed an infamous indulgence peddler, John Tetzel, to recover the money by selling souls from purgatory to heaven. In that year 1517, on October 31, about noon, an Augustinian monk of Wittenberg nailed Ninety-Five Theses to the door of the Castle Church in Wittenberg. From that time on much of the world's attention was to be centered on Martin Luther. But the troubles of the world continued unabated.

In 1518 the aging Emperor Maximilian I tried in vain to get a commitment from the German princes that they would elect his grandson, Charles of Spain. When the emperor died in January 1519 there was a long struggle for the selection of his successor, a struggle in which the pope was deeply involved. This struggle materially helped the cause of the Reformation and protected Luther from the harsh demands of Rome. Finally, in 1520 Charles V was chosen emperor and Luther was invited to appear at the Diet of Worms the following year. He was promptly outlawed and spirited away, but the emperor was unable to enforce his Edict of Worms, because once more France was at war with the world. For the next ten years Charles V was busy with Francis I of France, with the ever scheming pope, and with the Turk. Thus during the years from 1520 to 1530 the Reformation could spread unhampered. And spread it did. By 1530 the larger part of Germany, large areas of Scandinavia, Holland, Poland, Bohemia, Hungary, Austria, Switzerland, France, and even Italy had been won for the evangelical cause. The terrible sack of Rome, in 1527, had brought the power of the Roman Church to its lowest ebb in history.

During this decade the conquistadores conquered the New World for Charles V. Hernando Cortez accomplished his brilliant conquest of Mexico, thus subjugating the first American country to the rule of the white man. Alvarez Pineda explored the Gulf of Mexico, sailing from Florida to Vera Cruz. Francisco de Cordillo advanced along the Atlantic coast as far as South Carolina. Ferdinand Magellan began his circumnavigation of the world, which was finished in 1522 by Sebastian d'Elcano, after Magellan had been killed in the Philippines.

During this decade also the Turks advanced to the gates of Vienna. After the death of Selim I his successor, Suleiman the Magnificent, had taken up the war against the west with a vengeance. While Charles was embroiled in his senseless wars with Francis I, Suleiman was able to take Belgrade, from which he ravaged the countryside unpunished. The Knights of St. John were driven from their last possession, the Island of Rhodes, which now became the hunting ground of ferocious pirates. In the battle of Mohacs, on August 29-30, 1526, King Louis of Bohemia and Hungary was defeated and killed. The death of Louis brought a contest for the succession in Hungary which lasted until 1528. When Ferdinand of Austria, the emperor's brother, defeated the cruel John Zapolya, the latter appealed to the Turks who supported him vigorously. In this struggle most of Hungary passed under Turkish rule and Zapolya became a puppet of the Sultan. In 1529 the Turks stood at the gates of Vienna, capital of the Empire. In the meantime the famous Turkish admiral Kaireddin Pasha, an apostate Greek, was attacking the soft underbelly of the Empire from the Mediterranean. He was able to wrest Algiers from Charles.

Charles had been busy with Francis I of France. The first of the wars had begun a few months after the coronation of the emperor when the French once more invaded Italy. The French under Lautrec were, however, driven from Milan, and Francesco Sforza, heir of Ludovico, was restored to his realm. As a result of this disastrous war the French Constable, Charles de Bourbon, trans-

ferred his allegiance to Charles V and became one of his most
brilliant generals. In Italy Charles was able to influence the election of the new pope. His former tutor, Adrian of Utrecht, became the last non-Italian pope in history. An earnest reformer,
he was, however, unable to carry out his reforms because he met
strong opposition on the part of his advisors and died already the
following year. The next two popes were unworthy Renaissance
creatures.

Francis I of France did not take his defeat lying down. He
tried once more to fight against Charles, but was captured at
the Battle of Pavia in 1525 and kept prisoner until he had renounced once more all claims to Milan, Genoa, and Naples, as
well as the overlordship over Flanders and Artois, had ceded
the Duchy of Burgundy to Charles and surrendered his sons as
hostages to the imperial court. But no sooner had he been released,
in 1526, than he broke all previous promises and began to plot
with the pope against the emperor. The sack of Rome under
Bourbon and Frundsberg was the sad result. The pope was captured, his family driven from Florence, and revolts spread throughout Italy, of which the most famous was the rebellion of Andrea
Doria of Genoa. Francis I now turned to the Lutheran princes
of Germany, but with little success. In February 1530 Charles
V was crowned by the pope Emperor of the Holy Roman Empire,
the last emperor to be crowned by a Roman pontiff. When the
Diet of Augsburg met during the summer of 1530 to settle the
religious disputes, Charles had weathered ten years of hard, but
victorious, struggle and was at the height of his power. He felt
that he was now able to impose his will upon the heretical subjects of his realm. After the reading of the Augsburg Confession
—the real birthday of the Lutheran Church on June 25, 1530—
the emperor decreed that the Lutherans would be given until
the spring of the following year to return to the Catholic fold.
The Smalcald League of Lutheran princes was the answer.

The Turks and Francis I of France saved the day for the Lutheran Church and postponed the religious war between the
emperor and the Smalcald League until after the Reformer's
death. In 1532, the religious peace of Nuremberg revoked the

harsh Augsburg Edict and permitted free exercise of religion until the meeting of the next Council. From this time on all efforts were bent on convoking a Reform Council, but the popes continued to oppose these efforts, and when the Council finally met at Trent in 1545 it was much too late to do any good. It had become a mere Roman rump-Council.

In these years Henry VIII of England, who had once received the title "Defender of the Faith" for his valiant attack against Luther, broke with the pope over the issue of his divorce from Catherine of Aragon and founded his own Church. Before he died a few years later he had been married six times and had killed several of his wives. For a time he tried to form an alliance with the Lutherans of Germany, but with little success. Frustrated he killed some of his erstwhile Lutheran advisors. Francis I, too, who began his wars against the emperor once more, tried to claim the friendship of the Lutherans, showing understanding for the Evangelical concern while he was ruthlessly persecuting the Evangelicals in his own country. But his efforts, too, came to naught. After several more wars, all of them unsuccessful in the end, Francis I of France died poorer than he had been when he first became king thirty years before.[7]

The Great Turk who was anxious to crush some of his eastern rivals, gave Ferdinand and Charles a breathing spell. However, the war in the Mediterranean continued unabated. Charles was able to capture Tunis and other African ports.

During these years John Calvin of Noyon, France, not yet 25 years old published his "Institutes of the Christian Religion," and a Spanish nobleman, Ignatius de Loyola, founded a small society of fanatic followers which was recognized a few years later, in 1540, by Pope Paul III and received the name "Society of Jesus." In Portugal the infamous Inquisition was reactivated and soon spread throughout Catholic Europe. In Switzerland the Protestants, after initial defeats—during the battle of Cappel the Swiss Reformer Zwingli was killed—succeeded in winning the important cities of Geneva and Berne under the leadership of William Farel and subdued Vaud, Chablais, Lausanne and other territories which had formerly belonged to the Duke of Savoy. Bullinger, Bucer, and Capito wrote the First Helvetian Confession and attempts were made, partly successful, to heal the rift between the two main branches of Protestantism.

In 1537 Pope Paul III called a council to Mantua and Luther wrote his "Smalcald Articles" for this council, but the pope changed his mind and the council never met. The Reformation was still continuing its victorious march. Denmark, Sweden, and Norway were now completely Lutheran. Christian III of Denmark became the first prince outside the Empire to join the Lutheran league. But at Nuremberg a Catholic League was formed and the emperor who had just defeated Francis I had his hands free to turn against the heretics. The first great loss for the Lutheran cause—since the Peasant War and the defection of the fanatics and humanists—came when the immoral Philip of Hesse contracted a bigamous marriage and thus compromised his standing in the Empire. From then on the most energetic of Lutheran princes became an ineffective lame-duck onlooker. In Saxony, where Duke George had died in 1539, the Lutherans lost their advantage due to the stupidity of Elector John Frederick who offended his Dresden cousins to the point of starting a war which, however, was averted at the last minute by the intervention of Philip of Hesse. This lack of diplomacy on the part of the Saxon elector drove the young Duke Maurice into the arms of the Emperor Charles who used him to defeat the Lutherans in the Smalcald War.

On February 18, 1546, Luther died in the town where he had been born 63 years before. He died on the eve of the first great religious war between the followers of the old faith and of the evangelical faith. When he was born in 1483, the light of the new age had just begun to shine in Germany. Humanism was still in its infancy. The Turk was still far away. America had not yet been discovered. The Renaissance popes had just made their appearance in Rome, but the worst were yet to come. The authority of the Church which had been shattered a century before his birth had been re-established to some extent by a succession of Reform Councils in the fifteenth century. The merchant princes and the great cities had not yet seen their greatest power.

Greek and Hebrew were still forgotten languages. There were many misconceptions about the world. Copernicus had not yet made his appearance. The mind of the world was—at least north of the Alps—largely medieval.

When Luther died the world had witnessed the greatest upheaval in the religious sphere since the days of the Apostles. Large parts of Europe had rediscovered the light of the Gospel. No country, not even Spain, had fully escaped the impact of the Reformation. Even in the new world there were settlements of Lutherans, notably in Venezuela. Copernicus had changed the understanding of the world, and before him Columbus and a score of others had put to a test the theory that the world is round. A whole new world had been found and conquered, and while Christianity had spread in many lands, it had also lost much ground which it had claimed in the past. The Turks had advanced to the gates of Vienna, the greatest threat to western Christendom since the days of the Great Khan. When Luther died the great humanists had come and passed from the stage of history. Erasmus had revived the study of Greek and Reuchlin the study of Hebrew. Hundreds of great scholars had enriched the culture and civilization of the world in Luther's lifetime. Great universities had been established, even in such far-off places as Wittenberg, Frankfurt-on-Oder, and Koenigsberg. And above all, there was Charles V, ruling over the greatest empire the world had seen since the days of the old Roman emperors, an empire in which truly the sun never set.

Luther's world did not change entirely during his life time. The social structure remained largely the same. The fate of the lower classes, especially the peasants, had become worse rather than better. Serfdom was now firmly established not only in Germany, but in many other places. The light which the age of the Renaissance had brought to many countries was slowly being extinguished in Italy and Spain under the impacts of twin forces of Jesuitism and Inquisition. The superstitions of the Middle Ages were still strong. The worst was yet to come for witches and other unfortunate human beings, and in some years more witches would be burned in Lutheran territories than heretics in the notorious autodafés of the Catholics. In Luther's lifetime there began also divisions within the Lutheran Church which led to squabbles and controversies strangely reminiscent of the darkest Middle Ages.

Yet these reminders of things past could not hold back the dawn of a new age. The world around Luther had changed radically during his lifetime.

II

A Century in Ferment

The Reformation did not come upon the world without preparation. The whole century before the birth of the Reformer had been a century in ferment, a century which conditioned the minds of men for the great struggle that was to break the unity of the visible Church.

In the city of Worms there is a famous Luther monument, erected in the last century. In the center the well-known heroic figure of Martin Luther which has been copied many times in Luther monuments in this country and elsewhere, surrounded by his chief lieutenants. Looking a bit farther we notice four figures who at first glance had nothing to do with the Protestant Reformation, yet they were important nevertheless. They represent the unrest of the dying Middle Ages and the dawn of the religious consciousness of modern times. Three of these four Pre-Reformers lived within the century before the birth of Martin Luther.

The supreme power which the Roman Church had attained under Innocent III in the early thirteenth century, faded quickly away within three or four generations after his death. When Boniface VIII, the last great pope before Julius II, tried to assert the supremacy of the Vicar of Christ, his authority was boldly challenged by Philip of France and the Roman pope became a prisoner of the French king on September 7, 1303. After that Rome never regained its former place of honor.

The popes, forced to reside in Avignon in southern France, during the "Babylonian Captivity of the Church," soon became the playball of the French kings and their minions, the French cardinals. Rome, during the next seventy years, became a giant ruin both physically and spiritually. Cows were grazing on the grounds where the greatness of the medieval Church had been manifest only a few generations before, the Orsinis and other reckless Roman nobles were fighting murderous pitched battles in the deserted streets of the once great city, and its population declined until it was smaller than that of many of the cities of western Christendom over which it had lorded throughout the centuries. At Avignon, immorality, greed, and heresy invaded the worldly papal court. When some seventy years later the Roman clique tried to re-establish the papacy in Rome, there were two popes who damned and excommunicated each other in a running battle of bulls during the closing years of the fourteenth century. Finally, the emperor stepped into the fight and appointed a pope to end the rules of the counter-popes, but the result was, that there were now three popes. This condition continued until the second decade of the fifteenth century when the issue of the papacy was settled at the Reform Council of Constance.

Thus the revolt against the papacy began within the Church. The first marionette of Philip of France, Clement V, formerly archbishop of Bordeaux, was forced to abolish the order of the Knights Templar who had become too powerful for the French king. At the Council of Vienna in 1312 Clement V confiscated the immense assets of the Knights Templar and distributed them among others. Hundreds of Knights Templars were tortured and slowly put to death. Thus the most powerful allies of the pope were destroyed by the pope himself. Similar outrages continued throughout the century. The papacy seemed anxious to kill off its friends and to hasten its dissolution. The heralds of the young Renaissance could rejoice that papal superstition and arrogance was a thing of the past.[1]

More dangerous and of more lasting effect than the disintegrating external power and increasing folly of the popes were the attacks which were leveled against the theological foundations of the papacy from within the Church. At the Sorbonne, always the stronghold of Catholic theology, an opposition to the claims of the papacy arose which was to shake the whole structure of medieval theology. Under the leadership of Gerson, chancellor of the university, and Peter d'Ailli, its outstanding theologian, a powerful party arose which denied the claim of the pope that he was the final authority in matters of faith, and which demanded that the Ecumenical Councils should once more assume their historical role as arbiters of faith. During the latter part of the fourteenth century John Wycliffe, who died less than a century before the birth of Luther, called the pope the Anti-Christ. He asserted that the Bible was the sole authority of faith, and by translating the Word of God into the vernacular—a process forbidden in previous centuries—and by sending out travelling preachers of the Word, Wycliffe spread his doctrine throughout the western world, even to Bohemia. Through his assertion that Christ is the only Mediator between God and men Wycliffe gave a fatal stab to the medieval Church from which it was never to recover. He also attacked the Roman practice of withholding the cup in Holy Communion, the veneration of relics, and monasticism, three of the main pillars of the papal edifice which had been erected with so much care and under such great difficulties during the centuries of its highest power.

After Wycliffe's death his doctrines were taken up by John Huss, son of Bohemian peasants, whose attempted reforms were to reverberate throughout Europe right up to the time of Luther. Huss, born in 1369 at Hussinetz, and his friend, the Czech nobleman Jerome of Prague, had especially espoused Wycliffe's demand for the lay cup. Other matters entered, since the locale of Huss' reforms, the University of Prague, was at that time a hotbed of German and Czech nationalism. The result was, that the religious issue was somewhat buried under the animosity which existed between the German and Czech professors. The Czech populace took up the cause of Huss in a fashion very similar to that in which the German populace, even the religiously indifferent, espoused the cause of Martin Luther before the Peasant War brought a separation of the spirits. The matter was further aggravated by the fact, that Prague was also the residence of a German king, recently deposed for being unfit to rule, who tried to win Czech support against his German relative who had supplanted him. Finally, the conditions under which Huss went to the Council of Constance and to his death were just the reverse of of the conditions which prevailed a century later when Luther made his appearance at the Diet of Worms. The German Emperor Sigismund who broke his pledge of free conduct to Huss —and blushed for it—was of a different stripe than his descendant Charles V. His chief interest was to keep the prelates and bishops who were anxious to depart in Constance and to unite them behind the pope whom he had chosen, while Charles V was still rankling under the slap which Leo X had given him during the election maneuvers and was aware of the fact that the papacy was plotting his downfall through secret and open alliances with France. Thus Charles V could well afford to give Luther some kind of protection, slapping the hands of the pope and his nuncio, while Sigismund, a weak politician, could ill afford to antagonize the Roman Church by protecting the lonely professor from far-away Prague. Thus Huss was foredoomed.

The whole decay of the Church can be best illustrated by casting a quick look at this so-called Reform Council of Constance which met from 1414 to 1418. Even before the emperor arrived, Pope John XXIII had put Huss into jail, scarcely realizing that he himself would be jailed within a few months. The city of Constance with perhaps 4,000 inhabitants was crowded with thousands of knights, laymen, and prelates, among them many princes of the Church and scholars whose fame was voiced throughout Europe. There were also hundreds of minstrels, clowns, and prostitutes, camp followers of Lords Spiritual and Temporal. When Sigismund arrived at the end of 1414 Pope John XXIII had already started the process against Huss, thereby wishing to divert the attention of the council from his own problems. But Sigismund succeeded in recapturing the leadership of the council after his arrival. The pope who realized what was in store for him, secretly escaped from the city, dressed as a farmer, and was promptly excommunicated. Later he was captured and put into prison with Huss. For the first time in centuries an Ecumenical Council had dared to assert that the council had its power from God Himself and therefore was superior to the pope. This so-called Bulla Sacrosancta was to haunt the Roman Church in generations to come.[2]

Huss was given an opportunity to recant, but in vain. He was firmly resolved to sacrifice his life for the truth. On the 8th of July, 1415, he was bound to the stake, and while hymns and psalms resounded from his lips to the glory of God, the flames slowly consumed his earthly form. A year later Jerome of Prague suffered the same fate. The Moravian Church is a lasting testimonial to their faith.

Sigismund and the Roman clerics had thought that with the burning of the two arch-heretics the issue had been settled. They could not have been more mistaken. The murder of Huss and Jerome unloosened the greatest and most cruelly fought religious war of the fifteenth century, the memories of which reached right to the Leipzig debate of 1519 when Duke George of Saxony turned furiously on Luther after Luther had confessed that Hus had been right in some of his doctrines. This war, a blending of religious fanaticism and national fervor, was to devastate not only large parts of Bohemia, but also Saxony and surrounding territories during the next forty or fifty years. It started with the defenestration of the councillors—a historic Bohemian custom which two centuries later was to start another, even more bloody war—and was not to end until the Hussites had split up into so many splinters that the Catholic reaction was able to subdue them one by one. At the beginning the Calixtines, after Latin "Calix" (cup), had won the support of the ruling classes of Bohemia, but the more fanatical Taborites, named after Mount Tabor, who demanded Christian communism and apostolic simplicity, soon aroused the antagonism of the landed gentry, who assembled an army against them. The Taborites, however, under their gifted leader, the one-eyed Ziska, took bloody revenge, destroying their own cities and cultural monuments in their numerous forays from Mount Tabor. In vain did Sigismund try to root out the Taborites. Their strongholds were impregnable. Only after Ziska had died of the plague during a campaign in Hungary, did things look up. The Taborites split into two groups, each under a leader called Procopius. The pope now felt that it was the opportune time to call upon Christianity to wage a crusade against the Hussites, and in 1427 a general armament against them began. Again the imperials and the assorted crusaders were beaten and in 1431 the Hussites ravaged Germany, putting everything to the torch. At last the Roman see entered into colloquies with the more temperate Calixtines, making the concession of the lay cup. After that it was not difficult to defeat the more radical Taborites. Both of the leaders and over 13,000 Hussites were butchered a few years later at the Battle of Prague. The aging Emperor Sigismund finally seemed to have succeeded and was readying himself to wipe out the last vestiges of Hussite heresy, when a new revolt by the remnant of the Taborites forced him and the Empress Barbara to flee from Prague. He died in 1437 on the flight.[3]

The revolt against the Roman Church took other forms, too. Jeanne d'Arc, a peasant girl of Domrémy in Lorraine, born in 1412, at the age of 18 had a vision in which she was told by the Archangel Michael to save her country and her king. The background of this episode, the Hundred Years War between France and England, belongs to history. Its significance lies in the fact that this young peasant woman acted against the Church and the Inquisition and defied the ecclesiastical authorities unto her death on the stake. To be true, later she was canonized, but only after all of France had rallied to her memory and had declared her a national saint against the wishes of Rome. The fact remains that France's greatest heroine was burned as a heretic, who had concluded a pact with the devil. Under the merciless torture of the Inquisition she at first recanted, but later repented of her weakness and went heroically to her death, her eyes fixed to the Crucified on the Cross. Later the French Church all but broke away from the control by the Roman pope and became a national Church under the direct supervision of the French king. At the time of Luther's birth the influence of the Vicar of Christ in France was at its lowest ebb.

In Italy, the home of the pontiffs, the contempt stemming from closest familiarity with the Roman curia knew no bounds. Poets and thinkers condemned the "cesspool of Rome" in the most forceful indictments. Potentates often murdered unwanted clerics, including sometimes archbishops and even cardinals. Defiance of the pope was rather the rule than the exception. Petty princes used their relatives and even concubines to gain influence in Rome. For generations the papal see was to be had by the highest bidder, and future cardinals and popes often made their first impact on history by being related to prostitutes and money-lenders. It is significant that the greatest Italian Renaissance poets took the party of the foreign German emperor against the native minions who happened to be popes at that time.

The revolt against the papacy came to a head in Florence after the death of Lorenzo il Magnifico, grandson of the great Cosimo, one of the most cruel Renaissance princes and a Medici. Lorenzo himself had ruled without regard for law and order, had often been threatened and once was almost stabbed to death while attending mass in the cathedral. He escaped and had the archbishop, who was merely carrying out the pope's orders, hung in full regalia from a window in the Palazzo Vecchio. With the archbishop more than 300 faithful followers of the pope were dispatched to death. Yet, Lorenzo was one of the greatest patrons of the arts, a statesman, scholar, and student of antiquity. He drew to his court the philosopher Marsilio Ficino, a believing Christian, the famous humanist Pico della Mirandola, the poet Angelo Poliziano, and many others. He sponsored festivals and carnivals, especially to please his paramour, Lucretia Donati, and mixed with the populace dancing in the streets and singing his own compositions.

But after the carnival the fast! In 1491 the Dominican monk Girolamo Savonarola had preached for the first time in the Cathedral of Florence. Soon the whole city was terrorized by his predictions of heavenly punishment. Attacking Lorenzo and the Medicis, he refused to call upon the prince when he was first appointed to his office as cathedral preacher. Yet when Lorenzo died a short time

John Wycliffe, a forerunner of the Reformation, sends out his itinerant preachers with his English translation of the Bible in 1381. (After a painting by W. F. Yeames.)

John Huss, a forerunner of the Reformation, burned at the stake in 1415. At the invitation of the emperor, Huss presented himself at the Council of Constance to answer for his defiance of the papal bull, only to be imprisoned, tried as a heretic and burned. His martyrdom provoked a political and religious revolution in his native Bohemia.

Girolamo Savonarola, a forerunner of the Reformation, preaches against luxury in Florence in 1494. (After a painting by Ludwig von Langenmantel.)

Pope Julius II, a great patron of the arts, and his court admiring the Apollo Belvedere. (After a painting by Carl Becker.)

later, he called to himself the monk who had spoiled the gaiety of Florence and asked him for his absolution. This Savonarola was ready to give under three conditions, first that Lorenzo should confess his faith in God, secondly that he should make restitution of all things which he had stolen, thirdly that he should restore freedom and the old constitution to Florence. The first two Lorenzo was willing to do, at the third condition he turned to the wall and died without the absolution and the sacrament of the Church.[4]

From that day on Savonarola's ascendancy over the Medici was secure. In 1494 Lorenzo's son, Piero, and the other Medicis, including two later popes, were driven from the city, and Florence was declared a Republic. Savonarola was now the undisputed leader of a theocracy. "Thy sins, O Florence, thy sins, O Italy, cry to heaven!" With the fervor of a moral reformer he turned against the rotten hierarchy, castigating Alexander VI, the Borgia pope, and the "cesspool of Rome," the "Babylonian whore." In 1497 his influence had reached its zenith. Florence had become a city without festivals, without laughter. Its citizens walked about in sackcloth and ashes. Young men and even children walked from house to house, collecting godless books, pictures, statues, and other works of art, carrying them to the market place where they were burned. Soon, however, the Florentines got tired of their reformer, and while they had no love for the Pope and the Medici, they used the ban which Alexander VI had hurled against the Florentine monk as a pretext to rid themselves of the uncomfortable companion. In 1498 the Dominican was burned on the same market place where during the previous year great fires had consumed the worldly vanity of Florence, and his ashes were scattered on the Arno River. Soon the Medici were called back and gave to the Church Pope Leo X and later Pope Clement VII, who having learned nothing and having forgotten nothing, made it easy for the Reformation to spread like wildfire.

Only in Germany, among the great powers—if we leave aside Spain which was still involved in the struggle against the Moors—only in Germany did the spirit of ferment not erupt into rebellion. This was partly due to what Luther called "the stupidity of the Germans," who were "simpleminded" and did not know what was going on in the world. Partly it was due to the weakness of Emperor Frederick III who ruled during half of this century. But mostly, it was due to the excesses of Hussite troubles which prejudiced princes and knights against revolt and reformation. If the Hussite cause had been fought on a religious plane, rather than a national or racial one, the Reformation of the Church which took place in the sixteenth century might well have occurred a hundred years before. Huss might never have burned, the Emperor Sigismund would never have fought against the Czech patriots who rose in support of Huss, and Germany would have been infused with the spirit of reform. The time was ripe. England, France, Italy, Bohemia, and other countries had declared their independence from Rome, but the Germans remained inactive, the German spirit remained dormant. It has been said that no changes of permanence can be brought about in Europe without the vigorous support, if not the initiative, of the Germans, because they form the heart of Europe, not only in the geographical sense. This has never been more true than in the history of the Church. The Reformation did not take place until it was inaugurated in the heartland of Europe, by Luther, Zwingli, and others.

Germany, as usual, suffered more during the fifteenth century from the ferment of the times than any other country. It suffered invasions and bloodshed, because its emperor had forsaken the Bohemian Reformer. It suffered an ever increasing distintegration of political power, bordering often on anarchy. Ecclesiastics openly defied imperial laws, even electors were turning against their emperor. This was nothing new, but in the fifteenth century, the century of Reform Councils and Counter Councils this took on new meaning. Even after the pope had been forced to grant the national states autonomy in the administration of their ecclesiastical affairs— and France was quick to take advantage of this opportunity—the weakness of an emperor, Frederick III, the guile of an ecclesiastic, Aeneas Sylvius Piccolomini, and the disharmony among German princes combined to lose this golden opportunity for Germany to rid itself of papal interference in its internal affairs. Piccolomini, later Pope Pius II, at that time confidential secretary of Frederick III, prevailed upon his master to make peace with the discredited Pope

Eugene IV who in turn promised to crown the emperor in Rome. All reforms were abandoned, much against the wishes of the German princes, who, however, could not agree to concerted action against the weak emperor and his wily councillor. Thus for the empty gesture of a coronation in Rome all reforms were junked and Rome was allowed to use Germany for its ends until the deed of Martin Luther put an end to this rapacious exploitation. No wonder that the news of Piccolomini's triumph was received in festive Rome with the ringing of bells, the sound of trumpets and fireworks. In 1458 Piccolomini was awarded with the tiara.[5]

During the last half of the fifteenth century and the first two decades of the next, Rome exploited its victory to the utmost. With sources of revenue drying up everywhere else, with Spain and Portugal too busy with their own adventures in becoming world powers, Germany was the only major source of revenue for the papal see. The conquest of Constantinople by the Turks gave the excuse for levelling the first of many "Turkish Taxes" on the unsuspecting Germans. Later, the taxes were used unscrupulously to fill the coffers of the Roman pontiffs, to pay for their immoral lives, for hundreds of courtesans, for their artistic whims, and for briberies.

There was, of course, much opposition to this abuse of ecclesiastic powers among the Germans, especially among the learned and well-to-do. But the great masses of the "simple folk" continued to believe blindly in the miraculous powers of the indulgences and the score of other wares which the salesmen of the Church were peddling throughout Germany. Only once in a while a sly farmer or a brash young fellow succeeded in outwitting the busy salesmen of Roman power. The struggle against these abuses was confined almost exclusively to the printed and spoken word of the humanists, the preachings of a few conscientious priests, and the clear, if often theoretical, statements of a few theologians. Erasmus, Hutten, Mutianus, Crotus, and scores of others knew what should be done, but Luther did it. The faith of an Erfurt preacher who in 1508 preached against indulgences, the discovery of a Staupitz who be-before Luther knew that we are saved by grace alone, the clear statement of a Gabriel Biel who theologically proved that Christ is our sole mediator, all these did not take practical effect, until the peasant son from Eisleben with his hammer blows on October 31, 1517, aroused the world and brought about the Reformation of the Church.

In many other ways the century before the birth of Martin Luther was a century of ferment. Some of this, the Rebirth in the Renaissance and humanism, the great discoveries and conquests, which followed it, will be shown in subsequent chapters. Other manifestations of ferment, as for example, the birth of Swiss democracy, the delivery of the Russian peoples from the yoke of the Golden Horde, the many national crises in the eastern countries of Poland, Hungary, and the Baltic nations, the colonization and Christianization of the north-east by the Teutonic Knights, the interminable wars between France and England, the English civil strife, the birth of the Spanish nation, the social upheavals, the decay of knighthood, the ascendancy of the cities, the degeneration of the peasants, the formation and dissolution of leagues and alliances, the rise and fall of the Hanseatic League, do not belong within the scope of this presentation. They had little, if any, influence upon the birth and subsequent development of the Reformation. Some of these developments were wholly unknown to Luther, others interested him at times, but none of them influenced his actions. Luther was a child of the fifteenth century, an heir to the religious unrest exemplified in the three pre-Reformers Wycliffe, Huss, and Savonarola, a man who was burdened with everything that the century before his birth had done and not done, with all the heresies, and vile actions of the Church. But he was also a child of the Renaissance, of humanism, and of the age of the great discoveries. Whether he realized it or not, Luther, the great religious Reformer, was effective because he shook off the shackles of the Middle Ages and its limitations and was a modern man, perhaps the greatest of all. He brought to fruition the growth of a century in ferment.

III

The Rebirth

The ideal which had dominated the Middle Ages for over a thousand years can be circumscribed in one word: Asceticism. Man beware of man! Passions must be suppressed, marriage is a necessary evil, but celibacy is more God-pleasing. The Church Father Jerome who died in 420 left us, in his letter to the noble Laeta, a description of this all-pervading ideal. Advising her about the education of her daughter, the Church Father admonished Laeta to take John the Baptist as her example, who wore a coarse garment and ate locusts and wild honey. Thus a Christian girl should wear the shirt of a penitent. "Do not pierce her ears," he wrote, "and do not use rouge on a face which is consecrated to Christ, do not adorn her neck with gold chains and strings of pearls, do not dye her hair, if you do not want her to burn in hell." He forbade her to take baths, to uncover her body even in private. Let her eating and drinking be frugal, let her not listen to worldly music, but let her read only the Word of God, utter prayers and sing psalms.

In the lives of pious people throughout these dark ages we read again and again of how they sinned against nature, by cutting the bonds of family and friendship. An old woman throws herself at the threshold of her house to keep her son from entering the monastery. He walks over her. A mother takes her children to the monastery church to induce the father to return to the duties which he has forsaken. "I do not know you," he answers firmly. There was nothing on earth that was worth striving for. The world, instead of being accepted as God's revelation, became the enemy of God, to be shunned and to be hated.

Everywhere this strict division: God and the world, man and woman, children and parents, church and state. In the political arena this led to countless futile battles, in the world of the individual to countless heartbreaks. The true follower of Christ had neither home nor loyalty on earth. The monks and clerics were the "Knighthood of God," the nobility of Christendom. Asceticism, mortification of the flesh, which often, especially in times of stress —as the Black Death—took epidemic proportions, were the ideal. Even Luther thought to reconcile his God by beating himself bloody into senselessness.

This dark and joyless ideal was shattered by the dawn of the Rebirth of the Western world, the Renaissance of Greek and Roman ideals. To the Greek the human body had been a work of art, often idolized and perversely misused. He had tried to educate it to the greatest perfection. He had envisioned a world of light and gaiety. The practical sense of the Romans had created wonders of splendor and glory. But their world had fallen into idolatry, egotism, luxury, cruelty and perversion. Christianity, emerging from the bloodbath of the martyrs, had all but obliviated the memory of it.

It is strange that the crusades, one of the highest forms of medieval piety, should have given birth to the revival of antiquity. Frederick II, emperor from 1215-1250, and his son-in-law, the unscrupulous Ezzelino da Romano, were perhaps the first modern rulers who in their domain—mostly in Sicily—tried to introduce a modern personal rule based on antique concepts.[1] They were probably the first who had imbibed the poison of scepticism if the words of the bull of Gregory IX can be believed. For when this pope excommunicated the disobedient emperor he accused the "pestilential king" of having said "that the world has been deceived by three deceivers, Moses, Mohammed, and Christ . . . that the Almighty God was not born by a Virgin . . . that man does not need to believe what he cannot grasp with his own natural reason."

Ezzelino da Romano became the example for a long list of Italian tyrants during the next three hundred years. Fratricide, tyrannicide, extermination of whole families more often were the rule rather than the exception whenever there was a change of princes and dynasties. Take, for example, the history of Filippo Maria Visconti, duke of Milan, who lived some fifty years before Luther.

Filippo ascended the throne after his brother Gianmaria had been murdered by a relative. Gianmaria is famous in history for his hounds which had been trained to tear people to pieces.[2] When his subjects demanded peace by crying in the streets "Pace! Pace!" he had his mercenaries kill hundreds of them and ordered the priests of Milan to change the liturgical phrase "Donna nobis pacem!," give us peace, into "Donna nobis tranquillitatem!," give us tranquillity, an order which was punctiliously obeyed by the whole clergy of Milan. Filippo kept himself safely behind the walls of his fortress. Diplomats and lackeys often were not able to see him for months. Everyone in his employ had to pass constant security checks. His ministers and generals were under sharp supervision of political commissars, who constantly fanned jealousies among them in order to prevent any alignment which might be dangerous to the prince. His means of torturing his subjects were truly satanic. Yet he was a great admirer of Dante and Petrarch, and conversed learnedly with poets and humanists who called this monster a "divinely virtuous ruler." He was replaced by the Condottiere Francesco Sforza, the illegitimate son of a general, who had married the illegitimate daughter of Filippo. But illegitimacy was no bar to the highest offices in state and church.

One of the greatest condottieri was Sigismondo Malatesta, prince of Rimini, the conqueror of popes and cities. He called himself "Invincible Warrior" and possessed tremendous physical power. It was he who commissioned Leon Battista Alberti to build the famous S. Francesco Cathedral in Rimini, a monument to himself and his mistress, Isotta degli Atti, the "diva Isotta," the divine Isolt, as she is eulogized in marble in the Cathedral. Sigismondo never missed early morning mass, yet he killed two of his wives, one by poison, the other by sword. He raped nuns, Jewesses, and even bit a piece of flesh from the arm of a German princess who resisted

his advances. The pope excommunicated him for, among other
things, parricide, incest, adultery, and sacrilege, and burned Sigismondo in effigy. But Sigismondo, during a banquet, asked scorn-
fully: "Do meat and wine lose their taste because the person eating
and drinking them is banned?" For twenty years he was the terror
of popes and princes until he was brought to bay by the wily
Pius II, twenty years before the birth of Luther.[3]

The names of powerful Renaissance princes are legion. Not all
were bad, but all were independent. For practical ends they bowed
to the dogma of the Church and acknowledged the pope as Vicar
of Christ, but it has been truly said, that perhaps not one of these
great condottieri, dukes, princes, and princelings took the pope's
claims seriously.

The Rebirth also brought about a radical change in the position
of women in human society. The medieval ideal, so aptly postulated
in the above mentioned letter of Jerome, was most beautifully ful-
filled in the life of the humble Griseldis. Daughter of a cottager
she had become the wife of a prince who used every imaginable
trick to test her obedience, even to the point of taking away her children, but she remained steadfastly the obedient servant of her husband and master, until the doubting husband had satisfied his curiosity and a happy ending ensued. The place of the medieval woman
was strictly circumscribed by the four walls of her abode and the
will of her husband or father. Only a few nuns and a sprinkling of
emancipated princesses were able to burst through the iron curtain
of illiteracy and virtual serfdom.

The Renaissance changed this. Woman was put on an equal footing with man in education. She was allowed to study literature, singing, music, and even painting without restrictions. Her dress, once
modest, became revealing and often more shamelessly so than in the
twentieth century. Vittoria Colonna, the witty friend of Michelangelo, and Lucretia Borgia, the illegitimate daughter of Alexander
VI, corresponded in Latin and wrote beautiful poems. Later Catherine dei' Medicis, relative of two popes of the Reformation period,
became the most outstanding political force in France. Catherine
Sforza, niece-by-marriage of Pope Sixtus IV, served as a general de-

fending Forli until the year 1500, when she was defeated by Cesare Borgia, another child of Alexander VI.

Even prostitutes like Tullia d'Aragona, illegitimate daughter of Cardinal Luigi d'Aragona,[4] or the "Princely Whore," Beatrice de Ferrara, excelled in literature. They knew large portions of Petrarch and Boccaccio by heart, read voraciously from Virgil, Horace, Ovid and other Latin writers, and some even studied Greek. In the churches and cathedrals they occupied seats of honor next to the altar. Painters of renown vied in painting their likenesses.

During these years when knowledge and learning spread to even the lower middle classes, the Church—with the exception of a few high eccelesiatics—remained for the most part in the dark ignorance of the Middle Ages. Priests were wholly uneducated. The experiences which Luther and his friends had during the first church visitations in Germany were nothing specific German. Many priests actually did not know the Lord's Prayer, the Ten Commandments, the Creed. Neither had many read the Bible. Their sermons were often crudely comical, they were in the words of Faust "good comedians." One famous preacher, for example, told the story of Noah and his ark, imitating the animals as they entered, neighing, mooing, barking, yelping, grunting. Stories picked up in the gutter, or at best, edifying legends, served as a poor substitute for the Word of God which was not known to them. The moral life of many priests, probably the majority, was without reproach. Yet the literature of the Renaissance is abundant with scorn for the immoral lives of monks and nuns and their bastards. One writer wrote that to send a girl to a convent was to dedicate her to a life of shame, whereupon Bishop Bandello soothingly replied that at least nuns had intercourse only with monks. Of course, some of these descriptions must be taken with a grain of salt, but they are indicative of the moral climate of the Church.[5]

There was also a great deal of gluttony, especially in the Church. Monks who were supposed to walk on bare feet in truly apostolic fashion had their feet shod with expensive slippers and were riding obesely on little donkeys and ponies. Miracles were performed on alleged "blind" and "deaf," and devils were driven out. One of these

mendicant miracle priests made so much money that he was able
to buy a bishopric from a cardinal in which he and his helpers
spent their remaining days in peace and comfort.

And yet, in the midst of this degrading and perverse rebirth
there was the true rebirth. Dante Alighieri who is remembered
through his immortal "Divine Comedy" was a man of impeccable
morals and high ideals, who gave the world also such works as his
book "On the Monarchy" and "On the New Life," setting forth most
beautifully the ideals of the Renaissance. Francesco Petrarca, Petrarch, another great writer from Florence, but born in exile, the
true father of humanism, who revived the study of Cicero and introduced Homer to the new age, who wrote a great epic on Scipio
Africanus, but who is known to posterity through his exquisite
sonnets to Laura. Or Boccaccio whose Decameron is not only a
sensual thriller, but contains many of the rationalistic ideas which
the humanists embraced in the following century. The parable of
the Three Rings, later popularized by Lessing, the ideal of religious
tolerance, is contained in this book whose pages otherwise breathe
levity. Lorenzo Valla, editor of a Latin grammar and translator
of Greek texts whose work influenced Luther. Aeneas Silvio Piccolomini, Pope Pius II, above mentioned, who began after his coronation to write a History of the World, its geography, political
history, and civilization.

There were many misconceptions which these scholars corrected,
corrections which also aided the cause of the Reformation. In the
Middle Ages many had believed that Socrates, who died 399 B.C.,
had been born in Rome and had been married to a daughter of the
Emperor Claudius (41-54 A.D.). He was considered almost a Christian. Plato, on the other hand, was counted among the eight greatest
physicians of antiquity. No one knew that he had been a philosopher.
Virgil became the greatest magician of the world, who had prevented the vulcan Vesuvius from erupting by erecting on the
mountain the giant statue of a marksman which scared the mountain
into behaving. Kings and princes, even as late as Charles I of
England, tried to divine their future by studying the alleged writings of Virgil. The story is also told that Ignatius Loyola, the founder
of Jesuitism, drove out an evil spirit by reciting verses from Virgil.

One of the great humanists of the fifteenth century was Poggio Bracciolini, who served eight popes over a period of fifty years as secretary and apologist. He died a generation before Luther's birth. None other could be as scornful as he in dealing with his enemies. When arguments failed, he was able to convince through lies. He was an extortionist in the grand style, buying and selling the services of his pen. He was one of the greatest collectors of all times. As papal secretary the cellars and attics of monasteries were always open to him. What he found he kept. When he suspected that certain volumes or manuscripts would not be loaned to him, he without much ado let them disappear in the large folds of his cloak and was able to carry away his treasures unchallenged. Although this was plain thievery, he thus preserved to posterity innumerable valuable treasures of the past which otherwise would have been lost.

Later his collector's rage extended to other objects. His villa was filled with works of art, busts, inscriptions, which he had "borrowed," legally and illegally, throughout Europe.

Yet this man possessed a deep humanity. One of the finest things ever written during this turbulent century is Poggio Bracciolini's account of the martyrdom of Jerome of Prague, at the Council of Constance in 1416. "With high head and happy mien I saw him face his last hour on earth. No stoic ever went to his death with such strength of soul. When he came to the stake, he took off his cloak himself, bowed his knee before the stake to which he was bound with soaked ropes and a chain. Around him large pieces of wood were heaped. When the fire was lighted he began to sing a psalm, until fire and smoke forced him to be silent. When the executioner wanted to light the fire behind him, so that he may not see it, Jerome said: 'Come to the front and light it before my eyes. For if I were afraid, I would never have come here!' Thus died a man who is worthy of imitation, except for his heretical beliefs." Thus wrote the right hand man of the pope.

Poggio Bracciolini's frankness was often embarrassing to his popes. Repeatedly he was rebuked for living openly with a lady, not his wife, with whom he had fourteen children. But he replied bitingly that having mistresses was a hallowed custom among

priests. At the age of 55—he had never taken the clerical vows—
he finally married an eighteen-year-old noble, virtuous Florentine
girl. At the age of 73 he moved to Florence, the city of his youth,
highly honored, where he died a few years later, at the age of 79.
His portrait was hung in the Palazzo Signoria, the Florentine seat of
government.[6]

The greatest achievement of the Renaissance, however, is in the
field of the arts. Luther, on his trip to Rome, saw some of the
great architectural masterpieces of the period, he undoubtedly also
beheld some of the paintings. The artistic development of the Renaissance was not completed until after Luther's death, even after the
reaction of Jesuitism and the Inquisition had put an end to the expression of free thought.

Renaissance architecture was not a slavish imitation of antiquity.
Leon Battista Alberti (1404-1472) had expressed the ideal of beauty
in these words: "Beauty is a kind of consonance, harmony between
different parts, which does not permit that anything should be left
out or added which would disfigure the whole."

The Renaissance adapted and used freely the best it could find
in older styles. Thus St. Mark's of Venice, built in Byzantine style,
served as a pattern to the Renaissance architects who built five
centuries later the beautiful library of Venice. Northern Italy which
had never been home to any particular style, but had been the
crossroads of many streams of art, now became the center of
Renaissance architecture. Filippo Brunellesco (1377-1446) who
built the Palazzo Pitti in Florence became the real father of Renaissance architecture. At 26 he had gone with the ten years younger
Donatello to Rome where they studied in the ruins of antiquity, the
Pantheon, the Colosseum, and others. Upon his return to Florence
Brunellesco built one of the wonders of the world, the great dome
of the Cathedral. During the whole fourteenth century the Florentines had been building their Cathedral, but it stood there, a
giant ruin, until the genius of Brunellesco crowned it with the
famous dome which later served the builders of St. Peter's as a
pattern.[7]

While the greatest works of early Renaissance architecture were
erected in Florence and other north Italian cities, the popes and

patrons of Rome were soon able to draw the great builders to the
eternal city. The famous Palazzo Farnese was built on orders of
Cardinal Alessandro Farnese, later Pope Paul III, the last of the
Renaissance popes and the first of the popes of the Counterreforma-
tion. On the Monte Pincio the Medicis built the Villa Medici which
already forms the transition from Renaissance to Baroque and Jesuit
styles.

The greatest building project of Rome was St. Peter's. Luther
still saw it without its giant dome, but he was aware of the tremendous sums which were being lavished on its construction. The
building of St. Peter's had led to the embezzlement by the Church
of the funds which had been collected for the crusade against the
infidel. To the obsession of the popes to finish this giant project
may be credited the widespread simony which led to—among others
—the deplorable indulgence deal of Albert of Mainz.

Bramante (1444-1514) had begun the magnificent edifice upon
the ruins of an old church erected by Constantine the Great on
the grave of St. Peter. A hundred years later the work was finished.
In the meantime the Church to whose unity in Peter this was to be
a memorial had been hopelessly split. St. Peter's had lost its symbolic
sense, and what remained was a magnificent building, largely the
work of Michelangelo, the greatest of all Renaissance artists, who
had entered upon this work in 1546, the year of Luther's death.

Besides architecture, sculpture achieved its highest development in
two thousand years during this period. Although there had been
a few good sculptors, mostly anonymous, during the Middle Ages.
sculpture had been largely neglected since the decline of the Roman
Empire. There is nothing during those one thousand and more years
preceding the Renaissance, or even in the five hundred years since,
that can be compared with Lorenzo Ghiberti's magnificent doors
of the Florentine Baptistery. Michelangelo called them the "gates
of Paradise." For twenty-two years, 1425-1447, Ghiberti worked on
them, off and on, until they were completed. Luther may have seen
them on his Rome journey. He almost certainly saw the statue
of St. George, created by Donatello (1386-1466), the friend of
Brunellesco, which he erected in 1416 and which found its niche in
the Gran-San-Michele Church in Florence. The greatest works of

sculpture were yet to be born, created by Luther's contemporary, the mighty Michelangelo.

The paintings of the Renaissance are well known. Even today they are considered the most precious paintings of all times and thousands of dollars are spent each year selling and buying them. Filippo Lippi (1404-1469), the painter of etherial angels; Sandro Botticelli (1446-1510), his disciple, over whose pictures lies a mystic chastity, as in the "Birth of Venus," his most famous work; and Ghirlandajo (1449-1494) who painted the unbelievably beautiful frescos in Santa Maria Novella in Florence; and many others. The two greatest of the painters were Luther's contemporaries. Leonardo da Vinci (1452-1519), was the last "Homo Universalis," not only painter, but sculptor, architect, scientist, mathematician, a man accomplished in all arts and sciences. But he is remembered today by his Mona Lisa and the Lord's Supper, the first in the Louvre, the latter deteriorating in the moist cenacolo of Santa Maria delle Grazie in Milan. On both paintings da Vinci spent years of painstaking work, so many years indeed, that at the end of his life he saw the painting of the Lord's Supper disintegrate before his eyes. When Francis I of France bought the Mona Lisa from the artist he paid probably the largest sum ever paid for a portrait till this time.

The other great painter, Raphael Santi, for whom the whole era is divided into pre-Raphaelites and post-Raphaelites, was born in the year when Luther was born, 1483, but died already before Luther gave his confession before the Diet of Worms, in 1520. Unlike the lives of most of his great contemporaries, notably da Vinci's and Michelangelo's, his was a sunny path. Born in Urbino, he came in 1504 to Florence and in 1508 to Rome. Here he served as painter for Julius II and Leo X, was architect at the building of St. Peter's for a time, and devoted himself to archeology excavating the remnants of antiquity in and around Rome. His frescos in the Vatican belong to the most remarkable paintings of the period. Worldly and heavenly themes are freely mixed. But his greatest claim to fame are his Madonnas, of whom the most famous are the Madonna della Sedia and the Sistine Madonna.

There were great painters after Raphael, Titian who lived to the ripe old age of 99 (he died 1576), the painter of Charles V and of many great men of his age. His fame was so great, that once when he dropped the brush while working on Charles' portrait, the Emperor himself bent down and picked it up for the painter. There were Giorgione (1476-1510), Correggio (1494-1534) and Tintoretto (1518-1594). But the greatest of all Renaissance artists, some say the greatest artist of all times, was Michelangelo Buonarotti, born eight years before the Reformer whom he outlived by 18 years.

There are many parallels between the lives of the great Artist and the great Reformer. Both had a hard youth, were often harshly treated, both had inclinations to melancholy, both went through changes in occupation necessitated by circumstances. Both were never satisfied. Both worked exclusively for the glory of God. Under the influence of Savonarola Michelangelo became a serious Christian, a conversion similar to that of Luther who in 1505 entered the monastery. The works of the great man are too numerous to be mentioned even adequately. There is the powerful figure of Moses on the monument of Julius II which had to remain unfinished due to the niggardly schemes of succeeding popes. But Moses, the only figure finished for this great monument, gives an impression of the powerful conception of Michelangelo. On the other hand there is the gentle Pieta, Mary with the body of the Lord, perhaps the most beautiful expression of motherly sorrow, which the master created when only 25 years old. To Florence he gave the giant statue of David which still adorns the Piazza today. Or who could forget the monument to Giuliano de Medici, brother of Leo X, with the twin figures of Dawn and Dusk. But Michelangelo's fame rests upon the work which he did for St. Peter's, as architect, painter, and sculptor. The Sistine Chapel will always be his great memorial. The paintings which adorn its ceiling and walls are a song of praise to the God whom he loved with all his heart and whom he continued to serve in spite of all the machinations of greedy and worldly popes who made life sour for him. When he died, exactly eighteen years after Luther, on February 18, 1564, the world had lost the last of the great men of the Rebirth. His ashes rest at Santa Croce in Florence, the mausoleum where the greatest of the sons of the greatest Renaissance city are buried.

Besides these great artists the writings of Lodovico Ariosto (1474-1533) and Torquato Tasso (1544-1595), important though the "Orlando Furioso" of Ariosto and the "Gerusalemme Liberata" of Tasso are, do not reach the greatness of former times. The Renaissance which had begun with the pen long before painting, sculpture, and architecture created its immortal works, ended with the nefarious writing of two Italians, Niccolo Machiavelli (1469-1527) and Pietro Aretino (1492-1556). Machiavelli, a harmless man of limited talents, created "Il Principe," the Prince, the picture of an unscrupulous ruler, a brutally frank treatise which gave to posterity a new word: "Machiavellianism." Aretino, on the other hand, a scoundrel and one of the most feared men among high and low, left nothing worthwhile in spite of the incessant labors of his poison pen. Called "the Scourge of God" by popes who were powerless against him, he boasted that he had become the "Oracle of Truth and the Secretary of the World," while God was the highest truth in heaven, he, Aretino, was the highest truth on earth. In spite of extortion and secret police methods he had many loyal friends, among them Titian and Sansovino who built the library of Venice. In his palace in Venice kings, princes, courtesans, poets, artists met and waited on him. He received innumerable presents. Even Charles V paid the extortioner "silence money." He lied and poured out poison which at any time could upset the balance of power in Europe or turn husbands against wives, bishops against cardinals, popes against artists. He said, that he worked "in the sweat of my face." Always attired with a coat of mail, he was nevertheless pricked by daggers many a time and his body was full of scars. But he, like others of the Renaissance period, had outlived his time.[8]

Rome, once the gay city of Sixtus IV (1471-84) who had bought the pontificate with a large sum of money, and of his nephew, Pietro Riario, who died of immorality at the age of 28, the city where Innocent VIII (1484-1492) had legally acknowledged his bastards and had dined with his mistresses, the city of the Borgia, Alexander VI (1492-1503), the murderer of cardinals and father of the incestuous Cesare and Lucretia, the Rome of Julius II, Leo X, Clement VII, was no more. Gone were the mistresses, the "Brides of Christ," gone were the banquets with their naked dancers. When Leo X died in 1521 the coffers of the Church were so empty that there was no money to buy new candles for his funeral. Thus old candles had to be used. His successor, Adrian VI, Charles' former tutor, though earnest in his desire to reform the Church, had accomplished nothing, and the next pope, Clement VII, had seen the sack of Rome, imprisoned in St. Angelo's Castle in the heart of Rome, while cardinals, archbishops, bishops, and abbots, without shoes, in bloody clothes, often without noses or ears were forced to carry water for the mercenaries who wore gorgeous robes and drove them like slaves. He had to witness the day when a drunken soldiery proclaimed Martin Luther pope of Rome and of all Christendom. And even though he escaped with his life and his ears and his nose, Rome never regained its old spirit.

In place of the Renaissance, the rebirth of the world, a new force took over. In 1540 Paul III officially recognized the Society of Jesus, founded by Ignatius of Loyola (born 1491), and in 1542 the infamous Inquisition, dormant during the enlightened period in all but one country, was re-established throughout Roman Christendom. And even though the Jesuit Order was attacked during the eighteenth century and dissolved by one pope, it was re-established in its old power in the nineteenth and the Inquisition was newly organized as recently as 1908. For over four hundred years these two sinister forces have been the main architects, the new powers, on whose skill Rome relied. In 1545, the year before Luther's death, the Council of Trent constituted itself, not a council wished for so longingly for almost thirty years, but a council under the strict and uncompromising guidance of the Jesuits.

The Rebirth, for a large part of the Western World, had come to an end.

IV.

New Lands to Conquer

The discovery of America by Christopher Columbus on October 12, 1492, stands at the end of a long development and at the beginning of a new era. It focuses one of the great forces that formed the age of Martin Luther: the religious and cultural forces, which we discussed in the last two chapters, are complemented by the work of the Great Discoverers and the Conquistadores. The geographical boundaries are pushed back, the face of the world is changed and with it the attitudes and interests of men. This age of discovery and conquest finally changed also the great mystical entity of the Middle Ages, the Holy Empire, which now with the rise of new world powers loses its meaning completely, having lost its actual power long ago.

During the Middle Ages the geographical knowledge of the old civilizations of the West was limited and centered around the Mediterranean. The "Orbis Terrarum," the "Erdkreis," the world then known, was a radius that took in the countries bordering on the Mediterranean to the far ends of the world, which was not far. Perhaps a few score miles west of the Pillars of Hercules, the Rock of Gibraltar, England and Ireland and Norseland, parts of Russia, the Black Sea, Asia Minor, a dim knowledge of India, Persia, parts of the Indian Ocean, and northern Africa. All this surrounded by water which borders the rim of the flat cake called the earth. In the center, like a birthday candle, the Tower of Jerusalem. This is the picture of medieval man as it appears on a famous map of 1417.

The Phoenicians and Carthaginians had discovered what was essentially the core of this world. Alexander the Great had widened the circle somewhat and had founded, in Egypt, the first geographical institute. Under the Antonines in the second century A.D., war almost broke out between Rome and China. Through the crusades, the contacts with the Arabs, and the scourge of the Mongols, the Norse voyages to Vinland, the great exploratory trip of the Polos, this picture of the early geographers was only slightly changed. The system of Claudius Ptolemy stood firm for 1600 years until it was radically changed and overthrown by Copernicus, Luther's contemporary.

Marco Polo, with his uncles Niccolo and Maffeo, had visited the palace of the Kublai Khan in Peking in 1271 and remained in China 20 years. His description which was loosely incorporated in future world maps had a tremendous influence upon the decision of Columbus to find new worlds by travelling west. Columbus, however, had no knowledge of the Viking expeditions to Greenland and Vinland which may have antedated his discovery of America by almost 400 years.[1]

The main reason for the new discoveries was the growing might of the Turkish Empire which cut the vital trade route between the Italian trading cities and the East. Thus in the late fourteenth century the leaders of these merchandising enterprises became restless. Finally, the fever caught on after Prince Henry the Navigator, born in 1394 as the third son of John I of Portugal, entered upon his labors which he pursued determinedly for 45 years. His endeavor, to encircle the Moorish Empire in Africa and to defeat the infidel, led to many discoveries, and when he died, in 1460, the happy intelligence that the countries of the East could be reached by sea was accepted by many. Vasco da Gama, another Portuguese, born in 1469, was to verify Henry's assumption half a century later. On July 8, 1497, he began his great voyage, sailed around the Cape of Good Hope, and reached India at the Malabar Coast on May 20th of the following year. Eighty-four years after Henry the Navigator had sent his first expedition to discover the African "Black Ocean," the task had been accomplished. The second expedition to India, under Cabral—Vasco da Gama had met the common fate of explorers, distrust and fear by his prince—established the Portuguese Empire in India. But it was not until da Gama had been reinstated and sent on a third expedition, that the Portuguese, in 1505, were able to force their first viceroy, Francisco d'Almeida, upon the natives. During the next 80 years the Portuguese conquered many countries, defeated Egyptians, Turks, Moors, until they were finally, in 1580, conquered by the Spaniards who quickly lost interest in the Indian Empire which passed into other hands.

If the Portuguese would have discovered the sea route to India ten years earlier, Columbus might never have discovered America. The discovery of America, although eventually it would have occurred, might have been postponed for another century or more, until the rise of English power. It was fortunate that Columbus, born in Genoa, Italy, in 1446, as the son of a weaver, was able to persuade the reluctant Isabella of Castile and her even more reluctant husband, Ferdinand of Aragon, in 1492, that he could find a sea route to India by sailing West. For these monarchs, as almost all princes, were not interested in the discovery of new worlds, but in the practical issue of establishing a sea route to India, taking as much commerce away from the Italian and Portuguese competitors. Columbus had tried for many years to interest kings and princes in his "mad" scheme, but without success. He was about to give up, embarking at a Spanish port with his son for the voyage home, broken in spirit and bereft of finances. However, a Spanish monk, Juan de Marchena, and a physician, Garcia Hernandes, succeeded by a last attempt to change the mind of Isabella. The moment was propitious. The last Moors had been driven from Granada in January of that year. Columbus was sent. On August 3, 1492, the Santa Maria, Pinta, and Nina left Palos. After a difficult voyage land was sighted on October 12, 1492, and America, at least one of its outlying islands had been discovered. After establishing the first Spanish colony at La Navidad, and after suppressing a mutiny among his cut-throat sailors, many of them former criminals,

Columbus succeeded in the even more difficult task of reaching home, on March 15, 1493.[2]

The Portuguese, fearful that the Spaniards would establish an empire in the West while they were busy in the East, now induced Pope Alexander VI to divide the world between the two nations which he did in the Treaty of Tordesillas, 1494, in which the world —as far as it was not owned by a Christian prince at Christmas time 1492—was divided between Spain and Portugal at the 46th meridian. East of it the Portuguese were to have a free hand, west of it the Spaniards.[3]

Columbus, who had brought home from his first expedition a few samples of American products and a few naked "Indios," but no gold and spices, was not as enthusiastically supported on his second voyage as before. Later, on his third voyage, at San Domingo, where his brother Bartolomeo had just put down an insurrection, he was put in irons and sent back to Spain. Although he was freed and treated honorably, his star was rapidly declining. The discovery of the sea route to the East by Vasco da Gama, in 1499, put his life's work completely in the shade. And although a fourth voyage followed after the first three, in 1502, during which he discovered the central American mainland at Honduras and revived hopes that gold was abundant among the Mayas, Columbus returned as a shipwrecked captain and died a few years later. His remains were buried in Hispaniola, the pearl of the Antilles, but after the Spanish War of 1898, were returned to Spain. The new continent was not called Columbia, but America, after another Italian, the Venetian Amerigo Vespucci, who gave the first complete travelogue of the New World.

The discovery of Columbus gave rise to a whole generation of conquistadores, some important, some not, some good, some bad. In 1495 the Spanish government had given to all Spaniards the right to go to the "New World" and to find and keep under the Spanish crown what could be found and kept. Thus the knight Alonso de Hojeda discovered, in 1499, Surinam, Dutch Guiana. Juan de la Cosa drew the oldest map of America. Vespucci went to South America and returned with his famous description. Pinzon discovered the mouth of the Amazon. Balboa, a nobleman from Estramadura, discovered the "South Sea," which was later named the Pacific

Ocean. Deeply in debt and a failure in earlier adventures he gladly listened to the stories of the Indians, describing the existence of an ocean at the other side of the mountains. With the help of blood hounds which were used to tear unfriendly Indians to pieces, Balboa finally succeeded in crossing the Isthmus, and with a Spanish flag in his hand he ran into the surf and declared the "South Sea" part of the Spanish realm. That was in 1513.

In 1511 Diego Velasquez had accomplished the conquest of Cuba, the first American territory completely subjugated. In 1517 Francisco de Cordova made contact with the Mayas again whom Columbus had seen 15 years before. This eventually led to the conquest of Mexico and Peru. Juan de Grijalva, while coasting along the coast of Mexico, came for the first time face to face with the terrible custom of the Aztecs to sacrifice human beings to their gods, a custom which had been unknown among the more gentle Mayas.

Among the minor explorers must also be mentioned Ponce de Leon who discovered Florida, but was repelled by the wild Seminoles. South America was known as far south as the La Plata estuary, but the much searched for passage to the "South Sea" had not been found.

At that time a Portuguese in Spanish employ, Ferdinand Magellan (Magelhaens), undertook the task to complete the work which Columbus had left unfinished. On September 20, 1519, he left Spain with five boats and 280 men, sent by Charles, the later Roman emperor. Magellan had to fight the same mutinous attitudes —like Columbus he was considered a "foreigner"—but by ruthless suppression and abandonment of the mutineers he succeeded to reach the southern tip of Argentina. During the South American winter he remained for over 5 months in Patagonia, and after leaving the mutineers to their deadly fate and losing one of his ships, he continued on October 21, 1520, through the straits which are named after him. He did not see much of the inhabitants of these wild regions, only their fires at night which caused him to call the land "Tierra del Fuego." During the navigation of the straits he lost another boat, but on November 28, 1520, reached the open sea which he called "Mare Pacifico," not aware of the fact that another Spaniard had named it "South Sea." The following months were months of privation and starvation. Although he sailed through the Polynesian islands, he sighted only two. On March 6, 1521, he reached a group of islands where the natives, good naturedly, but curious, stole everything from his ships that they could lay hold of. In retaliation the native villages were burned and the island group named "Ladrones," which means Thieves' Islands. Later they received a more honorable name, Marianas. Finally he arrived at the Philippines, between Luzon and Mindanao, where his sick could be cared for and his stock refurbished. One of the native kings swore an oath of allegiance to the Spanish king and had himself baptized. But during an ensuing skirmish Magellan was killed and most of his men with him. The rest, under the leadership of Carvalhos and Espinosa, continued their voyage, under many hardships, persecuted not only by infidels, but also by Portuguese rivals whose territories they were now touching off and on. Most of them were captured, but a small remnant under the leadership of d'Elcano returned to San Lucar, Spain, on September 6, 1522, almost three years after Magellan had left. Of the 280 who had sailed, only 13 were left. The circumnavigation of the world was accomplished, the globe had been spanned, its size was now known.[4]

While Magellan and his successors had accomplished their task, the first great nation of America had been subjugated to the Spanish king. Apart from Cuba, a comparatively small country without a national existence, no country of the new world had been effectively colonized during the first quarter century after the discovery. It was not until 1519, that the first great attempt was made to conquer this world for the king. And to be sure, this was the greatest and most brilliant exposition ever carried on in the New World by the greatest of all conquistadores, Hernando Cortez.[5]

Born in 1485, two years after Luther, he studied at the University of Salamanca, but decided to find his fortune in the New World where he landed, only 20 years old, and participated in the conquest of Cuba. Trusting in his brilliant young lieutenant, the Cuban governor, Velasquez, sent Cortez with 400 soldiers, 200 Indians, 16 cavalry men and 14 canons to the main land. Velasquez regretted his choice, but too late. Cortez had left, before Velasquez could stop him. On the mainland he conquered Tabasco and appropriated an Indian slave girl, who is known to history by her Christian name, Donna Marina. Without her unselfish love for the conquistador and her services as spy and interpreter Cortez could never have succeeded in the great task which he now set out to accomplish. After landing on the Mexican coast on March 21, 1519, he built a fort which he called Villa Rica de la Vera Cruz, now the most important harbor of the Republic of Mexico.

Little was known about the state against which Cortez now proceeded. On the high plateau of the hinterland which arose terrace-like behind the coastal plains occupied by the Spanish, in the earlier Middle Ages the Mayas, a peaceful, agricultural nation, had developed a high civilization. But a few centuries before the discoveries this nation had retreated to Yukatan and Honduras, and the country was now occupied by the Aztecs, who about 1300 had built the lagune city of Tenochtitlan, the present-day Mexico. The Aztecs were a warlike and cruel nation who sacrificed their prisoners in bloody sacrifices to their gods among whom Huitzilopochtli or Mexitl was the most feared. Among the many other gods, Quetzalcoatl deserves special mention, for he was the mystical reformer of the faith, the man of light skin, bearded and darkhaired, of whom one told that he would some day return. At the time when Cortez arrived in Mexico this return was anxiously awaited since the Aztec empire had fallen upon evil days. It was, therefore, easy to mistake the darkhaired bearded Cortez for Quetzalcoatl.

The empire of the Aztecs was in decline, the restive captured nations were ready to rise. Nothing could restrain these people, not even the cannibalistic ceremonies of their conquerors. Thus the Aztecs had sacrificed 70,000 people at the dedication ceremony of the great Teocallin, the pyramid temple, of Mexico. They had by an excellent system of postal service tried to protect themselves against surprises, and in fact, their emperor Montezuma knew of Cortez's arrival with lightning speed. They had an excellent army, and this army was now ready to oppose the handful of Spanish adventurers who had landed at Vera Cruz.

Montezuma who with the news of Cortez' arrival also had received detailed descriptions and even sketches of his face was, however, undecided. The idea that this man may be a messenger of

Magellan landing in the Philippines, 1521.

Victory of Cortes over the Aztecs at Otumba, Mexico.
(After a painting by Manuel Ramirez.)

Vasco Da Gama received by the Samorin in Calcutta, India, 1498.

Balboa discovering the Pacific Ocean. The explorer claimed the unknown sea for the King of Castile.

effort to restore order, prevailed upon the captive emperor to address his restless people from the ramparts, but the plan misfired. Montezuma was badly wounded by rocks thrown by his people, and this and the feeling that he was rejected by his people caused his death a short time later. In the night of July 1 to July 2, 1520, Cortez and his army fled from Mexico's capital.

This night is remembered in history as "la noche triste," the night of sadness. The Spaniards succeeded in reaching the dam without being discovered. But suddenly alarm was sounded from the height of the temple of Huitzilopochtli, the Aztecs attacked furiously and the melee began. The Spaniards, pressed together on the narrow straits, burdened by booty, were unable to use their weapons to the fullest extent. They succeeded in reaching the first drawbridge which fortunately was down, but subsequently they had to use a self-made portable bridge which proved inadequate. The exact circumstances of the disaster are not known. Suffice it to say, that the portable bridge either fell into the water or broke, a panic ensued, the canals were filled with the bodies of men and animals, over which the remnants of the retreating Spaniards fled to safety. The few who escaped were either wounded or deadly tired. The rest were either killed by the arrows of the Aztecs, or had drowned during the panic, or what's worse, were now being sacrificed at the altar of the great Teocallin. Nevertheless, Cortez continued his retreat with great dispatch and was able to defeat an Aztec army which had been sent out to cut off his route. He reached the safe walls of Tlascala which had kept faith with him and started immediately to prepare a new assault on Tenochtitlan by building portable boats which were to be carried over the passes to the capital.

Before the catastrophic retreat from the Aztec capital Cortez had defeated a Spanish rival, who had been sent by his one-time protector, Velasquez, to punish the insubordination of the conquistador. In this way he received from Velasquez who did not know that his messenger had been defeated from time to time new troops so that the forces of the Spaniards gradually increased to 600. With these and about 100,000 Tlascalan and other Indian auxiliaries Cortez undertook at the beginning of 1521 his second assault on the Aztec capital and was able to capture it after bloody battles during which the horrified Spaniards beheld the sacrifices of their captured friends on the top of the pyramid of the great Teocallin. The battle lasted 75 days, over 100,000 Mexicans were killed, and the last emperor of the Aztecs, Guatimozin, was captured and tortured. Without saying a word or uttering a cry the proud Indian suffered the supreme humiliation.

Charles V rewarded his most successful conquistador royally. Cortez was later able to subjugate Yukatan and Honduras, but the fate of all conquistadores in the employ of faithless Spain was also his. Charles V, afraid of Cortez' growing power deprived him gradually of his positions. Deeply offended Cortez spent most of his remaining years on his estates in Oaxaca, only rarely occupying himself with further explorations. Thus he explored the California peninsula. But when the new Spanish governor forbade him further expeditions, Cortez in 1540 returned to Spain to find justice at the court of Charles V. The emperor fed him empty promises, took him to Algiers with his army, but did not allow him to continue his expeditions. Thus the greatest of all conquistadores died like the greatest of all Spanish admirals before him: Forsaken by his erstwhile friends, forgotten by the world. Death came on December 2, 1547, less than two years after Luther's.

There were other great explorers and conquerors. The conquest of Peru by Francisco Pizarro is equally glorious and infamous. Here too the Inkas had been divided, as were the Aztecs of Mexico before them, and were ripe for conquest. Pizarro's expedition which began in 1532 is strangely reminiscent of Cortez'. But his methods were cruder and more cruel. Furthermore, he was killed. His lieutenants continued the conquests, with much glory for Spain and little credit to their humanity. Again Charles V intervened and had some of his most faithful generals disqualified and even executed.

From Peru Gonzalo Pizarro, brother of the famous Francisco, conquered Colombia. Quesada, another Spanish warrior, founded Bogota and the colony New Granada. In Chile Pedro de Valdivia pushed back the fierce Araucas, many of whom are still unconquered today. At the end of the reign of Charles V the conquest of South and Central America was on the whole complete. Charles, who had ascended the throne of Spain before the great exploit of Cortez was destined to see the Spanish empire reach its greatest extent.

All these conquests seem to have had little effect upon the life of Martin Luther, but they vitally influenced the course of the Reformation. Not only was the evangelical doctrine transplanted to the new world, thus for a time to Venezuela where the Augsburg banker Welser settled some Lutherans, or to Brazil and Florida where around the middle of the sixteenth century colonies of "Lutherans," rather Calvinists, were found, but it was also aided in the old. The center of the old world which for 2,000 years had been around the Mediterranean, now had shifted to the coasts of the Atlantic Ocean. Northern Germany, Scandinavia, Holland, Flanders, let alone England, suddenly found themselves in the center of commerce. The rising power of England and the declining power of Spain under Charles' successor, Philip II, the liberation of the Netherlands and the defeat of the Armada favored the Reformation which otherwise would perhaps have been crushed under the power of Spanish Catholicism. The intellectual horizon widened perceptibly, the superstitions of the dark ages were left behind. Most of the world view of the Middle Ages was gone forever, and even Jesuitism and Inquisition were only partly successful in restoring it by resorting to blunt political terror. A new age had dawned, an age which unlike the era of the Renaissance had not crept upon Western man slowly and almost imperceptibly, but had come upon the world within the lifetime of Martin Luther: The age of the great world powers, of new nations where ultimately free exercise of religion, the evangelical principle of faith, would be victorious.

V

The Holy Empire

The Holy Roman Empire of the German Nation was at the time of Luther largely a religio-mystical force without any real power. Yet it continued to wield a tremendous influence in the minds of men, and the dream of long-lost glory was still very much alive among the best of them.

Conceived as a successor to the Roman Empire, extinct since 476 in the West, but continuing as a rival to the papacy in the East for another 1000 years, the Holy Empire was born from the alliance of emperor and pope. Charlemagne had received the crown on Christmas Day 800 in Rome from the hands of the pope, and throughout the Middle Ages to the time of Luther, when Charles V, the last great emperor, received the crown in 1530 from Clement VII, the desire to ally the worldly and the ecclesiastic power in the Holy Empire had been the dream of succeeding generations through 700 years. The Reformation finally brought this dream to an end, and although the empire continued to exist in a kind of shadow existence for another 300 years, to round out the millennium, the dream was never revived.

But so strong was the dream that Luther himself attempted to realize it by urging Charles V to become the true spiritual leader of the nations united under his scepter. In this he failed, due to Charles' vacillating policy, for although the emperor was not a friend of the popes and of Roman arrogance, he was still a faithful, and even fanatical member of the Church of which the pope was the head. It is the tragedy of the Empire, that Charles V was unable to emulate the example of Henry VIII—not his moral, but his practical, example—or even the example of the Danish and Swedish kings, to break away from the tutelage of Rome. How different would have been the outcome for the whole world! For Charles did not only rule Germany, Austria, Hungary, Bohemia and large parts of Italy, but also the Netherlands, Spain and the vast continent of America, newly discovered. He, and he alone, could have given the death blow to Romanism. But he too was unable to break away from the magic of the dream which had dominated his predecessors through the ages, and had himself crowned by the worthless Medici pope whom he had nearly annihilated three years before during the Sack of Rome.

The Holy Roman Empire as a political force of definite meaning really had not existed for nearly 300 years. Built first by Charlemagne upon the premise that the emperor, though receiving his crown from the pope, was the ruler of the realm, revived under the Ottos of the tenth century, it had slowly lost its power during the ensuing battles between popes and emperors. When Henry IV was banned by the pope and had to do penance before Gregory VII, standing barefooted before the castle gate of Canossa, the power of the Holy Empire received a blow from which it did not recover.[1] Neither the numerous expeditions to Italy in which the pope was often defeated and the emperors' powers asserted, nor the cooperation with popes during the crusades, could restore the ancient splendor of the Holy Empire. The captivity of the popes in Avignon, the schism of the Church did not alter this fact. For new states, until now mere satellites receiving their light from the Holy Empire, had arisen, placing themselves on an equal footing with it. France had been able to capture the pope. Before, France had claimed the blood of a Roman emperor, and the last Hohenstaufen had died, a victim of French intrigues, on the executioner's block in Naples. Switzerland had freed itself from the Empire, when the terror of the Hapsburg emperors proved unbearable. New nations had arisen in Bohemia and Hungary which were, for a time at least, independent of effective control by the emperor. Even within Germany mighty cities and combinations of cities had arisen which challenged the sovereignty of the emperor. In many parts anarchy and internecine wars were rampant. And the empire bled itself to death in constant battle and forays into Italy. Yet the dream persisted.

Frederick II, the first modern and at the same time the last truly universal emperor, had died in Sicily in 1250 and a few years later his dynasty had lost the throne when Conrad was beheaded in Naples. After the death of Conrad IV the empire was for a long time without a head. The newly elected King William was killed during a campaign against the Frisians in 1256 and until 1273 the "Great Interregnum," the rule without a ruler, made Germany a battleground of darkness. There were kings and candidates for kingship, there was Alfonse of Castile who was elected by one party of electors, while Richard of Cornwallis was elected by another. But order was not restored until finally the pope threatened to appoint a king for the orphaned empire. Then, and only then, did the princes agree on the person of Rudolph of Hapsburg (1273-1291), a minor prince whose ancestral castle was in Switzerland near the Rhine and Aar Rivers. Rudolph was able to assert himself, especially against his powerful rival, King Ottokar of Bohemia, who paid for his ambition with his life and from whom Rudolph obtained the countries of Austria, Styria, Carinthia, Crain, and Eger, the base of future Hapsburg greatness. Ottokar's son, Wenceslas II, was allowed to retain Bohemia.

With the help of strict laws Rudolph changed anarchy into order, but was unable to obtain the crown for his son Albert, so that the rule passed, at least temporarily, to another dynasty, represented by Adolph of Nassau (1291-1298), who, however, had to fight a hard fight for his throne and was finally defeated and killed in a battle against Rudolph's son Albert. During his reign Adolph had restored the Swiss privileges which had originally been granted by Frederick II in 1240. This letter of privilege and the subsequent refusal by Albrecht, whose ancestral home, as we have seen, was in Switzerland, to honor these letters was the reason for the birth of the Swiss Confederation which led to the first large breakaway from the Holy Empire.[2]

Albert I (1298-1308), at the same time cruel and undecided, was able to defeat the archbishops on the Rhine who upon instigation of Pope Boniface VIII, recently defeated and captured by Philip of France, had accused him of regicide, the murder of King Adolph of Nassau. He used this victory to increase the power of the House of Hapsburg, and also made overtures against Bohemia. But just as he was getting ready to advance his claim upon Bohemia by force of arms, he was murdered by his own nephew, the Duke John of Swabia, who in history has received the name John Parricida.

After Albert's death several pretenders to the throne appeared upon the scene, but finally the electors united their vote on Henry VII of Luxemburg (1308-1313), whose first ambition was to go to Italy and to receive the imperial crown. But Italy was now without a pope and the robber barons of the house of Colonna and Orsini ruled the streets of Rome. Henry VII who had crossed the Alps at Mt. Cenis in 1310 and had been received with great jubilation by the populace of Northern Italy—and by Dante himself—was able, with the help of the Ghibellines, to enter Rome, but was unable to reach St. Peter's Church. Thus the Roman Emperor received his crown in the Lateran Church during a bombardment by the Roman outlaws (1312). The following year he died, poisoned —it was rumored—by a Dominican monk. His last resting place is in Pisa.[3]

Again the electors were unable to unite their votes. One party, under the leadership of the archbishop of Cologne, elected Frederick the Fair of Austria, the son of Albert I, while the majority crowned Louis of Bavaria. The contest was finally settled by force of arms, Frederick the Fair was defeated, and Louis the Bavarian became emperor. Magnanimous and forgiving he appointed his fallen rival co-regent and was not deceived in his trust. Frederick died in 1330, having served his erstwhile rival faithfully. Louis (1313-1346) ruled with a strong hand, but again the dream of Rome almost was his undoing. He succeeded in winning the eternal city by force of arms and was crowned by the Colonnas—there was still no pope—but had to leave Rome in a hurry when he tried to impose upon the Roman populace a pope whom they did not like.

In order to put an end to the influence of the pope in the selection of kings, an influence which had been disastrous in past elections, Louis called together his electors to Rense and established the law by which future kings and emperors were to be elected by the electors of the empire, independent of the approval of the pope. The pope, even though a prisoner at Avignon or because of the intrigues of the French king, did not give in. He persuaded five German electors to depose Louis and elect his old enemy Charles, son of the king of Bohemia, king. The archbishop of Cologne actually crowned Charles king, but the cities and the other electors stood faithfully by Louis, the Bavarian. A civil war was seen unavoidable, when Louis suddenly died of a stroke and Charles IV (1346-1378) became undisputed ruler of the Empire.

Charles IV, founder of the first German university in Prague, ruled during the terrible Black Death which more than decimated the population of Europe.[4] It is estimated that more than 25 million people died during this scourge which was introduced to Europe by the hordes of the Mongols who had thrown the corpses of their dead into a city which refused to surrender. The plague spread like a forest fire. No city was left untouched. Petrarch has created a lasting monument to it in his Decameron. Often the whole population of a village or small town would die in one night. Even centuries later villages were "rediscovered" of whom there was no record. This terrible plague marked also the first large scale pogrom of Jews which was the beginning of a series of persecutions which were to besmirch the history of Western civilization to the present time. The bishop of Strassburg, for example, had 2,000 Jews burned to the greater glory of God and for reconciliation and deliverance from the plague. In France, Germany, Switzerland unnumbered Jews were killed. Only Poland, whose king had a Jewish mistress, gave asylum to the persecuted race.

Charles IV also went to Rome to receive the crown. But having made an agreement with Pope Clement VI to leave the city within 24 hours and having received his crown from a papal legate, the emperor hastily left the eternal city, cursed by the hatred of all true Italian patriots who had expected him to bring an end to the anarchy and civil strife in their country. After this experience Charles issued the "Golden Bull," which again reiterated the prin-

ciple laid down previously for the election of an emperor, adding
to this the provision that one of the seven electors should serve as
regent of the Empire after the death of an emperor, that three of
the electors should be Lords Spiritual and four Lords Temporal,
and that the presiding officer of the electoral council should be the
King of Bohemia who was to call his colleagues to Frankfurt for
the election. If after 30 days the electors could not agree on a
candidate they should be given nothing but bread and water until
they had united their votes. The Bull furthermore stipulated that
the electors should meet every year to discuss imperial matters of
policy, that electorates should not be subdivided and that the oldest
son of an elector should follow him in this dignity. Thus the first
real constitutional reform was instituted which was strengthened by
Maximilian during the lifetime of Luther and remained into effect
until the demise of the Holy Empire in 1806.

During the reign of Charles IV the first great combinations of free
cities victoriously resisted the encroachment by territorial princes.
In Swabia the Swabian cities were able to force Count Eberhard of
Wuerttemberg, a rapacious prince, to grant them the right to co-
determine the future policies of the land. In Northern Germany the
Hanseatic League, an alliance of 70 cities, defeated Waldemar
Atterdag of Denmark, and obtained in the Peace of Stralsund
(1370) a great influence which extended even to the election of a
Danish king. Charles, in the meantime, had been able to enlarge
his family possessions considerably. He saw his son, Wenceslas,
elected king. He even invested the French crown prince with the
Kingdom of Burgundy, thus obtaining a voice and influence in
French politics. The influence of the Emperor, if not of the Empire,
was greater than at any time since the days of Frederick II, when
Charles IV died in 1378 in Prague.

His son and successor Wenceslas (1378-1400), a cruel, worthless,
lazy king, was to undo much of what his father had accomplished.
He was completely unable to cope with the schism in the Church
which had begun in 1370 when a pope was elected in Rome, while
the pope in Avignon refused to yield. During the next half century
there were two, sometimes three, popes who cursed each other and
excommunicated each other. He was also unable to preserve the

peace in the Empire. Finally he retreated to his castle in Prague where he lived in virtual retirement while his princes and nobles ravaged the country. In the battle between Huss and the Roman see he took the side of Huss, not for religious, but for political reasons. When Wenceslas had been captured by the forces of the electors who wanted to get rid of him, the Czech populace had taken his side against the Germans and freed him. Finally, in 1400 he was dethroned, but continued to live lazily in Prague.[5]

Rupert of the Palatinate (1400-1410), the new emperor, like most of his predecessors had no greater desire than to obtain the Roman crown in Italy. In 1401 he crossed the Alps, but was defeated at the walls of Brescia by the experienced condottieri of Galeazzo Visconti, the chief Italian supporter of his rival Wenceslas. The defeat of Rupert encouraged his German enemies to plot for his overthrow. They concluded a League in Defense of Peace, as they called it euphemistically, which under the leadership of the archbishop of Mainz made a treaty with France. Everything was ready to bring Rupert's rule to an end, with the help of foreign mercenaries and native robber barons, when the emperor suddenly died in 1410.

The electors, not heeding the stipulations of the Golden Bull, again divided their votes between two contenders, Sigismund, the younger brother of the deposed Wenceslas, and his cousin, Jost of Moravia. Since Wenceslas still considered himself legal king, the empire for a while had three kings, as the Church had three popes, but Sigismund finally succeeded in 1411 to settle the dispute and was elected unanimously emperor. Sigismund was of a different caliber than many of his predecessors and not infected with the mystical power of the Roman crown. His foremost concern was to bring to an end the schism in the Church and to curb the heresy of Huss. In both he succeeded at the Council of Constance which was the first general council completely under the dominion of an emperor in the memory of men. Hus was treacherously killed, the popes deposed and a new pope appointed, but the religious ferment, as we have seen in a previous chapter was not brought to an end. Most of Sigismund's reign was consumed in this religious ferment and he died, while fleeing from Prague, in 1437. His son-in-law, Albert of Austria (1437-1439), had the distinction of recapturing the crown

for the Hapsburg dynasty with which it remained until the end
of the empire 400 years later.

Albert of Austria, after a reign too short to be effective, died
fighting against the Turks in 1439. He was followed by Frederick III
who ruled longer than any Roman emperor, a weak and easily
influenced monarch, who was interested primarily in Hapsburg's
future which he tried to guarantee by a series of more or less fortunate marriage deals. He lost, however, Hungary and Bohemia
which were not recovered until a century later. Hungary passed, in
1457, under the rule of its greatest son, Matthias Corvinus, while
Bohemia was captured by George Podiebrad, one of the Hussite
leaders. Equally ineffective were his attempts to deal with the
Roman question and a new schism was in the offing. However, his
able secretary, the wily Aeneas Sylvio Piccolomini, later Pope Pius
II, understood to handle these matters to the aggrandizement of
Roman power and the detriment of the empire.

Thus the long reign of Frederick III is one of the saddest chapters
of German history.[6] While France and other countries emancipated
themselves from Roman tutelage, Frederick accepted a large sum
as a bribe against all reforms in the Empire. No wonder that the
German princes and knights rose in rebellion against such unworthy
emperor. When Frederick went to Italy in 1451 to take a bride,
Eleonora of Portugal, and to be crowned in St. Peter's Church in
Rome, a free-for-all war broke out in Germany. The Hungarians
asked for the surrender of Vladislaw Posthumus, the son of a
former prince, Albert, and of the crown which Albert's widow had
surrendered to Frederick after her husband's death. In Germany
itself anarchy was rearing its ugly head, cities challenging knights,
knights robbing merchants and peasants, and princes looking on
helplessly. Achilles, Burggrave of Nuremberg and a Hohenzollern,
tried in vain to subject the proud city to his will. Nuremberg appealed to the Empire. Other cities joined the battle. The electors
demanded the election of a new Emperor, since Frederick III had
proved himself unfit for the high office, but due to the lack of
unity among the electors nothing was done. Aeneas Sylvio Piccolomini knew how to play elector against elector.

During this time the terrible news reached Germany that Constantinople, the Eastern Rome, had fallen to the infidels and that the Hagia Sophia was now no longer a temple of the Triune God. Fear and anger was the reaction. The pope admonished the Christians to fight against the infidel and demanded a Turkish tax for a Holy Crusade. But the money, mostly raised in Germany, was used for other purposes, especially the enrichment of the Roman coffers. The emperor was willing to help, but was unable to do anything effective on account of the anarchy in the Empire. His own brother, Albert of Austria, tried to take that country away from him and to detach it from the Empire. The Emperor Frederick himself was besieged and bombarded in his castle in Vienna and was forced to surrender Austria for eight years to his rebellious brother. Fortunately, Albert of Austria died before he could do more harm.

The King of Bohemia, George Podiebrad, had been offered the crown of the Empire by the dissatisfied electors, but when nothing came of it, this ambitious prince turned East to win the crown of the Eastern Roman Empire which had just been overthrown by the Turks. This induced him to conduct his affairs independently of the Empire and against the wishes of the pope. The pope, in turn, excommunicated him and in the ensuing rebellion the King of Hungary, Matthias Corvinus, invaded Bohemia to wrest the crown from Podiebrad. The latter, however, was able to defend himself successfully, but died soon thereafter, in 1471, whereupon a son of the King of Poland, Vladislaw Jagello, was elected king of Bohemia who later also became King of Hungary (1490). Hungary remained under this dynasty until Jagello's son, Louis II, was killed by the Turks in the battle of Mohacs, in 1526, and in the following years, both Bohemia and Hungary returned to the control of the Hapsburgs. But that was long after the death of Frederick III.

Frederick in the meantime tried to find new allies in his battle against the discontented princes of his empire. He turned to Charles the Bold of Burgundy, a brother of the French king, who by marriage had gained control of Antwerp, Flanders, Artois, Franche Comté, Brabant, and Limburg, to which were later added Holland, Zeeland, Hennegau, Namur, Boulogne, and Luxemburg. Thus the Burgundian duke was in possession of the entire German western frontier, a rich territory upon which Frederick now directed his attention. The ambitious Burgundian prince was coveting a royal crown and Frederick promised to help him to get it, if he would give his daughter Mary to the emperor's son, Maximilian. In November 1473 the two sovereigns met in Trier, but when Charles demanded to be crowned before he would give his daughter to Maximilian, Frederick was forced to leave Trier hurriedly, whereupon Charles invaded Germany plundering and ravaging, but the Swiss mercenaries who successfully stemmed the invasion, were able to complete the marriage arrangement. Charles himself was killed near Nancy in 1477 when he tried, unsuccessfully, to resume the war. The king of France now claimed Burgundy which lawfully belonged to Mary, the only daughter of the late Duke of Burgundy. She appealed to Maximilian who, after celebrating his nuptials with her, defeated the French forces in 1479; but already in 1482 the young couple was separated when Mary died after a fall from a horse. Maximilian, father of their two year old boy, Philip, now assumed the reign of Burgundy and its outlying possessions in the name of his son, but had to face the opposition of the Burgundian nobles.[7]

In the meantime, Matthias Corvinus, King of Hungary, had invaded Austria from the east. He forced the emperor to acknowledge him as King of Bohemia which after the death of George Podiebrad had become rulerless. Again in 1485 the same king, Matthias Corvinus, invaded Austria and conquered in a short period Austria, Carinthia, Crain, and Styria, while the aged emperor, robbed of his own lands, fled from city to city, from monastery to monastery and had to live from the mercy of his subjects. In vain he looked for help at the Diet of Frankfurt, which in 1486 elected the young promising Maximilian king and co-ruler of his father.

Maximilian tried, first, to reestablish order in the Netherlands where the rebellious nobles were still unwilling to acknowledge him as legal heir of his late wife, Mary. But the rebels caught him at Bruges and kept him imprisoned. Only with great difficulty was he able to extricate himself, and now turned against Hungary where Matthias Corvinus had just died. Maximilian was able to reconquer Austria from the leaderless Hungarians, but was unable to regain Hungary, which had passed under the rule of Vladaslav Jagello, as we have seen above. Frederick III was able to enjoy the possession of his old lands of Austria two more years. In 1493 he finally left the scene of history.

Thus was the condition of the Holy Roman Empire of the German nation at the time when Luther was born. Its magic name still existed, but its glory had long since departed. The reigns of Maximilian and Charles, who tried to recapture some of the old mystical meaning of the Holy Empire, will be described elsewhere. They and all the following emperors never succeeded. It has been alleged that the Reformation split the Empire and gave the death blow to the unity which existed during the Middle Ages. Nothing could be farther from the truth. The Reformation did not even break the alliance between the German rulers and Rome which had been broken centuries before. As a matter of fact, Charles V, the greatest opponent of the Reformation, probably also was the one emperor who was most independent of Rome and freely warred against the pope. On the other hand, the pope did not support this faithful son of the Church, but allied himself with the King of France and other enemies, thus making Charles' battle against the heresy of Lutheranism futile. As for the unity within the empire, the Reformation rather helped it. For before the Reformation there had been scores of alliances, disorders, petty wars, while with the Reformation order was restored not only in Protestant territories but also in the lands whose princes clung to the old faith. It is true, of course, that this ultimately led to the two great alliances of Protestants on the one hand and Catholics on the other, resulting in terrible wars. But these wars were no worse than the constant anarchy which prevailed throughout the Empire during the century of Luther's birth.

It has also been said that the Reformation turned back the clock of progress, that the Empire remained an ineffective political agglomeration of petty interests, while France, Spain, England, and other countries were able to unite under strongly centralized governments. This too is a false concept. France's struggle for unity had begun as early as the fourteenth century and by the time of the Reformation France was already a fairly centralized country under the able leadership of a strong king, Francis I. Nowhere was royal absolutism more complete than in the England of Henry VIII who was able to force his brand of Reformation on the whole country. The unity of these two countries had been born in the blood of interminable wars of the past. Spain, too, was unified, but not because it was a purely Catholic country, but because it had no history of power politics and dissensions. Only twenty-five years before the start of the Reformation the last Moors had been driven from its soil and the Spanish king was now occupied to establish his country as the world's leading power. The Scandinavian countries, the lands of the Lutheran Reformation, were able to maintain their unity and increase their power. Within one hundred years Gustavus Adolphus became the terror of the Catholic princes. The Netherlands, though fighting a relentless war of religion, were able to constitute themselves as one of the first powers during the century after the Reformation. Switzerland, too, emerged in the form in which it exists today in spite of the fact that it was religiously divided.

Thus the Reformation had nothing to do with the impotence of Germany. Germany had been divided for hundreds of years before the Reformation, and no religious division could add to this impotence. Similarly, Italy, which was religiously united, continued in its impotence until modern times. What caused the slow-up was not the Reformation, but in both countries the battle between emperors and popes, the mystical dream of the Holy Empire, which made it impossible for modern ideas of statehood to find an expression. Thus while France, England, Holland, the Northern Kingdoms, and even Spain, changed into modern political entities, the heart countries of the Holy Empire, Germany and Italy, remained backward because they could not shake the sentimental dream of the Holy Empire.

This, of course, in some way affected Luther and Lutheranism. Luther's political views often seemed impractical. His trust in Charles V, misplaced, but obstinately adhered to, his distrust of political alliances, his "old-fashioned" ideas against rebellion which made the more practical Swiss Reformed laugh, his hope for the re-unification of Christendom, for a Reform Council to reform the whole Church, never really left him, and he bequeathed them to the Lutheran Church. Thus while the Swiss energetically engaged in religious wars as early as 1531, and Zwingli died on the battlefield, and while Calvin established his theocracy in Geneva, and while the foreign kings, both Catholic and Evangelical, used all the resources of their royal power to force upon their people an order which they determined was best for them, Luther and his friends were reluctant to form even a defensive alliance against the Hapsburg emperor who sought their doom, and after the alliance had been formed, they were not willing to make it effective. The Smalcald League died before the Smalcald War began, and John Frederick was defeated, because he argued with himself whether it would be right to start a war against Charles V whom he knew to be his mortal enemy. This also caused Melanchthon and others to continue the useless discussions with the Catholics for the unity of faith, which continued even after the Smalcald War, to the detriment of the Lutheran Church. Even a century after the Reformation, the mystical dream was still so strong that the Protestant princes refused to rally to the side of their liberator, Gustavus of Sweden, until they were forced to do so and valuable time had been lost which the Protestants were never able to regain.

Even without the terrible Thirty Years War Germany would not have emerged as a powerful European power until the dream of the Holy Empire, a good dream in the times of Charlemagne and the Ottos and even of Frederick II, had died. Thus, while the power of the Empire had vanished long before the Reformation, the dream continued to occupy the minds and hearts of the "impractical" Germans until the day of Frederick the Great, not a Lutheran and not a Catholic, but a pure rationalist, who established the first modern state within the boundaries of the old Holy Roman Empire. The fact that Napoleon I finished the existence of this empire officially by degree, two years after the last emperor, later his father-in-law, had taken the title "Emperor of Austria," is merely accidental.

It is idle to speculate what would have happened, if the dream of the Holy Empire would have been extinct at the time of Luther. But it is not inconceivable to assume that all of Germany and probably Austria would have become a Lutheran nation, that Charles V would have been challenged and would have been forced to pursue a national policy or relinquish his throne. It is conceivable to assume that Charles V, the Spanish king, would not have been elected emperor in the first place, but that the electors would have pressed the election of Frederick the Wise of Saxony to whom they had proffered the crown. Frederick then would have united his country, both politically and religiously, as did the Nordic kings and Henry of England.

But this was not to be. The world around Luther despite the religious ferment of the preceding century, despite the rebirth of arts and sciences, despite the new vistas opened by discoveries and conquests, was still largely captive to the medieval ideas which had been inherited through a seven century history of glory and heart-ache, religious fervor and political callousness, but which was not willing to yield to the new age as yet and thus confined the Lutheran Reformation, for better or for worse, to the religious arena.

PART TWO

The Men
Around Luther

I.

Luther and
His Contemporaries

Large was the number of people who came into contact with the
Reformer during his lifetime. There is no common denominator
by which the relationship between Luther and his contemporaries
could be determined. Ordinarily the men around him divided into
friends and foes and Luther's dealings with them was accordingly
friendly or hostile. Yet his behavior was often irregular and unpredictable. He would be drawn to his enemies while growing cold
towards his most ardent supporters. Often other factors but religious
convictions entered into Luther's relationship with the men around
him: ethical factors, economic factors, political factors, or what
may be called "likes and dislikes." Thus, Luther would at times
think more of his most outspoken enemy among the princes, Duke
George, than of his most fervent supporter, Landgrave Philip. He
dwelt more often on his debt of gratitude to Staupitz who forsook
him than on the same feeling towards others who fought his battles.
Tetzel he comforted in his last sickness, while later he refused to
forgive Agricola and others who penitently knocked at his door. He
remembered gratefully his teachers Trutvetter and Usingen who did

everything in their power to minimize his influence in Erfurt, while
some of the men close by had to suffer from his increasing irascibility. In all this Luther was not a "Saint without blemish," but an
eminently human being, a "saint" who was a sinner, saved only by
the blood of Christ.

But no matter whom he addressed, the pope, the emperor, princes, theologians, laymen, friend or foe, Luther was always concerned about the Word of God and the salvation of man. Often we
know little of these men except what Luther said about them. Vice
versa Luther's life has been distorted by inaccuracies which often
present insurmountable or difficult problems. But while great pains
has been taken by contemporaries and writers since the times of the
Reformation to give us a fairly complete account of the life of the
Reformer, no one has given much thought and effort to supplement
the meager data which we have on most of the men around Luther.
Often the picture which we have of them has been colored by the
animosities of those who lived with them.

Few people in that intensely religious century could remain neutral in the battle of the Reformation. Almost all were forced to take
sides, even the humanists and artists. Not only popes, emperors,
kings, princes and statesmen spent the better part of their lives
struggling with the problems which Luther had raised, but also the
common man of the street, the quiet scholar, the obedient burgher,
the humble peasant. Never since the days of the great migrations
and the fall of the Western Roman Empire had man been so stirred
to the very depths of his soul as during the first half of the sixteenth
century. Political and economic wars were fought for or against the
Gospel, man's mind was liberated from the narrow confines of
medieval thought, a new day was dawning, in a word: The world
changed during Luther's life-time.

In these chapters we are not so much concerned with the biographical data of the men around Luther as we are interested in the
role which the Lutheran Reformation played in their lives or the
influence which they had upon Luther. This inter-relationship
formed his life, prepared him for his work, and above all enabled
him to carry through the great task to which he had been called.
Thus, in a sense, these men, from his father and friends to the far

distant emperor and pope were important for the Reformation of the Church.

Of Luther's family we know little. His father and mother, Hans and Margaret, who had him baptized by Pastor Rennebecher at SS. Peter-Paul Church in Eisleben. At least three brothers and three sisters. Only two of Luther's brothers lived to maturity. His three sisters later married three Mansfeld burghers, Polner, Mackenrod, and Kaufmann. The son of the Kaufmanns later lived with Luther for a time in Wittenberg. Of Luther's grandparents we know only the names.

In Mansfeld

Less than a year after the Reformer's birth John and Margaret Luther moved to Mansfeld where they lived the rest of their lives, the father dying in 1530 and the mother during the following year. Here in Mansfeld Luther received his first, somewhat less than satisfactory, schooling. The sixty year old Luther later recalled that he was sent to school at a very tender age and that an older schoolmate, Nicholas Oemler, carried him piggy-back through the bottomless muddy main street of tiny Mansfeld. Oemler later married into the Luther family.[1]

Luther's parents were brawny, strong, dark-skinned, and stubborn. The Swiss John Kessler who visited them in 1522 has given us a good picture of them, as did Melanchthon who talked to Luther's mother. Both parents were extremely strict. Yet Luther remembered them with fondness and gratitude. When his father temporarily disowned him after he had entered the monastery, Luther was anxious to become reconciled to him. They did not see each other for two years, and when they met it was unfortunate that old wounds had to be opened. A complete reconciliation between the two headstrong men seems to have been effected only after the dawn of the Reformation.

Of the teachers and pastors at Mansfeld we know little. Besides Oemler Luther had at least one other friend, John Reinicke, son of the Mansfeld bailiff Peter Reinicke. This boy accompanied him to Magdeburg.

In Magdeburg

Luther's father who had become moderately prosperous as a miner and part-owner of mines had decided that the Mansfeld school was not good enough for his oldest son for whom, in spite of the severe treatment which he meted out to him, he had fond hopes for the future. Young Martin was to become a lawyer. Therefore, after consultation with his fellow-townsman Peter Reinicke, both men sent their oldest sons to Magdeburg where an excellent school had been established some years before by the Lollards, the Brothers of the Common Life. Here Luther and John Reinicke stayed during the year 1497 to 1498. In Magdeburg Luther came into contact, probably for the first time in his life, with deeply religious people, the teachers of the Lollard school. Here he saw the penitent life of a Prince of Anhalt who went through the streets of this metropolis of Northern Germany begging *panem propter Deum*, "bread for the love of God." Here he was invited into the home of Dr. Mosshauer, a learned legal officer of the Archbishop of Magdeburg. Here, perhaps, his decision to enter the monastery may have received its first impetus, for, although he did not become a monk until eight years later, his father seems to have been alarmed by the overly religious influence of the Lollards and transferred his son after one year to the more secular surroundings of Eisenach.[2]

In Eisenach

The Eisenach years have been embellished with many beautiful stories. This was partly the fault of Luther himself, who as an old man liked to hold forth with all kinds of stories at table which were to haunt historians to this day, but to a larger extent it is the fault of the good citizens of Eisenach who seem to have been equipped with a more than average desire to boost the fame of the little city at the foot of the Wartburg by inventing fables about the beloved Reformer. This was excusable in the sixteenth century.

It is possible, and even probable, that Luther led a quite average life in Eisenach. His father was by then considered prosperous. Thus the stories about the "poor student" who lived by the mercy of Frau Cotta and even stole a ring of sausages from the local butcher, ate dry bread and sang with an empty stomach, all these stories may be nothing but beautiful weeds of pious legends. There is also no evidence that Luther was then a deeply religious teen-ager. The fact that he remembered the pious Prince of Anhalt 35 years later does not prove that he thought about him in Eisenach. Quite the contrary, there seems to have been during his Eisenach years and especially during the early years in Erfurt a conscious turning away from any preoccupation with the religious life. We do not know. Luther's parents were religious, but in an average sense: Religious to the point of superstition, more interested in indulgences, for which his father applied during those years, than in true faith and trust in God, afraid of witches and demons, grumbling against the clergy, but loyal to the parish church. The only definite religious influence during the three Eisenach years could have come from the Vicar of St. George's Church, John Braun, who befriended the boy and who remained a life-long friend of the maturing Reformer. But Braun's interest in Luther may have been more that of a pastor in a gifted choir boy than that of a devoted priest in the winning of a new convert. However, Luther remembered Braun with gratitude after he had entered the monastery in Erfurt and even after he had moved to Wittenberg.

Frau Cotta, the object of so many beautiful garlands woven around Luther's Eisenach years, was the wife of Kunz Cotta, a pillar of the Eisenach society, a daughter of the Schalbes, one of the first families of the little town (perhaps 2,000 inhabitants at that time), and a lady who had a good heart. The Schalbes and Cottas, not just Frau Cotta, took Martin into their homes probably for a very prosaic reason: They needed a combination baby-sitter and tutor for their children. Thus, young Luther worked for his "keep" very much like modern American high school students do. The fact that he also sang in the *Kurrende*, a group of students, was nothing unusual. While these students gladly accepted the bread which was offered to them by those who either appreciated their vocal efforts or wanted them to move on to the next house, they did not sing because they were starving, but because it was the beautiful custom of the day. Fully undocumented is

the suspicion that Father Luther transferred his son from Magdeburg to Eisenach so that he could sponge off some of his numerous relatives. There were some Luthers in Eisenach, among them
his Uncle Conrad whom he invited later, in 1507, to attend his ordination to the priesthood, but there is no evidence that Luther lived
with any of his relatives during the three Eisenach years.

Luther always remembered the Cottas with great affection. In
1540-41 Henry Cotta studied in Wittenberg and was a table companion at Luther's house. He and his brother Bonaventura, both
born after 1511—the death date of Frau Cotta—may have been
nephews of the Cottas with whom Luther lived during his Eisenach
years. The refined atmosphere in the Schalbe and Cotta homes
must have benefited the young Mansfeld miner's son.

Here in Eisenach we also meet by name for the first time two
of Luther's teachers and two outstanding ones at that. John
Trebonius was not only a scholar and poet, but also a very original
gentleman of great personal charm, a *unicum,* who tipped his hat
each time he entered the classroom because he felt that some of
the boys who were now sitting at his feet may some day be
famous doctors, mayors, chancellors, or regents. Since he was the
senior among the teachers at St. George's School—we would call
him the principal—he enforced this rule among all teachers. We
hasten to add, however, that this beautiful story has come down
to us from the pen of the unreliable Matthew Ratzeberger and must
be swallowed with a grain of salt. The other teacher whom
we know well was Wigand of Gueldenapp with whom Luther kept
in close touch during the stormy years of the Reformation. Wigand
later became Lutheran pastor in Waltershausen. When he retired
in the mid-twenties of the sixteenth century the grateful Reformer
saw to it that his "old schoolmaster" was granted a pension from
the Elector's court.[3]

In 1501 Luther left his "beloved city."

In Erfurt

In the summer of 1501 *Martinus Ludher ex Mansfeld* registered
at the University of Erfurt, one of the most renowned schools of

his time. Erfurt had opened wide its gates to the influence of humanism and Renaissance spirit and may have recommended itself to Father Luther—who almost certainly made the decision for his son—by the excellent law faculty which was then housed within its ancient walls.

Here Luther took at first the common general course. Melanchthon's statement that young Luther had developed into a brilliant student during his Eisenach days is contradicted by Martin's standing during the B.A. examination. He was then just an average student. But he was inspired by two outstanding teachers who later played an important part in his life: Jodocus Trutvetter and Bartholomew Arnoldi von Usingen. Both were then at the zenith of their careers and both were teaching philosophy. Trutvetter, in 1501, had just published his *magnum opus*, the "Sum of Logics." Even though Luther later had to break away from both men he kept for them a high regard. Another, less famous teacher, Hecker who taught at Erfurt in 1502 later followed his pupil into the camp of the Reformation and died as Lutheran pastor of Osnabrueck.

Perhaps of greater importance than the influence of these teachers upon the young Luther was the friendship which he formed with some of the men who were then studying at the University. As has been said Erfurt was a citadel of humanism. Maternus Pistoris had lectured here before Luther's time on the Roman classics and Nicholas Marschalk, a native Thuringian, had introduced Greek studies. These men and others had attracted to Erfurt a number of outstanding young students who were not interested in the old scholasticism of a Trutvetter and Usingen, but had come to Erfurt in order to be liberated from the medieval spirit, liberal arts students in the true sense of the word. Among these were the famous Crotus Rubeanus who later edited the most biting attack against the Church before 1517, the "Letters of the Obscure Men." He had just received the B.A. degree when Luther arrived in town. George Spalatin, later one of Luther's closest friends, had registered in 1498 at Erfurt, but left it one year after Luther's arrival and went to the newly established University of Wittenberg, returning to Erfurt in 1505 at about the time when Luther disappeared behind the walls of the Augustinian cloister.

There were the two brothers Peter and Henry Eberbach and John
Lang. The latter followed his friend Luther into the monastery.
Finally Eobanus Hessus and Mutianus Rufus, two distinguished
scholars of later years, were then young poets at Erfurt.

It is difficult to assess the influence which these men may have
had on Luther. Melanchthon later claimed that they inspired young
Luther to read Cicero, Virgil, Livy and other Latin authors. This
may well be true. For Erfurt, in spite of its renown, was a small
university with a close-knit faculty and student body. Thus all our
humanists were familiar with Trutvetter and Usingen, probably took
their courses, and praised them in their poems. Luther, in spite
of his restrained life in the *bursa* or because of it, lived in closest
contact with these people. It is thus probable that the Reformer's
life-long love for the languages was born during these four years
before he entered the Augustinian monastery. Also whatever knowledge he had of Greek and Roman secular authors was largely
acquired during the years when he mixed freely with the humanists
at Erfurt.

One other man must be mentioned in this connection: Jerome
Emser. Emser, who was a chronic liar, later claimed that in 1504
he had been Luther's teacher. This may well be true. But it is
doubtful that the superficial, vain man left any impression upon
the young scholar, for Luther later never recalled, either nega-
tively or positively, any indebtedness to the "Leipzig Goat."[4]

If we ask what Luther's influence has been upon these people
at this time we are not able to give any definite answer. There is
evidence that Lang even at that time was influenced by his friend
Luther and that Usingen followed Luther and Lang into the
monastery because he was persuaded by them. But while all the
other men whom Luther met during this period at Erfurt were
later deeply influenced by him, we must not assume that this influence was there "at first sight." As a matter of fact Luther must
have appeared to some of his fellow students and teachers as a very
ordinary type of man, because some of them could not believe
their own eyes when they later saw the Reformer emerge from
the cobwebs of scholasticism.

In the Monastery

On July 17, 1505, the portals of the Augustinian monastery in Erfurt closed behind the young postulant who had knocked at them during the night. Luther was to remain a member of the Augustinian order for almost twenty years, until seven years after the beginning of the Reformation, and he was to live out his life in the monastery in Wittenberg at the side of his faithful wife and children, surrounded by many table companions. Yet when he entered the monastery he had no vision of future happiness and greatness, but only *Anfechtung* and a feeling of unworthiness. The events which led to his decision do not need to be repeated here. We will never know what turned the friend of the happy humanists of Erfurt into a sorrowful monk. The seed may have been sown in that Magdeburg school of the pious Lollards, or it may have been—as some claim—the sudden death of a friend, or the storm of Stotternheim early that month. But decisions like these do not come suddenly, they grow slowly. Whatever it was that led Martin Luther to the Augustinian monastery, it was the decisive decision of his life. The young Master of Arts, the promising law student, in one night destroyed the dreams of his father, disappointed the expectations of his scholarly friends, and disappeared behind the walls of a monastery, renowned for its religious, but not for its scholarly, attainments. If Luther had wanted to devote his life to the Church and at the same time develop his intellectual powers there would have been better places than the Convent of the Augustinian Hermits. From his later accounts we must conclude that with few exceptions the monks were narrow and simple, that none of them had other religious problems except the faithful observance of the rules of the order, and that they could not understand the anxieties of the young brother who had joined them. Yet it was here that Luther learned the greatest lesson of his life: self-discipline and submission to the will of God, patiently waiting for many years until God would speak to him. And here he also met the man who had a decisive influence upon him: Staupitz. It is difficult to see where Luther's religious development would have ended without Staupitz pointing him to the patient

waiting and the grace of God. Without Staupitz Luther's religious
fervor may have run out with the blood of self-castigation or may
have ended in the lifeless acceptance of a devotion to God without
hope for release. In any other religious community, the Dominicans,
the Franciscans, and so on, Luther may have developed into just
another cog in the wheel of Romanism, but the religious seriousness of the Augustinian Hermits, especially the Erfurt monks who
opposed every kind of convenient accommodation to the demands
emanating from Rome (Luther was sent to Rome to oppose the
dictatorship of his superiors there!) prepared Luther for his later
work as the Reformer of the Church. It is significant that almost
the entire Augustinian Order dissolved after the hammerblows
of 1517 and had to be reorganized by Rome from the grass-roots
up.

Little is known of the men with whom Luther lived in close
communion during those years. Winand of Diedenhofen was
prior of the Erfurt monastery when Luther was received into
the order. John Genser von Paltz was master of studies. He died
in 1511 the year Luther moved to Wittenberg. He may have been
the "Old Brother" who befriended the troubled monk. We do
not know. Besides these two men only Prior Lohr and George
Leiffer, reader at meals, are known to us by name.

In Wittenberg

In 1510 Luther had been in Rome to plead for his brethren at
Erfurt and for the other Augustinian monasteries belonging to
the strict observance that they might be allowed to continue their
independent existence. The mission was unsuccessful. Erfurt and
the other monasteries were told to conform with the decision of the
curia and were put under the direct supervision of Staupitz.
There has been much speculation that the journey to Rome and
especially the moral conditions at the center of the Christian
Church which Luther encountered during his month-long stay
at Rome may have started him on the road to Reformation. This
seems unlikely. Luther returned from Rome, a convert to the Roman
ideas of centralization. He turned against his own independent

fellow-monks at Erfurt and life soon became unpleasant for him. Staupitz who had used him on a temporary basis in Wittenberg before the journey to Rome, now transferred him permanently to the new University. Some of his fellow-monks at Erfurt never forgave Luther for his desertion as they called it, and later Erfurt remained for a long time one of the chief centers of opposition to the Reformation, and this opposition was centered in the University and at the monastery.

Wittenberg, in the "Sandbox of the Holy Empire," as the border-lands of northern Saxony and Brandenburg were derisively called, became Luther's home for the rest of his life. It was a dingy little town, a few blocks wide and a few more blocks long. It lacked the industry of Mansfeld, the natural beauty of Eisenach, and the openness of Magdeburg and Erfurt. The University, the pride of Elector Frederick the Wise, was a second rate school and shed its mediocrity only during a few decades when Luther, Melanch-thon, and their friends became the shining stars on the intellectual sky of Europe. Soon after the Reformation it relapsed into its old sleepiness, wilted away and finally closed.

When Luther arrived at Wittenberg, however, there was promise of greatness for the new school. Pollich of Mellrichstadt, one of its founders, was considered one of the great minds of Germany. Nicholas Marschalk, the same who had introduced Greek studies at Erfurt, had come to Wittenberg in 1502, bringing a young student, George Spalatin, with him. There were the two Schurffs, Augustine the anatomist and Jerome the lawyer. Augustine Schurff was somewhat famous and "notorious" because he was one of the first anatomists to use corpses for his experiments. Jerome be-came Luther's faithful counsel. John Oldecop, unwilling to cope with Luther's new-fangled ideas, moved soon away and died as Catholic bishop of Hildesheim. But the noisiest of all—and some have called him a "genius"—was Andrew Bodenstein of Carlstadt who was rector of the University when Luther was created a Doctor of Theology. Carlstadt first fought the mounting influence of the young Augustinian professor, but when he realized that he could not stem the tide, he jumped on the bandwagon and rode along merrily and noisily until 1522, when he broke with the conservative

Reformer who moved too slowly for him, joined the fanatics, was almost killed in the Peasant War and finally found himself as Zwinglian professor in Switzerland. By that time many other great lights had appeared in Wittenberg and Carlstadt's antics were soon forgotten as a bad dream.[5]

These were the men who were famous at Wittenberg at the time of Luther's early lectures, so famous that a renowned compiler of a sixteenth century "Who's Who in Education" forgot to include the name of Professor Martin Luther when he visited Wittenberg three years before the dawn of the Reformation. Paul Lange, the forgetful chronicler, later made up for this slip by first praising Luther to the highest heaven and finally damning him to the lowest hell.

There were from the beginning a number of people, besides Staupitz, who recognized Luther's greatness very early. By 1515 or 1516 Luther was the leading theologian of the little University. Men like Amsdorf were won to Luther's theology through the serious study of St. Augustine. Others followed, like Carlstadt, for more external reasons. Spalatin, Lang, and Wenceslas Linck accepted Luther because they felt personally drawn to him. Eager students like Francis Guenther and Bartholomew Bernhardi wanted to learn from him, and gave him an opportunity to express himself in the theses which he prepared with them and for them in 1516 and 1517. The brethren in the Black Cloisters realized that there was something going on in the professor's mind which placed him at opposite ends to the prevailing Catholic theology and practice. Luther had not only tried repeatedly to dethrone Aristotle, but he had attacked the whole system of Catholic scholasticism. He had preached against indulgences and other abuses. But when the hammerblows of October 31, 1517, had died down the first reaction of his friends was that of being utterly stunned. Schurff earnestly rebuked him, some left him, others after the first shock rallied around him, and by April 1518 it seemed as though he had not only won the approval of the entire Augustinian order but of his Bishop, Jerome Scultetus of Brandenburg, of his Elector, Frederick the Wise, and of Archbishop Albert of Mainz who with his indulgence traffic had triggered the shot which started the Reformation.

The success of the Reformation before the Diet of Worms (1521) was still largely local. No effort was made to introduce the new teaching of the Wittenberg professor on a large scale, not even in Wittenberg. While Christian II of Denmark and Norway had toyed with the idea of reforming his domain as early as 1520 and while Carlstadt had instituted some violent reforms in Wittenberg in late 1521 and early 1522, the Reformation of the Church did not begin to be pushed systematically until Luther's return from the Wartburg (March 1522). The men who carried the torch of the Reformation were the men who had worked with Luther during his maturing years at Erfurt and Wittenberg, and many others who were won during the great years of 1518-1521. Later younger men joined the Reformation, studied under Luther and returned to their homelands, carrying the Gospel with them. But while Luther's ideas had spread like wild-fire immediately after October 31, 1517, and while his works were collected, read, hidden, and proclaimed (and at times burned), the official introduction of the Reformation took the form of a gradual evolution from Roman Catholicism to Lutheranism, in Saxony during the last years of Frederick the Wise, in Hesse shortly after Frederick's death (1525), in South Germany and Switzerland in the late 1520's, in East Prussia and the Baltic states from 1524 on, in Scandinavia during the early 1530's, and in some territories, especially nearby Brandenburg and Ducal Saxony, not until the eve of the Reformer's life. Wherever the Reformation was victorious it was due to the consecrated efforts of men who had been inspired by Luther, either personally or through his writings.

II

The Inner Circle

Wittenberg, a sleepy little town in the "Sandbox of the Holy Roman Empire" woke up one day and found itself famous. The faculty of the university, smaller in number than the faculty of a four year liberal arts college, bathed in the limelight of world attention. Students from all parts of Germany, from Scandinavia, Austria, Switzerland, Bohemia, the Baltic States, the Netherlands, and England came in great numbers to hear the famous professor, Martin Luther, who had dared "to touch the belly of the monks and the crown of the pope." Printers and other artisans moved their shops to the "Little Athens on the Elbe River." Humanists, religious enthusiasts, scholars and quacks, including the almost legendary Dr. Faustus, swelled at one time or another the confines of the little walled city which was scarcely able to bear all this excitement.

In these years Martin Luther continued to live where he had lived as a monk and unknown professor. He taught regularly at the University and preached the Gospel faithfully. He was absent less than the other major Reformers. After the first exciting years when he went to Heidelberg, Augsburg, Altenburg, Leipzig and Worms, Luther remained in Wittenberg by choice and the force of circumstances. He spent ten months at the Wartburg and six months at

the Coburg. He attended a few meetings through the years, at
Marburg, at Smalcald, at Torgau, and elsewhere. But these absences were rare and far between. He refused to leave the city which
in spite of all the chagrin which its local citizens caused him
he had begun to love. He remained there even during the periodic
plagues. During the plague of 1527 he wrote the famous Battle
Hymn of the Reformation. Only once, in his old age, did he leave
the city of the "whoring students" never to return. But he was
persuaded by a deputation of his sorrowing townsmen to come
back.[1]

Wittenberg served, besides Torgau, as a secondary residence for
the Electors Frederick the Wise, John, and John Frederick. Here
the important Saxon officials, the chancellors Brueck and Beyer, the
lawyers and courtiers, including the Chaplain of Frederick the
Wise, George Spalatin, often resided. Here Amsdorf, Bugenhagen,
Cruciger, Jonas, Melanchthon, and many others congregated.
Here it was that during Luther's protracted absence at the Wartburg, Carlstadt created the first organized disturbance when he
forcefully changed the Mass. To Wittenberg came the Heavenly
Prophets, Storch and Stuebner of Zwickau, to support the revolution of Carlstadt and had soon persuaded Melanchthon and other
moderates that they possessed the "Inner Light." In Wittenberg
the most important sermons of the Reformation period, the Eight
Invocavit Sermons, were delivered by an angry Reformer after he
had returned from the Wartburg in March 1522, and here he
preached almost all of his more than two thousand sermons. To
Wittenberg one day Leonard Coppe and Wolf Domnitsch brought
the nuns of Nimbschen whom they had "liberated" by devious
means from servitude. Luther was able to find a husband for
all of them, but one, Katherine von Bora, was jilted by her Nuremberg lover, Jerome Baumgaertner, and refusing to take the second
choice, one Professor Glatz, insisted on marrying Luther. In the
big Black Cloisters which a grateful Elector gave to the Reformer,
Martin and Kate Luther had six children and lost two, little
Elizabeth and young Magdalene. Here they lived a happy life
with their relatives and table companions which at times may have
numbered more than twenty. Luther's Table Talk is a lasting testi-

mony to all the joys and sorrows which Martin Luther experienced
during more than twenty years as husband, father, and friend.

In the lecture hall of the University Luther continued his work
as teacher to the end, with very few interruptions caused by sickness and travel. His great commentaries on Biblical books form a
large part of his literary heritage. In the Castle Church and more
often in the Town Church he continued to preach his regular
sermons, special sermon series on Biblical books, and substituted
for Bugenhagen who was often absent. In his study he collected
over four hundred "canned sermons" into Postils which were
edited by his friends, Roth, Cruciger, and others. In his study
he also wrote many important treatises, some brief, some long,
over seven hundred titles in all. While the transcripts of his Table
Talk by Dietrich, Medler, Roerer, Schlaginhaufen, Rabe, Cordatus,
Zwick, Wolf, Lauterbach, Weller, Khummer, Mathesius, Heydenreich, Aurifaber, and others, contain many inaccuracies and thoughts
which Luther may have never uttered, the treatises which he sent
out in great profusion give a well-rounded picture of the man
Martin Luther, with all his strong points and weak points, his
deep theological insights, his ways of hurried composition, often
colored by his aroused wrath, but more often stimulated by his
great love for the Church and the truth of the Word of God.[2]

During all these years Luther was part of the small community
which his work made famous. He was annoyed like other small
town citizens by the chicanery of a hateful street commissioner,
or rather: "City Wall Commissioner," who hated him because
he had rebuked him for his immorality. He foolishly bought ad-
ditional real estate—he didn't need it—and Kate made him sell it
again, at a loss. He ran out of money because so many students
and visiting scholars sat at his table. He repeatedly asked for and
received help from his Elector. He gardened and made his own
beer. He liked and disliked his physicians who with the crude tools
at their disposal could do very little to help him in his many
physical distresses. He had quarrels and patched up feuds. He invited the Lotthers to come to Wittenberg to take over the printing business in the place of the ineffective printer Gruenenberg,
but when the Lotthers got the "big head" Luther gave almost all

of his work to a young printer, Hans Lufft, who afterwards became the Printer of the Reformation *par excellence.* The Lotthers were forced to move away from Wittenberg. The faithful Vitus Dietrich, as headstrong as Luther, was "told off" and moved away. Agricola who had attacked his friend Melanchthon became *persona non grata,* not only because he was against the preaching of the Law, but because little "Grickel" had dared to challenge the theological wisdom of one of the great men of Wittenberg. And the Old Luther was sometimes considered difficult by even his best friends. Painful bouts with sickness made him grouchy and impatient. The only "crony" who always got along with him was Lucas Cranach, the Painter of the Reformation. The two old men comforted each other in their sorrows.

Yet it is amazing that during all these years Luther lost very few of his friends—and those whom he lost forsook him because their vanity had been touched or they were jealous of the Reformer —and gained many more. The procession of men to Wittenberg between the years 1518 and 1546 is truly impressive. It includes most of the great names of the Reformation. But Luther made little distinction between the great and the lowly. The papal Nuncio Peter Paul Vergerio who visited Luther in the mid-thirties was received with the same lack of formality as the "Master Barber" who shaved the Reformer regularly and to whom he dedicated one of his books. It seems that this informality coupled with Luther's theology started Vergerio on the road of becoming a simple Lutheran pastor in his later years. In his letters Luther was frank to the point of insult whether he dealt with Pope Leo X, the Elector, Thomas Muenzer, or the horse thief Hans Kohlhase. His pastoral concern was the same with persons of all stations: Queen Mary of Hungary, Prince Starhemberg of Austria, Duke Albert of Prussia were given the same attention, as but not more, than Wolfgang Sieberger, his servant, or the Jew Bernard who had married a Wittenberg servant girl. Thus Luther was the prototype of the ideal Christian pastor. In his sermons he praised and rebuked wherever the need arose. The "guzzling" of his most devoted protector, the Elector John Frederick, was an abomination to him, while the "honesty" of his fiercest enemy, Duke George of Saxony, was held up as an example to other princes. This does not mean that Luther had no blind spots: He supported the carnal desires of Landgrave Philip farther than a conscientious pastor could answer for, he covered up again and again for the heretical weakness of Melanchthon, and he was often unjust to those who crossed his ways. He enjoyed telling stories, even gossiping without always verifying the contents. Luther was not a saint without sin and blemish. His halo was not untarnished. But he was a "saint" in the evangelical sense, a sinner saved by grace to bring the Reformation to the Church. This human side of Luther, probably more than any of his accomplishments, was the reason for the tremendous impact of his personality on the men of the sixteenth century and of our times.

Among the thousands of men around Luther there were a few who emerged as his closest co-workers, the Inner Circle. They included Nicholas von Amsdorf, John Bugenhagen, Caspar Cruciger, Justus Jonas, Philip Melanchthon, and George Spalatin.

Nicholas von Amsdorf (1483-1565)

"I have joined the Reformation not on account of my love for the man Martin Luther, but on account of my love for truth,"[3] Amsdorf said later. He was a "Lutheran" even before the beginning of the Reformation. As a colleague of the young professor at the University of Wittenberg he had been persuaded to study St. Augustine and had arrived at the same conclusions as Luther: Man is saved without works by grace alone. Amsdorf never forgot the debt of gratitude which he owed to Luther.

Born less than a month after our Reformer, on December 3, 1483, Nicholas von Amsdorf (his birthplace probably was Torgau in Saxony) studied theology and earned his master's degree at the newly established University of Wittenberg, a year before Luther received his master's degree at Erfurt. Soon Amsdorf lectured on theological and philosophical subjects and became a well-known and highly respected scholar. When Luther arrived in Wittenberg Amsdorf befriended the young Augustinian and by him was led to the study of St. Augustine, as we have seen. On the eve of the Reformation the two men had become very close friends.

Amsdorf, like Luther, was an inveterate letter writer. In one of his letters to Spalatin he rejoiced "Luther has brought me to true theology." He accompanied the Reformer to the Leipzig debate in 1519 and was at Worms with him in 1521. On the return trip Luther was captured and taken to the Wartburg. Neither Melanchthon nor others at Wittenberg knew at first the whereabouts of the intrepid Reformer. Many believed that he had been killed. Amsdorf, with Spalatin, may have been one of the few who were informed of the secret hide-out. During Luther's absence from Wittenberg he took over most of the Reformer's duties as preacher and teacher. He never forsook the true course of the Reformation, even after Melanchthon began to waver under the influence of Carlstadt and the Heavenly Prophets.

After Luther's return from the Wartburg in March 1522 Amsdorf became the quiet but effective right-hand man of the Reformer. Today he is numbered among the four or five greatest Lutheran Reformers, although he was not a creative personality in the true sense of the word. Yet his strength was his unwavering loyalty to the Gospel, his industrious energy, and his personality which was above reproach. At many important junctures of Luther's life he exerted a restraining and irenic influence without sacrificing the essence of Reformation theology. In the great task of Bible translation Amsdorf became one of Luther's most trusted helpers.

Although Amsdorf did not stay in Wittenberg for long, he always remained close to Luther. During the fifteen-twenties he was busy with many assignments. On June 26, 1524, he preached the Gospel in Magdeburg, later the most important citadel of Lutheranism in northern Germany whose influence extended to Sweden and the Netherlands. In spite of the determined opposition from Catholic reactionaries and Anabaptist fanatics, Amsdorf refused to leave his post and carried the Gospel from Magdeburg to Goslar, Einbeck, Meissen, and many other cities. Luther tried again and again to win him back for Wittenberg, but Amsdorf remained at his post until 1542 when a new challenge arose.

During these years the Reformer and his friend kept up a run-

ning correspondence. On November 1, 1527, during the Wittenberg plague—Luther had refused to leave the city—the Reformer
wrote about "A Mighty Fortress," the only allusion which we
have to the writings of the famous hymn. A few years before
Amsdorf had been the first to inform his friend Spalatin that
"nine, fair, fine nuns, all of noble birth, and none of them fifty
years old" had arrived in Wittenberg and that he was reserving
one of them, "the sister of my gracious lord and uncle, Dr. Staupitz,
to be your wife . . . but if you wish to have a younger one, you
shall have your choice of the fairest of them." Later, on June 21,
1525, Luther had written to Amsdorf in Magdeburg: "The report
is true that I suddenly married Catherine to silence the mouths
which are accustomed to bicker at me. I hope to live a short time
yet, to gratify my father, who asked me to marry and leave him
descendants . . . On next Tuesday I am giving a wedding banquet
to celebrate, at which my parents will be present. I am very desirous of having you also, wherefore I invite you and beg you
not to be absent if you can possibly come." Now, on November
1, 1527, he had to report to his friend that the plague was in his own
house, but soon he was able to report "The plague no longer rules
us."[4]

Amsdorf was unable to accompany his friend to Marburg to
the colloquy with Zwingli, but Luther sent messengers to him to
report on the negative outcome. Throughout these years he comforted him in all adversities, especially in his difficulties with
Albert of Mainz and the Magdeburg clergy, and Amsdorf in turn
encouraged Luther when the latter felt melancholy.

In 1542 the "great challenge" came to Amsdorf. The Elector
John Frederick appointed him first bishop to the Lutheran diocese
of Naumburg-Zeitz, because, as he said in his decree, "he is gifted,
scholarly, of noble birth, and without a wife." For in spite of his
concern about marrying off his friends the gentle Amsdorf had
never married. This new assignment was even more difficult than
his work at Magdeburg. During several years Amsdorf managed
to hold on to his new office against the able Catholic contender
Julius von Pflug who refused to give up his claims to the diocese.
But at the beginning of the Smalcald War the valiant Lutheran

bishop lost his diocese which he, in his own words, had administered "without chrism, butter, lard, bacon, tar, smear, incense, and coals."

By this time Luther had died. Amsdorf followed the electoral family to their new residence in Weimar which had been assigned to them by the victorious Emperor Charles V at the conclusion of the Smalcald War. Once more he returned to Magdeburg, opposing with great zeal the compromising tendencies of his one-time friend Melanchthon and the Philippist party. Melanchthon who had accommodated himself to the changed conditions and cooperating with the "Judas" of the Lutheran Church, the turn-coat Elector Maurice of Saxony, had remained at Wittenberg. Amsdorf went into voluntary exile with his old Elector John Frederick.

His final years, from 1552 on, were spent at Eisenach, the "beloved city" of his master. There he lived, without defined office, the acknowledged "Secret Bishop of the Lutheran Church." He was instrumental in setting up the rival University of Jena where Luther's theology was faithfully taught while Wittenberg lapsed into crypto-Calvinism. Sometimes his stubbornness carried him away to make extreme statements. Against Major's thesis that good works were necessary for salvation—Major had been a follower of Melanchthon—Amsdorf maintained that "good works are detrimental to salvation." Against Pfeffinger's theology who proposed that man must co-operate with the grace of God Amsdorf came close to being a predestinarian. But he never went as far as his good friend Flacius, the Jena theologian, who declared that sin was the created substance of man. "To remain faithful to the doctrine of Luther" was his foremost concern. While others were driven from their positions on account of their extreme polemics and misstatements of doctrine, Amsdorf remained in Eisenach, ever watchful, always charitable, but uncompromising. He died there on May 14, 1565.

Luther called his friend "a natural-born theologian." This is perhaps the most beautiful epithet which Nicholas von Amsdorf earned during his long life. Much has been made of Melanchthon's influence upon Luther's theology, too much to be true. But while Melanchthon came from humanism and returned to it and in a sense was never a "good" theologian, Amsdorf remained untouched by the conflict between philosophy and theology and thus was enabled to guard the heritage of the Lutheran Reformation more faithfully than the more brilliant Philip Melanchthon. Many Reformation scholars today consider Amsdorf the greatest among those who preserved the light of the Reformation after the death of the Reformer.

John Bugenhagen (1484-1558)

"It remains for you," Luther instructed his friend Spalatin on September 20, 1522, "it remains for you to accept the task of securing from the Elector for John Bugenhagen one of those stipends that have heretofore been thrown away on the sophists. For next to Philip (Melanchthon) he is the best professor of theology in the world."[5] Thus began the close association of Martin Luther and John Bugenhagen. But the roots of it had their beginnings much earlier.

John Bugenhagen, called *Dr. Pomeranus* by his contemporaries, was born on June 24, 1484, at Wollin where his father was city councillor. He studied at the University of Greifswald and in 1503 became a teacher at Treptow. Later, after his ordination, he gave lectures at the convent school at Belbuck. His prince, Duke Bogislav X of Pomerania, commissioned him to write a history of his native land, and in 1518 the book "Pomerania" was ready for publication.

Independently of Luther, Bugenhagen had always been interested in the reform of the Church. For a time after the publication of the Ninety-Five Theses and the resulting upheaval he remained faithful to the old Church. However, after reading Luther's book "On the Babylonian Captivity of the Church" (1520), he immediately wrote a letter to the Wittenberg professor in which he declared himself for the Reformation. In 1521 Bugenhagen moved to Wittenberg where he arrived shortly before Luther's departure for Worms. He lectured at the University and preached during Luther's absence. When the Reformer returned he obtained for Bugenhagen a permanent position.

As interpreter of Old Testament books Bugenhagen followed

closely his famous friend, publishing in 1524 his lectures on Psalms which earned him the title as the "foremost interpreter of Psalms." Later he also published a commentary on Jeremiah (1546), Jonah (1550), and other exegetical works. But quite early during his Wittenberg ministry Bugenhagen's interest turned more and more to the practical field. As pastor of the Town Church since 1523 he re-organized the congregational service and cleansed it of the confusion which the Roman Mass on the one hand and Carlstadt's fanaticism on the other had caused. He was active in the re-establishment of schools. He was the first Lutheran to write against Zwingli during the Communion Controversy when, in 1525, he published his "Open Letter Against the New Errors."

Bugenhagen was a versatile man, a compiler, organizer, translator. In 1524 he wrote a Gospel harmony on the Passion story, the "Passionale," which was used in the Lutheran Church for many years and is used in principle still today. This important work was written in Latin, High German and Low German. He also translated the Bible into Low German, a language which then was used quite widely in Church services.

When, in 1523, Bugenhagen got married Luther asked the Elector to send game for his wedding. But Frederick the Wise, fearing that "he might lay himself open to the charge of favoring the marriage of priests," did not provide the meat. On January 2, 1523, Luther again complained to Spalatin that Bugenhagen is still "teaching for nothing, and yet his students think it a hardship to have to buy what they are not willing to do without. Meanwhile those who receive the stipends are either not lecturing at all, or else they are men who are not to be compared with Bugenhagen in any respect." Therefore, the students were complaining, "not about Bugenhagen, for they know that the stipends of those swine ought to go to him, but because they are not getting their lectures free." Luther enjoins his friend: "Mention this to the Elector; perhaps he may be willing to remedy the matter."[6] When Spalatin wanted to retire to the parish ministry in order to get away from all the troubles of the court, Luther seriously thought of recommending Bugenhagen to the Elector. But Spalatin stayed on until after the death of Frederick the Wise.

In 1525 Bugenhagen received the call to come to Danzig to help reform the Church there. From that time on he was recognized as the foremost organizer of the Lutheran Church. Luther himself did not put any obstacles in his way, but wrote to Spalatin: "I could have wished Bugenhagen to stay here, but in such circumstances and for the Word's sake I think we ought to give him up. Who knows to what use God may wish to put him there? We might not recognize, and therefore might stand in the way of, the clear calling of God." He need not have worried. Frederick the Wise

BUGENHAGEN

did not permit Bugenhagen to leave. But later, after Frederick's death, he was often called away. In 1526 he was in Hamburg, in 1528 in Brunswick, in 1530 in Luebeck and Lower Saxony. His Church Order became the model constitution for many Lutheran Churches. It was introduced in Minden, Osnabrueck, Goettingen, Soest, Bremen, and many other places. In 1534 Bugenhagen was called to Pomerania by the two Dukes, one of whom, Barmin, had been Luther's companion at the Leipzig Debate with Eck (1519). Although he found more opposition in his native land than anywhere else he succeeded in carrying out his assignment.

Each time Bugenhagen had returned after his work was finished and had resumed his duties as parish minister of the Town Church of Wittenberg, where Luther usually substituted for him during his absences. But when he was called to Copenhagen by Christian III to reform the Churches of Norway and Denmark it looked for a time as if he would never return. Elector John Frederick had to put all the pressure of his office on his reluctant colleague in Copenhagen to let Bugenhagen go. Finally, after almost two years of absence he arrived back in Wittenberg. In these two years he had reorganized the University of Copenhagen, had served as its rector, had given a new Church order to the Scandinavian Churches, had crowned Christian III in the first Lutheran coronation on record, and had consecrated the Bishops of Denmark and Norway. In 1542 Christian III called him back once more to reform the Duchy of Schleswig. Again he tried to keep him by offering him the bishopric of Schleswig, but Bugenhagen returned to Wittenberg.

The relationship between Luther and Bugenhagen was somewhat different from the ordinary relationship between friends, for the leader of the Reformation was at the same time the parishioner of the pastor of the Town Church and often in need of pastoral counsel, of *Seelsorge*. As Luther grew older he was plagued by many illnesses and was subject to long spells of melancholy. Bugenhagen who had been one of the few who had been present at the Reformer's wedding shared the joys and sorrows of the Reformer's family. Luther, in turn, always saw to it that his pastor was well provided with the necessities of life, that he was made a Doctor of Divinity as soon as the University of Wittenberg began again to confer degrees, and that he finally was elevated to the position of Superintendent General of Saxony (1539). At Luther's funeral Bugenhagen preached the sermon.

Bugenhagen's life after the Reformer's death was under the shadow of the Cross. During the troubled months of the Smalcald War he remained faithfully at his post while many others fled. During his last years as pastor in Wittenberg he had to endure much physical suffering. Finally the Lord called him home during the night from April 19 to 20, 1558.

Caspar Cruciger (1504-1548)

"When the entire German Bible had been published," we read in Mathesius' sermons on Luther's life, "Dr. Martin Luther again took the Bible and reviewed it from the very beginning, with great industry and prayer and . . . at once gathered his own Sanhedrin of the best persons available, which assembled weekly, several hours before supper in the doctor's study, namely, Dr. John Bugenhagen, Dr. Justus Jonas, Dr. Cruciger, Magister Philip Melanchthon, Matthew Aurogallus; Magister George Roerer, the *Corrector* was also present. Frequently other friends, doctors and learned men came to take part in this important work . . . Then when Dr. Luther had reviewed the previously published Bible and had also gained information from Jews and friends . . . and had inquired of old Germans about appropriate words, as when he had several rams slaughtered in his presence, so that a German butcher could tell him the proper name for each part of the sheep, he came into the conference room with his old Latin and his new German Bible, and always brought the Hebrew text with him. M. Philip Melanchthon brought the Greek text with him, Dr. Cruciger a Chaldean Bible in addition to the Hebrew. The professors had their rabbinical commentaries. Dr. Bugenhagen also had the Latin text with which he was very familiar. Each one had studied the text which was to be discussed and had examined Greek and Latin as well as Hebrew commentators."[7]

This beautiful picture of teamwork which Mathesius has left us not only shows the care with which the Bible was translated and revised, but also introduces us to the Inner Circle of Luther's friends, among whom Caspar Cruciger was the youngest and most precocious. Unlike the others he stayed close to the home-base once he had settled in Wittenberg and thus with Luther was the most regular professor of theology at a university whose work was often handicapped by the frequent absences of its very important people.

Caspar Cruciger was born in Leipzig, on New Year's Day 1504. He was twenty years younger than Luther, Amsdorf, Bugenhagen, and Spalatin, ten years younger than Jonas, and Melanchthon's junior by seven years. His was a precocious childhood. As a little child he was instructed by the humanists George Helt and Caspar Borner, and enrolled at the University of Leipzig at the age of nine. As a teenage "scholar" he was present at the disputation between Luther and Eck and became a fervent Lutheran. As a teenager he moved to Wittenberg where he began to study theology in earnest. Not satisfied to study only one subject, he also took up mathematics and natural sciences in which he became as proficient as in theology.

On April 16, 1525, Luther complained to Spalatin: "The Magdeburgers have called Caspar Cruciger . . . Thus we are scattering, and our school is running down. What will become of me I do not know; but this I do know, that in this matter you are not to blame. Satan alone is at the bottom of it," he added humorously. Thus, at the age of twenty Cruciger had been appointed rector of one of the most renowned schools in northern Germany, the City School of Magdeburg. Luther's fears, that he would be lost forever to Wittenberg, fortunately were unfounded. Four years later he was back upon the request of Melanchthon who had him appointed professor of theology. He also served as pastor of the Castle Church—at half salary—a position which offered him the opportunity to employ his talents as one of the outstanding speakers of the Reformation era. While his audience at the Castle Church was not as large as Bugenhagen's congregation at the Town Church, Cruciger often preached to a select group and influenced Reformation preaching deeply. He was the foremost authority on sermonizing, editing most of Luther's "canned sermons" in several postils.

But more important than his sermonizing was his work as theologian. He was an indefatigable worker, literally burning himself out. Originally he had lectured on philosophical subjects, but when he returned to Wittenberg he specialized more and more in purely theological courses. In recognition of his scholarly work he was created upon the recommendation of Luther a honorary Doctor of Divinity on June 17, 1533, the same day when Bugenhagen also received his degree.

More than Melanchthon who has been called the "Quiet Reformer" Cruciger deserved that title. While Melanchthon often was unjust and hasty in his judgments and showed rancor not only towards his enemies, like Agricola, but at times also towards his friends, as at the time of Luther's marriage, and had many other personal failings, Cruciger strove to remain humble. He liked anonymity, quietly working in the background, stepping into the limelight only when called to do so by Luther. His character was more firm than the vacillating character of his friend Melanchthon, yet he had to suffer more from the irascibility of Luther who continuously spared the feelings of Melanchthon and vented his anger on some of his more reliable followers, like Dietrich, Cruciger, and others. But Cruciger, unlike Dietrich, did not argue back. He recognized the causes for Luther's mounting irascibility and stayed at his post.

Luther recognized the depth of Cruciger's scholarship and his sincerity, although he was at times exasperated with his quiet passiveness. In 1529 he took him along to Marburg where the final break between the Lutherans and the Zwinglians took place. Cruciger's influence on the preaching in the Lutheran Church has been mentioned above. He did carry out in practice what Melanchthon had postulated in his "Visitation Articles" in theory: That the preaching of the Law and Gospel should be rightly divided. He took his stand at Melanchthon's side against John Agricola who had proclaimed that the preaching of the Law was no longer required for Christians. But his opposition against Agricola's teachings was not colored by his personal antipathy, as in the case of Melanchthon and later Luther. In all the controversies and discussions Cruciger remained ever charitable. This was acknowledged even by the Catholics. One of the strongest opponents of the Reformation, the Imperial Chancellor Granvella, said of him: "The Protestants have a secretary who is more learned than all Papists, for he does not only write down all the words which are spoken by Melanchthon, but also reminds him of all omissions in his speech."[8]

In spite of the disappointment which the Marburg Colloquy had brought to the Wittenberg theologians Melanchthon and Cruciger continued to work for a reconciliation. After Zwingli's death they persuaded Bucer, Capito, and other mediation theologians to persuade the Swiss to come to Saxony for a new meeting. The meeting finally took place in May 1536, but its success was far from complete. Most of the Swiss had refused to come and the Wittenberg Concord was worked out mainly between Bucer and Capito on the one side, and Luther and his friends on the other, whereby we must keep in mind that Bucer and Capito were Lutherans of a sort. Nevertheless, the meeting did much to heal the wounds which the clashing personalities of Luther and Zwingli had inflicted upon the Church. Although it changed the atmosphere in which both confessions were now living side-by-side, it yet did not bring about a basic change in theology, however much Melanchthon, and perhaps Cruciger, may have hoped for a softening of Luther's thinking.

During these years Cruciger supported faithfully Melanchthon's desire to go to Paris and London. But the Elector John Frederick who in spite of his many limitations may have had a clear understanding of Melanchthon's weaknesses did not consent to let him go. When the Smalcald Articles were written Cruciger was one of the first to affix his signature before they were sent to the Elector. When shortly thereafter Luther became critically ill, he asked Bugenhagen: "Pray ask for me my dear Philip, Jonas and Cruciger, that they will forgive me whatever I have sinned against them . . ." In his First Testament he remembered the friend whom he had wronged with unjust reproaches. Yet the irritation continued. Luther's suspicion had been aroused by the unjust accusation of Cordatus that Cruciger in his lectures on I Timothy had taught synergism, co-operation of man with God in the work of salvation. Although Cruciger's words had been grossly misconstrued, the attack by Cordatus led to one of the most serious controversies in the Lutheran Church and finally to a re-opening of the old controversy between Melanchthon and Agricola. All this must have been as painful to Luther as it was to Cruciger and misunderstandings led to harsh words. The matter was finally settled during the promotion disputation of Peter Palladius, the young Danish theologian, which took place on June 1, 1537. Luther acknowledged that good works are "necessarily the result of faith," but rejected the idea that they are "necessary for salvation." Cruciger who had never taught anything different gladly agreed with his friend. Cordatus who was also present remained quiet.

Luther who had called Cruciger his "Elisha," the man "who will teach theology after my death" did not openly hold a grudge against him, but beneath the surface the fires of suspicion were kept smoldering. Nevertheless, he sent Melanchthon and Cruciger to the Worms and Regensburg Colloquies of 1541, the last sincere meetings to bring about a reunion between the Old and the New Church. Here both men labored for many days under increasing pressure. Melanchthon had been injured during the trip when his carriage tipped over and had broken (or sprained) his hand. Luther who at Wittenberg was passing through another painful sickness wrote sharp and uncompromising letters. Melanchthon was at the end of his endurance, but Cruciger comforted him and strengthened him. Finally the Lutheran emissaries and their Catholic counterparts arrived—in spite of Eck's vigorous protests—at a compromise which however pleased neither the Elector John Frederick nor the Reformer. On May 11, 1541, Luther asked the Elector to reject the agreement, asking him to "write gently to Melanchthon and the others that they may not be grieved to death; for they have stuck to our Confession and have upheld firmly the pure doctrine."

With this last great effort Cruciger's work was finished. The man of peace had not been able to reestablish peace between Lutherans and Zwinglians and Lutherans and Catholics. His last years were spent under a cloud. He felt drawn closer and closer to Melanchthon, without sharing his character weakness. Thus after the death of Luther and during the Smalcald War he did not flee, but remained at his post. When Wittenberg was conquered by the enemy Cruciger was rector of the University. In these critical days he showed great courage. Almost singlehandedly he saved the University from oblivion. Unfortunately Melanchthon returned to Wittenberg shortly before Cruciger's death. Together the two friends drew up the infamous Leipzig Interim at the command of the turn-coat prince Maurice of Saxony. However, God intervened and Cruciger died before the full repercussions to this compromise could be felt, on November 16, 1548. He was buried two days later in his church, mourned by hundreds of sincere friends.

Justus Jonas (1493-1555)

In a postscript to a letter to John Lang, written on April 13, 1519, Luther wrote: "P.S.—Especially remember me to our Jonas, and tell him I like him."[9]

Thus began the life-long friendship between Jodocus Koch, called Justus Jonas, and the Reformer. Jodocus Koch had been born on June 5, 1493, in Nordhausen and, inspired by the humanist Eobanus Hess, he had taken, after the fashion of his day a "scholarly name," Justus Jonas. By this name he is known to us today.

After attending school in Nordhausen Jonas enrolled at the University of Erfurt when he was only 13 years old. Like Luther he first studied law, but later changed to theology. In 1507 he was awarded the bachelor's degree and in 1510 the master's degree. Then he continued his studies at Wittenberg, but soon returned to Erfurt where he became a lecturer in law. It was here that he met John Lang.

In his younger years Jonas was an enthusiastic follower of Erasmus and other humanists. He made a pilgrimage to Basel to visit "the most famous scholar" of his day and returned to Erfurt with such prestige that he was promptly elected rector of the university. This was in 1519 when Luther wrote his postscript to Lang sending greetings to Jonas.

In the meantime Jonas had changed from law to Biblical lectures and began to rely more and more on the advice of the Wittenberg professor who congratulated him that he had "escaped from the sea of human law into the quiet harbor of Holy Scriptures." In 1521 he accompanied the Reformer to Worms in spite of the opposition to Luther by some of his Erfurt colleagues.

During these years the bonds between Jonas and his humanist friends had been strengthened rather than loosened. On April 17, 1521, Ulrich von Hutten wrote him an enthusiastic letter in which he praised his decision to follow Luther. "And so," wrote the valiant humanist knight, "you have followed the preacher of the Gospel to be in his garden! O piety worthy of love! Truly, Justus, I loved you before, but on this account I love you a hundred times more."[10]

Erasmus, however, was more careful in acknowledging the news of his disciple's new fondness for the Reformer. "There has been a persistent rumor here, dear Jonas," he wrote from Louvain on May 10, 1521, "that you were with Martin Luther at Worms; nor do I doubt that your piety has done what I would have done had I been present, to assuage the tragedy with moderate counsels, so that it would not in future burst forth with greater damage to the world." Then he pontificated: "And as we easily believe what we vehemently desire, men thought that Luther was a man raised up pure from all temptations of this world, to bring a remedy for such great evils. . . . At the first taste of the books published over Luther's name I feared that the affair would bring on a tumult and strife throughout the world. So by letter I warned both Luther and those friends who I thought would have most influence with him. . . . I greatly wonder, Jonas, what god inspired Luther that with so licentious a pen he should attack the pope, all universities, philosophy and the mendicant orders. . . . I have not yet had time to read Luther's books, but from the little I have glanced at . . . , his method and argument by no means pleased me." Jonas did not take the hint. Subsequently the concern of Erasmus for the young Erfurt scholar cooled noticeably. Jonas, however, did not pay much attention to this change, comforting himself with his motto: "If I should please men, I would not be Christ's servant."[11]

In 1521 Justus Jonas was called to Wittenberg. He was installed as professor at the university on June 6th, during Luther's absence at the Waitburg. From this time on he lectured exclusively on theological subjects. During Carlstadt's rule in Wittenberg he was as helpless as Melanchthon and the others. But as soon as Luther returned from the Wartburg Jonas rallied from his weakness and became a strong pillar of the Reformation.

Always a faithful and indispensable helper of the Reformer, he was next to Bugenhagen and Melanchthon the closest collaborator in the work of the translation of the Bible. During the Church Visitations his practical advice was often sought. He was a good preacher and an excellent exegete, but, as Luther put it, "Dr. Jonas has all the virtues which a preacher should have, but he clears his throat too often."[12]

In personal friendship the two men drew closer as time went on. On June 13, 1525, Jonas was present at Luther's wedding, reporting the next day to Spalatin: "Seeing that sight I had to give way to my feelings and could not refrain from tears. Now that it has happened and is the will of God, I wish this good and true man and beloved father in the Lord much happiness." When Luther was critically ill in July 1527 Jonas was with him. "He complained of a loud and troublesome roaring in the left ear," Jonas reported, "which the physicians said was a precursor of a fainting spell, and when he suddenly perceived that roaring the doctor said he could not sit because of it, and, going to his bed-chamber, lay down on the bed. I alone followed him to the door, his wife stopping at the lower step to ask the maids for something, and before she reached the door of his room, though she hurried, he was seized with a faint. Suddenly he said: 'O Doctor Jonas, I am not well; give me some water or anything you have or I shall die.' Then terrified and trembling I poured cold water now on his face, now on his bare back. While I was doing this he began to pray: 'O Lord, if it be Thy will, if this is the hour Thou hast set for me, Thy will be done.' With great ardor and with his eyes raised to heaven he prayed the Lord's Prayer and the whole psalm, 'O Lord, rebuke me not in Thine anger,' etc. Meanwhile his wife came in, and seeing him lying there almost lifeless she, too, was in consternation and called loudly for the servants. . . ." After further describing Luther's patient suffering, the arrival of the doctor, Augustine Schurff, and the pastor, John Bugenhagen, Jonas concluded: "When the hot bags were applied, Luther said his strength was coming back and he hoped he could sweat. They were bidden to go away that he might have quiet. May our Lord Jesus Christ long keep this man for us. Amen."[13]

In 1527 the Jonas family was blessed with a little son while the Luther family had a little daughter, Elizabeth, who was soon taken from them again. From the first the two fond fathers had decided that little Justus and little Elizabeth should become husband and wife. In God's providence this plan was not realized. Justus Jonas Jr. later met a tragic fate. He was beheaded in Denmark in 1563. But in 1528 Father Jonas wrote from Nordhausen to Wittenberg:

"I will bid farewell to all the pleasures that my native place can ever hold in order to see you again and hear you talking about the fatherland of which the man in the Epistle to the Hebrews talks so confidently and so splendidly. . . . I am glad to hear that your little son John is well and strong and active, and runs around and chatters, and is the joy of his parents. I am sending him as a New Year's present a silver John [coin with the image of Elector John], that he may have a little gift from Jonas and a token of the love I bear to him and his father. . . . My son sends greetings to your daughter, his future wife."[14]

During the first great controversy in the Lutheran Church, the Antinomian Controversy between Agricola and Melanchthon, Jonas stood faithfully at the side of the Reformer. "The contention between Philip and Agricola grieved me deeply," he wrote, "because I knew that it would be distasteful to you and add to your already heavy trials, which we, your disciples, ought to lessen, not increase." He also reported that the "poison of the sacramentarians and Anabaptists" had not yet reached Nordhausen.

Jonas accompanied Luther to the colloquy with Zwingli at Marburg. His reports from the Castle of Landgrave Philip still make interesting reading today. "On the day after Michaelmas (September 30, 1529) we arrived at Marburg and were graciously received by the Prince of Hesse with every sort of kindness, right royally. Comfortable lodgings had been provided for us in the town, but the Hessian lord changed his mind and took us all to quarters in the castle and to his regal table. . . . I hope that everything will turn out to Christ's glory. . . . On the Friday after Michaelmas the leaders of the opposing parties conferred privately, by order of the prince, Luther with Oecolampadius, Philip with Zwingli. But they failed to come to agreement, and the next day—the Saturday after Michaelmas—the colloquy was begun. It was not open to all, but was held before the prince, and only the councillors of the Prince of Hesse and those whom the debaters had brought with them, were admitted. On the one side were Zwingli, Oecolampadius, and Hedio, and with them Jacob Sturm, head of the Strassburg Council, . . . Ulrich Funk . . . and Rudolph Frey. . . . On the other side were Luther, Philip (Melanchthon), Eberhard von der Than, prefect of

Eisenach, I, Jonas, Caspar Cruciger, and the rest of our party. Before the prince, with all the councillors sitting around was placed a table at which sat these four—Luther, Melanchthon, Zwingli and Oecolampadius. When the colloquy began . . . Oecolampadius urged the argument for almost two whole days: 'Christ has a true body and is in heaven, but no true body can be in many places.' He dwelt also on John 6 which speaks of the spiritual eating of the flesh and drinking of the blood, as though this were merely saying the same thing in other words. Luther would not permit Christ's words about the Supper to be distorted, by force or craft, from the clear words of Him who said, 'This is my body," and the words of St. Paul, 'This I receive from the Lord.' . . . On the Sunday after Michaelmas the colloquy was resumed. . . . Today, Monday, the prince through his councillors and scholars is seeking a way to some compromise, but the matter of the Sacrament will not be patched up on anybody's account, and there will be no agreement."[15]

Jonas then continued to describe the main actors on the scene: "Zwingli is somewhat boorish and presumptuous; Oecolampadius is a man of wonderful gentleness of spirit and kindliness; Hedio is no less suave and broad-minded; Bucer has the craftiness of a fox, making a perverse pretense of wisdom and keenness. The prince was the most attentive of all onlookers at this display, and is said to have declared openly: 'Now, I would rather believe the simple words of Christ than the shrewd imaginings of men.' "

Although Jonas followed his friend Luther in the Communion Controversy he was, like Melanchthon and Cruciger, always willing to mediate between the two parties, "for Satan can hurt the Gospel only by splitting us into sects."

At Augsburg he again and again propped up Melanchthon's failing courage. With Luther at the Castle Coburg, Jonas was the strongest Lutheran theologian during the fateful months of the Diet of Augsburg. Later he signed the Smalcald Articles, was active during the introduction of the Reformation in Naumburg, in 1536, and during the visitation of Ducal Saxony after Duke George's death, in 1539. He wrote a widely used Church Order.

In 1541 Jonas went to Halle, until then the residence of Albert of Mainz, and introduced the Reformation there, forcing Albert to move his residence to Mainz. Here Luther often visited Jonas. The two friends became especially close during the last hard years of Luther's life. Jonas was with Luther on his last trip to Eisleben and stood at the side of the Reformer in the hour of death. When the Reformer's life was ebbing away Jonas asked him with a penetrating voice: "*Reverende pater*, are you willing to die in the name of the Christ and the doctrine which you have preached?" Luther rallied his last strength and replied "Yes" so distinctly that the whole group heard it. The next day, February 19, 1546, Jonas preached the first funeral sermon for the departed friend at Eisleben.[16]

After Luther's death Jonas parted company with Melanchthon and Cruciger and followed Amsdorf, Cranach, and others into the exile of their beloved prince, Elector John Frederick. At the height of the Smalcald War Justus Jonas left out the name of the Emperor Charles from the General Prayer and put his name next to Pilate's in the Apostles' Creed as "the cruel Diocletian, the persecutor of Christianity." He was forced to flee to his native Nordhausen and from there to Hildesheim. In 1548 he tried to return to Halle, but the intimidated City Council did not dare to take him back. Therefore, he turned south to Thuringia, the realm of Duke Ernest and lived for a while at Coburg taking part in the Osiandrian Controversy. In 1552 he organized the Lutheran Church in Regensburg, but again was forced to leave, taught for a while at the newly established Lutheran university of Jena, and finally found a haven in Eisfeld-on-Werra where he died peacefully, after a decade of many disappointments and hardships, on October 9, 1955.

Philip Melanchthon (1497-1560)

The most controversial and least understood friend of Luther whose later activities brought more harm to our Church than all his labors at the side of the Reformer had brought blessings, was born at Bretten in Baden on February 16, 1497. He was the son of a famous armourer who numbered among his customers the Emperor Maximilian I and many princes and knights of the Holy Roman Empire. Philip Schwarzerd came early under the influence of his great-uncle John Reuchlin, the renowned humanist and Hebrew scholar. In keeping with the custom of the times Reuchlin changed the prosaic name of his nephew to "Melanchthon," the Greek equivalent for "Schwarzerd."

In 1509, at the age of twelve, Melanchthon enrolled at the University of Heidelberg, took his bachelor's degree, but unable to obtain a master's degree at such a tender age he transferred to the more liberal University of Tuebingen where he soon received the coveted degree. The only other academic distinction which Melanchthon ever received was a Bachelor of Divinity degree which the University of Wittenberg conferred upon him in 1519. He refused to accept an honorary doctorate. Thus the man who is known in history as the "Preceptor of Germany" never held a doctor's degree.

Upon the recommendation of Reuchlin Melanchthon was called to Wittenberg and was installed as professor on August 29, 1518. Under him Wittenberg University which up to this time had been a second rate school became one of the finest in Europe. Melanchthon set aside the traditional scholastic methods. His discourse "On Reforming the Studies of Youth" caught the spirit of the Renaissance and the best in humanism. His contribution to the Reformation in the field of higher education cannot be overestimated.

Melanchthon was primarily a Greek scholar. At first he lectured on Homer and other Greek authors, but as time went on he concentrated more and more on Biblical lecture courses. Luther was deeply impressed by Melanchthon's methods of interpretation, but it is wrong to say—as has been done in the past—that Melanchthon influenced the theology of Luther to any great extent. Melanchthon was primarily a philologist, a craftsman with the word, a master interpreter, a systematician. But he never freed himself from his humanist heritage. Whenever he was tested as a man of the Church he failed, especially after Luther's death. It is perhaps the tragedy of the Lutheran Church that the Reformer did not see this weakness of his good friend or when it was called to his attention stubbornly refused to see it.

Nevertheless Melanchthon's theological works are impressive.

They are a strange mixture of philosophical and theological thought, very much like some of the important theological works of the mid-twentieth century. The present revival of Melanchthon, like the revival during the period of Enlightment, can be best explained by the kinship which many theologians may feel to the humanist-reformer. Melanchthon stood half-way between Erasmus and Luther, but remained faithful to the latter—without breaking with the former—because he admired Luther's work for the Reformation of the Church. Luther in turn transformed the layman Melanchthon

MELANCHTHON

from a mere "great Greek scholar" into a theologian of sorts who wrote the *Loci,* the first Lutheran dogmatics, and lectured on Romans and other Biblical books.

Melanchthon's marriage to Catherine Krapp of Wittenberg gave a domestic center to the Reformation. When Luther was at the Wartburg in 1521 and 1522 the 24 year old Greek scholar became the natural leader of the orphaned Lutherans at Wittenberg. Here for the first time he revealed his weakness: He failed to meet the issues raised by Carlstadt and was almost persuaded by the fanatical Heavenly Prophets Storch and Stuebner to join their ranks.

In regards to their claims of personal inspiration Melanchthon replied: "Luther alone can decide. Let us beware of quenching the spirit of God and let us also beware of being led astray by the spirit of Satan."[17]

But in spite of this indecision on the homefront, Melanchthon valiantly defended his friend against the attacks from abroad. When the Paris theologians condemned Luther's teachings as heresy he wrote a bold "Apology of Luther Against Paris" which Luther liked so much that he translated it into German and published it side by side with the Paris condemnation. Yet Luther was deeply disturbed by the seeming inability of his friend to take a strong stand in Wittenberg. In December 1521 he made a secret and hurried trip to Wittenberg to put some backbone into his friend, but a few weeks later we again find Melanchthon faltering. Luther finally returned in March 1522, sent Carlstadt and his prophets away, and relieved Melanchthon from a task which he was unable to perform.

In spite of this experience nothing changed in the relationship between the two men and Melanchthon was soon again considered the heir-apparent of the Reformer. The reason may have been that Melanchthon's scholarship became almost indispensable. He revised the New Testament which Luther had translated at the Wartburg in 11 weeks. It was published a half year after the Reformer's return to Wittenberg, in September 1522. He also assisted Luther in preparing the first installments of his Old Testament translation for publication. In the meantime he remained, next to Luther, the star attraction to the University of Wittenberg, a valuable public relations position since Wittenberg was off-limits for students from most surrounding states, including the subjects of Duke George of Saxony and Elector Joachim of Brandenburg.

Since Melanchthon had, under proper guidance, the ability to keep his head even during the most heated arguments and to argue the cause of the Reformation convincingly, he was often chosen to head the delegations which during the next two decades defended Lutheran doctrines at various colloquies and disputations. In 1524 Campeggio, the wily papal delegate, had met Melanchthon during a vacation which the Wittenberg professor spent in his native South Germany and had asked him openly to forsake Luther. This

Melanchthon had refused to do and had set forth his theological views in the treatise, "The Sum Total of Lutheran Doctrine." But throughout his life the thought of re-uniting the Christian Church under the Bishop of Rome whom he recognized as supreme shepherd "by human right" even after the Smalcald Articles never left him.

In this year 1524 the first Lutheran controversy had its beginning. Melanchthon rightly saw that the Biblical theology on which Luther's teaching hinged was the proper distinction between Law and Gospel. Many Lutheran preachers, especially in the Lutherlands of central Germany, had discarded the Law and were preaching the Gospel only. This lopsidedness was partly due to a misunderstanding of Luther's earlier works, especially the "Freedom of a Christian" of 1520, partly to influences from the outside and an aversion to the laws of Rome. In 1524 Melanchthon discussed the importance of the Law of Moses with the Eisenach theologian, Jacob Strauss. This controversy was taken over later by John Agricola who renewed it again and again, but Melanchthon remained firm and Luther supported him.

The year 1524 also established closer relations between Wittenberg and the South German theologians who were wavering between Wittenberg and Zurich. Strassburg and Basel now became the centers of mediation theology.

Although Melanchthon had been married happily for five years he did not approve of Luther's marriage. On June 16, 1525, he wrote to Joachim Camerarius: "You might be amazed that at this unfortunate time when good and excellent men everywhere are in distress" [it was the time of the Peasant War], "Luther not only does not sympathize with them, but, as it seems, rather waxes wanton and diminishes his reputation. . . . The man is certainly pliable; and the nuns have used their arts against him most successfully; thus probably society with the nuns has softened or even inflamed this noble and high-spirited man. In this way he seems to have fallen into this untimely change of life. The rumor, however, that he had previously dishonored her is manifestly a lie. Now that the deed is done, we must not take it too hard, or reproach him. . . . The mode of life, too, while indeed humble is, nevertheless, holy and more pleasing to God than celibacy." This from the pen of the best friend of Luther.[18]

In December of 1525 Luther launched his counter-attack against Erasmus and the humanists by publishing his treatise, "On the Bondage of the Will." While Melanchthon never was able to understand fully Luther's theological concern for the utter inability of man to co-operate with God, he remained faithful also this time. The break with the many friends whom he had among the humanists must have been painful to him. He managed to remain personally on good terms with most of them. He was unwilling to divest himself completely of his humanistic past.

The next crisis in Melanchthon's career followed soon thereafter. It was the crisis which caused him greatest heartaches in the years to come. Again he chose the side of Luther, although temperamentally and philosophically he should have gone over to the Swiss. He would have felt happier with them and the Lutheran Church would have been spared the interminable troubles of the post-Luther era which plagued her into the nineteenth and even into the twentieth centuries. Zwingli's personality, half humanist philosopher, half Biblical theologian, was closer to Melanchthon's than Luther's uncompromising stand on the revealed Word of God. Luther had called the Zwinglians "willful enemies of God and His Word," was opposed to making an alliance with them, for "in the first place," he wrote to the Elector John on May 22, 1529, "it is certain that such an alliance is not of God and does not come of trust in Him, but is a device of human wits. . . . In the second place, the worst thing of all is that in this league most of the members are those who strive against God and the Sacraments. . . . By making a league with them we take upon ourselves the burden of all their wickedness and blasphemy. . . . In the third place, in the Old Testament God always condemned leagues for human help." And on June 23, 1529, he wrote to Landgrave Philip of Hesse who had invited both parties: "I should like to speak out in time and tell your Grace dryly what I think. It seems to me that our opponents are seeking to use your Grace's diligence to accomplish an end from which no good will come, namely, that they may hereafter be able to boast that it was not their fault . . . If, then, we were to part without agree-

ment, not only would your Grace's expense and trouble and our
time and labor be lost, but they, too, would not cease their boast-
ing. . . . In that case it would have been better if things had been
left as they now are. In a word, I can expect no good of the devil,
however prettily he acts." How true were these prophecies of the
Reformer![19]

Yet the meeting took place, partly because Melanchthon suc-
cumbed to the flattery of Landgrave Philip. On July 1 the Landgrave had written, "We ask that you do not refuse this invitation or
hinder the meeting. . . . Thereby you will, without doubt, be comforting weak consciences and doing a good and Christian work. . . .
Since in matters of this kind we can propose no special measures
that will be proper, as you who are experts can well understand,
it is therefore our gracious desire that you will yourselves consider
ways and means by which harmony and unity may be reached."

After the meeting Melanchthon reported to his elector: "In order
that the discussion [the Colloquy at Marburg] might not be fruitless, however, articles were adopted dealing with other subjects. . . .
We have found that there have been improper utterances about the
articles. . . . They have accepted our views on all points except the
presence of the body of Christ in the Lord's Supper. We think, too,
that if this matter is not to go too far it ought never to be taken up
again; it is to be hoped that if they are dealt with in the right way
they will yield. For in other respects they have showed themselves
not unfriendly to us. . ." For the rest of his life Melanchthon tried
to "deal with them in the right way," not the way of Luther, but by
constantly compromising the doctrine of the Real Presence and
even changing the official Augsburg Confession of the Lutheran
Church.

In 1526 Melanchthon had attended the First Diet of Speier which
had ended favorably for the Lutherans. Immediately after this he
embarked on the work for which he will at all times receive just
credit: The work of Church Visitations, the cleansing of the Church
from the impurities of false doctrine and ignorance which had left
a residue of un-Lutheran preaching and practice even in the heartland of Saxony. The first Antinomian Controversy was a by-product
of this cleansing. In March 1529 Melanchthon voiced strong op-

position to the contemplated Edict of the Second Diet of Speier. His courageous stand led to the "Protest" for which Protestants are named today. But the greatest and most memorable year of his entire life was the year 1530 when, after initial hesitation and timidity, he rose above himself and wrote the Augsburg Confession and its Apology, the two central Lutheran confessions. Although he received some prodding from Luther, the Elector and Landgrave, and from Jonas and other theological colleagues, these two documents were his masterpiece for which the Lutheran Church will always be indebted to him. Luther later summed up Melanchthon's role at Augsburg when he stated that no one else could have stepped as softly as he and therefore no one would have accomplished what he alone could do. The Confession was read to the Emperor Charles on June 25, 1530. Fortunately the Lutherans had made copies of it, because the Emperor promptly confiscated the original. Shortly after delivering the Confession Melanchthon wrote a scholarly Apology, or defense, of it which in spite of the storms which were to engulf Master Philip's head during the next thirty years has remained one of the most cherished Lutheran Confessions.

The desire of Melanchthon to work for union among all Christian Churches led, in the late thirties, to his tampering with the wording of the Augsburg Confession, to a revision of his *Loci*, and to his refusal to sign the Smalcald Articles without reservation because they did not accept the pope's supremacy by "human right." He was busy arranging with the Strassburgers and others for the Wittenberg Concord which, however, remained ineffective since most of the Swiss theologians had refused to co-operate. He tried for a while to win Henry VIII of England for the Lutheran Reformation, to influence Francis I, wily, two-faced, double-dealing king of France, and to come to an understanding with the Catholics at various colloquies long after Luther had given up hope. The seed which had been sown in his heart came to full fruition after his friend's death when, in 1548, he sponsored the infamous Leipzig Interim in which he surrendered the most precious doctrines of his Church and later engaged in Crypto-Calvinistic activities which almost led to the disestablishment of the Lutheran Church in the heartland of Saxony. These activities, whether born of weakness or inability to think theologically, called upon his head the *"rabies theologorum,"* the furor of the theologians, from which he was saved by a timely death.

But perhaps the greatest trial of Melanchthon took place during the lifetime of Luther. It was partly Luther's fault. In 1539 the licentious Landgrave Philip of Hesse had decided to enter a bigamous marriage with the consent of his original wife whom he abhorred. In spite of the sanction which he received from the fickle court chaplain Melander he felt in conscience bound to seek the advice of Luther and Melanchthon. The latter hesitated, but Luther who on the basis of Old Testament precedent considered bigamy preferable to divorce gave his consent and persuaded Melanchthon to do likewise. When the matter was noised abroad and the Landgrave incurred the wrath of the Emperor (bigamy was punishable with death), Luther committed the second grave error by advising the Landgrave to deny that he, Luther, had given his consent. This advise, although based on the false concepts of the Roman Catholic doctrine concerning confessional secrets, was equally inexcusable. The result was that Melanchthon fell gravely ill and was at the point of death while on a journey to Weimar. Luther who was summoned to his bedside prayed fervently that his friend might be spared. This prayer was quite different from the prayers which he prayed during his own bouts with sickness. "I rubbed the Lord's ears with all the promises which I recalled from Scripture so that He must hear me if I were to believe His promises." Then he took Melanchthon's hand and told him to cheer up, for now he would not die. Thereupon, Melanchthon who had been lying in his bed ashen-pale began to take deep breaths, and although he was unable to talk for a while yet, the crisis had passed. Luther had a meal brought into the room and told his friend, who had not eaten for several days: "Listen, Philip, you must eat or else I am going to excommunicate you!" Four days later, on July 2, 1540, the Reformer was able to report to John Lang: "We found Melanchthon dead, but behold, now he lives again!"[20]

When Melanchthon heard that Luther had fallen asleep in Eisleben he posted the following notice to the bulletin board of the University of Wittenberg: "Alas, gone is the chariot of Israel and the horseman thereof (II Kings 2:12), who has ruled the Church in these latter days; for it was not human reason which discovered the doctrine of the forgiveness of sins and trust in the Son of God, but God has this revealed by this man whom God, as we have witnessed, has brought forth among us. Therefore, let us cherish this man's memory and his doctrine and let us be disciplined and watch for the great visitations and changes which will follow this event. But you, O Son of God, crucified and risen Immanuel, rule your Church, preserve and protect her. Amen." On February 22, 1546, the mortal remains of Luther were brought to Wittenberg through the Elster Gate to the Castle Church where many years ago he had nailed the Ninety-Five Theses. Catherine, her children, his brother James and other Mansfeld relatives, the heads of the city and university, hundreds of students, and many, many friends followed the coffin. After Bugenhagen's sermon Melanchthon took the word to say a final farewell. "We have become orphans," he said, "who have had a wonderful father and are now deprived of him." Then the coffin was lowered into the grave under the pulpit.

"We are orphans." These words of Melanchthon characterized the Lutheran Church of the next decades. No one felt this more than Melanchthon. He was utterly helpless. We do not want to mention all the troubles which he and the orphaned Church endured during the next fourteen years. The evening of Melanchthon's life was filled with suffering and grief. His enemies attacked him to the day of his death which occurred on April 19, 1560. His mortal remains were laid to rest at the side of Luther's in the Castle Church of Wittenberg.

George Spalatin (1482-1545)

"Please commend me to Dr. Martin. I think so much of him as a most learned and upright man, and what is extremely rare one of such acumen in judging that I wish to be entirely his friend." This wish written by George Spalatin to John Lang in 1515 was fully realized.[21]

It has been said that without Spalatin's enthusiastic and faithful support Luther would not have survived the crucial years of the Reformation from 1517 to 1521. It was Spalatin who protected him, who won the Elector Frederick the Wise for the Reformer. Although Frederick did not confess his Lutheran faith until the day before his death, he saved Luther from the wrath of the Emperor and the wrath of the Pope.

Luther saw the Elector only once, and then only from afar off. Spalatin served as the go-between between the Reformer and his Prince. As secretary and court chaplain he was in an eminent position to influence Frederick the Wise who during the early years of the Reformation was often exasperated by Luther's actions. Therefore Spalatin must be counted among the friends of the Inner Circle.

George Burkhard was born at Spalt near Nuremberg in 1482, a year before Luther. He came of a poor family which he supported for many years financially, even after he had moved to Saxony. Following the humanist custom he discarded his German name and called himself *Spalatinus* after his birthplace, meaning "The Man from Spalt." After elementary and secondary education at home and at Nuremberg he enrolled, in 1498, at the University of Erfurt, but soon after Luther's arrival he followed his beloved teacher Marschalk to Wittenberg where he received the master's degree with the first graduating class. Soon he returned to Erfurt and became tutor as was the custom among penniless young scholars. However, at the two universities which he had attended he had formed many valuable friendships with leading humanists, and although his endowments were more modest than those of the first rate humanists of his time, his good qualities recommended him in high places.

Strangely, Spalatin was without ambition. In the same year 1505 in which Luther entered the Convent of the Augustinian Hermits, Spalatin became a monk in the nearby St. George's Monastery. After three years he followed a call to become tutor of the heir-apparent to the Saxon throne, the son of Duke John and nephew of the Elector. This young man, the later Elector John Frederick, received a thoroughly Christian education at the hands of the young Erfurt scholar and later became the greatest champion of the Gospel among the German princes. From the time when Spalatin entered court life to the end of his life he served faithfully three Electors, Frederick the Wise, John the Constant, and John Frederick the Magnanimous. Although he left the immediate service of the court in 1525 in order to become pastor in Altenburg he remained one of the most trusted advisers at court, a clear indication of the high esteem in which he was held.

But the beginnings of Spalatin's career at court were not easy. He had to struggle against an influential clique of ultraconservative advisers who took undue advantage of the piety of Frederick the Wise. The Elector soon recognized his personal merits and appointed him his personal chaplain, used him as special ambassador, trouble shooter extraordinary, censor, and general handy-man. Besides these many functions he also served as historiographer of Saxony, a coveted position at sixteenth century courts. He immortalized his princes and their ancestors in his "Annals of Saxony" which rate among the better annals of that unscientific age.

Yet Spalatin would have died without ever attaining fame, for he was a very modest man, had not Luther and the Reformation catapulted him into the limelight. He was one of the earliest friends of the Reformer. He never wavered in his loyalty to him. For a time he was practically alone among the partisans of the Wittenberg professor at the Saxon court and had to fight an uphill fight. But in the end he won, not only the support of his own prince, but through him the protection of Luther by the most important princes of the Empire. It is Spalatin's work which kept the pious Frederick the Wise from following in the reactionary footsteps of his Leipzig cousin, Duke George. Frederick's hobby of collecting relics—he had the largest relic collection in Germany—certainly would have prejudiced him against Luther had not Spalatin turned his mind to the greater thing, the Word of God.

Spalatin interfered when Pope Leo tried to persuade Frederick to give up Luther by dangling before him the promise of the imperial crown. He was present when Miltitz through promises tried to buy Luther's silence. But diplomatically he stayed away from the Leipzig Debate with Eck. He strengthened the hand of his Elector whom he had accompanied to the coronation of Charles V in Cologne. He was in Worms in 1521 and probably was instrumental in making the arrangements for Luther's abduction to the Wartburg. But when he saw that the cause of the Reformation was victorious in Saxon lands and that his help was no longer urgently needed, he tired of court life and tried again and again to obtain permission to become a simple parish pastor, to serve the Lord as true "Man of God." During the seventeen years at the Saxon court Spalatin had become famous and moderately well-to-do, he was known throughout Germany and more highly respected than many of those who were superior to him in intelligence and scholarship, he was wooed by both Catholics and Lutherans, but in his innermost heart he was never really absorbed in the role which history and his friendship with Luther had thrust upon him.

Luther at first objected to Spalatin's retirement from active court life. However, at the death of Frederick the Wise and the accession to the throne of the determinedly Lutheran Elector John he permitted him to "retire to Altenburg."

On August 25, 1525, three and a half months after the death of his beloved Elector, George Spalatin became pastor of St. Bartholomew's Church in Altenburg. He was the second resident Lutheran pastor, his predecessor, Wenceslas Linck, having left in the midst of grave disturbances. Although Altenburg was one of the alternate residences of the Elector, the Catholic reaction of the town had by no means given up the fight. It took a man of the infinite patience of a Spalatin to bring about complete reformation of this city. At the time of his death in 1545 Altenburg was solidly Lutheran. He was aided in his often difficult work by his faithful wife, Catherine, whom he had married on November 19, 1525, a few months after another monk, Martin Luther, had cast off the false vow of celibacy.

Spalatin's influence upon the course of the Reformation did not diminish during the twenty years which he spent in Altenburg. Even as a parish pastor he was often called on to advise the two Electors John and John Frederick. He remained throughout these years a close personal friend of Luther and most Reformation scholars. He was at Speier when the Lutherans "protested," he helped frame the Augsburg Confession, he was at Smalcald when the Lutherans organized a defensive alliance against the newly formed Catholic league. When one reads Spalatin's voluminous correspondence one cannot help but wonder that he had time left for work in his parish. And yet he was one of the finest pastors.

His most outstanding contribution to his Church during the second part of his active life lay in the field of Christian education. He was an indefatigable "Church Visitor," a position which required an unusual amount of patience and tact. He established libraries and schools, trained pastors in practical theology and taught the young people. He was called "Loquax," the Talkative One, not because he rambled and talked all the time, but because he contributed so much to the organization of the Church through his tremendous output in letters which he wrote to many men. While he was not a systematic theologian or a deep exegete, he had the capacity of communicating to others and of inspiring others.

In the fifteen thirties the effects of his untiring activity began to tell. We hear of his desire to retire for the first time in 1536. In that year he wrote his will. But he stayed at his post until the end of his life on January 16, 1545. His body was laid to rest under the altar of the St. Bartholomew's Church.

Spalatin's voluminous correspondence has only partly been published. Most of his literary legacy is still in manuscript form at Weimar in the Soviet zone. We have at least 800 letters which he exchanged with Luther, but many others may be lost. Even so, these letters constitute a valuable aid to the understanding of Luther and of the Reformation period. In these letters Luther confided to his friend his innermost thoughts from the pre-Reformation controversy between Reuchlin and the Cologne inquisitors to the serious visitations of Luther's last years. In them are shared not only the sorrows, but also the joys of the two friends. They speak of the great things of life as well as the small details of everyday living. Through them Spalatin participated in the work of the Reformation. As a sample may serve this excerpt from a letter of Luther, written on December 12, 1522, when he and his Wittenberg co-workers were stumbling through the book of Leviticus. "Dear Spalatin," he wrote, "Grace and peace . . . Please do us the favor of describing the following animals and giving us their names according to their species:

"Birds of prey—Kite, vulture, hawk, sparrow-hawk, falcon, and any others of this sort.

"Game animals—Roebuck, chamois, ibex, wild goat or *silvestris hircus*.

"Reptiles—Is *stellio* properly called a newt, and *lacerta limara* a viper? In Hebrew and Latin and Greek these things are all so confused that we have to guess at them from the genera and species of the animals. Therefore I wish, if possible, to learn in German the names, the species and the nature of all the birds of prey, the game animals and the venomous reptiles. I shall tell you the poisonous vermins that I have. They are: weasel, mouse, toad, viper, newt, lizard, snail, mole. Moses calls them, *crocodylon, mygalon, chameleon,* and numbers them, shamelessly enough, among the 'creeping things' of Leviticus XI.

"The names of the night birds are these: Owl, raven, horned owl, tawny owl, screech owl.

"Of the wild animals I have the stag, the roebuck and the chamois, which our author makes *bubulus*. Of the birds I have the vulture, the kite, the hawk and the sparrow-hawk. . . . I do not know what he is dreaming of when he numbers among the edible animals the *taragelaphus,* the *pygargus,* the *oryx* and the *camelopardus*. I wish that you would undertake this part of the work, take a Hebrew Bible and work all this out carefully and try to reach some certainty about it. I have not the leisure. Farewell, and pray for me.

MARTINUS LUTHER."[22]

III.

The Larger Circle

The chief centers of the Reformation during the fifteen-twenties were Electoral Saxony with Thuringia, the heartland of the Reformation. Here Wittenberg, Magdeburg, Weimar, Erfurt, Gotha, Altenburg, Eisenach, Coburg, Torgau, Zwickau, and Chemnitz served as main bastions of Lutheranism. Ducal Saxony with Leipzig, Meissen and Dresden remained officially hostile to the Reformation until 1539 when Duke George died. To the north Brandenburg with Berlin and Frankfurt-on-Oder was under the rule of Joachim I of Hohenzollern who hated Luther because Wittenberg had given refuge to his estranged wife, the Electress Elizabeth, and because Luther had attacked the house of Hohenzollern when he threw the gauntlet at the feet of Albert of Mainz, Joachim's nearest kin. After the death of Joachim I his son, Elector Joachim II, introduced a type of independent Lutheranism in his country, formed by the theology and personality of John Agricola. East of Brandenburg there were a few outposts of the Lutheran faith in Silesia with Breslau and Liegnitz as centers. Pomerania, the home of John Bugenhagen, now under the rule of Duke Barmin, who had accompanied the Reformer to the Leipzig Debate, soon joined the Reformation, but it was not until the thirties that the movement was completely victorious.

119

Still farther to the East and North the realm of the Teutonic
Knights, under the leadership of Albert of Prussia, another Hohenzollern, but more worthy than his cousins in Mainz and Brandenburg, had accepted the Reformation in 1525. The last Grandmaster
of the Teutonic Order married and became the first Duke of
Prussia. Koenigsberg and Danzig were the chief cities from where
the movement spread throughout the country. Farther North
the Baltic States had accepted the Gospel still earlier. The names
of Dietrich von Cleen, Lohmueller and Plettenberg—among others
—come to mind as we think of the victory of Lutheranism in
Riga, Dorpat and Reval.

Turning now to the Northwest of Wittenberg we have as the
most important hedge-hog of Lutheran doctrine the great city
of Magdeburg. To the north and west are the Hartz Mountains
with Goslar, Nordhausen and Klausthal, then Lueneburg, Hamburg and Bremen. After the Reformation in Scandinavia which
took its own independent course in the late twenties and mid-
thirties, Schleswig and Holstein became Lutheran. There were
also pockets of Lutheranism in the Lowlands in spite of the determined opposition of Charles V.

West of the domain of Frederick the Wise and John the
Constant, Hesse with Marburg was probably the most important
bastion of the Reformation outside Saxony-Thuringia. Landgrave
Philip of Hesse was one of the most fervent and ablest supporters
of Luther. After the death of Frederick the Wise he was the greatest statesman among the Lutheran princes and shaped the events
in Germany—for better and for worse—during the last twenty
years of Luther's life. The Marburg Colloquy, the League of
Smalcald, the reconquest of Wuerttemberg from the Catholic
Hapsburgs, the prevention of open warfare between Electoral
and Ducal Saxony in the early fifteen-forties, these are his greatest contributions to the Reformation.

South of the Main River—the Mason-Dixon Line of Germany—
the Catholic resistance was strong from the beginning, due mainly
to the efforts of the Bavarian dukes and the brother of Emperor
Charles, King Ferdinand. Here Albert of Mainz, the Bishops of

Salzburg and Passau, and other princes of the Church were successful in stemming the tide, at least for a time. Exceptions were the great Free Cities, especially Nueremberg and Augsburg, where Lutheranism was strong. Minor potentates, like the rulers of Ansbach-Bayreuth and of the Palatinate were willing to tolerate the Lutherans and often joined them. Wuerttemberg became openly Lutheran after the Hapsburg governors had been driven out and Duke Ulrich had been reinstated. Strassburg and large parts of the Alsace occupied a mediating position between Wittenberg and Zurich. Even in Switzerland the Lutheran influences were strong among the Zwinglians. Oecolampadius, Kessler and numerous other Zwinglians had come directly from Luther. Lutheran influence in Switzerland never ceased, even after Calvin had taken over the Reformation movement in Geneva.

The story of the remaining regions is mostly a story of persecution and martyrdom. The greatest Lutheran theologian of the "Younger Generation," Flacius, came from Istria, driven from Italy by persecution. Vergerio who later served as pastor in Wuerttemberg was likewise an Italian exile. Lambert and others had come from France. Most of the so-called English Lutherans spent the years of their lives in exile or were martyred. All of the Spanish "Luteranos" who survived were forced to live abroad. Only in Hungary, Transylvania and—for a time—Czechoslovakia do we find flourishing Lutheran congregations.

These then were the centers of the young movement during Luther's lifetime. In these centers hundreds of men were working for the Reformation, men who had been in contact, directly and indirectly, with Martin Luther and the other Wittenberg Reformers. Many of them had studied under Luther and even lived in his house. Others had become acquainted with him through his works, had corresponded with him or visited him. These were the men of the Larger Circle.

In Wittenberg

In Wittenberg congregated the men who carried the Gospel into all the lands. From Denmark had come Peder von Swaven and later Hans Tausen, from Norway Torbjorn Olafsson Bratt, from Sweden the two Petris, from Finland Michael Agricola and long before him Peter Saerkilahti, and many others from Scandinavian nations. There were students from the Baltic States, East Prussia, Poland, Bohemia and Moravia, Hungary, Transylvania, Austria, Switzerland, France, the Netherlands and England, but most of the men of the Larger Circle had come from nearby towns and neighboring territories and Free Cities. The Black Cloisters became the center of their contacts with Luther. To the home which had served as his monastery but had been emptied of monks during the first five years of the fifteen-twenties and had been given to the Reformer by a grateful prince, hundreds of men came for spiritual counsel, for social conversation and for good food and beer. At times the table companions numbered a score or more. It is difficult to see how Kate Luther managed this large establishment. Often money was lacking completely, although Luther received a good salary. Some of these companions paid for their fare, others sat at the table of the large Luther family for weeks and months without paying. Luther who was no financial genius managed to entertain them all, holding forth with his Table Talk which the grateful boarders took down in notebooks and which now serve us as a source book for the study of the Reformation.[1]

These men shared the joys and sorrows of the Luther home. Kate did not always look upon them with favor, but in deference to her famous husband she and an aunt, Muhme Lene, who managed the kitchen, Wolfgang Sieberger, the former monk but now the servant of the house, and the others did their best to make the big house a place where men of all stations and conditions could meet with Luther. During the illnesses of the Reformer which occurred more and more frequently as he grew older this house full of guests was sometimes a severe test to the faith and patience of its occupants, but at other times the companions helped to cheer up and to assist the Reformer in his hard work.

Besides these table companions, the Dietrichs, Medlers, Roerers, Schlaginhaufens, Rabes, Cordatusses, Zwicks, Wolfs, Lauterbachs, Wellers, Khummers, Mathesiusses, Heydenreichs, Aurifabers and

the many others we have the steady Wittenberg friends and co-
workers who kept in close and often daily touch with the occupants of the Black Cloisters. The men of the Inner Circle have
been mentioned in a previous chapter. There were others, men
like Aurogallus, the Hebrew scholar, who helped translate the
Old Testament and spent many hours in Luther's study. Cranach,
the painter and close personal friend of Luther, who painted
him again and again, who visited and comforted him and was
in turn comforted by him when the death of a son in far-away
Italy almost broke his heart. There was Hans Lufft, the Bible
printer, who had more to print than he could manage, and
before him the Lotthers, the forgotten printers of the Reformation. There were the officials of the court and the leaders of the
community, men like Gregory von Brueck and Christian Beyer,
the chancellors, and a large number of others. Finally the friends
who were living far and near and were returning to Wittenberg
from time to time to see Luther.

Through Wittenberg passed people who would have never
looked a second time at the dingy little place, had not Luther
been there. Here were Christian II, deposed king of Denmark and
Norway who for a time served as a deacon of the Wittenberg
Church; the Electress Elizabeth, who had been exiled by her
husband, Elector Joachim I of Brandenburg. Before her her
husband had passed through Wittenberg on his trip to Worms.
Other princes and knights came throughout the years, among
them Albert of Hohenzollern, cousin of the famous Albert of
Mainz, the last Grandmaster of the Teutonic Knights who, after
a chat with Luther, decided to introduce the Reformation in his
domain. Even a papal nuncio, Peter Paul Vergerio, arrived here
in the mid-thirties to interview Luther and to sound him out on
the proposed Ecumenical Council. It has been said that Wittenberg was "the most important city in Western Christendom" in
the thirty years between 1516 and 1546, not only because Luther
carried on the work of the Reformation from there but also because more people of importance visited the little town on the
Elbe and received inspiration and direction of their lives here than
anywhere else.[2]

In Saxony

From Wittenberg the Gospel spread as we have seen above. Near the city the towns of Kemberg and Niemegk are often mentioned in the history of the Reformation. Bernhardi who had disputed the theses "On the Human Will," one of the earliest followers of Luther, became pastor in Kemberg. Carlstadt lived after his downfall for a while in Niemegk, causing some trouble, as did George Witzel who as pastor in Niemegk from 1526-1531 slowly returned to the Catholic fold. But the Lutherans of Niemegk forced these men to leave and remained true to the Gospel. At Torgau where Frederick the Wise and his successors resided most of the time George Spalatin and later Gabriel Zwilling, the "Second Luther" of the Wittenberg disturbances who had reformed after Luther's return from the Wartburg, were the most outstanding champions of Lutheranism. There were many others, both clergy and lay-people, who faithfully supported the Gospel. Altenburg, another residence of the electors, did not fare so well at the beginning. The Catholic reaction was strong. Here Luther and Miltitz had met in 1519. Here Luther appointed a reformed Zwilling as first pastor only to be told by the Elector that Zwilling could not be entrusted with such an important post. Wenceslas Linck was sent to Altenburg in his place, but was unable to overcome the opposition. He moved on to Nuremberg. George Spalatin himself took over the pastorate and superintendent's office in the divided city and labored here with great blessings until his death, twenty years later. In Zwickau, hot bed of fanatics since the previous century and now plagued by Heavenly Prophets, Thomas Muenzer was the first Lutheran pastor, but had soon to leave because of his involvement with the *Schwaermer*, went to Alstedt, Muehlhausen and his doom. At Zwickau Hausmann and Weller worked with varying success. Nicholas Hausmann, the fearless pastor of Zwickau, became one of Luther's dearest friends. Luther mourned his death more than that of any other contemporary. Jena and Weimar did not really become important centers until after the Reformer's death, Jena as the seat of a strictly Lutheran university, Weimar as the residence of the dispossessed Saxon princes. Many illustrious names are connected with the development of Jena as a center of Lutheranism. Of those who had lived with Luther we mention especially George Roerer, later the editor of Luther's Works, and Matthias Flacius, the most fiery defender of orthodoxy after his master's death. Muehlhausen which had suffered much spiritual *Anfechtung* during the time of Muenzer and Carlstadt was kept in the faith by Matthew Hitzschold; Eisenach had two great pastors in Menius and Amsdorf; Gotha became a Lutheran stronghold under Frederick Myconius; while Eisleben and Mansfeld, Luther's home towns, had a great number of outstanding leaders, beginning with John Agricola, Major, the two Spangenbergs, Coelius, Guettel, and many others.

In Erfurt, Magdeburg, and Halle

These three important centers of the Lutheran Reformation, although located in the heart of Lutherlands occupied a special position in the history of the Reformation because they were in part or completely under non-Saxon control. Erfurt, nominally also under the control of Albert of Mainz, the city where Luther had entered the monastery, remained for many years a thorn in the flesh of the Reformer. Here Nathin, Trutvetter and Usingen and many of his former associates continued to oppose him. But here was also one of his ablest lieutenants, John Lang, who with the younger John Aurifaber and Menius and a great number of others worked unceasingly to win Erfurt for the cause of the Reformation. In the end he was successful, but not until after many trials. In Magdeburg we have seen the fine work which Amsdorf carried on for many difficult years. But his efforts were crowned when Magdeburg became a bastion of Lutheranism stronger than even Wittenberg. Here Major worked, and much later Flacius. From here the efforts of the Emperor to force the Interim upon the Lutherans were met with defiance. Here a hundred years later the most determined effort was made to stop the avalanche of the Catholic armies overrunning northern Germany.

Halle, the favorite residence of Albert of Mainz, was the most difficult city in the Lutherlands, more difficult than Erfurt and

Magdeburg. The first Lutheran pastor of Halle, George Winkler, was assassinated by men in the employ of the archbishop. Whether Albert knew about this planned assassination or not is a mute question. Many contemporaries believed that he inspired it. However, he was left to regret his rashness. Before his death the powerful cardinal was forced to move his residence to Mainz, leaving Halle to the Lutherans. Among the later Halle pastors Andrew Poach was the most outstanding.³

In Brandenburg

One of the reasons why Joachim I of Brandenburg did not like Luther was that Luther had openly rebuked this immoral prince for his adultery. Joachim had been married to a daughter of the Danish king but was unfaithful to her almost from the beginning. When Electress Elizabeth sought solace in religion and had the Lord's Supper given to her by her court chaplain under both kinds, the Elector promptly drove her and all Lutherans from his realm. But like his fellow-prince, Duke George of Saxony, Joachim had to realize before his death, in 1535, that his people were solidly behind the Reformation. When his son, Joachim II, became Elector he almost immediately introduced the Reformation, retaining a great deal of the Catholic ceremonial. In 1551 he gained possession of the diocese of Magdeburg which with Halberstadt and Mainz had belonged to his late uncle Albert. From that time on the victory of the Reformation in northern Germany was complete, in spite of the vacillating policy of Joachim's foremost theologian, John Agricola, who with other mediation theologians had helped draft the infamous Augsburg Interim. When the Lutherans were granted full religious tolerance at Augsburg in 1555 Joachim II was the most powerful among the Lutheran princes and played an outstanding part in the negotiations.

The Duchy of Saxony

Ducal Saxony became officially Lutheran in 1539, twenty years after the Leipzig Debate. Duke Henry the Pious, co-regent with his brother Duke George, had already introduced the Reformation in Freiberg and other cities several years before the death of his brother. In 1539 he reformed his whole domain, a mere formality, since over 90% of his subjects had been Lutheran for years. When Luther officially introduced the Reformation in Leipzig, a large number of Lutheran theologians from Electoral Saxony and Hesse assisted him in this work; the visitations which had been carried on in Electoral Saxony and Thuringia in the late twenties were repeated, and all of Saxony was henceforth Lutheran and remained Lutheran, in spite of the changing policies of future generations of dukes, electors and kings. The Leipzig theologian Pfeffinger had later a part in the Interim, but repented and returned to stricter adherence to the confessions. Like Pfeffinger many other theologians of Leipzig, Dresden and Meissen were under a cloud of suspicion. After 1547 the spirit which had been prevailing in the former Duchy was transferred to the lands which Maurice had taken from John Frederick when he stabbed his Lutheran brethren in the back and helped Charles V win the Smalcald War. Wittenberg became part of his domain and quickly lost its former lustre with its integrity.[4]

In Silesia and Pomerania

In Silesia Bishop John VI von Thurzo of Breslau had been one of the first supporters of Luther among the Roman bishops. Before Worms he had sent a number of his priests to Wittenberg to study under Luther. Later strong Lutheran centers were established, especially in Breslau and Liegnitz. Caspar von Schwenkfeld early in his career was influenced by Luther's theology; however, his later deviations hurt the cause of the Reformation. Schwenkfeld was finally forced to leave his native land and became a restless wanderer, clinging to his mystical beliefs. John Hess who had had much trouble with Schwenkfeld and his sect carried on the work in Breslau. Later he was joined by the elder John Aurifaber who had retired from the Osiandrian controversy and found a new field of quiet labor among the Silesians. In spite of beginning Jesuit persecutions the Lutheran faith survived as a vital force among the Silesians. The largest number of hymn

writers during the next century and a half were found in that
province which did not regain religious freedom until after the
province passed from Austrian rule under the rule of Frederick
the Great, in the eighteenth century.

The part which Duke Barnim, then only 18 years old, played
at the Leipzig Debate has been referred to. After he had finished
his studies at the University of Wittenberg he returned to his
native land and soon followed Duke Bogislav, former protector
of Bugenhagen. Various efforts to introduce the Reformation in
his backward land proved futile. Finally he and his co-regent
called John Bugenhagen back to his native country and the great
organizer of the Lutheran Church was able to establish firmly
the preaching of the Gospel in Pomerania, the most difficult
task of his long career.

In East Prussia and the Baltic States

Albert von Hohenzollern, last Grandmaster of the Teutonic
Knights, had passed through Wittenberg on his way to the
Diet of Nuremberg and had met Luther who advised him to
secularize his country and get married. Since East Prussia and
the Teutonic Knights were still under the suzerainty of the
fanatically Catholic kings of Poland the change-over presented
some problems. But with the help of enlightened Catholic prelates, led by John Dantiscus, Bishop of Culm and friend of Copernicus, who served as canon in his diocese, the secularization
of the Teutonic territory was accomplished with a minimum of
trouble. George von Polentz became the first Lutheran bishop in
East Prussia. A large number of outstanding theologians and
pastors followed the invitation of Duke Albert of Prussia—as he
styled himself now—especially after the University of Koenigsberg had been founded. We mention here merely the names of a
few: Briesemann, Poliander, Osiander, Amandus, and Seehofer.
There were repeated disturbances, especially the Osiandrian Controversy which rent the Lutheran Church not only of East Prussia,
but of all of Germany.

In the Baltic States Dietrich von Cleen, Lieutenant Grandmaster of the Teutonic Knights, had been an early follower of Luther and had made overtures to Wittenberg even before Albert von Hohenzollern visited Luther. The letters which Luther wrote in the early fifteen-twenties to the Christians at Riga, Dorpat and Reval give an eloquent testimony to upsurge of Reformation sentiment in Livonia and Latvia. Melchior Hoffmann, a mystic who later joined the Anabaptist movement, had been the first Lutheran to preach the Gospel in Livonia. It was in answer to questions raised by his preaching that Luther admonished the people of Riga, Dorpat, and Reval to remain faithful to the pure doctrine of the Word and to organize their congregations along evangelical lines. John Lohmueller, secretary of the city council of Riga, who had contacted Luther in 1522, became one of the finest laymen of the Lutheran movement in this territory. Walter von Plettenberg carried through the Reformation.

In Northwest Germany

The number of Reformers in northwest Germany is not large. Henry of Zuetphen, the Lutheran martyr, was the first pastor in Bremen. He was followed by James Propst, called Praepositus, who served the Hanseatic City faithfully for many years. The most outstanding layman among the citizens was John von der Wyck who was later martyred when he tried to lead the people of his native city of Muenster back to sanity. There the former Lutheran pastor, Bernard Rothmann, had joined the Muenster Madness and become a fanatical Anabaptist. If we add to this incident the wanderings of Carlstadt in Frisia and of Hoffmann in Holstein we can easily see that the Lutheran religion was widely discredited in these areas. Bugenhagen's tireless efforts in the years after 1526 bore fruit especially in these regions which were in danger of falling victim to the teachings of the Anabaptists. He established sound Lutheran church orders in Hamburg, Brunswick, Luebeck, Lower Saxony, and finally in Schleswig-Holstein. The Hartz Mountains, closer to Wittenberg in geography, but farther removed in spirit, had as their Reformers the unhappy Amandus and the two Spangenbergs, father and son, who

worked among the superstitious people for many, many years. The
Hamburg Reformer Matthew Delius established one of the bridges
between Wittenberg and Canterbury even before the Strassburgers
were becoming interested in the English Reformation.

In Hesse

Philip of Hesse, as has been pointed out, was probably the
most energetic supporter of the Lutheran Reformation among
the princes of the Empire. But his tendency to mediate between
the warring factions of Protestants, coupled with his weakness
of the flesh, attracted a number of weak Lutherans to the court
of Hesse and the newly established University of Marburg. The
best known example of this type of spineless clergyman was the
court preacher Melander who encouraged the prince in his immoral practices which finally led to the disaster of his bigamous
marriage. After that Philip of Hesse was a lame duck in the Lutheran Church and a liability. He suffered a great deal after
the Smalcald War and showed great courage, but his usefulness
to the Church was past. Hesse became one of the centers of
unionism which entered Germany by way of Strassburg and other
Upper German cities during the latter part of the century. Yet
during the early years we find in Hesse a large number of notables,
among them John Drach, called Draconites, who had suffered
persecution under Albert of Mainz and became now professor
in Marburg; Erasmus Alber who soon moved on to Brandenburg; Erhard Schnepf, one of the Swabian Reformers; John Hess
the Younger, called Montanus, who served as rector of the University of Marburg; the Frenchman Lambert who later turned
Zwinglian; and many others. Marburg, the first university to be
founded under Lutheran auspices, became a renowned seat of a
type of learning which was a mixture of Lutheran theology and
humanistic philosophy.[5]

In Augsburg and Nuremberg

At the beginning of the Reformation support for Luther and
his theology had been stronger in Augsburg than in any other

city of the Holy Empire, Wittenberg excluded. Here Luther was met by many friends during the stormy days of October 1518 when he was confronted by the ultimatum of Cajetan. Augsburg, the city of the Fuggers and the Welsers, richest men of the world, was a center of western commerce. Popes and emperors owed large sums and much gratitude to the great merchant princes. But this preoccupation with the commerce of the country also showed up the weakness of Augsburg as a center of Lutheranism. Fugger had no room for Lutheran theology. Welser cautiously evaded the issue by leaving the city several times during the crucial days of her history in order not to be caught in the net of an imperial ban or a papal interdict. Here lived the Prior John Frosch, a fervent Lutheran, Stephen Agricola who later moved to Eisleben, Arsacius Seehofer who later moved to Swabia, Urbanus Rhegius who later moved to Lueneburg, and Wolfgang Musculus who later moved to Zurich and Berne. Most of the Lutheran leaders of Augsburg were there only temporarily, but when the trouble arose they left and went elsewhere. Finally Zwinglianism made deep inroads in the city which had never had the courage to stand up wholeheartedly for her convictions. The many glorious events of the Reformation associated with the name "Augsburg" are no indication of the religious convictions of her inhabitants.

The situation was quite different in Nuremberg. This city, too, played an important part in the affairs of the Empire. During the critical years of the Reformation two imperial Diets were held within her walls. But the Nurembergers were more enduring Lutherans than their brethren in the rival city of Augsburg. Their chief interest was not commerce, although Nuremberg was then as now a flourishing center of commerce. But the city was better known for her achievements in the arts. Here Hans Sachs became an early follower of Luther. His "Wittenberg Nightingale" is one of the finest tributes to the Reformer. Albert Duerer, the great German painter, was a Lutheran at heart although he continued—like Cranach—to paint faces of Roman prelates and princes. The language of art was interdenominational. Duerer, like Holbein and Cranach, was highly esteemed by both Lutherans and Catholics. At Nuremberg we find Dietrich after his quarrel with Luther. In spite of his differences with the Reformer he remained faithful to the cause of the Reformation. Here also Osiander began his work, long before his teaching became suspect in Lutheran circles. Camerarius was pastor in Nuremberg, but later moved on to Tuebingen and Leipzig. The faithful Lazarus Spengler, devoted father of his nine children and happily married husband, gave Nuremberg her visitation articles and her church order. But perhaps the greatest among the Nuremberg Lutherans was Wenceslas Linck, Luther's good friend and successor to Staupitz as vicar general of the Augustinian order, who after a brief pastorate in Altenburg had moved to Nuremberg. His position in Nuremberg can be compared with that of John Brenz in Swabia.[6]

Swabian Lutherans

Swabia—mostly the Duchy of Wuerttemberg with parts of present day Bavaria and the former state of Baden—was situated between the strongly Lutheran centers of south Germany and the strongly Zwinglian centers of Switzerland. At the outer edge of Swabia was the city of Strassburg with its mediating theologians. To complicate matters further Swabia was until the midthirties under Hapsburg rule. The legitimate prince of the realm, Duke Ulrich, had been driven out by the Swabian League, and Ferdinand of Austria ruled the country under the league's mandate. Finally, Philip of Hesse succeeded in restoring Ulrich to his throne, forcing the Austrians to renounce all but their titular authority over the Wuerttemberg duchy. After that Swabia became strongly Lutheran.

John Brenz had been won for Luther's cause at the Heidelberg Convention of 1518, at the same time when Bucer, later the Reformer of Strassburg, turned to the new doctrine. Bucer, however, later leaned heavily towards Basel where he and Oecolampadius made common cause in the Communion controversy, while Brenz remained staunchly Lutheran. Thus we find Brenz in Luther's corner at the Colloquy of Marburg. The position of Brenz in Wuerttemberg was precarious until the return of Duke Ulrich in 1534. The loyalties of the Swabians were divided between the followers of Ambrosius Blaurer, the Zwinglian spokesman, and Erhard Schnepf, the strict Lutheran. Finally Brenz with the help of his friends succeeded in establishing a moderate, open-hearted, pietistic strain of Lutheranism which was to bear good fruit in the years of strife which the Church had to face after Luther's death. Brenz' theology bore rich fruit also in England where it was incorporated many years later in the Thirty-Nine Articles of the Anglican Church (1563). Besides Brenz and Schnepf we should mention especially Alber, Seehofer, and Andreae, the father of the Formula of Concord. Here in Wuerttemberg Peter Paul Vergerio found refuge, after he had left the service of the Curia. At the University of Tuebingen many Lutheran theologians of the sixteenth century taught or received their schooling.[7]

We can only briefly talk about the men of the Larger Circle, for there are too many of them.

John Aurifaber

During the last years of the Reformer one of his constant companions was John Aurifaber the Younger—to be distinguished from the other John Aurifaber, who was two years older and lived in Rostock, East Prussia and Breslau. In contrast to his older namesake (they were not related), the younger Aurifaber remained a faithful Lutheran even after the Reformer's death while the older Aurifaber followed in the path of Melanchthon who was his good friend. The younger man had been present at Luther's deathbed in Eisleben, he had accompanied the unfortunate Elector John Frederick as chaplain during the Smalcald War, had shared his prison, and had refused to return to Wittenberg, preferring to serve at Weimar where John Frederick's son was residing. During the Melanchthonian and Osiandrian controversies John Aurifaber the Younger had to suffer much. But this tribulation gave him strength to edit Luther's works (the Jena Edition) and his Table Talk. Unfortunately he became involved in a controversy with another Table companion, Andrew Poach, and the two men quarreled almost to the end of their lives. Aurifaber dying in 1575 and Poach in 1585.

Andrew Poach

Andrew Poach was a year older than his table companion (b. in 1516 in Eilenburg). From 1530 until 1541 he had taken his meals with the Luthers, but in 1541—about the time when Aurifaber arrived in Wittenberg—Poach had been sent to Halle from where he was expelled by the Catholics in 1547. In 1550 he went with his wife, two children, and the physician Ratzeberger, another close friend of the late Reformer, to Erfurt where he became pastor. Like Aurifaber he was strictly orthodox, but the Erfurters, though they were by this time Lutherans, still retained their proclivity for loose morals, and drove the faithful pastor from their town. He wandered, separated from his family, through the countryside until he was finally reunited with his loved ones in a little hamlet near Jena. There began the unpleasant, purely personal controversy with Aurifaber. Today Poach is remembered chiefly as the editor of Luther's House Postil which for many years was one of the best loved devotional books of the Lutheran Church.

Matthew Aurogallus

Another faithful Wittenberg helper of the Reformer was Matthew Aurogallus. He was the greatest Hebrew scholar at the university. His help in translating the Old Testament became almost indispensable. There had been a number of Hebrew scholars in Wittenberg, Matthew Adrian, the converted Jew from Spain, who taught Hebrew from 1520-1521; Caspar Aquila who during his stay in Wittenberg (1523-1527) often was consulted in the work of translation; and John Boeschenstein who was probably the first "Lutheran" Hebraist. He left Wittenberg early in 1519 under unpleasant circumstances. But Aurogallus was the Lutheran Hebraist *par excellence*. He had come to Wittenberg from Comotau in Bohemia in 1519, shortly after Boeschenstein had left. By 1521 he was already instructor in Hebrew. With the men of the Inner Circle he was one of the regular co-workers of Luther between the years 1523 and 1532. The work of translation was often extremely difficult, for Luther was a perfectionist, and if a passage was not clear the Hebrew word was usually written into the text until Luther was satisfied that the correct German word had been found. Luther rewarded the faithful man by entrusting him with the revision of the Bible in 1540

DIETRICH

and by having him appointed rector of the university in 1542. The following year Aurogallus died. His Hebrew Grammar (1523 and 1539) was considered the best grammar of the post-Reuchlinian period.

Vitus Dietrich

Vitus Dietrich who was born and died at Nuremberg came to Wittenberg in 1527. In due time he became one of the regular table companions of Luther. He accompanied the Reformer to

Marburg and stayed with him at the Coburg during the Diet of Augsburg in 1530. But unlike the other men who lived with Luther Dietrich had a hot temper (like his master) and loved to argue. After an especially hot argument with the Reformer he left Wittenberg and returned to his native Nuremberg where he became pastor of St. Sebaldus Church in 1536. Here he remained to the end, a strong partisan of orthodox Lutheranism against all enemies. He fought the first skirmish against Osiander whom he considered "popish." He objected to private confession, to the elevation of the elements in Holy Communion, and other Romanizing practices. He was present at Smalcald where he signed on behalf of the city of Nuremberg and at Regensburg (1546). During the Smalcald War he preached so sharply against the intentions of the emperor to re-introduce the Catholic religion that he was forced to resign from his pastorate. He died soon after the Interim had been imposed upon Nuremberg, in March 1549. His Old Testament commentaries were considered by many—including Luther—as the best products of Old Testament scholarship.

John Mathesius

The finest Luther biographer of the sixteenth century—more reliable than Melanchthon and Ratzeberger—was John Mathesius, born at Rochlitz on June 24, 1504. His parents had sent him to Munich and Ingolstadt in order to strengthen his faith, but after some years Mathesius went to Wittenberg in order to investigate for himself the teachings of Luther. There he became an intimate friend of the Reformer. From 1532 to 1540 he served as rector of the Latin school in Joachimsthal in Bohemia, returning to Wittenberg for a year's stay (1540-41). During this year the plan took shape to write his "Life of Luther" which was to make Mathesius famous throughout the Lutheran world. After his return to Joachimsthal Mathesius exchanged the teacher's desk for the pulpit, married and lived a happy life, working on and completing his biography. Mathesius is also well known as a hymn-writer. He died in 1565.

George Roerer

George Roerer (1492-1557) was the "first ordained Lutheran pastor," having been ordained by Luther himself on May 14, 1525. Until that time priests ordained in the Roman Catholic Church had filled the pulpits of the Lutheran Church. Thus Roerer was the first Lutheran pastor in the history of the Church. Later he participated in the Church Visitations and often served as ordainer for pastors. After 1537, however, Roerer retired to Wittenberg where he was a daily guest at Luther's house. He held no office, remaining a pastor without call. After the debacle of the Smalcald War Roerer followed his elector into captivity, but in 1551 he took leave to go to Denmark where he tried to persuade King Christian III to print his edition of Luther's works. Called back to Germany to join the faculty of the brand-new Lutheran university at Jena, Roerer began editing Luther's works in earnest. But while Aurifaber's "Jena Edition" enjoyed great popularity, Roerer's painstaking work remained in manuscript form until the eighteen-nineties when its 33 volumes were discovered in the library in Zwickau. While Roerer did not have a creative mind, he was probably the most faithful collector of *Lutheriana*.

Jerome Weller

At about the time when Roerer was ordained by Luther another former student of Luther returned to Wittenberg. Jerome Weller (1499-1572) had studied in Wittenberg, taking his master's degree in 1519. Now in 1525 he returned to Wittenberg, forming a strong friendship with the Reformer who appointed him soon as tutor to his son John ("Hänschen"). When Weller was offered a good position in Dresden he refused to leave Wittenberg. Luther later created the faithful man Doctor of Theology in recognition for his services. Later he became pastor in Freiberg. Among the theologians close to Luther, Weller was the most peaceloving. After the Reformer's death he was able to mediate between the two parties of Lutherans who were at each other's throats. He refused many honorable calls to Meissen, Leipzig,

Nuremberg, Vienna and Copenhagen, in order to be able to serve his Saxons at Freiberg, his native city.

Besides these men the best known companions of the Reformer were Medler, Schlaginhaufen, Rabe, Cordatus, Zwick, Wolf, Lauterbach, Khummer, and Heydenreich. All of them collected pieces and parcels of the Table Talk, sometimes reliable crumbs from the table of Martin Luther, sometimes quite unreliable. The career of Conrad Cordatus may serve as an example for the life stories of these men.

Conrad Cordatus

Conrad Cordatus was born in 1475 in Wiessenkirche, Austria, as a child of Hussite parents. After studies in Vienna he was ordained to the priesthood in 1505, became licentiate in Ferrara, went from there to Rome and finally came to Budapest where, on account of his burning interest in the Reformation, he was imprisoned. Finally he was released, but only after a long period of mental and physical suffering. In May 1524 he arrived in Wittenberg, exhausted and sick, but determined to study Lutheran theology. In 1525 we find him once more in Hungary. Again he is caught and is imprisoned for thirty-eight long weeks. After his release from prison he once more returned to Wittenberg, where Melanchthon took pity on him and sent him to Nuremberg to teach at the new school. But again the urge to return to Hungary was stronger than his fear of imprisonment and torture. By way of Liegnitz Cordatus re-entered Hungary, found, however, no congregation to which he could preach. Shipwrecked, he came back to Wittenberg where Luther received him kindly and, in 1529, sent him on to Zwickau, formerly the troublous city of Storch, Stuebner, Muenzer and other fiery spirits. Driven from the city by the city council Cordatus once more returned to Luther who now appointed him pastor at Niemegk to take the place of George Witzel who had rejoined the Catholic fold. Later Cordatus went to Eisleben. Finally he became one of the Reformers of Brandenburg under Joachim II. He died as superintendent in Stendal, two months after Luther's death.

Luther paid him this tribute: "When I have to pass through the fire, Bugenhagen will accompany me to the edge of the flame, but Cordatus will go with me into the fire."[8]

And Others

Others who lived in Wittenberg for at least some time were Camerarius, who came to Wittenberg in 1521, but later, in 1525, became pastor in Nuremberg; Simon Drach, called Draconites, in Wittenberg in 1523, but later professor at the new Lutheran university of Marburg; the faithful Hausmann, one of the warmest friends of Luther, who spent most of his ministry in Zwickau; John Lang, in Wittenberg from 1513 to 1516, but later Luther's lieutenant in Erfurt; Wenceslas Linck, the former Wittenberg prior of the Augustinians, who became the greatest of the Nuremberg reformers; the Bavarian John Pfeffinger who studied in Wittenberg and later was one of the outstanding theologians of Leipzig; Erasmus Alber, in Wittenberg since 1520, but later in the service of Philip of Hesse and Joachim II of Brandenburg; Bartholomew Bernhardi who wrote the theses "On the Human Will" (1516), the first theses known to have been written under Luther's guidance, later pastor in Kemberg; Coelius who followed Luther to Wittenberg after the Leipzig debate, for many years the peaceloving chaplain of Albert of Mansfeld whose lot it was to fight the pernicious influence of the renegade George Witzel in Eisleben; the Hungarian Aegidius Faber who after his studies in Wittenberg served as pastor in Schwerin; Flacius, student in Wittenberg in 1541, professor there in 1544, the strongest Lutheran fighter after the debacles of the Smalcald War and the Interim; Francis Guenther who under Luther's guidance wrote the important theses "Against Scholastic Theology" (September 1517), by many regarded as more important than the famous Ninety-Five Theses; Hitzschold, the Benedictine monk who came to Wittenberg at about the time when the former Augustinian vicar-general, John von Staupitz, left the Augustinian order and retired to a Benedictine monastery in Salzburg; the controversial Major, former page boy of Frederick the Wise, relative of Carlstadt, who after Luther's death began one of the great controversies in the Lutheran Church, the controversy on the necessity of good works for salvation; the unhappy Jacob Schenk, who after a brilliant career in Wittenberg went to Freiberg and Leipzig where he became involved in the Antinomian Controversy and starved himself to death; the younger Spangenberg who after studies in Wittenberg helped his father to bring the Reformation to the backward Hartz Mountains, but ended his life as an enemy of the Book of Concord; Gabriel Zwilling, who during Luther's absence at the Wartburg became the "Second Luther," got involved with the Heavenly Prophets, but later repented and spent a fruitful life in Torgau; Jerome Baumgaertner who jilted Catherine von Bora and later became an important supporter of the Reformation in Nuremberg; the prior John Frosch who accompanied Luther to Cajetan and later served as pastor in Augsburg and Nuremberg; Arsacius Seehofer, student of Eck and Luther, former professor at Ingolstadt, who after his expulsion from Catholic territories helped reform East Prussia and Wuerttemberg; John Agricola whom Luther called "Grickel" and who later was one of the chief authors of the infamous Augsburg Interim; Briesemann, later the nominal leader of the Lutheran Church in East Prussia; Matthew Delius, since 1520 in Wittenberg, who was sent to Hamburg and became one of the truly Lutheran contacts between Wittenberg and Canterbury; Andrew Musculus who came to Wittenberg in 1538 and lived long enough to help draft the Formula of Concord; James Propst (Jacob Praepositus) from Flanders, Augustinian at Erfurt who sought out Luther in Wittenberg in 1521 and became the Reformer of Bremen after Henry of Zuetphen's martyrdom; Bleicard Sindringer, rector of the University of Wittenberg and later one of the founding fathers of the strictly Lutheran university in Jena; Stephen Agricola who fled from his prison to Luther's house and later served as pastor in Augsburg and Eisleben; John Apel who abducted a nun, married her and was imprisoned, and found refuge in Wittenberg, where he became professor; the Doebeln pastor Bruno Brauer from whom Luther bought a house in Wittenberg in 1541; Eberhard Brisger, the last monk to share the large monastery with Luther until his marriage in 1525; Gottschalk Crusius, doctor of theology at Wittenberg in 1521, who in 1524 became pastor in Celle; Caspar Glatz, the older colleague, whom Luther suggested as a fitting partner to Catherine von Bora, but whom she refused to take (rightly so, because he turned out "rather badly"); Gottschalk Gropp, at Wittenberg in 1521, later pastor in Eimbeck, and James Gropp whom Luther in 1520 sent to Lochau as pastor; Augustine Himmel, since 1516 in Wittenberg who succeeded Spalatin as pastor in Altenburg many years later; Justus Kern who was sent from Wittenberg to Alstedt where Meunzer had wrought havoc, but whose matrimonial unhappiness caused much grief to himself and to the Reformer; John Lonicer, former Augustinian fellow-monk of Luther at Wittenberg who for a time taught at Freiburg-Breisgau until driven out by the Catholic reaction, and finally became one of the finest Greek and Hebrew scholars of Germany, teaching at the new Lutheran University of Marburg; the Celestine prior John Mantel who fled to Wittenberg and got married under Luther's protection; the monk Petzensteiner, Luther's *viarius* or road-companion on his trip to Worms; Wolfgang Reissenbusch who had come to Wittenberg 10 years before Luther, married in 1525 at the time of Luther's marriage, and became teacher in Lichtenberg; Wolfgang Sieberger, the former fellow-monk and faithful life-long servant of the Reformer; and Stephan Roth, Luther's literary helper and secretary.

The long list of men who met Luther in Wittenberg, studied under him and lived with him, could be lengthened by the scores and hundreds. Most of them are not much more than names to us. But during his lifetime each one of them was a wheel in the great clock-work of Reformation history, each one of them was important for the cause of the Gospel.

In conclusion we can only give the brief biographies of a few of the "biggest wheels" in this clock-work.

Nicholas Hausmann

Foremost among the minor theologians of the Reformation era was Nicholas Hausmann. He is said to have been closer to Luther than even the friends of the Inner Circle. Yet his life was spent far away from the center of things. The home of Hausmann was in

Freiberg, and here he also died. But his most important years were spent in turbulent Zwickau where he carried on a valiant fight against Muenzer, Storch, Stuebner and the other fanatics. In this fight he became a convinced Lutheran, celebrating Holy Communion in both kinds for the first time on Palm Sunday 1524. He wrote an excellent Church Order of Zwickau and suggested visitations as early as 1525, long before Melanchthon warmed up to the idea.

Hausmann, a mild and peaceloving *Seelsorger,* pleaded for mercy for the defeated peasants. The Zwickau authorities put more and more stumbling blocks into his path. Finally, on the advice of Luther, he left the rebellious city in 1531 and went to Wittenberg where he stayed several months at the house of his good friend. Later he served in Dessau and finally accepted a call to Freiberg where, however, he died during his first sermon.

No one mourned Hausmann's death more than Luther. Only gradually did his friends dare tell the Reformer that his friend had passed away. Of him Luther said: "What we teach, he lives—Christ."[9]

John Lang

John Lang of Erfurt had been a friend of Luther of long standing. Luther may have met him as early as 1501 when he enrolled at the university. After that the two were inseparable in spirit, although they lived most of the time in different communities, Luther in Wittenberg, Lang in Erfurt. During Luther's formative years, however, Lang spent a few years at the Wittenberg monastery where he instructed Luther in Hebrew and Greek. He returned to Erfurt as prior of the Augustinian monastery, Luther's old monastery. In spite of the difficulties which he experienced as an administrator— especially of monastery finances—the relationship between him and his district vicar (Luther) was never disturbed. In fact Lang assembled around him men like Jonas, Sturz, Drach who later became staunch supporters of the Reformation. In recognition of this loyalty Luther sent to his friend one of the copies of the Ninety-Five Theses. This spurred Lang to new efforts. In the end he was

successful in counteracting the negative attitude of Usingen, Trutvetter and others. In 1518 he accompanied Luther to Heidelberg,
in 1519 he seconded him at the Leipzig Disputation. After Worms
Lang had much trouble. So, in 1522, he finally demitted his office
as prior, reorganized the city of Erfurt along Lutheran lines, divid-
ing it into eight parochial districts with himself as pastor of the
former Augustinian Church. Here he served 24 years, dying shortly
after his great friend.

Wenceslas Linck

Wenceslas Linck, the last vicar-general of the Augustinian Order
(after Staupitz had retired into a Benedictine abbey) was, like Luther and Lang, a Saxon, but he did his greatest work in Nuremberg.
From 1511 to 1516 he had been Luther's prior at the Wittenberg
monastery. Then, after a brief stay in Munich, he settled in Nuremberg where he died many years later, in 1547.

In 1518 Linck had accompanied Luther to his colloquy with
Cajetan, the papal legate, but unlike Staupitz he had not been afraid
of the threats of the Roman. In 1520, when Staupitz resigned, Linck
became his successor, but later resigned the position in order to become the first Lutheran pastor in Altenburg. When on January 4,
1521, Staupitz wrote despairingly to his successor "Martin has begun a hard task and acts with great courage, divinely inspired; I
stammer and am a child needing milk. Do not desert me under this
dark star," Linck assured him that all would be well with the people
who love God. In March of the same year Luther assured the new
vicar-general, "The matter is not yet in the nest of the papists." And
again, a few months later, he strengthened Linck with the words,
written from the Wartburg: "My God lives and reigns."[10]

In 1523, two years before Luther, Linck married and settled in
Altenburg for a brief and stormy stay. After Spalatin's arrival on
the scene, Linck moved back to Nuremberg, where after initial disagreements with his Nuremberg fellow-pastor Osiander, he became
the undisputed leader of Lutherans not only in Nuremberg but
throughout Franconia. He stayed there until the end.

The correspondence between Luther and Linck is significant for its frankness. In Luther's letters to the friend we find for the first time an expression on Luther's part of his suspicion towards Melanchthon. One of the most beautiful letters ever written by the Reformer was however the letter written to Wenceslas Linck in 1532 when he comforted his friend at the death of his son.

Matthias Flacius

Matthias Flacius (1520-1575), the greatest Lutheran theologian of the post-Luther era was not a German. Born at Albona in Istria Flacius was first educated by his father and later at Venice. The young serious man decided—like Luther—to find salvation in a monastery, but was advised against this step by an uncle, Lupetinus, later one of the first Lutheran blood-witnesses in Italy. By way of Basel and Tuebingen Flacius now found his way to Wittenberg where he arrived in 1541, five years before Luther's death. His conversion from the old to the new faith was as slow and as painful as that of the Reformer had been twenty-five years before. It was accompanied by great soul struggles. Thus Flacius, better than Melanchthon and others who had found the easy road to Lutheranism, was later able to carry on the tradition of the great Reformer. Although at Wittenberg he had been closer to Melanchthon—with whom he shared the love for languages—than with Luther, he later turned completely away from the vacillating philologist and became a strict Lutheran. In 1544 he had become professor of Hebrew at Wittenberg and in 1545 he had married. After the Smalcald War and the acceptance of the Leipzig Interim he refused to return to Wittenberg, broke all connections with his former mentor Melanchthon and became the pillar of the Lutheran University of Jena which was established by the dispossessed Saxon princes in opposition to Wittenberg. Due to his stubbornness in matters of faith he had to suffer a great deal, lost his position, was driven from town to town, and finally died on March 11, 1575, in the convent of the White Ladies near Frankfurt-Main where the Prioress Catherine von Meerfeld had harbored him in spite of all threats.

George Major

George Major, together with John Agricola, shared the dubious distinction of having started the first controversies within the Lutheran Church. Major's controversy was on the necessity of good works for salvation, while Agricola had wanted to do away with the preaching of the Law. Yet during most of his long life (1502-1574) Major was one of the finest Lutheran theologians, a friend of Luther, although he had been married to Carlstadt's sister-in-law, Margarethe von Mochau. He introduced the Reformation in Magdeburg where he was teacher for seven and a half years. In 1536 he became professor and a colleague of Luther in Wittenberg. The Reformer had him appointed rector of the university in 1546. In 1546, Luther's death year, he was an honored member of the consistory. For some years Luther had visibly preferred him over Melanchthon. He was one of the few friends invited to the Reformer's last birthday party on November 10, 1545. But after Luther's death he became—with Melanchthon—responsible for the drafting of the Leipzig Interim which orthodox Lutherans found impossible to accept. From then on he became involved in more and more controversies. Probably in an attempt to justify his part in drafting the Interim Major began to teach the necessity of good works for salvation. He was strongly attacked by Amsdorf, Flacius, Gallus, and others. Later, to be sure, he retracted some of his statements, but the damage had been done. When the Crypto-Calvinists plotted against the Lutheran religion in Saxony he was an unsuspecting accomplice in the odious affair. His former colleagues forced him to sign the Torgau Articles against the Crypto-Calvinists on May 30, 1574. Yet to the end Major protested his faithfulness to Luther's doctrines. He died a few months later, "of old age and of grief."[11]

Gabriel Zwilling

Gabriel Zwilling, the "Second Luther," who had been involved with the fanatics in 1521 and 1522, died a staunch defender of Lutheran orthodoxy. On account of his opposition to the Interim and to the turn-coat prince, Elector Maurice, he was deprived of his office and died in straitened circumstances in Torgau in 1558, where he had worked most of his life after repenting of his part in the Wittenberg disturbances.

Zwilling was admired by his contemporaries as the most outstanding pulpit orator of the Lutheran movement. Luther himself said of him: "He has the gift of preaching second to none."[12] He had known Luther since 1517 when he had joined the Wittenberg monastery. A few years later, during Luther's stay at the Wartburg, he was the first monk to leave the monastery, very much against Luther's will. On October 6, 1521, he proclaimed that henceforth no mass would be celebrated unless the Sacrament would be distributed as it was instituted by Christ Himself. After that the populace gathered around the inspiring former monk and followed his preaching. His spellbinding came to a rude end when Luther returned from the Wartburg, drove out the troublemakers and restored peace and good order in Wittenberg with the preaching of the eight Invocavit Sermons. Zwilling, unlike Carlstadt, took Luther's rebuke and repented. Luther had him appointed to Altenburg, but the Elector Frederick the Wise, who did not trust the spellbinder away from home, had him transferred to Torgau where Zwilling worked with great blessings, until imprisoned for his faithfulness by the faithless Elector Maurice.

John Brenz

Besides Linck, the greatest south German Lutheran of the Larger Circle was John Brenz, the Swabian reformer. Brenz, born at Weilder-Stadt in 1498, was a student at Heidelberg when he met Luther during the Heidelberg Convention. He became so outspoken in his Lutheran convictions, that the Catholic party, then still in the majority, forced him to leave the city. Brenz went back to Swabia, to Schwaebisch-Hall. From here he did most of his great work. His warm heart and his concern for his parishioners won for him many a battle. He pleaded for clemency for the peasants. He wrote an excellent catechism, "A Questionnaire on the Christian Faith for the Youth of Schwaebisch-Hall," years before Luther published his own catechisms. In the Communion Controversy he was firmly Lutheran, against many of the Swabian fellow-theologians and the

Strassburgers and Baselers. His "Syngramma Suevicum" is one of the finest expositions of Lutheran doctrine.

Besides being an exemplary pastor Brenz was a great churchman. He served his church in many important functions, at Nuremberg and Brandenburg-Ansbach, where he helped introduce the Reformation. But his greatest accomplishment was that as the Reformer of Wuerttemberg where he became the chief helper of Duke Ulrich after the latter's restoration in 1534. He also reorganized the University of Tuebingen, which later became one of the centers of Lutheran teaching.

In the wake of the Smalcald War Brenz was forced to flee from Schwabisch-Hall. The imperial chancellor, Granvella, had put a price on his head. Fleeing across the border into Switzerland he was befriended by Calvin who comforted him when the news reached Geneva that Brenz' wife whom he had left behind with their six children had died of the hardships of imperial terror. Brenz tried repeatedly to return to Wuerttemberg. Finally he reached Stuttgart, its capital, where he lay in a hide-out with a loaf of bread and an egg. The latter he had taken from a hen who shared his quarters. Duke Ulrich was able to obtain a pardon for him and Brenz was reunited with his children, living at the duke's castle at Hemberg.

Later Brenz wrote the "Swabian Confession" for the Council of Trent which, however, was rejected by the Catholic Church. In 1553 he became provost in Stuttgart from where he reformed the whole life of the Church of Wuerttemberg. His Wuerttemberg Church Order became the pattern for many church orders throughout Germany. Under the influence of his friend Alber he insisted on simplicity in the service, but retained strict Lutheran doctrines. He established schools, homes for the poor and orphans and theological pro-seminaries which have survived to this day, a source of strength for the Church of Wuerttemberg. He died in 1570.

John Agricola

John Schnitter, called Agricola—Luther called him "Grickel"—was born, like Luther, in Eisleben. For a time he was Luther's table companion, sitting among a group of students who ate regularly at Luther's table. He was with Luther at the Leipzig Disputation in 1519.

A man of great ability and greater ambition, Agricola was at first an instructor at Wittenberg, but was soon sent by the Reformer to Eisleben, a position which he considered inferior to his talents. In spite of the fact that the Elector John took him along as advisor to the Diet of Speier in 1526, Agricola chafed under the removal from Wittenberg for which he blamed—rightly or wrongly—the professional jealousy of Melanchthon. Therefore, when Melanchthon published his Articles for Visitors in which he stressed besides the preaching of the Gospel also the teaching of the Law, the Eisleben professor strongly objected. This controversy, the first to rent the young Lutheran Church, is called the Antinomian Controversy, because Agricola rejected the Law (nomos). Luther settled this controversy, but nine years later it broke out with renewed vehemence when Agricola suddenly appeared in Wittenberg and published a series of theses in which he attacked not only Melanchthon, but also Luther. Luther answered with a series of Antinomian Theses which were publicly discussed, for the most part. Instead of recognizing his error Agricola now proceeded to complain about Luther to the Elector John Frederick and in consequence was forced to leave electoral Saxony. Joachim II of Brandenburg received him into his realm after effecting a formal reconciliation between the warring factions (1540). But when a few years later Agricola came to Wittenberg to pay his respects to Luther, the Reformer refused to receive him.

After Luther's death Agricola became one of the chief authors of the infamous Augsburg Interim and is known—with Maurice—as the "Judas who betrayed the Lutheran Church."

Andrew Osiander

Andrew Osiander, whose real name was Heiligmann, came from Gunzenhausen near Nuremberg, and had studied in Leipzig, Altenburg and Ingolstadt. Ordained a priest in 1520 and for a time instructor in the Augustinian convent in Nuremberg, Osiander, in

1522, became pastor of St. Lawrence Church and publicly came out in favor of the Reformation. He married at the time of Luther's marriage.

Although he had had difficulties with Linck, more on personal than on theological grounds, he attended the Marburg Colloquy in 1529 and the Diet of Augsburg in 1530. He also signed the Smalcald Articles of 1537. However, from the beginning of his ministry he had many enemies, due mostly to his hot temper.

OSIANDER

During the troubles which followed the issuance of the Augsburg Interim Osiander stood firm and was forced to leave Nuremberg. He first went to Breslau and from there to Koenigsberg. Here he served as professor at the university. In 1550 he published two disputations "On the Law and the Gospel" and "On Justification" which aroused one of the most violent controversies in the Church after Luther's death. Fundamentally at one with Luther's position against Romanism and Calvinism Osiander's interpretation of justification was that it was not by imputation, but by the infusion of the essential righteousness of God. While he personally was saved from the consequences of his teachings by a timely death (1552), his followers did not fare as well. His son-in-law, John Funk, was even executed for his beliefs by the Duke of Prussia. Yet his son and two of his grandsons became well-known Lutheran theologians.

These, then, are the best known of the many men of the Larger Circle of Martin Luther's theological helpers. But there were also many lay-people who helped Luther and the Reformation. Of them we shall speak in the next chapter.

IV

Lutheran Laymen

Throughout his life Luther did not only associate with theologians and churchmen, but from his earliest years he had had and continued to keep up many contacts with lay people of all walks of life. There were his relatives in Mansfeld and Eisenach, the friends at the Cotta and Schalbe homes, Oemler who had carried him to school when he was too small to walk and John Reinecke, his school friend, who accompanied him to Magdeburg. Later, at Erfurt and at Wittenberg, he met many lay people with whom he remained in constant contact until the end of life. Many of them became ambassadors of the good news who spread the Gospel throughout the countryside, each one in his own way, in government, in the lecture rooms, through art and literature, or by various other means.

Professors and Teachers

Among the people with whom Luther had naturally more contact than with others were the colleagues at the universities and teachers at other schools who corresponded with the Reformer or visited him at frequent intervals. When Luther came to Wittenberg the famous Martin Pollich of Mellrichstadt, one of the founders of the university and court physician of Frederick the Wise, was still living. He was present when Luther received his doctor's degree. He died the following year. One of his successors on the medical faculty of the university, Augustine Schurff, the first to perform an anatomical dissection, later became one of the most fervent supporters of Luther. His brother Jerome, professor of law, accompanied Luther to Worms and insisted that the titles of the books which were spread before the Emperor and were attributed to Luther should be read. The two Saxon Chancellors Brueck and Beyer who later read the Augsburg Confession (1530) at the Diet of Augsburg had both been professors of law at the university in the earlier years. There was Hermann Tullich, to whom Luther dedicated one of his writings; Balthasar Fabricius von Fach, rector of the university in 1517 and 1520; Peter Lupinus, an early follower of Luther (he died in 1521); Sebald Muensterer who with his wife died during one of the Wittenberg plagues and whose children Luther took into his home; Ulrich Pinder, who was not only a professor, but also an ambassador of the elector to the court of Charles V; and Jodocus Wilck, for a time at Wittenberg and later the outstanding Lutheran professor at Frankfurt-Oder, who not only taught medicine, but also studied and taught theology.

Besides these men who worked with Luther in Wittenberg there were a number of others: John von Memmingen (Oeder), who became rector of the Princes' School in Grimma; John Hess, called Montanus, professor at Marburg; and the various theologians of the Larger Circle who were serving at one time or another as school teachers in the communities of Saxony and Thuringia.

The Common Citizens of Wittenberg

More numerous than professors and teachers were of course the common citizens of Wittenberg, all of whom were Lutherans after a fashion. Luther's relationship with them was not always pleasant. John von Metsch, bailiff of Wittenberg, who did everything in his power to irritate the Reformer, had often been rebuked by Luther for his immorality. On the other hand Luther's relations with the two converted Jews around him were cordial. There was no anti-semitism in Luther's personal behavior towards the Jews, although late in life he objected strenuously against the efforts of outside Judaizers, i.e., people who tried to convert Christians to the Jewish religion by spreading lies about Christ. The violent treatises which Luther wrote in the last years of his life have often obscured the fact that he wrote and dedicated one of the finest treatises on the Jewish race to a converted Jew, the Jew Bernard who had married Carlstadt's maid in the early twenties. Then there was the tax collector, the converted Jew William Reifenstein, who was a close friend of Luther. Of the Spanish Jew, Matthew Adrian, who taught Hebrew at Wittenberg, we have already spoken in the last chapter. Even his barber, "Master Barber," was close to him, for he dedicated one of the finest books of his later years to him.[1]

Among the city officials who ruled at one time or another the little city on the Elbe we may mention besides Hans Lufft, the Bible printer, and Lucas Cranach, the painter of the Reformation, the town clerk Urban Baldwin, the school master Tilo Dene who served as mayor of the city, the Wittenberg judge Bernard von Hirschfeld, Blasius Matthaeus, the town councillor, and again Christian Beyer, who was not only professor at the university and chancellor of the elector, but also served as mayor of Wittenberg.

Then there were a large number of common folks living outside of Wittenberg, men like Leonard Coppe and Wolf Dommitsch, who kidnapped the nuns from the convent at Nimbschen—including Catherine von Bora—and took them to Luther's house in Wittenberg; Matthes Busch, the bailiff at Buchholtz on the border of ducal Saxony whose work on behalf of the Reformation constantly annoyed Duke George; Michael von der Strassen at Borna with whom Luther stayed on his return from the Wartburg; and others.

Saxon Officials and Others

Besides Beyer and Brueck we find at the court of the electors many men who supported Luther's work. There was John von Dolzig, the treasurer of the elector, who was present at Luther's wedding; Hans von der Planitz, an important Saxon diplomat who was used on many delicate missions; John Walther, the electoral music director, who assisted Luther in composing tunes to his

hymns; John von Minkwitz, the Saxon councillor, who drew up the
protest at the Diet of Speier (1529); the castellan at the Wartburg,
Hans von Berlepsch, to whom Luther dedicated one of his books,
and Paul Bader, at the Coburg; the councillor Philip Feilitsch who
accompanied Luther on his trip to Augsburg to meet Cajetan;
John von Greffendorf, another Saxon councillor, who was the first
to suggest the Lutheran Church visitations; John Loeser, hereditary
marshal of Saxony, at whose marriage to Ursula von Porzig Luther
officiated and to whom he dedicated his exposition of Psalm 147;
John Mohr, the castellan; and others.

There were the great painters, Cranach, Duerer, and Holbein
the Younger; the printers, Gruenenberg, Lotther, Lufft, Froben,
Rhau, Amerbach, Anselm of Hagenau, Doering, Martens, Setzer,
and Nesen; the poets, Sachs, Hutten, Corvinus, Francis Faber, and
Moibanus; the knights and soldiers, Sickingen, Kronberg, Hutten,
Kram, Lantschad, Boskowitz, and Armstorff; the officials of the
great cities, Baumgaertner, Spengler, Auer, Bock, Lohmueller, and
others.

These are just a few of the names that occur again and again
in the history of the Reformation—and often they are only names.
Like the men of the Larger Circle, these lay people were important
to the cause of the Reformation. In the following pages we shall
give details on a few of them.

Gregory von Brueck

The two Saxon chancellors, Gregory von Brueck, the "Old Chancellor," and Christian Beyer, his assistant, called the "Young Chancellor," together with Luther's electors were the most powerful
protectors of the Reformer during the years of his life after Worms.
Gregory von Brueck, born near Wittenberg in the year of Luther's
birth (1483), was a lawyer at Wittenberg, associated with the famous Henning Goede, when Luther arrived in the small town on the
Elbe River. Later in the decade Brueck accompanied Frederick the
Wise to Cologne where he met Erasmus, who in turn recommended
the lawyer warmly to the elector. Thus we find him in Worms, in
1521, engaged in negotiations with Glapion, the father-confessor of

Charles V, and the papal nuncio Aleander. In recognition for his work at Worms the University of Wittenberg awarded him the doctor of laws degree. During Luther's absence at the Wartburg Brueck and Beyer tried to curb the excesses caused by the religious fanatics in Wittenberg. In the following years he served at various delicate missions to the elector's cousin Duke George and helped settle the notorious Pack Affair. At Augsburg he was at the side of the Elector John who commissioned him to read the Confession to the assembled Diet in the Latin language, while Beyer read the German version. During the discussions with the Catholic princes he told his counterpart, the Chancellor Tuerk of Mainz: "On our side we are not afraid of any repercussions to our religious convictions, for our doctrines have penetrated too deeply among the people. Everyone now knows what is right and what is wrong." Later, in 1532, Brueck—in opposition to Luther's cautious stand—gave the opinion that it was right "to oppose the emperor when he was meddling in our faith."[2]

The activities of Brueck were manysided: He participated in the church visitations, he helped establish the Church Order and was one of the founders of the Wittenberg consistory, the first church government in the Lutheran Church. He lived through the Smalcald War, remaining faithful to his elector, John Frederick. He died in 1557.

Christian Beyer

The "Young Chancellor" Christian Beyer was really a few years older than the "Old Chancellor" and died long before him. But he did not enter the service of the elector until 1528. That was the reason why he was called the "Young Chancellor."

Christian Beyer was not a Saxon by birth, but had come to Wittenberg from Franconia. In Wittenberg he began to lecture in the law faculty in 1507 and became a regular professor in the year when Luther arrived for the second time in Wittenberg. In 1513 he served as mayor of Wittenberg.

Although Beyer was often used by Frederick the Wise to prepare official opinions during the stormy days before and after Worms, he continued his lectures at the university until he was appointed chancellor in 1528. At the Augsburg Diet he read the Confession "with a loud, ringing voice so that all people assembled in the square could hear it."[3] He died in 1535 after a brief, but distinguished career.

Hans von Dolzig

Another important Saxon official was Hans von Dolzig, one of the earliest supporters of Luther at the court. He and Hans von Minckwitz were entrusted with the important task of reforming the University of Wittenberg, making it (in 1525) the first Lutheran university in Germany (completed in 1536 under John Frederick). In his later years Dolzig represented the Lutheran cause at many pivotal meetings. He was sent to Frankfurt, to the court of King Ferdinand, and to Henry VIII. In 1541 he was the Saxon representative at Regensburg and in 1544 at Speier. His greatest deed for the Reformation was the negotiations which brought Naumburg into the electorate in 1542. We do not know what happened to him after Luther's death.

Luther thought very highly of Dolzig. In 1524 he requested him to write German Psalms, because "his German is so rich and elegant," but the timid Dolzig did not comply. However, he was annoyed by Dolzig's insistence on grammatical rules. When Luther translated *Du sollts mirs tun*, Dolzig insisted—rightly—on *Du solltest mir es tun*. In exasperation Luther exclaimed: "See what grace there is in my syncope and what nausea in Dolzig's rule!"[4]

Matthew Ratzeberger

Also connected with the court was the renowned physician Matthew Ratzeberger to whom Luther dedicated one of his last—and most abusive—books, "Against the Papacy Founded by the Devil." Ratzeberger later was the biographer of Luther.

He was born at Wangen near Lake Constance, was about 20 years younger than the Reformer, and had enrolled at the University of Wittenberg during the year before the Indulgence controversy broke out. Later he was court physician to the unhappy Electress

Elizabeth of Brandenburg with whom he fled to Wittenberg, when
Joachim I accused his wife of Lutheranism. With Boehmer and
other physicians he often attended Luther during his recurring
sicknesses. Luther sent him to his "beloved count," Albert of Mansfeld, where Ratzeberger became a close friend of John Agricola
until the latter turned against Luther. In 1538 he was back in
Wittenberg and subsequently became court physician of John
Frederick.

Ratzeberger was a faithful Bible reader and it is said that he
was one of the few men who had read all of Luther's Bible commentaries. Luther esteemed him highly. When the aging Reformer
in a fit of disgust swore to forsake Wittenberg, it was Ratzeberger
who went after him and led him back to the repentant city. He
died in Erfurt, in 1559.

The Schurffs

The two Schurffs, Jerome and Augustine, came from St. Gall
in Switzerland. Jerome, two years older than Luther, had at first
studied medicine with his brother, but while attending the lectures
of Ulrich Crafft in Basel, he had been converted to the study of
law. In 1500 he had gone with his revered teacher to the University
of Tuebingen, from where he accompanied the jurist Ambrosius
Volland to the University of Wittenberg, then in its first year (1502).
He stayed in Wittenberg almost all of his life until forced to flee by
the usurper, Elector Maurice. His last few years he served with
distinction at the University of Frankfurt-Oder in Brandenburg
where he died in 1554.

Schurff's legal knowledge was indispensable to Luther during the
early years of the Reformation. Although he chided Luther for having written the Ninety-Five Theses, he remained faithful to him
through all the storms of the next thirty years. Even after the
burning of the bull on December 10, 1520—of which he disapproved
—he accompanied Luther wherever he was needed. He was at
Worms, an active leader in the Wittenberg congregation, a church
visitor in Saxony. But his relations with Luther and especially with
Kate were never really smooth. Schurff did not like Luther's dis-

regard for legal fine points and wrote a rather tactless treatise against the marriage of former monks to former nuns. Sometimes the skirmishes between the two men—Kate would not have him in her house—got so hot that the Elector John Frederick had to step in. Yet Schurff was one of the most faithful Lutherans of all times.

Unlike his argumentative brother, Augustine Schurff was a quiet scholar. His dissecting of a corpse, strictly forbidden hitherto, however, caused a flurry of exitement. He was a good anatomist and wrote a number of medical treatises, among them a book "On the Plague." With Ratzeberger, Boehmer and others he often was consulted in Luther's illnesses. He died at the end of the Smalcald War, in May 1548.

Holbein and Duerer

Painters, like printers, played an important part in the Reformation. It is almost impossible to visualize the great happenings of the sixteenth century without men like Holbein, Duerer, and above all, Cranach. Holbein at Basel (later in England as court painter of Henry VIII) was important both for the work of Erasmus of Rotterdam whose various editions he illustrated and for the first edition of Luther's works by Froben (1519). Although he was Lutheran at heart, he did not play an important part in the later development of the movement. It is possible that the strife between Erasmus and Luther, or perhaps the controversies between the Zwinglians and the Lutherans, caused him to emigrate to England where he made his fortune and gained added fame as a painter of Henry VIII and his various wives and courtiers. Duerer, living in the free City of Nuremberg, was, like the poet Hans Sachs, an early and fervent supporter of Luther. However, like most artists—including Cranach—he continued to accept commissions from both sides. His patron, Willibald Pirckheimer, had been a lukewarm supporter of Luther and later, like many other humanists, faded away. The Nuremberg city council for many years was undecided. And while Sachs was forbidden to write in praise of Luther, Duerer reacted more cautiously to the changing times. But as early as February 1520 he had written to Spalatin: "If God help me I will go to Dr. Martin Luther and make his likeness in copper for a lasting memorial to the Christian man who has helped me out of my anguish." Unfortunately he never carried out his plan. When Duerer died in 1528 Luther wrote to Eobanus Hess at Nuremberg: "It is indeed a pious duty to grieve over Duerer, who was a most excellent man; but it was also right for you to call him happy, as one whom, well-prepared by a blessed death, Christ has taken out of these times . . . so that he, who was worthy to see only the best things, might not be compelled to look upon the worst. May he rest in peace . . . Amen."[5]

Lucas Cranach

The greatest painter of the Reformation, however, was Lucas Sunder of Cranach in Franconia, also called Lucas Cranach. Eleven years older than Luther he outlived the Reformer by almost a decade. Little is known about his early life. There are indications that he worked in Austria before he came to Wittenberg in 1505. He quickly made his fortune. In 1508, when Luther arrived in Wittenberg for the first time, Frederick the Wise bestowed upon the painter a coat of arms. In the following year he spent some time at the imperial court where he painted the grandson of the Emperor Maximilian, the boy Charles.

Frederick the Wise proudly lent his painter to neighboring princes. He painted the fierce Duke George with the Beard and even Albert of Mainz. But from the beginning he was drawn to Luther. He was proud of him. He attended the wedding of Luther and Catherine von Bora, and was a sponsor when Luther's first child was born. The Luthers and the Cranachs visited each other's homes often.

Cranach painted innumerable Luther pictures. His painting shop was a regular factory where helpers finished the paintings after Cranach had painted the face and the hands of the Reformer. He also painted Luther's parents, Kate, and the children of Luther. His famous picture of little Magdalene Luther who died an early death is one of his best.

It is true that Cranach was more an artisan than an artist. It has been regretted that neither Holbein nor Duerer gave us a likeness of Luther. When he ran out of work, Cranach even would paint houses. Still his pictures helped spread the Reformation throughout Europe. Hundreds of students took their "Luther" with them before returning home. Besides Cranach did a yeoman task in illustrating the Bibles which were printed by the Lotthers and Hans Lufft.

In their old age Luther and Cranach suffered much sickness and the loss of loved ones. They comforted each other. After Luther's

CRANACH

death he followed his captive prince, John Frederick, into prison. He was received with great honors by the Emperor Charles, whom he had painted many years before as a nine-year-old boy. Finally he moved with John Frederick to Weimar, the new Saxon residence city, where he began the altar painting which was finished by his son, Lucas Cranach the Younger, after his death in 1553. On this picture Christ is nailed to the cross, John the Baptist is pointing at the Savior of mankind, while Luther and Lucas Cranach the Elder adore Him whose blood is flowing upon them.

Luther's Printers

Next to the painters, printers played an important part in Luther's work. He kept several busy during his most productive years. John Gruenenberg was the first Wittenberg printer to receive work from Luther. But he was slow and his type was not too good. Therefore, Luther turned to the renowned Leipzig printing establishment of the Lotthers, father and two sons. After the Leipzig debate two Lotthers, Melchior, Jr., and Michael, moved to Wittenberg and did most of the printing for Luther until Hans Lufft appeared on the scene and became the Bible printer of the Reformation. But although the Lotthers moved away, one to Leipzig to help his father, the other to Magdeburg, Luther still gave them commissions. In the meantime John Froben, Europe's foremost printer (he had printed Erasmus' New Testament), had published the first edition of Luther's Works and continued to publish for the Reformers, both Lutheran and Zwinglian. And there were many other printers who have been mentioned above.

John Froben

Froben who had come to Basel from Bavaria was the best known printer of the sixteenth century. Erasmus read proof for him and was quite angry when Froben published Luther's works. Holbein was one of his artists. However, his greatest fame rests upon the publication not of the Greek New Testament or of Luther's works, but of the Church Fathers, especially Jerome, Cyprian, Tertullian, Hilary, and Ambrose, which he began and continued until his death (1527) and which was continued by his son-in-law.

The Lotthers

More important for the work of the Reformation was Melchior Lotther who together with his brother, Michael, established a printing shop in Wittenberg in late 1519, relieving Gruenenberg of some of the work which he was unable to handle. In those exciting days before Worms Luther had the habit of having his writings published as soon as he had written a few pages. This accounts sometimes for the difference between the beginning of a work and its end, e.g., in the "Treatise on Christian Liberty" and the accompanying letter to Pope Leo X. There was a reason for this "page snatching," as it has been called, because there was no copyright and type-setting was a slow process. The most outstanding work which the Lotthers published was the September Bible, the New Testament which Luther had translated in eleven weeks at the Wartburg. After 1522 the star of the two brothers was eclipsed by Lufft. They published a few installments of the Old Testament, but sometime during 1524 or 1525 Melchior left Wittenberg. Michael stayed on until 1529, trying to carry on without his brother. The reason for their departure is not known. Both Luther and Melanchthon had received them with open arms, especially since they were the first printers who had Greek letters. Melchior, Jr., died in Leipzig, Michael in Magdeburg, within a decade of Luther's death. Michael's stand against the Interim has been celebrated in a famous German short story by Raabe. He died in 1555, after having published books for Flacius during the last few years of his life.

Hans Lufft

The man who inherited the mantle of the early Reformation printers and who is known today as "The Bible Printer," was Hans Lufft. He was born in 1495. That is about all we know about his first twenty-eight years. It seems that he never wanted to talk about them, although he lived to a very old age. In 1523 he came to Wittenberg, already married, and with a great deal of ambition. Within two or three years he was the chief printer of the Reformation.

Lufft "began to live when he met Luther," at the age of 28. He outlived his master by nearly 40 years. He never forsook the trust which he had accepted when he printed the first complete German Bible. Ten years before his death—at the age of 89—he could boast that he had printed 100,000 complete German Bibles, a truly Gargantuan task in those days.

It is ironical that Lufft was a very poor man when he came to Wittenberg. He had neither Greek nor Latin type. But this very fact made him rich fast, as Luther published more and more German tracts which had to be printed in Gothic type. By 1530 Lufft printed all German writings of the Reformer. His German printing was superior to that of his competitors. Thus while Lufft became rich, others became poor, and Luther never received a penny for royalties (they did not exist in those days), except for occasional gifts from the grateful printer. In 1534, Lufft began publishing his masterpiece, the German Bible, to which he had applied himself during the past year with great zeal. He had stopped all other publications in order to devote all his energies and resources to this work. The book, when it appeared on the market, contained page after page of large, clear print, done with so much care that a contemporary critic could write that "no syllable, let alone a word, had been changed or omitted."[6]

After Luther's death Lufft, like the others, had to suffer during the Smalcald War. But the after effects of the war affected his work little. By 1550 he was a member of the city council and in 1563 he was elected mayor of Wittenberg.

Every year on Maundy Thursday—the anniversary of the first publication of the Bible—Lufft would invite all his co-workers and quench "the fires of hell" with beer. He and all his printers had long since been condemned by the Roman Church for the printing of the Bible. He died in 1584 and was buried in the Castle Church in Wittenberg.

Hans Sachs

Of the writers and composers of the Reformation period we may mention the great Mastersinger Hans Sachs (1494-1576), fellow-townsman with Duerer. His "Wittenberg Nightingale" is one of the finest early poems in praise of the Reformation. He lived for many years after that, writing hundreds of playlets and poems which dealt with themes in which his Lutheran convictions could be expressed. His shrovetide plays do not only assail the foibles of man in general, but especially the abuses within the Church. According to his own computation, a decade before his death, Sachs wrote 4,275 mastersongs, 1,700 tales and fables in verse, 208 dramas, and many other poems which filled no less than 34 volumes of his collected works. Luther liked especially Sachs' rhymes to a picture book on the papacy which Osiander published in Nuremberg in 1527. "I approve of the way in which he portrayed me with a sickle, for it shows that it was long ago foretold that I would be sharp and bitter."[7]

George Rhau

George Rhau, cantor at St. Thomas Church in Leipzig, was one of the best writers on music theory of the Reformation period. Born in Eisfeld-on-Werra, Rhau had studied at the University of Leipzig from where he received his B.A. degree in 1518. The following year he became cantor at the school where later J. S. Bach served for many years. After the Leipzig debate his sympathies for Luther became more and more known and Rhau was forced to flee to Eisleben where he taught music for some time. Later he made his home with his brother in Wittenberg, a deacon at the Town Church. In Wittenberg he founded a printing shop where he printed much of the music of the Reformation period. His greatest contribution to the Reformation, however, was his critical work. He helped Luther and Walther to make the Lutheran Church a singing church.

John Walther

John Walther, the electoral concert master, became a close personal friend of Luther. Although his talents were less abundant than those of the Nuremberg mastersinger and the St. Thomas cantor, his contributions to the cause of the Reformation had more lasting effect. At the request of Luther, Walther (b. 1496 in Thuringia) had been sent by the elector to Wittenberg to help with the composition of German Psalms, the first Lutheran hymns. The result of the collaboration between the two men was the publication of the Wittenberg Hymnbook of 1524 which contained the first 43 Lutheran hymns. When in 1526 the thrifty new elector, John of Saxony, threatened to dismiss Walther and to disband his orchestra, both Luther and Melanchthon protested. However, even though the elector gave in this time, he dismissed Walther in 1530. The citizens of Torgau promptly hired the dismissed band director to organize a municipal band for the city. During the next decades Walther set to music many Lutheran hymns. He also taught church music. Walther died after a long distinguished career, in 1570.

Knights and Soldiers

Finally, there were numerous knights, noblemen, and military men who supported the Reformation. The words of George von Frundsberg, the imperial generalissimo, which he said to Luther at the Diet of Worms, "Little monk, little monk, you are embarking on a difficult journey such as I and other seasoned fighters have never travelled. May God be with you," may be apocryphal. There is no evidence to show that Frundsberg ever was a Lutheran, although a large portion of his army was. When Rome was sacked in 1527 the soldiers proclaimed Luther pope of the church. Of course, they were drunk and Frundsberg took the disgrace so much to heart, that he died shortly thereafter. But there were many Lutheran knights, from Starhemberg and Armstorff in Austria, to Sickingen, Hutten, and Kronberg in Western Germany.

Franz von Sickingen

Sickingen, who died in 1523, was probably the most fervent and the most powerful supporter of Luther outside of Saxony. He had fought in the armies of the Emperor Maximilian I, had evicted Ulrich of Wuerttemberg, had taken on a good many enemies, including the cities of Worms and Metz until he found his death in fighting against the powerful Archbishop of Trier, Richard von Greiffenklau. Strangley, Philip of Hesse, who hated Sickingen and Hutten, was instrumental in bringing about the downfall of the most fervent Lutheran knight.

Franz von Sickingen was a combination of social reformer—he fought against Worms, Metz, and Trier in order to undo social injustices—religious independent—he was influenced by the humanists and Hutten—and selfish free-booter. He offered asylum to Luther before Worms, and again tried to protect him after the Diet. Luther tentatively accepted his offers, but nothing came of it, since Frederick the Wise was strong enough to look after his own professor. Luther dedicated his book "On Confession" (1522) to the valiant knight, but years later, in a letter to Philip of Hesse, he lumped Sickingen with Carlstadt and Muenzer saying: "It is nothing new that turbulent spirits cause bloodshed. They have proved it before by Francis von Sickingen, by Carlstadt and Muenzer."

Ulrich von Hutten

Ulrich von Hutten, the knight-errant and gifted humanist writer, died shortly after Sickingen. It is significant that he did not turn to Luther after Sickingen's defeat, but went to Zwingli in Zurich where he found a safe haven during his last few months. Yet none had written greater panegyrics about the Reformer than Hutten. After the bull had been issued by Leo X against Luther, Hutten wrote "to all Germans": "Behold, men of Germany, the bull of Leo X by which he tries to suppress the rising truth of Christianity, which he opposes to our liberty. . . . Shall we not resist him in this attempt, and take public counsel lest he should go farther and before we know it accomplish something for his insatiable cupidity and impudence? . . . Luther is not touched in this, but all of us; nor is the sword drawn against one only, but we are all threatened. . . . Remember to act like Germans!" And to Luther he wrote: "The Lord hear thee in the day of tribulation; the name of the God of Jacob protect thee! May He send thee help from His holy place and guard thee from Zion. . . . You see what is stacked on you. . . . You must never doubt me as long as you are constant. I will cling to you to my last breath. . . . This I write briefly in great anxiety for you. May Christ save you!

ULRICH VON HUTTEN.[8]

Ebernburg, April 17, 1521."

V

Scandinavian Lutherans

As the Reformation was dawning over the rest of Europe the peoples of Scandinavia were still largely living apart from the mainstream of sixteenth century problems. The pressing need for religious reform which existed elsewhere was not felt in these countries, the Roman Church had not degenerated to the same extent as elsewhere, and the primary concern of the Scandinavian nations was political rather than religious. Christian II had his troubles with the Swedes, massacred their leaders and lost their country. Gustavus Vasa established his dynasty and an independent nationhood for his people. The Danes, no longer satisfied with their discredited king, sent him packing and chose Frederick I, the Duke of Holstein, to be his successor. Christian II went to Wittenberg where he led a curious existence, served for a while as deacon of the local Church, became outwardly a good Lutheran, but never forgot his ambition to return to the thrones of Denmark and Norway and eventually to reconquer Sweden. He went to the Netherlands, where he came under the direct influence of the Hapsburgs, abjured his Lutheran faith, returned to the Catholic fold and tried with the help of the reactionary Norwegian bishops, who for religious and political reasons were opposed to the progressive government of Frederick I, to return to Copenhagen. Frederick I died and his son, Christian III, became king after a drawn-out civil war. The

Norwegians lost their battle and whatever nominal independence they had had under Denmark, became a province of the Danish realm under whose rule they remained until the days of Napoleon, and were forced to adopt Lutheranism. King Christian II was imprisoned at Sonderburg, the Norwegian archbishop Engelbrechtsson fled to the Netherlands taking most of his fellow-bishops and almost all the gold of the country with him, and new bishops were appointed for the defeated province. In far away Iceland the process of Reformation was somewhat slower and was not completed until 1600.

In the meantime in Sweden Gustavus Vasa had established his rule against great odds, a rule which was often threatened by the undisciplined Swedish populace and their ambitious chieftains. Since the Catholic Church had a hand in the constant troubles that harassed the king, Gustavus turned against her and imported Lutheranism into his country. His Reformation was somewhat likened to the Reformation of Henry VIII of England, although it did not take the form of extreme Caesaro-papism which it had taken in the British Isles. Yet there were many examples of royal interference and outright terror which were not quite in the tradition of Lutheranism. But we must take into account that the conditions in Sweden were different from the comparatively orderly conditions on the continent and that Gustavus Vasa was a self-made monarch who could not rely on the historical loyalty of his people. From Sweden the Reformation was introduced in Finland which was then part of Gustavus' realm.

From this brief description it may seem that the Reformation in Scandinavia was largely the work of two dynasties, the Danish-Norwegian and the Swedish. While it is true that the Scandinavian kings took the lead whereas the other European princes followed the events, it would be wrong to assume that the face of Lutheranism in Scandinavia was formed by them. They merely used the power of their office to insure that their countries would be 100% Lutheran, that there would be no dissension, that the organization of the Church would function smoothly, and that their royal prerogatives would not be touched or abridged by the new religion. But the Reformation of the cities and of the countryside was the work of men of great consecration, patience, and devotion. While there were similarities in the way in which the Reformation was introduced to all countries, there were also numerous differences, just as numerous personalities were involved in this work. Therefore, we must consider the Reformation in Scandinavia country by country.

In Denmark

We know from the history of the Reformer that Peder von Swaven accompanied him to Worms. Few biographies mention that this Peder von Swaven was a Danish student who had accepted the doctrines of the Reformation during the crucial years between 1518 and 1521. But even before von Swaven followed his master on the dangerous journey, Christian II, unworthy ruler of the Scandinavian countries, had called upon Luther "to cleanse religion and to lead the clergy and the magistrates back into the true service of the Church."[1] He had invited the Reformer in 1520—at about the same time as he perpetrated the bloodbath of Stockholm—to come to Copenhagen where he would find a secure haven from all his troubles. Luther, however, declined to come personally but sent Magister Reinhard, who stayed in Denmark for a short while without accomplishing anything. Martin Reinhard was a good man who later distinguished himself as pastor in Jena and Nuremberg. But the political situation in Denmark may have been the contributing factor to his failure. Christian II was shortly thereafter expelled, and Frederick I upon his accession to the throne had to promise not to change the *status quo*. Church historians also agree that the need for a thorough reform was not felt in Denmark at that time. Since, moreover, the attempts at reform were identified with the unpopular rule of the late king the Danish people may have been less ready to listen to the good news from Wittenberg.

Frederick I was by conviction a Lutheran and by political necessity a Catholic. The Danish episcopate had forced him to accept certain conditions before they would accept him as king. But while the former Duke of Holstein during the first years of his reign did nothing to further the cause of the Reformation, he also did not seriously hamper the preaching of the Gospel by those who had been "infected" by the Lutheran spirit. Thus the torch for the Reformation in the fifteen-twenties was carried by men who had rallied around Luther, foremost among them Hans Tausen. The Danish episcopate was either unwilling or unable to stem the tide. Archbishop Skodborg fell before the onslaught like a ripe plum. Other bishops used restrictive measures, but to no avail, since the king did not lift a finger either to assist them or to stop them. The most effective defender of Catholicism in Denmark, and perhaps in all of Europe, was Paul Helgesen who continued to defend his faith even after Lutheranism had been officially established under Frederick's successor, Christian III. Helgesen, one of the noblest figures of the sixteenth century Reformation history, a shining light on the horizon of Catholicism, was respected by friend and foe. His tragedy was that in Hans Tausen he had found his equal. For several years these two men fought their duel, an unequal duel since the councillors of the king were secretly supporting Tausen. What Spalatin did for Luther at the court of Frederick the Wise, Johan von Rantzau did at the court of Frederick of Denmark for Tausen. Influenced by Tausen, von Rantzau, and many others, Frederick I sought to establish a *modus vivendi* among the two religions, and at the Diet of Odense, in 1527, forced the Catholic opposition to accept toleration for the Lutheran faith. From then on the Gospel spread rapidly in Denmark, although fanatical sects like the Anabaptists did a great deal of damage to the cause of the Reformation. When Frederick I died the majority of the people had embraced the Lutheran faith, Christiern Pedersen had translated the New Testament, and the Forty-Three Articles of Copenhagen had become the confession of the Danish Lutheran Church. Helgesen and his co-worker, Nicholas of Herborn, had been unable to stem the tide.[2]

After the death of Frederick I the Catholics tried once more to regain the ascendancy. The "statue smashers" of the Anabaptist movement helped them unwittingly and for a time the Lutheran movement was in great jeopardy. But Christian III won the civil war, the cause of Christian II, for whose return many Danish

Catholics had secretly prayed, was irretrievably lost, and the Lutheran Church became the official Church. Bugenhagen was called to Denmark, consecrated the new bishops, crowned the new king, reformed the University of Copenhagen, the "powerhouse of the Church," and gave the Danish Church her Church Order.

Besides Tausen and von Rantzau there were a large number of men who played an important part in the Reformation: Peder Trane, Jacob Skønning, Jørgen Sadolin, Thøger Jensen, Mogens Gjøe. Sadolin is best known as the Reformer of Viborg. Oluf Gyldenmund reformed the Church of Malmø, while Knud Gyldenstjerne served as first Lutheran Bishop of Funen as early as 1527. Among the writers we have besides Tausen and Pedersen especially Peder Laurensen who wrote many of the important books of the Danish Reformation, Hans Mikkelsen who made another translation of the New Testament, and Nicholas Martini Mortensen, "Claus Tøndebinder," the leader of the Malmø Lutherans.

In Norway

The course of the Reformation in Norway was quite different from that in her sister country. There was no Tausen and Helgesen to cross swords. Rather the introduction of Lutheranism in the Land of the Midnight Sun coincided with the loss of national independence in 1536. The most influential Norwegian bishops, led by the unworthy and ruthless Olav Engelbrechtsson, Archbishop of Trondheim, had for political reasons underwritten the candidacy of the discredited King Christian II. There was no general support for this scheme. After the capture of Christian II the Danish Diet declared Norway a province of the realm, and the Catholics lost their bishops and their religion. However, we must not assume that this transition from the old faith to the new was a sudden transition. For while there had been many contacts between the Danish Reformers and Wittenberg, such contacts were largely nonexistent in isolated Norway. The Church had still a tremendous hold on the populace, especially since she was considered the champion of Norwegian independence against Copenhagen. Olav Engelbrechtsson fled the country and so did others, but Lutheran bishops and pastors

were not at once appointed. The Danes asked the Norwegians to
send their young men for training to the Danish University, but
the Norwegians were suspicious or unwilling to do so. There was
also a rumor afloat that Norwegians would never be allowed to return once they had set foot on Danish soil. Thus for a time the
Catholic priests continued to serve in their old parishes; the new
administrators sent over by Bugenhagen with the title of superintendents, later bishops, were unable to supervise their dioceses,
and many "Roman abominations" continued to be taught in Norway for some time. Only gradually were the Catholic priests retired, retrained, or supplanted by Lutheran pastors.

It is significant, however, that the first generation of Norwegian
Lutherans brought forth a number of excellent Churchmen who
knitted the divided Church together. Among the first bishops was
Magister Torbjørn Olavsson Bratt, one of the few Norwegian
Church leaders who had studied in Wittenberg. He had even
lived in Luther's house. He took the place of Engelbrechtsson as
Bishop (no longer Archbishop) of Trondhjem. Magister Geble
Pedersson, the new Lutheran Bishop of Bergen, was one of the best
Scandinavian educators, a very pious man, whose personal piety had
a tremendous influence upon future generations of Norwegian
Christians. Magister Jens Nilssøn, Bishop of Oslo, was a distinguished humanist. His great work in the Church of Norway was the
work of visitation which he established on the pattern of Melanchthon's Instruction for Visitors. All in all the Melanchthonian influence seems to have been stronger in Norway than anywhere else.
The most energetic and commanding figure of Norwegian Lutheranism in the sixteenth century, however, was Magister Jørgen Erichs-
søn, Bishop of Stavanger, who could keep his audiences spellbound.
He was called "The Luther of Norway" as Tausen was called "The
Luther of Denmark."

The Norwegian Church worked under a great handicap, suspicion. Suspicion by the people against the prelates who had been
appointed by the Danish king, and suspicion by Christian III, who
was wary of the Norwegians and kept close tab on their activities.[3]
Furthermore, the Norwegian Church leaders knew that they were
somewhat shunted to the sidelines while their Danish colleagues

not only were closer to the court, but very often helped to formulate the policies concerning ecclesiastic matters. The Norwegian Church labored under these handicaps for about 400 years, until early in the twentieth century Norway became once more a free country. But this dependence, first on Denmark, then on Sweden, has also been a blessing in disguise, since the Lutheran faith was more purely preserved in Norway than in Denmark and in Sweden or in Germany. The enlightenment which all but dechristianized the Danish Church did not make deep inroads in Norway. The deep piety which had characterized the early Fathers of the Lutheran Church remained a tradition in the Lutheran Church of Norway and led to many revivals of faith. Thus, while Norway may bemoan the fact that Lutheranism was introduced under duress, she can also rejoice that her isolation from subsequent Lutheran controversies saved her much spiritual anxiety.

In Iceland

Bishop Münter who wrote one of the best histories of the Reformation more than a century and a half ago, stated that we have more information on the Reformation in Iceland than on the Reformation in any other Scandinavian country. The Icelanders were the great chroniclers of the late Middle Ages and had not yet lost the touch to put everything newsworthy on paper when the new age dawned upon them. Yet Iceland was the smallest of the Scandinavian countries, containing very few people who lived far apart from each other and followed primitive customs, such as murdering their bishops and pastors when they wanted to rid themselves of them. Thus, when the Reformation was introduced, the Catholic Bishop of the Northern Diocese, Jon Arason of Holar, was dethroned and lynched. After Bishop Sigmund Eyolfsen had conveniently died a peaceful death, King Christian III experienced not much trouble when he officially introduced the Lutheran religion. Gissur Einarsson, a secret disciple of Luther, had already served for some time as Bishop of the Southern Diocese. But when the Icelanders caught their breath they began to resist the "Danish Bureaucrat Religion" and there was a relapse into the "old superstitions of the Catholic Church." The work during the next half century was extremely difficult, partly owing to the lack of able leaders, partly due to the rugged spirit of independence and the old heathenish superstitions among the Icelanders. Christianity was even more recent to them than to the other Scandinavian countries and being far away from the rest of their Norse brethren they had retained a good deal of Germanic idolatry which had been tolerated by the Church. Now Lutheranism demanded a more determined stand for Christ, coupled with a closer allegiance to Copenhagen, and the Icelanders did not like it. Therefore, the Reformation was not truly victorious until at the end of the century Gudbrandur Thorlakson, the greatest Icelandic Lutheran, worked among his fellow countrymen. Thus Iceland has the distinction of being the last country to be won for the Lutheran Church.[4]

In Sweden

It has been said that "The Reformation was a financial necessity for Sweden." Although this is an oversimplification bordering on libel, there is a kernel of truth in this statement. Of course, the same statement could be made with some semblance of verity of a great many realms which changed from the Catholic to the Lutheran side in the sixteenth century, including some territories and free cities very close to Wittenberg. We also know that Henry VIII was partly motivated by the same reason to introduce the Reformation in his country. Yet none of these other countries were in such dire financial straits as the realms of Gustavus Vasa.

Sweden was bankrupt and it was not the fault of the Catholic bishops or of St. Peter's Church in Rome. The abuses which had crept into the Swedish Church had not been more than the abuses which we had noticed in other Scandinavian countries. In a sense Sweden was less ready for a Reformation than any other Scandinavian country. The hated Christian II was associated with Lutheranism, so were Frederick I and Christian III. But unfortunately for the Catholic Church the Swedish episcopate did not like the strong personal leadership and sometime ruthlessness of the liber-

ator, Gustavus Vasa. Plots followed plots and the king's life was
often in danger. The king finally got tired of this opposition. And
he needed the money which the Church, as in every other European
country, had hoarded through the centuries. Two Catholic bishops
who did not agree with the reasoning of their monarch were
executed, the rest of the old prelates fled the country, and Gustavus
set out to divide his country into twelve dioceses, appointed the
faithful Laurentius Petri first Lutheran Archbishop of Uppsala.
Luckily for the Swedes who think so much of Apostolic Succession a man was found who had received episcopal ordination in
Rome. He was forced to ordain the new Lutheran Bishops, and
Sweden, like England, was able to boast ever after of the uninter-
rupted laying on of hands from Christ through Peter to the present
day.[5]

In other ways, too, there are similarities between the Reformation in England and in Sweden. Although the cruel Caesaro-papism
of Henry VIII did not succeed in Sweden, there were attempts by
Gustavus Vasa to bring the Church completely under his rule.
His interest in the Church was mostly political as was the concern
of Henry VIII, the "Defender of the Faith." He had very little
regard for the men of the cloth. Olavus Petri, the brother of
Laurentius Petri, and the greatest Reformer of Sweden, was condemned to death (with the consent of his subservient brother).
Although the king later commuted the sentence, he never apologized
for it and Olavus Petri never received justice. A similar fate over-
took Laurentius Andreae, the faithful chancellor of Gustavus, because he had dared to criticise the king for his dabbling in Church
affairs. That these men were not executed—as their counterparts
in England had been executed by Henry VIII—was largely due
to the fact that the Swedish king had to listen to the *vox populi*
which was raised on behalf of the Swedish Reformers and against
the king's reckless schemes. The king gave up his intention to
abolish the episcopate, reinstated the Lutheran bishops, and Petri
and Andreae were permitted to live out their lives in peace.

The influence of Luther's theology was strong from the very beginning of the Reformation. Both Olavus and Laurentius Petri had
studied at Wittenberg. The Gospel was preached at Strengnäs as

early as 1520 where Laurentius Andreae, later chancellor of Sweden, heard Olavus Petri. After the terrible bloodbath of Stockholm, in which Christian had killed all leaders but two, Strengnäs became for a time the center of Swedish resistance to the Danish terror. In the same year in which Frederick I issued the edict of toleration for the Lutherans of Denmark, Gustavus Wasa decreed in the "Vesterås Recess" (1527) that "God's Word should be preached pure and clear." Since neither Saxon Lutheranism, nor English Caesaro-papism, nor Zurich democracy, nor Geneva theocracy fitted the Swedish requirements, a new type of Lutheranism developed in the following decades among the Swedes. It was a strange mixture of religious concepts and political ideas. There was no Swedish Helgesen. As a matter of fact the Reformation in Sweden ran its course more smoothly than in any other Scandinavian country, once the initial blow by the king had been struck in its favor. By 1529 the change-over was complete.

Although Luther's influence continued through the two Petris, trouble arose when George Normann came to Sweden to abolish the episcopate. From 1538 to 1543 Gustavus Vasa was under the influence of this Pomeranian Reformer, appointed Lutheran superintendents in the former dioceses, but was finally forced to give the Swedes back their bishops. In 1553, in the Articles of Vadstena, an attempt was made to organize the Church of Sweden completely as Lutheran, an attempt which was only partly successful. In later years the Church became more decidedly Lutheran, especially after Gustavus Adolphus had rescued Lutheranism from defeat during the Thirty Years' War.[6]

In Finland

The herald of the Finnish Reformation, Magister Peter Särkilahti, had returned to Finland after having studied under Luther and Melanchthon in Wittenberg and after having married a German girl and began preaching the Gospel in his native land in 1524. But the people were not ready for the Reformation. Later, however, when Gustavus Vasa introduced the Reformation in Sweden, Lutheranism spread also to the Finnish possessions of the Swedish crown and Martin Skytte became the first Lutheran bishop of Finland. Skytte, whose personality resembled that of Melanchthon rather than that of Luther, was a quiet, humble servant of the Lord and did not set the country on fire. In his oath to Gustavus he promised to follow faithfully the teaching of the Gospel. Under him the Reformation made steady progress, but this progress was slow, since the people were not interested in change.

The greatest Finnish Reformer was Michael Agricola, no kin of John or Stephen Agricola, a poor fisherman's son from Finland. His position in Finnish Lutheranism was somewhat like Luther's in Germany. He was the father of Finnish literature, the writer of the most important Lutheran books in the Finnish language, the translator of the Bible into his native language. He had studied in Wittenberg and returning home a generation after Särkilahti found the climate more favorable and the ground better prepared than Saerkilahti a generation before him. By 1571 the Reformation was definitely victorious in Finland.

These were the men who brought the Gospel to Denmark, Norway, Iceland, Sweden and Finland. Often little more than their names are known, but they all played their part in the great changes that took place in those years in Scandinavia. Among them stand out the great students of Luther: Tausen, the two Petris, and Michael Agricola.

Hans Tausen (1494-1561)

Hans Tausen, the "Danish Luther," was the greatest Reformer of Denmark-Norway. He was born in Birkende on the Island of Fyn where his father was a smith, a strange man who was considered a kind of magician because he was credited with winning ore from the turf. Hans Tausen had a hard childhood. Once when he was twelve years old his father beat him as he was walking behind the plow and reading, because he believed that reading was of the devil. Hans promptly ran away from home and went to Odense, where he attended school for a while. Later he became a monk at Slagelse on Sjælland (Zealand).

The prior of the monastery which Hans had entered, Eskil

Thomesen, was an influential man. He took a great liking to the openhearted young man and, in 1516, sent him to the University of Rostock for further studies. There Hans earned the bachelor's degree in 1517 and the master's degree in 1519. In 1520 he was lecturing in Rostock. It may be possible that he also studied at the University of Cologne and Louvain, bastions of the Catholic faith. The young scholar attracted the attention of Christian II who called him home to teach at the University of Copenhagen. After the flight of the king in April 1523 Hans Tausen, too, left his native country.

In May 1523 we find him in Wittenberg where he heard "with an unbelievable enthusiasm to learn" the Gospel of Luther. His Danish friends soon became suspicious and called him home, in the fall of 1524. On Good Friday 1525 he was imprisoned for teaching "justification by faith alone." Sent to Viborg in Jylland (Jutland) where a patient prior tried to cure him of his enthusiasm, Tausen continued to preach and soon found a great following. The citizens of Viborg banded together and forcibly rescued the young monk from a living death in the monastery. He was received into the home of the mayor of the town, Peder Trane, who saw to it that the local priest opened him the doors of St. Hans' Church. This priest, Jacob Skønning, later became first Lutheran Bishop of Viborg.

St. Hans' Church soon was too small to hold the congregation which turned out to hear the eloquent "Luther of Denmark." Tausen went outside, holding open air services, perched on a tombstone in the church yard. The largest Church in town, the Franciscan Church, refused to admit the heretical preacher. The citizens forced the doors and Tausen with his congregation entered the building, refusing to preach from the pulpit, but rather standing on a bench. The congregation and pastor sang Psalms and antiphonies, the beginning of congregational singing in Denmark.

In 1526 King Frederick I came to Aalborg. Here Tausen visited the king and made a deep impression on the monarch. Soon he received a royal letter of protection naming him "our servant and chaplain." Nevertheless, the bishops of Jylland conspired to arrest the bold preacher. As Tausen was preaching one day in the Franciscan Church the bishops' soldiers arrived and told him to stop his sermon and follow them. Tausen answered: "I stand here in the service of a greater Lord; when I am finished, I shall come along."[7] The soldiers, however, not satisfied with this answer tried to seize him by force, a scuffle ensued, and Tausen was carried to safety by his fellow-citizens. Now many townsmen who had been undecided joined the Reformation openly. Among them were Magister Jørgen Jensen Sadolin, later his brother-in-law, Thøger Jensen, and the parish priest of St. Hans', Jacob Skønning. In 1528 Tausen published his first important Reformation writing, a Baptismal Booklet, an instruction for Confession and Holy Communion and several polemical tracts.

The Catholic bishops, however, did not give up without a fight. When the Bishop Jens Andersen warned the city council of Viborg against the "run-away monk and heretic of Luther" Tausen answered with bold defiance. With the permission of the king ten of the 12 Churches of Viborg were demolished, only two were left standing and converted into parochial Churches. Hans Tausen that year married Sadolin's sister Dorothea.

In 1529 Tausen turned up at Copenhagen, the capital. Here he preached at St. Nicolai's Church where his sermons and powerful hymns aroused the populace even more than at Viborg. The monasteries quickly emptied. When Christian II made known his intention to return to his lost throne King Frederick and his Lutheran supporters speeded the Reformation of Denmark. In 1530 the Forty-Three Copenhagen Articles were submitted and adopted as a confession of the new Church, at the same time at which in Germany the Augsburg Confession had been submitted to the emperor. The great Danish Catholic apologist Peder Helgesen, like Eck in Germany, wrote a Confutation of the Articles, but its result was nil. On July 14, 1530, freedom of evangelical preaching was officially decreed. "If anyone preaches or teaches otherwise than he can prove from Holy Scripture he shall be tried in court" the decree said.

Unfortunately the introduction of the Reformation in Copenhagen was accompanied by fanatical actions which hurt the cause of the Reformation among those who were of conservative inclination. The Copenhagen citizens, led by Mayor Ambrosius Bogbinder, on Christmas Day 1530 entered Our Lady's Church by force and

smashed all statuary. Tausen, like Luther, was against this radi-
calism, but the Catholic reaction held him responsible for the
outrages. Thus, when Frederick I died in 1533 and Christian III
was unable to claim the throne, the position of the Danish Reformer became precarious. Helgesen accused him openly at the
Diet in July 1533, the Minister Mogens Gjøe defended him and
Tausen was permitted to continue his activities during the interregnum, but was told to abstain from "uttering insults." During
this time he translated the Five Books of Moses into Danish.
They were published in 1535 at Magdeburg.

When Christian III came to power Tausen's troubles were over.
The king protected him, although for leaders of the Church he preferred other men. Thus, when Bugenhagen consecrated the first
seven "Superintendents" of the Lutheran Church the name of
Tausen was conspicuously missing. During these years Tausen,
like Luther, wrote "canned sermons," collected into the first Danish Postil, worked on a Church Order, and gave Old Testament
lectures at the University of Copenhagen. For several years he
served also as pastor at Copenhagen and Roskilde. Finally, on
April 30, 1542, the faithful man was consecrated Bishop of Ribe.
He died in 1561.

Tausen had been the most devoted disciple of Luther in Denmark during the Reformation period. His Baptismal Booklet had
been a reproduction of Luther's own. His great concern for the
translation of the Bible, a task which he could only partly undertake, his conservative character, his firm stand against the fanatics,
his insistence that the Word of God must be preached freely
against all opposition, all this is a reminder of Luther's spirit. Although he had returned from Wittenberg long before the personality of the German Reformer had fully developed, he kept
up with developments in Germany and thus was able to parallel the
Reformation in Denmark and Norway to that of Germany.

Olavus Petri (1493-1552)

Two brothers Olavus and Laurentius Petri are usually mentioned
in one breath when we consider the Reformation in Sweden. And

yet there was a great difference between them. Laurentius was primarily the professional churchman, the Archbishop. His role in Sweden can be compared to that of Cranmer in England. There was no one in Germany whose career would parallel his. Olavus, on the other hand, was the Reformer of the Church, the greater of the two, more akin to Luther in his stand against Gustavus Vasa, more concerned about the purity of the Church than about its organization.

Olavus Petri was born in 1493. In the fall of 1516 we find him in Wittenberg where he stayed for two years. Here he became a follower of Luther during the first few critical months of the Reformation. There were then as later other Scandinavians at Wittenberg, but Olavus stands out among them as the most serious and most consecrated. Although his temperament was more like Melanchthon's who during these years joined the Wittenberg faculty, his determination to defend the truth was learned at the feet of Luther. Olavus Petri was a peaceful man, faithful, very religious, but without humor.

In 1520 Olavus Petri returned to his native land and became deacon at Strangnäs which after the massacre of Stockholm was for some time the center of the Swedish Empire. Here in Strengnäs Laurentius Andreae, the great statesman of Sweden, heard the young preacher and in turn told Gustavus Vasa about him. When, in 1523, Swedish national independence was established in Strengnäs, Olavus Petri suddenly came into national prominence. Although the Old Church resisted any changes the intrepid preacher now found unexpected support from the king who was anxious to break the political and financial stranglehold of the Church on the state. Gustavus Vasa took over the Reformation of the Church of Sweden lock, stock, and barrel. Everywhere he introduced "the new doctrine" and at the Diet of Vesterås in 1527 officially proclaimed the right of the Lutheran Church to exist.[8]

In spite of the overpowering position of the king or because of it, the work of Olavus Petri and his helpers became more important as the years went by. The king had even less understanding for religious concerns than Henry VIII, who had at least received a theological education. Again and again political interests interfered with the preaching of the Gospel, again and again the king asserted himself against the servants of the Lord. Thus it became the arduous task of Olavus Petri to introduce Lutheran theology into the Swedish Church.

In 1524 Olavus Petri had come as pastor to Stockholm, once more the capital of the Empire. Here he edited, in 1526, Luther's Prayer Booklet, significantly the first Swedish Reformation writing. In the same year the Swedish New Testament made its appearance which became of equal importance for the Swedish language and civilization as had Luther's New Testament for the German language and civilization. Also during that same year Olavus Petri published the first Swedish hymnal containing 10 hymns. Its appearance can be compared to Luther's famous *Achtliederbuch* of 1524.

The following years, 1527-1528, saw the publication of a large number of writings by Petri. The Catholics of Sweden had no Helgesen. When the king appointed new Lutheran bishops in 1528 to take the place of the executed and deposed Catholic prelates it happened that a man was found who had received his consecration as bishop in Rome but had never functioned as bishop in Sweden. This man, Petrus Magni, insured the *Successio Apostolica* for Sweden, a very important point for Swedish Lutherans. In 1529, at the Council of Oerebro, Laurentius Andreae legalized the changes. During that same year Olavus Petri published his Church Handbook, one of the most important works of the Swedish Reformation, to be followed, in 1530, by a Postil and a Catechism and, in 1531, by the Swedish Mass. In this latter work he showed, like Luther in 1523, great piety and caution in liturgical matters.

In 1527 Olavus' brother Laurentius Petri had returned from Wittenberg. He now became his brother's greatest helper and soon his ecclesiastical superior. In 1531 Gustavus Wasa appointed the younger Petri Archbishop of Uppsala. Laurentius Petri was a man of mild disposition, like his brother, but unlike Olavus he became more and more subservient to the king. Nevertheless, the two brothers worked together for many years. In 1541 they published their greatest work: The complete translation of the Bible.

But the clouds were gathering which were to separate the two brothers. In 1538 George Normann of Pomerania had been called to Sweden. He was a sincere man, sponsored by a bold adventurer who had great influence at the court. Soon Normann was preferred by the king over his Swedish churchmen. Normann who had grown up in the tradition of Luther persuaded the king who by this time was annoyed by the dignified resistance of his bishops, to abolish the episcopate and to appoint superintendents who, lacking the ancient title of bishop, could be corralled more easily. Olavus Petri and Laurentius Andreae resisted, were promptly condemned to death, with brother Laurentius Petri concurring in the verdict, were pardoned, but, although the king was later prevailed upon and agreed to reappoint his bishops, the two men never regained their former influence. After a long period of living in comparative obscurity, both Olavus Petri and his first and greatest Swedish convert, Laurentius Andreae, died in 1552. Laurentius Petri, the churchman, carried on the work of the Reformation and succeeded through the Articles of Vadstena, in 1553, to organize the Church also outwardly more completely along Lutheran lines.

Michael Agricola (d. 1554)

The greatest Reformer of Finland, Michael Agricola, lived during his youth in abject poverty. Born as the son of a poor fisherman at Perna he received his schooling at Åbo, the second city of his native land. The fame of Luther and of Wittenberg attracted the young serious man and he enrolled at the university where he studied for some time. During these years the Reformation had made only slow progress in Finland, due mostly to the lack of proper literature in the Finnish language. Therefore, Agricola made it his special concern to supply this need as soon as he returned from abroad. He began to translate the Bible into the Finnish language.

In 1543 Agricola published his so-called ABC-Book, a Catechism which is believed to have been a translation of Luther's Small Catechism. There followed, in 1544, a Prayer Book, similar to Luther's and Petri's. In 1548 his New Testament was printed in Stockholm. He continued his Bible translation, publishing the Psalms and Prophets in 1551 and 1552, but was not able to finish the great work. The Baptismal Booklet, published in 1549, and some minor tracts round out his literary work. He died, in 1554, before he could finish his work.

Agricola was a quiet man, very much unlike his namesake in Germany to whom he was not related. The remoteness of his country, the difficulty of his language, have been contributing factors which have obscured his great merits for the cause of the Reformation. Like Luther and Petri he is today considered the father of his nation's literary language. Among the Scandinavian Reformers he ranks as one of the greatest.

VI.

The Martyrs
and the Persecuted

"The blood of the martyrs is the seed of the Church," wrote a Church Father 200 years after the death of Christ. How true this word was to become during the Reformation period! Wycliffe, Huss, a long trail of blood-witnesses, but the fires could not be quenched. The murder of the first Lutheran martyrs in the Netherlands brought forth the first Lutheran hymn and thus gave birth to the great tradition of hymnody in our Church. St. Bartholomew's Night led to the downfall of the *Ancien Régime* in France two centuries later and brought forth the present-day harvest of anticlericalism. Even Spain and Italy which all but extinguished the fires of faith in the fires of the *auto-da-fés* did not do so unpunished and the last chapter of Spanish and Italian Christianity is not yet written. In Austria and Bavaria the martyrdom of hundreds of faithful Lutherans gave the survivors strength to go underground for 200 years and to exist from generation to generation until their faith was once more tolerated. The terrible sufferings of the Hungarian pastors condemned to the galleys brought forth a stronger Church in that country. Similar stories can be told of almost all the countries

185

where true believers were persecuted by the "Ahabs" and "Jezebels" of the Old Church.

In the Netherlands

Even before the Diet of Worms, the Netherlands, personal domain of Charles V, had distinguished themselves by the zeal with which not only Lutheran faith but every kind of free thought was persecuted. Here the University of Louvain was the center of darkest reaction. At this university the future Adrian VI had taught for many years. The theologians of Louvain, Nicholas Baechem, Natalis Beda, Vincent Diercx, and others, had persecuted Erasmus of Rotterdam long before Luther came to their attention. When Luther's case was appealed to the judgment of the theological faculties, Louvain was the first to condemn the heresiarch. Charles V had grown up in this climate. His tutor had been Adrian of Utrecht, the later pope. The books of Luther were burned here earlier and with greater zeal than anywhere else in the empire.

Thus it was natural that the officials who ruled the Netherlands for the emperor persecuted the Church from the beginning. "The priests of Baal in the Low Countries have got their Jezebel," Luther wrote on August 3, 1523, to Spalatin.[1] The "Jezebel" was Margaret Princess Regent of the Netherlands. Her "Ahab" was Gattinara, Grand Chancellor of the Netherlands from 1518-1530. These people saw to it that the Inquisition was never idle in their domain. Some of the most infamous inquisitors of the Reformation period were Hollanders and Flemings. Hoogstraten, the ferocious enemy of Reuchlin and of the Jews, came from Holland. Roland van Berchem, bailiff of Antwerp, who persecuted the printers of Tyndale's Bible and other heretics, was a Fleming. The fact that the Netherlands were administered for Charles also led to the importing of a large number of Italian and Spanish officials who exploited the country and considered every sign of Lutheran faith as rebellion. This state of affairs lasted until, after Charles' death, under his son Philip II and the Duke of Alba, the bow which was strung too tightly snapped and the northern provinces of the Netherlands freed themselves from political and religious tyranny.

The first martyrs of the Lutheran cause were two Augustinians of Antwerp, Henry Voes and John Esch, who were burned at Brussels on July 1, 1523. This event not only inspired Luther to write his first hymn, the first hymn of the Lutheran Church, but also prompted him to write a letter of comfort to the Christians in the Netherlands, in which he rejoiced: "Praise and thanks be to the Father of all mercy who at this time lets us see His wonderful light, hitherto hidden on account of our sins while we were compelled to submit to the terrible power of Antichrist. But now the time has come when the voice of the turtle is heard in the land, and flowers appear on the earth. Of what joy, dear friends, have you been participants, you have been the first to witness unto us. . . . For among you those two precious jewels of Christ, Henry and John, have held their lives of no account for Christ's Word. . . . What little thing it is to be put to shame and slain by the world, so long as we know that their blood is precious and their death dear in the eyes of God. . . ." After reminding the Lutherans in the Netherlands of the beautiful promises of God's Word, he encouraged them, "Let us renew our hearts and be of good cheer and joyfully allow the Lord to slay us. . . . Our Judge is not far off, and He will pass a different judgment."[2]

The following January he wrote to Lambert Thorn who had been arrested with Henry Voes and John Esch and was still languishing in prison, "God has given me abundant testimony of you, dear brother Lambert, that you do not need my words, for He Himself suffers in you and is glorified in you. He is taken captive in you and reigns in you, He is oppressed in you and triumphs in you. . . . There is little need to burden you with my consolations. . . . Therefore, I rejoice with you and congratulate you with my whole heart, giving thanks to our faithful Savior. . . . May the Lord Jesus who has begun His glory in you, perfect it unto His own day. . . . Here in the realm of our Elector Frederick there is peace, but the Duke of Bavaria and the Bishop of Trier are killing and driving out and persecuting many. Other bishops and princes are abstaining, indeed, from blood but not from violence and threats, and everywhere Christ has become again 'a reproach of men and despised of the people.' You have become a member of Him by the holy calling of our Father. . . . All our friends and our whole Church sends you greetings, especially James Propst and the brethren from Antwerp, and they commend themselves to your prayers."[3]

James Propst, who was then at Wittenberg, had been one of the first Lutherans to feel the hand of the inquisition. He had studied at Wittenberg in 1519. Returning to Antwerp in 1520 he was arrested and forced to recant which he did after long imprisonment on February 9, 1522. Escaping from the Netherlands he again professed his Lutheran faith and in 1524 became pastor at Bremen where he took the place of Henry of Zuetphen who had been martyred on December 10, 1524.

Hundreds of martyrs followed in the footsteps of these men. There was Adrian of Antwerp who was killed in 1531, William Tyndale, the translator of the English Bible, who was surrendered to the inquisition of Antwerp in 1535 and after a long imprisonment was strangled at the stake on October 6, 1536, and Nicholas of Antwerp who was drowned in the River Scheldt on July 31, 1525. Of his martyrdom we have a detailed account by Sir Robert Wingfield to Cardinal Wolsey. "An Austrian friar at Antwerp," he wrote, "who had preached several times to those of Luther's sect, till he was forbidden in the Emperor's name, continued preaching in the fields, and at last in a boat on the river, and had always escaped, until at last a wait was laid for him by the lords of the town. He was taken in a pair of red hose and a Spanish cap, and soon after had a confessor given him. The lords caused a fire to be made in the market place, as if they meant to burn him openly, but as he confessed that his faction was of great number, the prison being at the waterside, he was carried out at the watergate which was shut behind him, 'and he fair sent to Luther in a sack by water.' Meanwhile, as the people in the market place lacked pastime, a riot got up between the adherents of Luther and the [Catholic] Church, whether done purposely or not is unknown; but the substantial folks were glad to reach their houses, and the unthrifts began to cry, 'Slay! Slay!' The lords of the town assembled all archers and the halberdiers, and brought four or five serpentines into the market place, 'and scoured the streets every way' all night, keeping the gates of the town shut till a search had been made and fourteen or fifteen of the band taken. It is hard to tell what will come of this, for the town is thought to be marvelously corrupt. . . ."[4]

In Western Europe

While there was no serious persecution in France until at least the middle of the century, after Luther's death, the true intentions of King Francis had become clear even before Calvin wrote his *Institutes of the Christian Religion.* The Protestants of all shades were called by the collective term "Les Luthériens" and every annoyance was laid at the feet of Luther. Still the king's wrath was quite ineffective since his own sister, Margaret of Angoulême, Queen of Navarre, herself a "secret Luthérienne," shielded the heretics and gave them asylum. After the Reformer's death the "Luthériens" which had included such diverse characters as Lefèvre d'Etaples, Briconnet, Roussel, Farel, Calvin, Coligny, and even the Unitarian Servetus, gradually developed into the Huguenot movement which suffered increasing persecution until the massacre of St. Bartholomew's Night almost, but not quite, extinguished the light of the Gospel in France.

In Spain and Portugal where most of the blood of martyrs was to flow during the next centuries, the brothers Alfonso and Juan de Valdes had appealed to Charles V to promulgate the Reformation in the Iberian peninsula. Juan who came to his Lutheran faith through the reading of Luther's Treatise on the Freedom of a Christian later continued his activities in exile in Naples. But as late as 1550 there was a "nest of Lutherans" in Valladolid, the capital of the kingdom. Here the Italian Carlos de Seso distributed Lutheran tracts. Even the imperial chaplain de Cazalla was infected by heresy and burned for the glory of God. The inquisition took drastic action and the *auto-da-fés,* literally "acts of faith," which burned in 1559 and 1560 are remembered as the most brilliant entertainments of that period. There were also the brothers Jaime and Francisco Enzinas who had studied Lutheran theology in the Netherlands. The inquisition caught Jaime in Rome while Francisco was able to escape to Strassburg where he became the most important translator of Luther's works into Spanish. Another Spanish martyr was Juan Diaz, the fearless preacher of the Word. Others among the Spanish martyrs included Juan Perez, Rodrigo de Valera, and Juan Egidio. It has been said that the fires of Christian freedom were extinguished in over 10,000 *auto-da-fés* under King Philip II and his hangman, the Duke of Alba. Whole countrysides of Spain were depopulated and Spanish world power declined quickly in the next century.

In the Land of the Pope

In Italy where the Renaissance scholars had made fun of the papacy it seemed for a time as if the "cesspool of Rome" would disappear under the earthquake caused by the Wittenberg volcano. But there was no Pompey! The Italians who had suffered less than the other nationalities under the financial pressures of the curia (they had shared in the flow of money from many countries) and who now realized that they had a national interest in the preservation of the *status quo* did not open their gates to the flood of new thoughts. There were small centers where groups of independent thinkers congregated, foremost at Venice, Modena, Ferrara, and Naples. We have seen that Juan Valdes continued to work at Naples after his expulsion from Spain. The most interesting circle was that of "evangelical ladies and monks" around Renata, Duchess of Ferrara. This circle included Olympia Morata and the famous poetess Vittoria Colonna. Its most important literary monument remains to this day the work of Benedetto da Mantova "Il Benefizio di Cristo," a strikingly Lutheran exposition of the doctrine of justification by faith alone. After Paul III reestablished the Inquisition in Italy these evangelical movements were quickly suppressed. Many outstanding "Lutherans" were imprisoned and burned. Galateo was put into a dungeon. Foncio, the translater of Luther's "To the Christian Nobility," was martyred. Baldo Lupetino, an uncle of the greatest theologian of post-Lutheran Germany, Flacius, was burned. Peter Martyr Vermigli and Bernardino Ochino fled into Switzerland. The last papal nuncio to visit Luther, in 1535, Peter Paul Vergerio, beholding the death of a near relative at the hands of the Inquisition, became a Lutheran convert and served the Lutheran Church in Wuerttemberg and elsewhere. By the time the Council of Trent opened in Northern Italy the land of the popes was once more safe for the Catholic Church.

In the East

In present-day Yugoslavia and Rumania there were only sporadic persecutions which did not change the picture of steady progress during Luther's lifetime. The Slovenes had their churches, their catechism, New Testament, Psalter, hymns, and freedom of worship until almost to the end of the century. The Transylvanian Germans and Magyars converted their "nationalities" to the Lutheran faith and did not encounter much antagonism on the part of the Greek-Orthodox of Wallachia. The great Reformer of the Transylvanians, John Honter, worked in perfect peace until his death in 1549. The Turkish puppet ruler, John Zapolya, and his family joined the Reformation and kept the Catholics at bay. Their reasoning may have been more political than religious. Ferdinand I claimed the throne of Hungary as did John Zapolya, and Ferdinand was the strongest partisan of Catholic suppression in southeastern Europe.

Hungary which passed more and more under the dominion of Ferdinand and the Hapsburgs, experienced severe persecutions. But since Ferdinand, the brother of Charles V, had to rely heavily on German troops to fight his wars against the Turks and since many of these troops were Lutheran, the final reckoning was postponed from year to year until the advent of the Jesuits. The most outstanding early Lutheran leader of Hungary was Matthias Biro Devay who was forced to spend part of his life in exile in Switzerland where he was converted to Calvinism. Later both Lutheranism and Calvinism suffered terrible persecutions. Most of the pastors were killed or sold as galley slaves.

Bohemia and Moravia enjoyed a period of comparative calm, due to the strength of the Hussites and strong Lutheran "nests" among the German population living in the Sudentenland and in some important cities of which Iglau became the center of the movement. But when, after Luther's death, the Bohemians and Moravians refused to fight in the Smalcald War against their German Lutheran brethren Ferdinand persecuted them severely. Yet he was unable to suppress the Lutheran and Utraquist movements. Hundreds of martyrs died in these persecutions.

Poland and Lithuania were religiously badly split between all types of Protestants, including the non-Protestant Unitarians and the Anabaptists on the one hand, and the Roman Catholics and the Greek Orthodox on the other; furthermore they felt themselves constantly threatened by East Prussia and the northern Baltic states of Livonia and Latvia which were largely Lutheran, and by Russia which was Greek Orthodox, that even the fanatical devotion of King Sigismund and the Jagellon family could not venture to engage in large scale persecutions. Not until long after the Reformation when the Protestants had hopelessly splintered their forces and an anti-Trinitarian Unitarian Church had made inroads among the populace did the Jesuits succeed to win back the majority of the people to the Catholic faith.

Since there were no Lutherans to speak of in Russia, there were also no persecutions. East Prussia, Livonia, Latvia were predominantly Lutheran and permitted both religions to live peaceably side by side. In Scandinavia there were—officially at least—only Lutherans and no persecutions.

In Germany

In Germany the Romanists were not without champions. The persecutions in Trier and Bavaria have been mentioned before. But even next door to Electoral Saxony the Lutheran religion was strictly forbidden, in Brandenburg-Berlin until the early fifteen thirties, in Ducal Saxony until 1539. Joachim I of Hohenzollern, Elector of Brandenburg, one of the worst rulers of his time, had driven his wife Elizabeth into exile, ostensibly because she had received Lutheran Communion, but in reality because he wanted to live undisturbed with his mistress. For the rest of his life he had to keep up the bold front of championing the Catholic religion, persecuted the Lutherans, exiled many of them and put others into prison. But his bark was worse than his bite. His son and successor, Joachim II, quickly rectified the mistakes of his father.

The behavior of Duke George with the Beard was more dangerous. His personal life and his piety were above reproach. He was
a cousin of the reigning elector. His people were separated from
their Lutheran fellow-Saxons by an artificial border drawn less than
fifty years before the Reformation. They were overwhelmingly
Lutheran. Yet George continued to send those whom he caught into
exile, imprisoned others, and used his city of Leipzig as the center
of anti-Lutheran propaganda annoying the Wittenberg professor.
Although Luther called him at times an "assassin" and George replied in kind, the two really respected each other, and George's
fine personality insured that no blood was shed.[5]

Matters were worse in Brunswick-Wolfenbuettel under the rule
of Duke Henry, whom Luther called "Jack Sausage." But the
Lutheran princes were strong enough to bring this persecution
under control before the end of the Reformer's life by the expedient
of dispossessing the rambunctious Henry. Albert of Mainz did not
recoil from using assassination to silence the Lutherans in his
realm, but he had the chagrin of being forced from his residence
in Halle and Magdeburg to live the last years of his life in far-
away Mainz. The death of Pastor Winkler, the dispossessing of
Hartmut von Kronberg, and many other acts of tyranny must be
charged against the amiable epicurean who humored Luther with
his letters and his wedding present. Cologne, after the death of
Hoogstraten, became more and more lenient toward the new faith
until, in the early fifteen-forties, its Archbishop-Elector joined the
Lutheran Church and tried to convert his diocese into a secular
domain. He failed, but for a long time a strong minority of the
people in the electorate were staunch Lutherans. The free cities
which for various reasons had persecuted Lutherans within their
walls—mostly, as in the case of Hans Sachs, by the strict order to
keep silence—were now for the most part won for the Reformation.
Wuerttemberg under Duke Ulrich, had expelled the Hapsburg
authorities and had become Lutheran. A few Catholic bishops
periodically drove out Lutherans, but the spirit of the Counter-
Reformation had not yet taken hold of the German episcopate.

Thus there were left Bavaria and Austria, with the Diocese of
Salzburg as the center of Catholic reaction. The Dukes of Bavaria,

especially Duke Ernest, made no secret of their fervent desire to reestablish the *status quo* in their domain. The University of Ingolstadt was to Bavaria what Louvain was to the Netherlands. Eck dominated the Bavarian scene. The martyrdom of Leonard Kaiser, one of the earliest on German soil, which took place under the personal supervision of John Eck, is one of the darkest blotches in the history of the Reformation in Germany. But even before Kaiser Austria had executed its first Lutheran martyr, Caspar Tauber, on September 12, 1524. These two executions were to form the pattern for the many, many persecutions and two hundred years of underground existence of the Lutheran Church in the domains of the Hapsburgs and the Wittelsbachs. Not until the days of Joseph II, at the end of the eighteenth century, were the Lutherans allowed to confess their faith and not until the beginning of the nineteenth century were Lutherans allowed to settle in Munich. Matthew Cardinal Lang, Archbishop of Salzburg, warm friend of Staupitz who received the former vicar general into his home after the Reformation, gave him a Benedictine Abbey, and permitted the "spiritual father of Lutheran heresy" to die a peaceful death, was a typical example of a bishop under Bavarian and Austrian protection. During the Peasant War he changed from an outwardly benevolent ruler to a cruel persecutor, made Salzburg the citadel of Catholic Counter-Reformation for all of Germany, where long after Staupitz' death his books were burned on the market square, where hundreds and thousands of people were imprisoned and where everyone who was suspected of secret leanings toward Lutheranism was expelled. The mass expulsion of the Salzburgers in the eighteenth century which formed the background to Goethe's *Hermann und Dorothea* and which gave valuable colonists to America, was the consequent conclusion and the worst example of the persecution of the Church in Germany.

The names of 99% of the martyrs for the cause of the Gospel will never be known. They died for their faith and that was all the world knew about them. Names? Only a few are remembered locally, only a few have been printed in books made of paper and ink. These are some of the martyrs about whom we know a few facts.

Henry of Zuetphen (about 1488-1524)

Brother Henry of the Augustinian Hermits, whose last name was "Moeller," was called Henry of Zuetphen after his hometown. In 1508 he came to Wittenberg where he became acquainted with Luther during the latter's brief first stay there. In 1509 Brother Henry was lector at the Black Cloisters in Wittenberg, but left soon thereafter to become sub-prior in Cologne. In 1515 he became Augustinian prior in Dortrecht in Holland.

The persecution of "heretics" in Dortrecht began as early as 1518, even before Charles had arrived from Spain. Brother Henry does not seem to have suffered at that time, for we find him in the retinue of the Elector Frederick the Wise during the election of Charles V. He was at Cologne when the papal nuncio Aleander delivered the bull against Luther to the elector. With the court he travelled to Wittenberg where he continued his studies under Melanchthon, taking his baccalaureate and licentiate in 1521.

After the completion of his studies Brother Henry returned to the Netherlands in order to preach the Gospel. In spite of the persecution just then raging at Antwerp he was not afraid to proceed to that city, but was arrested on September 22, 1522, on the banks of the River Scheldt during an open air meeting. He was able to escape, however, and went to Bremen where he preached the Gospel with great success. Upon the arrival of the regularly called Lutheran pastor he left Bremen continuing to Ditmarschen to assist the Lutheran pastor there, Nicholas Boje, who was experiencing great difficulties at the hands of the hard-headed East Frisians. The stubborn Frisian farmers whose ancestors seven hundred years before had slain St. Boniface this time too resisted all change and lent a willing ear to Dominican troublemakers who persuaded them to kidnap Brother Henry from the parsonage at night. They broke into his home, tortured him without mercy for several hours and burned him at the stake during the early morning hours of December 11, 1524.

Luther has left us a beautiful document in his description of the "History and Martyrdom of the Sainted Brother Henry" which he sent to the sorrowing congregation in Bremen.

He describes how the tormentors took him during the night, naked and cold, threw him into a cellar where the guards mocked and beat him while the villagers were getting drunk. In the morning they took him out of the cellar, but being intoxicated were unable to start a fire to burn him. Finally one of the men hit him with a sledge hammer until he did not move any more. Before he died Brother Henry prayed the Lord to forgive his tormentors because they knew not what they did. When a monk commanded him to confess he replied by reciting the creed, but was struck and kicked by the enraged mob. In conclusion Luther adds the ninth Psalm: "I will give thanks to the Lord with my whole heart; I will tell all thy wonderful deeds." "These wonderful deeds," he says, "are that God does not convert the world by force but through the blood of His saints and overcomes the living through the dying: this is the miraculous victory."[6]

Leonhard Kaiser (died 1527)

Leonhard Kaiser was an early convert to the cause of the Reformation but was not allowed to confess his faith in Passau in Bavaria where Bishop Ernest forced him to recant. Later Leonhard left the city secretly and went to Wittenberg where he enrolled at the University on June 7, 1525. Here he became a daily companion of Luther and stayed with him almost two years. Called home by the sickness of his father, Leonhard Kaiser was soon found by the soldiers of the bishop and imprisoned on April 3, 1527. The bishop appointed the most famous Bavarian theologian, John Eck, to serve as prosecutor, a task which Eck executed with great relish. However, this time Kaiser did not recant. Eck adamantly refused the request of Kaiser to be tried before an imperial court. On July 18, 1527, Leonhard Kaiser was sentenced to be burned at the stake. The verdict was carried out at Scharding, in the diocese of Passau, on August 16, 1527. In the years to come many other Lutherans were burned and drowned in Bavaria.

The Reformer had written to Kaiser a letter of comfort. Several princes, including Elector John, had interceded for him at the Bavarian court, but to no avail. Kaiser died with Christian courage and strong faith. Michael Stiefel who lived a few miles from Scharding sent Luther an account of his death which the Reformer published, adding: "How unfortunate I am that I cannot suffer like our Leonhard, I who preach with many words. . . . Who will deem me worthy that I with half the courage should overcome Satan and depart from this life? . . . Rightly he is called not merely *Koenig*, king, but *Kaiser*, emperor, because he has overcome him whose power is unequalled here on earth. He is not merely a pastor, but a high priest and true pope who has brought his body as a sacrifice to God. He is a real Leonhard, that is: Lion's heart."[7]

Caspar Tauber (died 1524)

Several years before the martyrdom of Kaiser there had been the first bloodwitness in the capital of the Hapsburg empire, in Vienna.

On September 18, 1524, Gasparo Contarini reported from Vienna to Anzolo Gabriel: "Yesterday, at the hour when there were not 30 persons in the market place, the Lutheran merchant was at length burnt, whereupon 4,000 persons came instantly to rescue him, but he was already consumed; so it is thought his Majesty will thus render himself very odious to the people, and that one day or other there will be some grave tumult."[8]

This brief report of the end of Tauber's suffering shows how far Lutheranism had advanced in the capital of the Catholic reaction. Tauber had been brought before the Inquisition in August 1524, accused of spreading heretical ideas in company with two other men, Peregrinus and Voysler. While the others were persuaded to recant, Tauber steadfastly refused to deny his faith. On the contrary, he wrote a set of theses in which he defended the evangelical doctrines. The Inquisition, far from being mollified, pressed the charges which were specifically that Tauber had taught that bread and wine did not become the Body and Blood of Christ through consecration, that Roman ceremonies were not essential and should be rejected, that there was no purgatory, that all laymen are priests before God and do not need the mediation of ordained priests, that oral confession was not commanded and was superfluous, that the intercession of Mary and the saints was a fable and not valid, and that the Keys of the Church had been given to all believers. This list of particulars is the most complete description of Lutheran teaching ever given by a court in the early years of the persecutions.

Weakened by continuous threats and promises, Tauber finally promised to recant. But when he was taken to St. Stephen's Cathedral to carry out the agreement before the public, he remained firm. Thereupon he was condemned to death "because he had publicly promised to do penance and had signed his confession with his own hand, but later had refused to carry out the agreement and had remained steadfast in his heretical beliefs."[9]

On September 12, 1524, Tauber was led secretly before the Stuben Gate, and at 6 o'clock in the morning he was beheaded and burned. When a Catholic priest tried at the last minute to obtain a confession from him, Tauber quietly refused and commended his soul to God. Immediately after the execution the events described by Contarini took place.

When Luther heard about the martyrdom of the Viennese merchant he wrote to his friend Nicholas Hausmann: "I believe you have seen the history of Caspar Tauber, the new martyr of Vienna. They write that he was beheaded and burned for the Word of God. The same thing happened to a certain George, a bookseller in Budapest, in Hungary. He was burned with his books piled around him and suffered bravely for the Lord. Blood touches blood (Hosea 4:2). It will smother the pope with kings and their kingdoms. Farewell, and pray for me a sinner."[10]

George Winkler (died in 1527)

George Winkler, a native of Bischofswerda, had been since 1523 a chaplain at the court of Albert of Mainz, then residing at Halle. Beginning in 1524 his sermons became more and more Lutheran, but for several years Winkler continued preaching the Gospel unmolested. Finally a fanatical canon, Hoffmann, denounced the pastor to the archbishop who called Winkler to Aschaffenburg. But before Winkler reached his destination he was waylaid and murdered by highway men who had been hired by Hoffmann with the

connivance, it was thought, of Albert of Mainz who hated to start
formal proceedings against the popular Halle pastor. Luther promptly asked the archbishop to punish Hoffmann and the other murderers, but nothing was done. Luther who had been with Winkler
on March 10, less than two months before the murder, now attacked Albert of Mainz personally. When Dr. Ruehel interceded
with the Reformer for his bishop, Luther boldly replied: "How can
a human heart consider the priests or the bishop innocent since
they are silent? I shall do whatever I can so that I do not become
guilty of hypocrisy." In his "Letter of Consolation to the Christians
in Halle" he set a monument to Winkler. He wished, he said, to cry
to heaven on account of the innocent blood which had been shed,
that God, the Just Judge, may hear his voice as He has heard the
blood of Abel and may punish and avenge . . . and that the blood
of the martyr should become a divine seed which will bear fruit
a hundredfold. As far as the human perpetrators of the outrage are
concerned he is willing to believe that Albert was not directly involved, but he is accusing the Mainz canons who are willing to
start a bloodbath in all of Germany, which they had openly advocated in 1525. He is comforted by the fact that Winkler died in
obedience to the higher authorities whose call he had heeded
although he knew the dangers that were involved, and that he died
in obedience to the Gospel and most of all to the right doctrine
concerning the Holy Supper. Luther admonished the Christians in
Halle to hold fast to their faith and to continue to celebrate the
Lord's Supper under both kinds.

There was a sequence to this martyrdom. Early the following
year a Councillor of Albert of Mainz, Dr. Krause of Halle, cut his
throat "because he despaired having denied his Lord by carrying
out the archbishop's order against the right celebration of Holy
Communion."[11]

John von der Wyck (died in 1534)

John von der Wyck was one of the most distinguished lawyers of
the Reformation era. He came from Muenster in Westphalia, but
we do not know whether he was born there. He first made a name

for himself as an attorney for Reuchlin, the great humanist and Hebrew scholar, who had been accused of heresy by the Cologne inquisitor, Jacob Hoogstraten, before the start of the Reformation. In 1515 von der Wyck was able to win an acquittal for his famous client by appealing directly to the curia in Rome. He returned to Germany in 1518. We do not hear of him for several years after that. When he appears again on the pages of history he is a syndic in Bremen.

It was here, in Bremen, where Henry of Zuetphen and Propst had worked with such great blessing, that Wyck became one of the outstanding defenders of the Reformation. He was instrumental in persuading the reluctant city council to join the Lutheran League of Smalcald in 1530. He attended various meetings in the interest of the Reformation and, wherever he went, the cause of the Gospel was victorious. Luther and the Wittenbergers held him in high esteem.

During the Anabaptist "Muenster Madness" John von der Wyck was returning to his native city in order to bring peace. Catholic enemies found out about his intentions, waylaid him and murdered him without trial in April 1534. His death was mourned throughout Lutheran Germany. "It is a pity," a friend of von der Wyck wrote to the Elector John Frederick, "that this pious, honest man who has always helped Your Grace and all the evangelical estates so faithfully, should have lost his life in this miserable and secret manner."[12]

After his return from Rome John von der Wyck had visited Luther in Wittenberg several days and had placed at his disposal all the facts gathered in Rome against the papacy. These facts Luther later used in his treatise "To the Christian Nobility" in which he made sweeping recommendations for the "betterment of the Christian estate."

To John von der Wyck and all the other martyrs of the Reformation the words of the Reformer's first hymn, "The Hymn to the Martyrs," apply:

> *Their ashes will not rest; world-wide*
> *They fly through every nation.*
> *No cave nor grave, no turn nor tide,*
> *Can hide the abomination.*

The voices which with cruel hands
They put to silence living,
Are heard, though dead, throughout all lands
Their testimonies giving,
And loud hosannas singing. . . .

Summer is even at the door,
The winter now has vanished,
The tender flowers spring once more,
And he, who winter banished,
Will send a happy summer.

Amen.

VII.

The Strassburgers

Strassburg, the beautiful cathedral city of the Alsace, straddles the border between Germany and France. In a sense its location became symbolical for its theology during the period of the Reformation, for Strassburg occupied a strange position in the history of Lutheranism. It may be said that the Strassburgers were the fence-sitters of Luther's time. This statement is not meant in any derogatory sense. The men of Strassburg belonged to the best representatives among the Reformation theologians. They were sincere and always willing to help. They were more active than most theologians. They were strong in their own way, preferring to suffer for their faith rather than to submit to dictation by emperor or pope. And yet Strassburg was the first seat of unionism in the history of the Lutheran Church. It served as a vestibule where Wittenberg and Zurich, Wittenberg and Cambridge, Wittenberg and Geneva, reformers and humanists met and talked amiably to each other. It also served as the window through which the light of the Reformation entered France and Spain.

In Strassburg Lambert of Avignon, illegitimate son of a papal secretary and former monk who had visited Luther in Wittenberg in 1523 and married a Wittenberg baker's daughter, translated Luther's work into French. To Strassburg came later John Witz, pupil of Lefèvre d'Etaples, greatest living French theologian who had influenced the theology of Luther and Calvin. Thus the spirit of French and German humanism merged in the educational system of the great city of which Witz became the most outstanding educator. Still later John Calvin himself arrived and served here for a while as Lutheran pastor to the French refugees, subscribing to the Augsburg Confession before he returned to Geneva. Francisco Enzinas, the greatest among the Spanish Lutherans, fled to Strassburg, became professor at the University and translated Luther into his native tongue. And Bucer, the most renowned Strassburg theologian, went to England in 1548 when he had been driven from the city on account of the Interim which he steadfastly refused to sign. He died as professor of theology at Cambridge.

The Strassburgers were remarkable people in many ways. Melanchthon who often was much more inclined to compromise his faith said of them contemptuously: "I hate the falseness of those people!"[1] He had been miffed when the Strassburgers did not sign the Augsburg Confession but insisted on presenting their own separate confession, the *Confessio Tetrapolitana*. Yet these same Strassburgers were among the first to join the Lutheran Smalcald League, and a few years later when Archbishop Hermann von Wied of Cologne tried desperately to introduce the Lutheran Reformation in that very important part of Germany and when Melanchthon and especially Luther were dragging their feet, the Strassburgers were the only ones who actively supported the frustrated archbishop-elector.

The thing which most annoyed non-Strassburgers was that they were utterly unpredictable and stubbornly independent. They not only got along with Wittenberg, Zurich, Geneva, and Canterbury, but also harbored within their walls Catholics, humanists, Waldensians, Anabaptists, and even Unitarians. At times they were tolerant and peaceloving while at other times they made those who disagreed with their theology languish in jails. Poor Melchior Hoffmann, the erring and wandering mystic and Anabaptist, sought refuge in Strassburg only to be imprisoned for the rest of his life. Constantly under suspicion by friend and foe, the Strassburgers were nevertheless liked and their help was often sought. Luther would call Bucer one day "a rascal" and listen to him the next. Erasmus chided them for destroying the unity of the Church and yet grudgingly conceded that nowhere had the Reformation been introduced with less tumult than at Strassburg.

Most of the men whom we call today "The Strassburgers" were not born in the city. Only Jacob Sturm, its mayor, was a real Strassburger. Bucer came from nearby Schlettstadt and arrived in Strassburg after the defeat of Sickingen, long after the start of the Reformation; Capito, from Hagenau in the Alsace, made Strassburg his home in 1523, after he had been fired by Albert of Mainz; Gerbel, whose birthplace we do not know, studied in Strassburg first in 1507 and made it his home in 1515; Hedio, from Ettlingen in neighboring Baden, arrived shortly after Capito, also fleeing from the wrath of Albert of Mainz; Lambert resided here several years in the fifteen-twenties; John Bock who conferred with Luther at Worms may or may not have been a native; Gregory Casel's origins are shrouded in darkness; Wolfgang Koepfel came from the court of Albert of Mainz; Witz came from France and from Schlettstadt; Enzinas was a Spaniard; and Calvin a Frenchman. It may have been that these men and many others, including Carlstadt, Hoffmann, Schwenkfeld, and Rhenanus, went to Strassburg because they hoped to find there freedom of expression.

The reputation of independence which Strassburg enjoyed during the Reformation period goes back to the Catholic era. William III von Honstein, Bishop of Strassburg, had tried in 1520 to reform the cathedral but was prevented by the pope. Luther spoke of this "Strassburg tragedy" in a letter to Spalatin and again described the episode in his address "To the German Nobility." At Worms in 1521 the representative of Strassburg to the Diet, John Bock, joined with others in an effort to persuade Luther to come to terms with the Emperor and was converted by him. And Jacob Sturm as a member of the Catholic city council was instrumental in introducing the Lutheran Reformation in Strassburg, although William III continued to reign in his cathedral until 1541.

Of the men who came to Strassburg during the fifteen-twenties and who settled there, Martin Bucer had been the first convert to Lutheranism. As a Dominican in Heidelberg in 1518 he was supposed to be Luther's enemy when the latter arrived in the city to dispute his doctrines. But on May 1, 1518, he reported to Beatus Rhenanus: "His sweetness in answering is remarkable, his patience in listening is incomparable, in his explanations you would recognize the acumen of Paul, not of Scotus; his answers, so brief, so wise, and drawn from the Holy Scriptures, easily made all his hearers his admirers."[2] A few months later, Capito, then at Basel, wrote to Luther: "Behold how my friendship has made me forget myself in telling you what to do. Pray forgive my solicitude. You have more than one champion. . . ."[3] Hedio, from Mainz, wrote to Zwingli in 1520: "The pope has sent a bull about Luther, a real bull, I hear. He urges the angels of heaven, SS. Peter and Paul, and every creature to take part against Luther. . . . But Luther will burst forth . . . and before the next fair we shall have thunder. Cease not, help good men and Christian piety as much as you can. . . ."[4] By 1524 these three men had joined Sturm and Gerbel in Strassburg which had been reformed in December 1523. Here Bucer introduced a German Mass, two years before Luther wrote his own. Together these men resisted the inroads of the Anabaptists and cleaned up the backwash of the Peasant Revolt. During the Communion controversy they stood together solidly for a compromise between Zurich and Wittenberg and enlisted the offices of Landgrave Philip of Hesse. Offended by Luther's suspicion at Marburg they worked out their own confession, keeping the gates of the city open to all non-conformists. But when the Lutheran cause was threatened they readily joined the Lutheran princes and free cities in a common defense front. In their second attempt to bring about unity between Wittenberg and Zurich they were even less successful than at Marburg. This time the Zwinglians refused to go along. Henceforth the Strassburgers drew closer to Wittenberg, both in personal friendship and theological agreement. In the fifteen-forties they were the most active propagators of the Lutheran cause, helping Hermann of Cologne and refusing to sign the Interim.

Bucer went to England where he died in 1551. His friend Capito had died in 1541. Gerbel continued in Strassburg until his death in 1560. Hedio died of the plague in 1552 and Jacob Sturm the following year. The minor characters, with the exception of John

Witz who died in 1561, had all passed from the scene long ago. After the fifteen-fifties when Luther's generation was gone Strassburg became one of the many avenues through which Calvinism entered sixteenth century Germany. Its great days were gone.

Martin Bucer (1491-1551)

Martin Bucer does not only stand alphabetically at the head of the Strassburgers, but was their foremost representative in the three decades which followed his decision of 1518 to cast his lot with Luther. In many ways he was closest to the Wittenberg Reformer to whom he remained loyal even after the latter's death. And yet he was eyed with greater suspicion by Luther and even by Melanchthon than any of his fellow-townsmen. Responsible for this mistrust was Bucer's zig-zag course in ecclesiastical politics.

Born at Schlettstadt of honorable parents who moved soon after the birth of young Martin, in 1491, to Strassburg, the young child was left behind to live with his grandfather in Schlettstadt and was instructed by him. In 1516 Martin entered the Dominican Order and became a monk. Soon his outstanding talents were recognized by his superiors who sent him on to Heidelberg where he had an opportunity to study at the university. There he took his bachelor's degree and was consecrated to the priesthood.

Soon after his ordination Bucer met Luther when he attended the Convention of the Augustinians in Heidelberg. Although he had been interested primarily in philosophy this meeting with the famous Wittenberg professor gave new direction to his life's interests. After this meeting he read all of Luther's books and was especially impressed by his exegetical commentaries. Having obtained a special papal dispensation Bucer left the monastery in which he had never been really happy. He first served as chaplain to the Count Palatinate, later accepted a pastorate at Landstuhl. In 1522—three years before Luther—he married a former nun and served for a time as pastor of Weissenburg where he recommended to his parishioners the reading of the New Testament and of Luther's works.

After the debacle of Sickingen's defeat and the victory of the Catholic forces under the Archbishop of Trier and his allies Bucer

retired to Strassburg where he stayed for over twenty years until
he was forced by the imperial Interim to leave the city to which his
presence had given so much luster and prestige. He had been one of
the busiest men of the Reformation, although he was not always
the most reliable person to turn to. One of his first acts upon reaching Strassburg was to help the city council introduce the Reforma-

BUCER

tion against much ecclesiastic opposition. For some time after this
he was more closely associated with Zwingli than with Luther.

In 1524 Bucer introduced the German Mass, a German service,
in Strassburg. In 1529 he succeeded in abolishing the Latin service
completely. In the meantime the Communion controversy had
broken out and Bucer had become the most fervent advocate of a
meeting between Luther and Zwingli which had been suggested to
him by Justus Jonas. But before this he had offended Luther by
publishing one of his books without the authorization of the author
and slightly changing a few passages. Luther never forgot this in-

cident and when he met him a few years later at Marburg he
wagged his finger at him and called out: "You are a rascal, Bucer."
This caused some hard feelings for a time and may have been a
contributing cause to Bucer's insistence on publishing a separate
confession in 1530.

Another matter which Luther resented was that even after the
Reformer's break with Erasmus and his friends, Bucer and the
Strassburgers kept on good terms with the humanists. In a sense
Bucer was a liberal, but when his faith was put to a test, as in the
Interim, he mustered strength to resist. Luther was probably some-
what unfair in his treatment of the Strassburg theologian, since he
chose to overlook graver faults in his friend Melanchthon.

The attempts of Bucer to bring the warring factions together in
the Wittenberg Concord of 1536 were abortive. His renown as a
mediation theologian had endeared him to Landgrave Philip of
Hesse who now turned to him when he wanted to take a second
wife without divorcing the first. Bucer agreed to go to Wittenberg
to win Luther's and Melanchthon's consent to the contemplated
bigamous marriage. Although Luther consented of his own free
will, he later was inclined to blame Bucer for his meddling. In the
fifteen-forties the support which was so urgently needed in the
Cologne affair was not forthcoming from Wittenberg. If Bucer
would have succeeded here, the whole religious map of Europe
might have been changed and the Thirty-Years War might never
have taken place. Certainly the Lutherans would not have been
defeated by Charles V five years later.

Although Melanchthon commented on "the falseness of these
people" the two men were drawn to each other. Some scholars
think that Bucer's influence on Melanchthon after 1530—the difference about the Augsburg Confession and the *Tetrapolitana* had
been patched up—may have been responsible for Melanchthon's
tampering with the Augsburg Confession. We do not know. But
the correspondence between the two became more and more important as the years went by. In 1534 Bucer won a great victory
when Augsburg adopted a stand similar to the Strassburg position
on Holy Communion. In 1535 Bucer tried with some success to
assuage the newly aroused suspicions of Luther, but by 1536 he and

Capito helped the Swiss write their First Helvetic Confession. That same year he signed the Wittenberg Concord. For the next two years he tried in vain to bring the Swiss into line, but by November 1538 he had to admit that the effort had failed.

Luther's death and the Smalcald War dealt a deathblow to the Strassburg theology. Forced to leave the city by the refusal to sign the Interim Bucer followed an invitation by Archbishop Cranmer and went to England where he taught theology until his death on February 28, 1551.

"Hail, reverend Father, sincerest of theologians and strongest of Christians," he had greeted Luther in 1520. "Received at dinner by you and your pious superior, John Staupitz, I was wonderfully refreshed, not only by the excellent delicacies of the table, but by the exquisite and sweet meat of the Scriptures, for which, indeed, I came more hungry than for the bodily food. Among the other excellent gifts of your mind, the genuine humility of our Lord Jesus manifested itself with special brilliance; your face, words, gestures and whole body testified to it."[5] Luther, the simple miner's son, who usually did not appreciate this type of language, was taken in and sent the letter on to Spalatin, on February 12, 1520, with the remark: "Here is the letter of Bucer, a young brother, who almost alone of his order gives some promise. At Heidelberg he received me eagerly and simply, and conversed with me showing himself worthy of love and trust, and also of hope."[6]

In these years the enthusiasm of Bucer continued unclouded by misunderstandings. Later in 1521 he wrote to Spalatin concerning Luther's book "To the Christian Nobility": "Good Heavens! what wise liberty is in it! There is not an iota of it to which I can oppose anything from Scripture." And to Rhenanus he wrote from the Ebernburg, Sickingen's fortress: "The wicked are in labor and with violent throes have brought forth a little mandate. They bear in their womb a great giant, Antichrist himself, who will not only hurl mountain on mountain, but with his own might will thrust from heaven Christ and all the gods. . . . [Luther] writes that he hopes no hands save those of the papists will be stained with his blood."[7] But at the same time he was impressed by Glapion's "sincerity" when the wily papist conferred with Sickingen to keep Luther away from

Worms. He reported to Spalatin in April 1521: "He desires only that
Luther may be able to defend himself. . . . But keep this secret, for
we have given our word to be silent."[8] Fortunately, Luther proceeded to Worms. After the Diet Luther greeted Sickingen from his
own Patmos, the Wartburg: "God have you in His keeping. I commend Sir Ulrich von Hutten and Martin Bucer to your Grace."[9]

But the idyll ended after Bucer became involved in the Sacramentarian Controversy, started by Carlstadt and now taken up by
the Swiss Reformers. In his letter "To the Clergy of Strassburg"
which followed nine months after his letter "To the Christians of
Strassburg" and many exchanges between Zwingli, Oecolampadius,
Bugenhagen, Pirckheimer, John Brenz and others, Luther admonished his Strassburg colleagues: "Be wise, beloved; Satan is . . .
the prince of this world. Who does not rejoice in the praise that
you accord to the sanctity of Zwingli and Oecolampadius and to
their churches? But see where Zwingli comes to in his doctrine of
original sin. . . ."[10] His wrath was kindled shortly thereafter when
Bucer not only did not heed his warning but tampered with Luther's
Church Postil by changing at will certain passages on the Lord's
Supper and publishing the work without Luther's permission at
Strassburg. Luther immediately wrote to John Heerwagen, the printer: "I was satisfied and still am satisfied that the translation [into
Latin] should be made by Bucer. . . . But alas! in the midst of these
praiseworthy labors he fell, by God's permission, into the horrible
blasphemy of the sacramentarian spirit, and his gift of facility and
insight is contaminated, nay, it is destroyed by that pestilential
poison. . . ."[11] Bucer apologized abjectly, but two years later felt
constrained to publish a "Dialogue" in which he attacked Luther's
"Great Confession of the Lord's Supper." Again, Luther complained,
this time to Bucer's Strassburg colleague Gerbel, "of Bucer's base-
ness" and continued: "Away with those vipers! I pray with all my
might that Christ may keep you safe who dwell in the midst of these
wild beasts . . . in almost greater peril than Daniel himself was
in the den of lions."[12] In spite of these sentiments which were known
to him, Bucer went along to Marburg in 1529, where Jonas described
him "crafty as a fox, making a perverse pretense of wisdom and
keenness."[13] It was here that Luther waved his finger in front of

Bucer's nose and exclaimed smilingly: *Tu es nequam,* "You are a rascal."

The two men crossed swords, figuratively speaking, many a time after that, but never again did Luther hit Bucer as hard as he had in the fifteen-twenties. His esteem of the "crafty fox" increased to such an extent that shortly before his death he omitted the sharp attacks against his Strassburg friend when he published the polemical treatises in his collected works. Asked why the long philippic against Bucer had been changed in Luther's treatise "That These Words Still Stand" Roerer, who supervised the edition of Luther's works, replied: "That such had been done with the knowledge and upon the request of Luther because in these passages Bucer had been attacked very harshly as an enemy of the Sacrament, but now had been converted."[14] This coming from a man who rarely admitted that he had wronged anyone was the finest tribute to Martin Bucer.

Wolfgang Capito (1472-1541)

On September 4, 1518, Wolfgang Capito, good friend of Erasmus, had written to Luther from Basel that he should go slow because the "Apostles urged nothing suddenly, nothing openly, but always preserved decorum and courtesy."[15] That same year he had prefaced the first edition of Luther's works published by Froben in October. "Here you have the theological works of the Reverend Father Martin Luther," he had written, "whom many consider a Daniel sent at length in mercy by Christ to correct abuses and restore the evangelical and Pauline divinity to theologians who . . . occupy themselves with the merest logical and verbal trifles."[16] In 1519 he offered Luther asylum in case of need and repeated the offer in 1520, after he had joined Albert's court in Mainz, predicting "Their end shall be death whether they were born of contention or whether they were begotten by guile."[17] And in another letter he begged his friend Erasmus not to disparage Luther's fame, "but let Luther's fame live."

Yet when Luther commented on this faithful disciple from The Wilderness (Wartburg), on September 19, 1521, he stated: "Neither Capito's nor Erasmus' opinion moves me in the least. They are only doing what I expected. [After the edict of Worms the two had tried to reconcile the two parties.] Indeed, I have been afraid that some day I should have trouble with one or the other of them. . . . Their books do no good because they refrain from chiding and biting and giving offence. . . . Jeremiah speaks gravely and terribly of them: 'Cursed be he that doeth the work of the Lord deceitfully.' . . . I, too, am afraid and my conscience troubles me because I listened to you, Spalatin, and to those friends at Worms and held my spirit in check and did not show myself a second Elijah to those idols. They would hear another story if I stood before them again."[18]

These excerpts from the early years of Luther's and Capito's acquaintance show at once the difficulties which their relationship encountered. Capito, the son of a poor smith in Hagenau who did not want his son to become a priest, had much in common with the son of the Mansfeld miner, but unlike Luther he followed his father's wishes, studying medicine and law, earning a master's and a doctor's degree and establishing himself as physician and licentiate at law. However, after his father's death, he followed the calling which had always been close to his heart, studied theology, and at 39 was a licentiate in theology. In 1511 he began to lecture at Freiburg.

Soon his preaching and teaching became suspect because it deviated from the accepted Roman norm. In 1514 he was transferred to a Benedictine Abbey in Bruchsal in Baden where he served as abbot. But here, too, he was attacked by his fellow-monks because his teaching on transubstantiation was not Catholic. In 1515 he went to Basel where he spent several fruitful years as pastor of the Minster, supported by his liberal bishop. He avoided all polemical issues, but slowly prepared the way for the Reformation long before the world had heard of Luther or Zwingli. Erasmus who was then at Basel made use of Capito's profound scholarship to verify Hebrew quotations from the Old Testament for his edition of the New Testament. In 1518 Capito was elected dean of the university.

In his work as professor Capito endeavored to push scholasticism into the background and to raise sound Biblical exegesis to its proper place in the Church. He printed a good edition of the Hebrew Psalter in 1516 and edited a Hebrew Grammar in 1517. His motto was: "Scripture must reign supreme in theology." Timid and retiring by nature, Capito was emboldened by Luther's courageous stand against the abuses in the Church. Within four months after the publication of the Ninety-Five Theses he got in touch with the Wittenberg professor. Less than two years later he supervised the first edition of Luther's Works to which we referred above. This edition helped to spread Luther's fame to Italy, France, Spain, and England. Erasmus, however, always jealous of his rank as the first among the scholars rebuked Capito for his "rash endorsement" of Luther. Capito complained, "There are a few people who suspect me of being a partisan of Luther, although I am doing my best to act with restraint."[19]

From 1520 to 1523 we find this "partisan of Luther" at the court of Albert of Mainz whom he served as chancellor of the archdiocese. Luther did not like it at all, that Capito thus became involved in Albert's schemes. When Capito heard of Luther's objections he went to Wittenberg and the two became reconciled. From Wittenberg he returned to Mainz. But finally, in 1523, he decided that the time had come to come out openly for Luther. He went to Strassburg, helped Bucer, Sturm, and others to introduce the Reformation and stayed here until the end of his life.

In Strassburg he preached the Gospel without fear and trembling. His congregation was very fond of him, protected him against the bishop (whose attempts to silence him were not more determined than those of Albert of Mainz had been), and strengthened him to such a degree that he could proclaim: "If we were servants of men we would not be Christ's followers!" At the University of Strassburg the education of Lutheran pastors was especially close to his heart.

During the Peasant War his heart went out to the unfortunate misguided peasants. Although, like Luther, he was strongly opposed to the use of violence, he understood their grievances and tried to protect them. When, in 1526, Carlstadt with wife and child arrived in Strassburg fleeing from Electoral Saxony, Capito took them into his house. But his pity for the unfortunate fanatic was changed to chagrin when he found out that Carlstadt brought unrest to his Church in Strassburg.

For the Communion Controversy he had no understanding.

"Posterity will smile on our desire to quarrel for the sake of the sign of unity which is Holy Communion."[20] Although, like Bucer, he had been closer to Zwingli than to Luther, he turned now more and more to the Wittenberg Reformer in whom he had recognized the greater mind. While assuring Luther of his orthodox beliefs, he tried to bring the two Reformers together. After the Colloquy of Marburg, however, he felt that he could not sign the Augsburg Confession in good conscience, and therefore worked out, with Bucer, the *Confessio Tetrapolitana* which the four cities of Strassburg, Constance, Lindau, and Memmingen submitted separately. In 1536 Capito attended the meeting between Zwinglians and Lutherans at Wittenberg. That year he also assisted in drafting the First Helvetian Confession. His "Church Constitution and Pastoral Instructions" belongs to the best documents for congregational organization published during the Reformation period.

Capito died in 1541, leaving his second wife, the widow of his friend Oecolampadius, free to marry his friend Bucer who then took care of all the children.

Nicholas Gerbel (about 1485-1560)

Nicholas Gerbel, a native of Pforzheim, studied in 1506 at Cologne and in 1507 at Vienna. He was a friend of many humanists, including Reuchlin with whom he carried on an extended correspondence. He took his Doctor of Laws degree in 1513 at Bologna, went to Basel and finally settled, in 1515, in Strassburg. After his marriage he became a professor of history at the university.

Gerbel had many interests. His avocation was painting, but he also was absorbed in the problems of theology. After the arrival of Bucer and Hedio he joined forces with them.

Since 1521 Gerbel had been in contact with Luther. His edition of the New Testament which he sent to the Reformer in the fall of 1521 and which Luther received at the Wartburg was used together with Erasmus' second edition of the New Testament for Luther's translation of the New Testament into German.

While Gerbel had a great personal liking for the Reformer he objected, like Capito, to his often violent language. During his long and distinguished career he wrote several treatises on theology, history and geography, participated in the disputations against the Anabaptists, and was closer to Luther's theology than any of the other Strassburg theologians, supporting Luther in the sacramental controversy, even against Bucer and Capito. He died in 1560.

Shortly after Luther had been spirited away to the Wartburg, Gerbel wrote him a worried letter. "Greetings in Christ Jesus the Crucified," he began. "About you everything here is so uncertain that you never saw or heard of anything more uncertain. A persistent rumor is going the rounds that you have been taken by treachery, and even that you were afterwards killed, stabbed in the neck with a sword. There are some who say that you have returned safe to Wittenberg. Between the two reports it is not known which is true. Certainly there is not a single learned and good man who does not hope for the latter. You would not believe how the adherents of the other party rejoice in the first story and how they thank their gods. The men are altogether crazy and do not know how much ill, nay, how much human blood your death would cost. But we who have aspired to salvation and true faith, are variously affected, and you would not believe how anxious we are for your life. Not that we grudge you the glory of living with the heavenly spirits and dying to the world . . . but because you seemed one of the few who treat the Gospel as it should be treated, and we cherished the hope that in you we had a leader who would not fail us, by whom all that had been lost by the wrong-doing and the negligence of the fathers could be restored."[21]

During the next few years Luther and Gerbel collaborated in many literary enterprises. The best known of these was probably the "theft" of Melanchthon's manuscript of "Notes on Three Epistles of St. Paul" (Romans and I and II Corinthians), actually a student's manuscript full of errors, which Luther had sent to the printer secretly. Melanchthon forgave him and the real manuscript was sent to Gerbel. "I sent you my booty, my dear Gerbel," Luther wrote, "so that you may do your best to make it known how unwillingly the author is. I hope John Setzer will print it more correctly and accurately than my former theft was printed."[22]

Yet the relationship was not always undisturbed by disagree-

ments. In 1525 Gerbel took Carlstadt's side, especially after Carlstadt had been attacked by Luther in the treatise "Against the
Heavenly Prophets." He wrote to John Schwebel on March 30,
1525: "What Luther thinks on the Sacrament of the Eucharist you
will have learned from his last book against Carlstadt which greatly
displeases almost everyone in Zurich, Basel, and here. . . . Shall we,
having given up faith and love, come to the same place as the
papists are with their quarrels?"[23] Later, however, he saw the real
concern of Luther, the seriousness of the question, and followed
him faithfully. When, in 1528, Luther did not know to whom to
turn in Strassburg after "Bucer's base betrayal" during the Communion Controversy, he wrote for help to Gerbel, whom he had
chosen as one of the sponsors of his first child, little Hans.

Caspar Hedio (1494-1552)

Caspar Hedio was born in 1494 in Ettlingen in Baden, attended
the University of Freiburg receiving his master's degree in 1518
and becoming a licentiate in theology in 1519. From Freiburg he
went to Basel where he was soon linked in close friendship with
Capito and came under the influence of Zwingli. At the same time
he helped spread the writings of Luther which had just been published by Froben in Basel.

In spite of his known zeal for the Wittenberg Reformer Hedio
was soon called to Mainz by Archbishop Albert to whom he had
been recommended by his friend Capito. He became court chaplain
and was so well liked that he stayed with Albert for a while even
after Capito had left Mainz for Strassburg. But as the restrictions
against the Lutheran "heresy" became more and more stringent at
Albert's court Hedio decided to follow Capito to Strassburg. Here
he met also Bucer and Gerbel with whom he formed lasting
friendships.

Like the other Strassburg theologians Hedio tried to mediate the
growing rift between Wittenberg and Zurich and was suspected of
lukewarmness in both camps. In 1529 he was present in Marburg
where he signed the articles. In the thirties he was again involved
in mediation efforts and in 1543 he helped Bucer and Melanchthon

with their labors in Cologne, labors which were defeated by the suspicions of Luther and the energetic opposition of the Cologne chapter and the Emperor Charles V.

The last years of his life were darkened by much suffering. Bucer had fled to England, Capito had died, and his other friends no longer understood his concern for unity. He died of the plague, faithful to the last at his post, on October 17, 1552.

Shortly after he had gone to Mainz in 1520 Hedio wrote to Zwingli at Zurich: "Although I am long absent from you, dearest Zwingli, yet would I be present in my letters. Capito called me to Mainz, where I shall be preacher until his return from the coronation of the king [Charles V], and perhaps afterwards, if Christ will, for Capito is going to give up this office, having been made chancellor of the Archbishop of Mainz. You will hardly believe how valuable he is in this position. Luther's books would long ago have been burnt in this district and Lutherans excommunicated, had he not persuaded the archbishop otherwise. . . ."[24] But at the end of the year he reported: "We burned Luther here in obedience to the pope's decree, but it was a ridiculous affair. Some swear that we did not burn Luther's books but those of Aeneas Silvius [a pope of the fifteenth century]; some that it was Eck and some Prierias. But whatever books were burned it was done to hurt Luther. The people almost threw Aleander into a cesspool. It has been decreed by the council of princes to summon Luther to Worms to give an answer for his writings. Good heavens, Zwingli, how the Roman legates withstand this! They don't want the heretic to be heard. They make many threats, but I think their efforts are vain. We shall soon see what will happen. . . ."[25]

In spite of Aleander's objections and machinations Luther was heard in Worms. During the years that followed Hedio remained the closest friend and follower of Zwingli among the Strassburgers. His connections with Wittenberg were very loose. Yet in 1529, before the Colloquy of Marburg, Melanchthon wrote in an opinion: "I know some of them who I hope could be moved to abandon their error—men like Hedio and Ambrose Blaurer; but the others would only become worse and there would be more disturbances afterwards, as it happened after the Leipzig Disputation."[26] At Marburg

Jonas described Hedio as "suave and broadminded." Luther was favorably impressed with him. Hedio signed the Articles. But his heart remained with Zwingli.

Due to his outspoken Zwinglianism Hedio's fame has been obscured, although he was more reliable than Bucer, milder than Capito, and a more effective teacher than Gerbel. He was above all a practical theologian, an excellent preacher, a generous man. More lasting than his theological labors was his work in education. He was Strassburg's outstanding schoolman and reorganizer of schools.

Jacob Sturm (1489-1553)

Jacob Sturm is credited with having first suggested a meeting between Luther and Zwingli at the First Diet of Speier in 1526. Duke Ulrich of Wuerttemberg, then living in exile, was anxious to see it accomplished. Landgrave Philip of Hesse approached Luther on the subject in 1527, but found him unwilling even to consider it. Raising the question again Melanchthon suggested that also some "honorable and reasonable papists" should be present. The meeting was finally held at Marburg with Luther and Zwingli discussing their differences and points of agreement as Sturm had suggested.

Jacob Sturm, a kinsman of Wimpfeling, was born at Strassburg on August 10, 1489, of a good family. After an excellent education at the Universities of Heidelberg and Freiburg-Breisgau Sturm entered the services of the Count Palatinate Henry of Wittelsbach, Provost of Strassburg. Soon after 1517 he was won for the Reformation. In 1524 he was elected councillor and provost and from 1527 on he was repeatedly mayor of the city. He was one of the most active men in the world of affairs. All in all he was sent on 91 diplomatic missions, a record in those days.

Sturm was the prime mover in introducing the Reformation in Strassburg. He was able to keep the disturbances of the Peasant War and the Anabaptist movement to a minimum. He was present at Speier and Marburg, and when the attempt to bridge the gulf between Luther and Zwingli failed Sturm was chosen to present the *Confessio Tetrapolitana*, drawn up by the Strassburg theologians,

at the Diet of Augsburg. However, he was not satisfied to stand
aside from the other Lutheran cities and princes when danger
threatened. Under his influence Strassburg joined the League of
Smalcald. Later, after the Smalcald War, Sturm succeeded in obtaining special terms from the Emperor Charles V which were less
stringent than those of the Augsburg Interim. A few years later, on
October 30, 1553, Sturm died in his native city which he had served
with unswerving loyalty to the cause of the Reformation.

VIII

The Swiss Reformers

When Luther nailed the Ninety-Five Theses to the door of the Castle Church in Wittenberg he was unaware that in faraway Switzerland earnest men were concerned about the same problems which he had raised in his Thèses. Although the Swiss Reformation was born of humanism and not primarily of theology the task of cleansing the Church of her impurities was taken as seriously there as in Wittenberg. The Swiss welcomed Luther's actions and accepted some of his theological thoughts, but they never wholly freed themselves from humanism and thus split the anti-Roman movement into two great historical branches which still exist today.

In Zurich

Since the beginning of the sixteenth century the life of the Swiss cities had been deeply influenced by humanism. The younger generation looked to Erasmus of Rotterdam for guidance. He was then teaching at Basel. From Erasmus came also Zwingli who had studied at Vienna under the humanist Celtes, at Basel under the humanist Thomas Wyttenbach and had become personally acquainted with the great Erasmus in 1516. Zwingli, an extremely practical man, world-wise and politically-minded like most Swiss leaders, endeavored even before 1517 to raise the Christian Church from the low estate into which she had sunk during the preceding generations. His ideal was a purified humanistic Christian piety which would slough off the impurities which had crept into doctrine and practice. In this endeavor he was supported by most Catholic leaders of Switzerland. Thus when he began to preach against the indulgence peddler Bernard Samson, the Bishop of Constance supported him and the pope recalled the peddler. There was not that sharp conflict which was felt in Germany immediately after Luther's bold adventure. There was no Albert of Mainz, no stubborn Tetzel and Wimpina, and above all no brilliant Eck in Switzerland. The preoccupation of the Catholic world with Luther also helped Zwingli during the first years of the Reformation.

Zwingli, like Luther, at first had no intention of breaking with the Church. In 1518 he applied for and was given the title of papal acolyte. But soon, especially after the Leipzig Debate of 1519, he felt encouraged to follow in the footsteps of Luther. During the next six or seven years, until after the break of Luther with Erasmus, Luther became the acknowledged leader of most Swiss Reformers. Many of the men who worked with Zwingli had come from Lutheranism. The best-known of the early "Lutheran" theologians of Switzerland was Oecolampadius.

Even during this period of theological occupation Zwingli's concerns were mostly practical. During 1519 and 1520 the big issues in Switzerland were not the freedom of Christians from papal tryanny, but abuses like the custom of sending mercenaries to fight the battles for other states and princes and the financial drain of the system of pensions. In 1520 Zwingli set an example to other theologians by voluntarily renouncing the right to a papal pension. In 1522 he persuaded the city council of Zurich to forbid the recruiting of mercenaries.

Early in 1522, while Carlstadt was promoting revolutionary changes in Wittenberg during Luther's absence, similar events took place in Zurich. This was a time of great excitement for the sober Swiss. Many citizens, encouraged by Zwingli, did not keep the fast during Lent. When the Bishop of Constance, who had backed Zwingli against the indulgence traffic, objected the Zurich Reformer published his first reformation writing: "Of the Choosing and

Freedom of Meats." Later that year, in his "Supplication," he advocated freedom to preach the Gospel and marriage for the priests. In January 1523 things came to a head and to a decision. In the First Zurich Disputation Zwingli was declared the victor and the Catholic representative John Faber the vanquished. Thereupon the city council decided that from now on all preachers had to preach the Gospel.

In the fall of 1523 revolutionary elements smashed the statues and pictures in the Churches of Zurich. Although Zwingli was opposed to such drastic action, this event gave him an opportunity to insist in the Second Zurich Disputation that all statues and pictures should be removed from the churches, but in an orderly fashion.

During the iconoclastic disturbances a new movement had appeared on the scene, the Anabaptist movement, led by Grebel, Hubmaier, and Stumpf. For a time these radicals were tolerated, but the break between Zwingli and the Anabaptist leaders was a foregone conclusion. They left Zurich, went underground or were martyred, and the city council once more took things firmly in hand.

The Anabaptist opposition had forced Zwingli to break radically with Roman customs and ceremonies, a break that was much more radical than in Lutheran lands. The Reformed attitude towards these external things was that nothing should be retained that had not been expressly commanded in the Bible, while Luther and his followers insisted that anything that had not been expressly prohibited by God's Word should be left free to the individual Christian to keep or to discard. Thus in Zurich not only the Catholic sacrifice of the Mass was abolished, but also the organs removed, hymn-singing, except the chanting of psalms, forbidden, and altars torn down. Of course, all types of processions, relics, pictures and statues, confirmation, and extreme unction were included in this list of forbidden customs. The council of the city was entrusted with running the Church.

In Other Cities

From Zurich the Zwinglian Reformation spread with irresistible force. To be sure, the original cantons, called the Forest Cantons, clung to the old faith. Besides Schwyz, Uri, and Unterwalden also the progressive cities of Lucerne, Zug, and Fribourg fought for the *status quo*. But Berne, Basel, St. Gall, Schaffhausen, Glarus, and many other cities followed Zwingli. His influence even spread across the border into Upper Germany.

The victorious progress of the Reformation was checked for a time when Zwingli received a defeat during the Disputation at Baden in May 1526. Here not only John Faber, but also John Eck and Thomas Murner had defended the Catholic position, while the evangelicals had as their champions Oecolampadius and Haller. For a time it looked as if Zwingli's Reformation would die. But the Disputation of Berne in January 1528 in which not only Haller participated but to which he brought along Bucer and Capito from Strassburg, gave it a new lease on life. The lines were drawn. Zurich, Basel, Berne, Constance and other cities made a military alliance. The Catholics with the help of Ferdinand of Austria lined up Schwyz, Uri, Unterwalden, Zug, and Lucerne on the opposite side. A war was only avoided when the Catholic Swiss—they were Swiss first and Catholics second—agreed to exclude the hated Austrians from their league. Peace was re-established for two short years at the Cappel Peace of 1529.

In the meantime the Basel and Zurich Reformers decided to promote unity among the "Protestants" in order to have a united front in the future. Zwingli's reasons for coming to the Marburg Colloquy were mostly political, Luther's primarily religious. The two men were farther apart than they had realized. Their meeting merely served to make the division final. When the Lutherans presented the Augsburg Confession to the emperor a few months later they did not include the Zwinglians. Zwingli had to submit his own separate *Fidei Ratio*. On October 11, 1531, he and the best men of the Zurich evangelicals were killed on the battle field of Cappel. Oecolampadius died a few weeks later. Henry Bullinger became Zwingli's successor and Oswald Myconius followed Oecolampadius. The Wittenberg Concord of 1536 checked the spread of Zwinglianism across the border into Upper Germany. The first Helvetian Confession tried to give new direction to the dying movement, but was only partly successful. In this year Calvin arrived on the stage at Geneva.

The weakness of the followers of Zwingli had been that they were humanists first and theologians second. Although Oecolampadius and Myconius can be compared to Melanchthon, the Zwinglian movement lacked the deep theological insights of a Luther. Bullinger, in many ways more able and more acceptable than his master, could not infuse new life into the dying movement. The bickering between Berne and Zurich had been responsible for the defeat of Cappel. Basel was still largely under the spell of Erasmus, although the famous humanist had moved away from his beloved city when the Reformation movement got too strong for him. But he returned often to Basel and the friendship between him and the Zwinglians continued. Other Zwinglians, like Kessler in St. Gall, were in reality good Lutherans. Luther's judgment that everything hinged on Zwingli's denial of the authority of Holy Scriptures in the Communion controversy became true after the death of the Zurich Reformer. Calvin saved the Reformation for Switzerland, but in turn he was influenced by Zwingli's followers who, in the *Consensus Tigurinus* of 1549, made the division between the two major branches of Protestant Christianity permanent.

Before Calvin's arrival in French Switzerland the Reformation had been largely carried on by William Farel, Anton Froment, and Peter Viret. Geneva which had joined the Swiss Confederation in 1531 had just recently become evangelical and driven out its Catholic bishop.

The Geneva Period

Jean Caulvin, from Noyon, France, had been converted through Luther's teaching. At first as secret disciple, as "Nicodemite," then openly he had proclaimed the Gospel in France but was soon forced to leave. In Basel, where Erasmus and Oecolampadius had given the theological-philosophical foundation to Zwinglianism, the French Reformer wrote a treatise which was quite different from anything ever produced before in that city. Calvin's "Institutes of

Christian Religion" put him into the same class with Luther. The Wittenbergers accepted him almost immediately. Luther had the highest praise for him. This had been in 1536. Shortly thereafter William Farel stopped him as he was passing through Geneva and with a terrible oath forced him to stay.

At first the work of Calvin and Farel prospered. But since Swiss Protestantism was disorganized and indifferent to the happenings elsewhere, the two Reformers soon found out that they could not carry out their plans in the gay city on Lac Leman. In 1537 Calvin had published his "Instruction and Confession of Faith" and had forced the city council to pass ordinances for strict observance of all doctrinal and moral maxims contained therein. But the lax members of the community refused to take the oath of allegiance required of them and also refused to leave the city. In February 1538 the enemies of Calvin and Farel won the majority in the council and exiled the two Reformers. Farel went to Neuchatel where he stayed and worked until his death with great blessings, while Calvin became Lutheran pastor in Strassburg. After three years he was back in Geneva as absolute ruler. In the "Ordonnances Ecclésiastiques" of November 1541 he established the theocratic government for Geneva which has come to be associated with the term Calvinism.

Geneva was still a boiling cauldron, but by 1545 the fanatical followers of Calvin had won their way. In 1544 the rector of the University of Geneva, Sebastian Castellio, an excellent humanist scholar, was expelled from the city and whatever had been left of humanism until this time no longer enjoyed the right of existence under Calvin's rule. The merchant Pierre Ameaux, who had voiced some "dangerous ideas," was forced to recant, dressed in a shirt and with bare feet. Jacques Gruet was executed for blasphemy in 1547. The syndic Ami Perrin, a former friend of Calvin, became the leader of the opposition. From time to time little revolutions broke out and Calvin's life was often in danger, but these outbreaks were cruelly suppressed. When Jerome Bolsec attacked Calvin's doctrine of predestination he was put into prison. Michael Servetus who had fled to Geneva did not fare that well. He was publicly burned on October 27, 1553.

Even during Calvin's lifetime Calvinism became a world power. Lutheranism had always been a religious movement, even though at times little territorial princes and the Scandinavian kings had abused it for political purposes. But Calvinism had, after the first few years, become a strange blend of politico-religious amalgam which it retained wherever it spread during the next decades and centuries. After 1550 the French Protestants were no longer called "Luthériens." They developed the Huguenot movement which in reality was a politically subversive religious state within the state. In England the state churchism of Cranmer, Somerset, and Edward VI was the result of Calvin's influence. In Scotland theocratic tendencies and religious terror became evident under John Knox, who had lived in Geneva with Calvin. The evangelical movement in Hungary became predominantly Calvinistic. His influence was strong in Poland.

The Swiss Reformation Completed

Calvin's strong personality forced itself upon the remnants of the Zwinglian movement. This led, as we have seen, to the final break with Lutheranism. By that time Luther had been dead several years.

The Consensus Tigurinus, written by Bullinger, brought about an agreement on the doctrine of the Lord's Supper between Zurich and Geneva. Its theology is somewhere between Zwingli's extreme position on the one side and Calvin's earlier leanings to the Lutheran doctrine on the other. Calvin sacrificed only what had been sacrificed by Melanchthon long ago. It was unfortunate for him that by then the star of Melanchthon had been eclipsed and that a strongly confessional Lutheranism had become dominant in Germany, not only in Lutherlands, but especially in Upper Germany which had formerly been Zwinglian. Brenz and the other Swabian theologians were staunchly Lutheran. The Strassburgers were either dead or had moved. Calvin was almost at once attacked by Lutheran theologians who, under the leadership of Joachim Westphal, launched a double-pronged attack against the Swiss and against the crypto-Calvinists, meaning Melanchthon and his followers. Yet during Calvin's lifetime there was hope that the breach might yet be healed. Calvin's successor, Théodore de Bèze and the ever active Henry Bullinger made the break official with the publication of the *Confessio Helvetica Posterior* in 1566. Calvin had died in 1564.

It is idle to ask what would have happened if Luther would have lived another 10 or 15 years, or if Calvin would have died 10 or 15 years earlier. Calvin considered Melanchthon Luther's legitimate successor. During his Strassburg stay the influence of the Melanchthonian brand of Lutheran theology had been profound. In his own theological thinking he was very much like Luther. He understood Scripture better than Zwingli. He was an excellent exegete. Although he never grasped the true distinction between Law and Gospel which is the basis of all Lutheran theology he never tried to put reason before Scripture as Zwingli had done and as Zwingli's followers were doing. Thus an alliance between Wittenberg and Geneva would have been more natural than the alliance between Geneva and Zurich which watered down Calvin's theology. That this alliance between Wittenberg and Geneva did not come about is partly the fault of the Lutherans. When Calvin looked for an alignment the Lutherans were split hopelessly. "Wittenberg" was no longer the seat of Lutheran theology.

Ulrich Zwingli (1484-1531)

"Though I must admit that Luther lacked moderation, yet by freely exposing and censuring the crimes of the prelates, if they continued to be bad, he would finally frighten them and put some sense of shame into them."[1] These words written by Zwingli to his friend Oswald Myconius, later the great theologian of Zwinglianism, on April 2, 1520, express more clearly than all later volumes and arguments the gulf that separated him from Luther. He admired Luther for the same reason for which Erasmus, Pirckheimer, Sickingen, and Hutten admired him. "He has touched the belly of the monks and the crown of the pope," said Erasmus. "He has cornered Eck," said Pirckheimer. And Hutten wrote to Melanchthon: "Sickingen loves Luther partly because he seems good to him and

to others and is therefore hateful to those men." To Luther he
wrote: "I, Hutten, will cling to you to my last breath. Many dogs
surround you and the council of the malignant besieges you. . . .
God, the just and strong judge, can no longer connive at such
wickedness."[2]

These were the sentiments of typical humanists in the early days
of the Reformation. Zwingli's were not different. He had been born
on January 1, 1484, less than two months after Luther, at Wildhaus

ZWINGLI

in the Toggenburg Valley, near St. Gall. Like Luther he came of
peasant stock. His father served as chief magistrate of the small
village. His mother, Margaret Moile, was related to an abbot. Unlike Luther, however, Zwingli was from his youth inspired with
enthusiasm for the classics. His heaven, like Dante's, was peopled
with heathen philosophers. There was room for Socrates, Plato,
Aristotle, and other "god-fearing pagans."

Zwingli studied at Basel and Berne and went, in 1500, to Vienna
to study philosophy. Soon he returned to Basel where for a time

he taught school. He was ordained to the priesthood at the age of 22 and became a parish priest at Glarus. There he stayed 10 years. During those 10 years he laid the spiritual and intellectual foundation for his later work. Vexed by the thought of his salvation he very systematically studied the Word of God, the Greek language, some Hebrew, the Church Fathers, and sought advice from Erasmus and other humanists. What a difference between the soul struggle of the monk in Erfurt and the professor in Wittenberg, and the leisurely attained assurance of salvation of the unhurried parson of Glarus. His friends gave the serene parish priest the name "Cicero."

While studying the works of Pico della Mirandola, Zwingli received his first shock. From then on we may detect an underlying scepticism towards Rome. But his chief interests were those of practical reforms, like the objectionable features of Swiss soldiering which he had experienced as army chaplain at the victory of Novara and the defeat of Marignano. When he came to Zurich in 1518 he promoted first those reforms which did not arouse Roman opposition. Thus his statement that he started the Reformation of the Church before Luther, spoken in anger and self-defense years later, is not quite true. However, once he got started he proceeded more radically than the German Reformer. The principle according to which the Zurich Reformation was carried out has been mentioned before: "Forbid everything that is not expressly commanded in the Bible," a principle which is still present in twentieth century Reformed theology.

After the Reformation in Zurich had been completed in less than two years Zwingli married, a year before Luther, Anna Reinhard. Little did he suspect then that he would be involved in a serious struggle with Luther and that the Catholic opposition in Switzerland would muster enough force to all but destroy the young Reformation movement.

In 1523 Zwingli had become acquainted with the doctrines of the Dutchman Cornelis Henrixs Hoen, from The Hague, who understood the words "this is" in the Words of Institution to mean "this signifies." Fascinated by this thought which appealed to his reason he obtained the consent of Oecolampadius and Bucer for his symbolical interpretation. In his "Commentary on True and False Religion," written in 1525, he publicly proclaimed his new ideas. After Luther's rejoinder to Erasmus which was published in December 1525 Zwingli became more and more resentful of the Wittenberg professor. Luther hated reason in all matters of faith, Zwingli was above all a rationalist who followed logic even if it conflicted with the Word of God.

The fight began inauspiciously. Brenz had championed the doctrine of the Real Presence, while Luther up to this time had been non-committal. Zwingli had advanced the symbolic interpretation. Bugenhagen had become involved, defending Brenz' position. It was not until 1527 that the great literary feud erupted. The two Reformers crossed swords again and again. In February Zwingli had written his "Friendly Exegesis," Luther answered in April with the abusive language he could at times muster: "That these Words 'This Is My Body' Still Stand, Against the Fanatics," which was answered in kind by Zwingli, in June, with the treatise: "That the Words . . . Still Have Their Original Meaning." Finally, in March 1528, Luther published his "Great Confession of the Lord's Supper." What angered Zwingli was the patronizing tone of Luther's treatises. Zwingli was a proud and self-confident man who did not like to be treated "like an ass," not even by Luther. On August 30, 1528, he complained to Conrad Saum at Ulm, one of the leading Zwinglians in Germany: "That rash man, Luther, keeps killing human and divine wisdom in his books, though it would have been easy to restore this wisdom among the pious. But since the heretics, that is his followers, together with the wicked, have become so deaf to all truth that they refuse to listen, I was for a long time doubtful about expending this enormous labor which I knew would be vain. . . . May I die if he does not surpass Eck in impurity, Cochlaeus in audacity, and, in brief, all the vices of men . . . ." Some years before Luther had written to Gregory Casel: "In a word, either they or we must be ministers of Satan! There is not room here for negotiation or mediation."[3]

These two excerpts, not written for publication, give an indication of the intensity of ill feeling, not to say hatred, between the two men who had greeted each other as fellow-Reformers in the

early years of the Reformation. But in spite of the fact that both
avowed that negotiations were useless, they did meet, in October
1529, at Marburg. The account which Justus Jonas gave of the
historic colloquy has been quoted in his biography. By the late
afternoon of the meeting the lines of demarcation were clearly
drawn. Walter Koehler reconstructed the proceedings from the
original sources some years ago. Here are some of the exchanges
which at the same time give a good insight into the mental pro-
cesses of the two antagonists. Zwingli and Luther were arguing
about the Real Presence.

Zwingli: Oecolampadius and I gladly admit: Certainly God can
make it possible for one body to be in different places at once, but
that He does this in the Lord's Supper demands proof. The Holy
Scriptures always place Christ in a specific place, such as, in the
crib, the temple, in the desert, on the cross, in the grave, on the
right hand of the Father.

Luther: With such passages one cannot prove anything except
that Christ at certain times was in a specific place; that, however,
He is eternally and always in a specific place and limited . . . that
can never be proved on the basis of these passages.

Zwingli: I have just proved that Christ was in one place. You
prove, on the contrary, that He exists without space or in many
places simultaneously. . . . It would be a shame to believe in such
an important doctrine [the Real Presence], teach and defend it,
and yet be unable or unwilling to cite a single Scripture passage
to prove it.

Luther (taking the cover from the inscription on the table):
"This Is My Body!" Here is our Scripture passage. . . . Since the
words of my Lord Jesus Christ stand here . . . I cannot truthfully
pass over them, but must confess and believe that the Body of
Christ is there.

Zwingli (leaping to his feet): Dear Doctor, you admit Christ's
Body is spatially in the Lord's Supper. You just said: "The Body of
Christ must be there!" There, there, there, that is an adverb of
space.

Luther: I simply repeated the words of Christ and did not look
for a snare. . . . Whether He is there in space or outside of space,

I do not wish to question. . . . No mortal can prove it one way or another.[4]

The meeting ended the next day. Luther thanked Zwingli, adding: "Pardon me, please, for now and then speaking rather harsh words against you, for I am after all flesh and blood." Zwingli, in tears, said: "I have always had the great desire to remain on friendly terms with you. . . . There are no men in Italy or France with whom I would rather be friendly than with you." They parted after signing the Marburg Articles.

Zwingli died two years later. He was killed by a band of mercenaries, his body was quartered and burned with dung by the bestial soldiery. A boulder now marks the place where he fell. "They may kill the body, but not the soul. Thus spoke Ulrich Zwingli who for truth and freedom of the Christian Church died a hero's death. October 11, 1531."[5]

Henry Bullinger (1504-1575)

Henry Bullinger, the man who inherited Zwingli's mantle, was born in Bremgarten, in 1504. He was one of the mildest and kindest among the Reformers, quite different from the arrogant Zwingli and the harsh Luther. He was firm but conciliatory. In his refusal to compromise he was more akin to Luther than to Melanchthon. His life was above reproach. He was thought of kindly by both friend and antagonist. He lived long enough to steer the faltering boat of Zwinglianism into the safe harbor of Calvinism and to give to the movement its final form, the Second Helvetic Confession.

At 19 years of age Bullinger was already teaching at the monastery in Cappel. He instituted the first monastic reforms in Switzerland. Having left the monastery he returned, in 1529, to his native town as evangelical pastor. He was loved by his fellow-citizens and highly esteemed, in spite of his youth. After the disastrous battle of Cappel and Zwingli's untimely death Bullinger was forced to seek refuge within the walls of Zurich.

He was only 27 years old at his friend's death. The orphaned congregations in Basel and Berne called him, but he decided to stay in Zurich. Thus he became the successor of Zwingli at the Minster. When the city council tried to muffle him Bullinger led a procession of his fellow-pastors to the council hall protesting that "the Word of God cannot be bound." From then on pastors were allowed to appear before the council at any time to talk over their problems with the city fathers.

To Luther whom he esteemed highly as a pious man of God, but of whose temper he was afraid, he never found a close relation. In December 1534 he thought that a compromise could be worked out in the Communion controversy, but when he was asked to send representatives to Wittenberg, he refused to do so. Bullinger and his followers did not sign the Wittenberg Concord which was to establish peace between Zurich and Wittenberg. Nevertheless, Bullinger and Luther remained on friendly terms because Luther thought more highly of Bullinger's firm stand than of Zwingli's, Bucer's, and Melanchthon's readiness to compromise.

After Luther's death Bullinger won over Calvin to the Zwinglian *Consensus Tigurinus*, the agreement of Zurich. He continued as the revered head of the Zurich Reformed in spite of Calvin's ascendancy. In 1566, two years after Calvin's death, he gave to the Reformed the Confession which holds a place among them comparable to that of the Augsburg Confession among the Lutherans.

Bullinger was an excellent exegete. Even in controversies he remained cool and dignified. He published Zwingli's works and glorified him in his "Chronicles of Switzerland." He was an important historian and a well-known literary figure. Best known among his works is his drama "Lucretia," written in 1533, which breathes a truly republican spirit. His home in Zurich was a refuge for many Italians, Frenchmen, Englishmen, and Germans who were persecuted for the sake of their faith. He died in 1575.

In 1534 Bullinger had written a confessional statement in which he took away some of the sharp edges of Zwingli's position on the Lord's Supper. This statement which followed more or less the wording of the *Confessio Tetrapolitana* of Bucer, Capito, and Hedio, admitted that in Holy Communion the Body of Christ is truly present for the believers as spiritual food. Melanchthon was immediately in favor of resuming the negotiations with the Zurich Reformers, Bucer and his friends pushed the project, Luther reluctantly agreed, and the meeting was set. After preliminary discussions in Kassel, where Landgrave Philip again took a very active part, the Swiss and their friends were invited to come to Eisenach. Bucer and Capito from Strassburg, Wolfgang Musculus and Lycosthenes from Augsburg, Schuler from Memmingen, Frecht from Ulm, Otther from Esslingen, Matthew Alber and Schradin from Reutlingen, German from Fuerfeld, and Algersheimer from Frankfurt soon arrived in Eisenach where they were informed that Luther, due to his recent illness, was unable to attend. They decided to continue the journey to Wittenberg where they arrived on Sunday, May 21, 1536. Bullinger and his friends were not with them. For the next week the two parties—on Luther's side Melanchthon, Bugenhagen, Jonas, Cruciger, Menius, Myconius, Weller, and Roerer participated—met and ironed out their differences, especially the question of whether the unworthy and unprepared receive the Lord's Body in the Sacrament. After much discussion which was carried on in a friendly way, the Wittenberg Concord was drawn up and signed on Monday, May 29, 1536.

Concerning the Lord's Supper the Concord stated that with bread and wine the Body and Blood is "substantially" present, is offered and received. The Body is not contained in the bread, but is there at the moment of Communion. Worthy and unworthy receive this Body, the former for salvation, the latter for damnation. To satisfy the partisans of Zwingli the word "unworthy" was substituted for "godless," because, as Bucer explained, those who did not at all believe could not possibly receive the Body of Christ. Luther for once did not object, whether from physical exhaustion or from theological considerations we do not know.

The greatest handicap of this Wittenberg meeting was, however, that Bullinger and his immediate circle did not show up and thus were not bound to the Concord. As a matter of fact Bullinger had just written a foreword to a new edition of Zwingli's "Exposition of Faith" in which the old heresies were not only repeated, but in which Bullinger praised the dead friend as "the teacher of the true faith." At the same time the letters of Zwingli and Oecolampadius were printed in Basel, in which many offensive statements and personal insults against Luther were contained. Bucer had written a foreword to this publication. The Swiss were once more proclaiming the obnoxious teaching that besides the saints of the Old Testament pious heathen like Hercules, Theseus, Socrates, Aristides, Numa, Camillus, etc., were enjoying the blessings of the Christian heaven. All this must have filled Luther with great misgivings. Nevertheless he did not rebuke Bullinger, but carried out his plans for the Wittenberg Concord.

After the signing of the Wittenberg Concord Luther tried again and again to win the Swiss. He pleaded with the Basel Mayor Meyer "to do his best" to influence Bullinger. But some of the Swiss, especially the Reformers of Zurich and Berne, were offended by the language of the Concord. Vadianus, in St. Gall, had just published an attack against the Catholic doctrine of transubstantiation which also attacked Luther's doctrine. Bucer's efforts to win his Swiss friends for the Concord hit a blank wall. The Swiss prepared a document which they sent to Luther and in which they voiced their objections. Surprisingly, however, Luther again wrote a friendly reply, on February 17, 1537, in which he did not touch on the dogmatic differences at all.

By this time Bullinger must have been overjoyed. This joy was heightened when Luther finally sent a detailed answer on December 1, 1537, in which he apologized for his former harshness and added: "I humbly beg of you to look upon me as a person of sincere heart. I shall do whatever I can to help the cause of the Concord. This God knows and I call upon Him as witness. For discord has neither helped me nor anyone else, but has done much harm."[6] He concluded by asking the Zurichers to stand together with him against the devil and the pope. Thus the man whom Bullinger and his friends had often labeled the "Lutheran Pope" wrote to them as a brother in faith.

Nevertheless, Bullinger and his friends discussed Luther's propositions with some hesitation at their Convention in Zurich. Some even insisted now that Luther should publicly disclaim his former attacks against Zwingli. But they were a minority. On May 4,

1538, they wrote Luther that they and he were, "God be thanked, agreed in the understanding and in substance and that there was no longer any quarrel between them." In the meantime Luther had written a personal letter to Bullinger which crossed paths with the official declaration of the Zurich convention. In this letter he had said that he had wronged Zwingli, that he had thought differently of him after the Marburg Colloquy, but that he still had his misgivings when Zwingli suddenly died without having seen the truth of the doctrine concerning the Lord's Supper. He also admitted that Bullinger's new edition of Zwingli's "Exposition of Faith" had hurt him. "This I write to you," he stated, "that you may see that I am honest with you. You may believe that we are wrong. God's judgment will decide. We on our part cannot go along with everything you propose, unless we are ready to burden our consciences. This you will not expect of us. But there is no greater joy which I may experience before my end than that we would speak the same language and think the same in Christ."[7] When he received the official communication from Zurich, he exclaimed: "Ah, these are pious people. We must have patience with them a little while until we can win them!"[8]

Bullinger, however, in spite of his joy reiterated Zwingli's doctrines in a letter which he wrote to Luther on September 1, 1538. The honeymoon was over. In his treatise "On Councils and the Church" of 1539 Luther again attacked Zwinglianism and in his "Admonition to Prayer Against the Turk" of 1541 he mentioned in one breath the Zwinglians and Anabaptists among the "desperate evil sects and heresies." Finally, less than two years before his death he published his "Brief Confession on the Sacrament" in which he made short shrift with "Carlstadt, Zwingli, Oecolampadius, Schwenkfeld and their disciples wherever they are found." The Zurichers replied in kind. But Luther did not answer again.

Thus ended the relationship between Luther and Bullinger which had given such great promise in the early years after Zwingli's death. No other choice was left to Bullinger but to lead the remnant of his movement into the camp of Calvin. Five years after the last sharp exchange with Wittenberg Zurich and Geneva were united into one movement.

John Oecolampadius (1482-1531)

John Hussgen, called Oecolampadius, the Melanchthon of Zwingli, was born at Weinsberg, Wuerttemberg, where he received his first schooling. Later he studied at Heilbronn and Bologna, but soon returned to his native country and enrolled at the University of Heidelberg, studying theology. He developed into an excellent Greek and Hebrew scholar. In 1503 he was awarded the Bachelor of Divinity degree.

In 1515 Oecolampadius became pastor of the Cathedral in Basel where he served directly under the tolerant Bishop Christopher von Uttenheim who later became a secret follower of the evangelicals. In 1518 Oecolampadius began preaching against introducing secular stories and legends into sermons. He was especially opposed to the so-called "Devil Stories" which, without Biblical foundation, were used abundantly in the Easter sermons. In 1520 he published a Greek grammar.

His fame spread rapidly. He was soon invited to introduce the Reformation at Augsburg, but instead he retired to a monastery in order to find clarity in his mind and peace of soul. In 1522 he was chaplain to the ill-fated Franz von Sickingen. After Sickingen's death he returned to Basel as Lutheran pastor.

Oecolampadius who in many ways was more like Luther than Zwingli, because he was more conservative than the practical and impatient Swiss, began gradually to introduce the Reformation in the city of Erasmus. At first he attacked only the monasteries, the false worship of God through good works, but finally—under the influence of Zwingli—his proposals became more radical. The city council joined him in 1525. In 1528 he married the well-known Willibrandis Rosenblatt, the marryingest widow of the Reformation era, who outlived four distinguished husbands: Keller, Oecolampadius, Capito, and Bucer.

The influence of Oecolampadius upon the Upper German Reformers had always been strong. After he became associated with Zwingli he served as the main connecting link between Zurich and Strassburg and other cities who were anxious to establish unity between Wittenberg and the Swiss. He took part in many impor-

tant meetings. He was at Berne in 1528 where the partisans of the
old faith were defeated, he was at Marburg in 1529 where he broke
the ice during a preliminary talk with Luther, and at various disputations with Anabaptist leaders.

Oecolampadius died shortly after Zwingli, on November 24, 1531.
Thus the Swiss lost their two greatest leaders in one year. Bullinger
took Zwingli's place. Oswald Myconius followed Oecolampadius
as the theologian of the Swiss Reformers.

On July 21, 1519, Melanchthon sent a report on the Leipzig Colloquy to his friend Oecolampadius, which he concluded with the
words: "In Luther, now long familiarly known to me, I admire a
lively talent, learning and eloquence, and cannot help loving his
sincere and entirely Christian mind. Greet our common friends. . . .
Do not believe all that is told you about the result of this debate.
Farewell."[9] Oecolampadius now wrote the "Answer of the Un-
learned Canons" in which he defended Luther against Eck. The
following year Luther asked Spalatin for a copy of this pamphlet.
A friendly correspondence between the two men resulted. In one
of his letters, written on June 20, 1523, Luther comforted his friend
who had been offended by Erasmus' adverse criticism of his work.
"Do not let his displeasure trouble you," Luther wrote. "What
Erasmus thinks, or pretends to think, in judging things spiritual,
is abundantly shown by his books, from the first to the last. I note
the pricks he gives me now and then, but as he does it without
openly declaring himself my foe, I act as though I were unaware of
his sly attacks, though I understand him better than he thinks. He
has done what he was called to do; he has brought us from godless
studies to a knowledge of the languages; perhaps he will die with
Moses in the plains of Moab, for he does not go forward to the
better studies—those that pertain to godliness. I greatly wish he
would stop commenting on the Holy Scriptures . . . for he is not
equal to this task. . . . He has done enough in showing us the evil;
to show us the good and to lead us into the promised land, he is, as
I see it, unable . . . ."[10] When this passage came to the attention of
Erasmus through the indiscretion of Oecolampadius he "was
excited with indignation." He retorted in a letter to Zwingli: "Luther has written him . . . that not much attention must be paid me

in the things of the Spirit. . . . He said, too, that I like Moses have
led Israel out of Egypt but would die in the plains. Would that
he were the Joshua who would lead us all into the land of
promise . . . ."[11] At the beginning of 1525 when Oecolampadius had
taken up for Carlstadt, the relationship between Luther and the
Basel Reformer cooled perceptibly. "Oecolampadius and Pellicanus," Luther wrote to Spalatin, "write that they agree with Carlstadt's opinions, and Anémond de Coct is so obstinate that he
threatens to write against me unless I give up my position. Behold
Satan's portents!"[12] And in October 1525 he cautioned Gottschalk
Crusius: "We must be the more suspicious of this doctrine [of
Zwingli] because Carlstadt was the first to proclaim it, and now
Zwingli and Oecolampadius reject all his proofs for it, though they
attempt to defend it on other grounds, and yet the foolish fellows
offer only the chief arguments of Carlstadt which they have already condemned. It seems to me a ridiculous spirit . . . ."[13] To the
clergy of Strassburg he wrote: "Who does not rejoice in the praise
that you accord to the sanctity of Zwingli and Oecolampadius and
to their churches? But see where Zwingli comes to in his doctrine
of original sin. Just what you mean by 'sanctity' and 'Churches' I
do not know . . . ."[14] From then on the names Zwingli and Oecolampadius were always associated in his mind with each other, although
he reserved most of his attacks for "Zwingel." In his hierarchy of
heretics he lists at that time: Carlstadt, Zwingli, Oecolampadius,
Cellarius, Krautwald, Schwenkfeld. Yet at the same time he wrote
to Nicholas Hausmann: "I am heartily sorry for Oecolampadius.
He is very much of a man, but held captive in that sectarian sacrilege by empty and worthless arguments. God have mercy on him!"[15]
and again, on January 10, 1527, "I am heartily sorry that that excellent man, Oecolampadius, has been pushed by Satan into this
abyss. . . . The Lord draw him out!"[16] The two men met face to
face at Marburg. After it was all over Luther wrote to Kate on
October 4, 1529: "I think God blinded them [Zwingli and Oecolam-
padius] that they could not get beyond these points,"[17] and to Nicholas Gerbel in Strassburg he sent the final word: "We ought to have
charity and peace even with our foes, and so we plainly told them
that unless they grow wiser in this point [of Holy Communion]

they may indeed have our charity, but cannot by us be considered as brothers and members of Christ."[18]

Two years later both Zwingli and Oecolampadius died.

John Calvin (1509-1564)

In 1539 Luther saw the treatise which Calvin had written in response to the open letter of Bishop Sadoleto to the Geneva Christians and was pleased to read that Calvin believed in the "true Communion of flesh and blood of Christ" and opposed the "local presence" of the body in the bread. In a letter to Bucer, on October 14, 1539, he expressed his joy that Calvin was serving in Strassburg at the side of the other friends. Melanchthon too reported that Calvin was high in Luther's favor. He liked the positive statements of Calvin and did not mind that the attack against the "local presence" might have been directed against him as well as against the Catholics. "I hope he will think better of us in the future," Luther said, "in the meantime it is meet that we should suffer a little from this excellent man."[19] When Calvin's Catechism, "The Instruction and Confession of Faith," had been translated into Latin, Luther was anxious to obtain a copy. He went into the store of a Wittenberg bookseller, took a copy off the shelves, read part of it right there and said approvingly: "The author is certainly a scholarly and pious man; if only Oecolampadius and Zwingli would have been as clear from the beginning, such a terrible quarrel would have never happened."[20] This was on April 13, 1545, less than a year before Luther's death.

We must not assume that this friendliness would have lasted, had Luther lived longer. His acquaintance with Calvin's theology was superficial. He esteemed him because he was a theologian's theologian. Zwingli and Oecolampadius appeared to him superficial, Calvin was thorough. Luther did not live to witness the alliance between Zurich and Geneva, the *Consensus Tigurinus* between Bullinger and Calvin.

Jean Caulvin, better known as John Calvin, was born in Noyon, Picardy, on July 10, 1509, the second son of Gerard Caulvin, a notary, and Jeanne Franc, a daughter of an innkeeper at Cambrai.

Little is known of his early years, except that he was educated in the home of the family de Montmor. In 1521 he received his tonsure and accompanied his patron to Paris where he attended the Collège de la Marche, studying under the famous Mathurin Cordier who later taught at Geneva. Calvin preserved a life-long friendship for his revered teacher and dedicated to him his commentary on the First Epistle to the Thessalonians. In Paris Calvin also attended the Collège de Montaigu showing great promise during disputa-

CALVIN

tions. The oft repeated story that the taciturn Reformer was anti-social as a youth has no foundation. At Montaigu he had many friends.

In 1527, at the age of eighteen, Calvin was appointed parish priest of St. Martin de Marteville. Two years later he moved to Pont l'Evêque. His father who had been influenced by "Lutheran" ideas and had begun to doubt the authority of the Church, sought to safeguard the future of his son by drawing him away from the life of a religious and enticing him to study law. Therefore, young Calvin, not yet 20 years old, moved from Paris to Orleans and later to Bourges where he studied under the brilliant Italian Andrea Alciati. At that time he read for the first time the New Testament in the original Greek.

After his father's death in 1531 Calvin returned to Paris and openly opposed scholasticism. After a visit to Orleans and his native Noyon he returned once more to Paris where in the meantime persecution against the "Luthériens" had broken out. One of his old friends, Nicholas Cop, now rector at the Sorbonne, was defending the doctrine of salvation by faith alone. The Sorbonne which 13 years before had condemned Luther forced Cop to resign. He fled to Basel in neighboring Switzerland. Calvin, on account of his friendship with Cop, was also forced to flee. He went to Angoulême as guest of Louis de Tillet. It was here while in hiding that he began to write the most important work of the Calvinist Reformation, "The Institutes of Christianity." At Angoulême he was also influenced by the famous theologian Lefèvre d'Etaples whose theology had influenced Luther almost two decades before, and whom he met now personally. On May 4, 1534, Calvin resigned his ecclesiastic offices, was arrested and imprisoned. After his release from prison and a last hurried trip to Paris, Orleans, Poitiers, Calvin took "Lutheran Communion" in a grotto near Poitiers, using a rock for a table. Since his life was now in grave danger he decided to follow his friend Cop to Basel. There both Lutherans and Zwinglians received him with open arms. Bullinger and Myconius became his friends.

As King Francis I of France was anxious at that time to win the support of the German Lutheran princes against Charles V, he assured the Lutheran princes that he was not fighting against Lutheran doctrine but merely against the Anabaptist revolutionary ideas. Calvin was angry at this falsehood and prepared his Institutes for publication, dedicating them with a famous letter to Francis I.

After a short visit to Ferrara where the Duchess Renata was harboring a number of exiled evangelicals, Calvin returned to Basel by way of France, saying farewell to his native country forever. He had intended to settle at Basel or Strassburg, but on account of the war between Charles V and Francis I he went to Geneva where William Farel "forced" him to stay. With the interruption of his short exile in Strassburg, Geneva now became the base and bastion of the Calvinist Reformation.

The work of Calvin at Geneva has been described elsewhere. His theology was as exclusive as Luther's. He brooked no contradiction. At times his character was sullied by unnecessary harshness. He burned Michael Servetus, the father of Unitarianism, at the stake. He had every Genevese spy on the morals and private behavior of his fellow-men. But he also did much to give moral greatness to the Reformation movement. His emphasis on the terrifying wrath of God, even his teaching of predestination put a definite stamp on Protestant Christianity. He was the lawgiver among the Reformers.

Exactly eighteen years after Luther had preached his last sermon in Eisleben Calvin preached also his last sermon, on February 16, 1564. The next few months he spent in constant prayer and died quietly in the arms of his faithful friend, Théodore de Bèze, on May 27, 1564. His grave is not known.

Other Reformers

Besides these great four there are others who helped in the work of the Reformation in Switzerland. Oswald Myconius, the theologian of the second generation of Zwinglians, William Farel, the fiery first Reformer of Geneva, who later left the field to Calvin and retired to Neuchatel. The Zurich associates of Zwingli and Bullinger, Rudolph zum Buhl, professor of Greek, Ulrich Funk, the glazier who was present at Marburg, Leo Jud, who supported Zwingli's reforms, Conrad Pellicanus, and others. There were Diebold III von Geroldseck and the numerous supporters who died with Zwingli at Cappel. There were the two Blaurers, Ambrose and Thomas, reformers of Constance, Otto Braunfels, the botanist who played a prominent part in the Reformation of Basel and Berne, Ulrich Campel who wrote the first Zwinglian Catechism, Rudolph Frey, the Basel merchant, also at Marburg, who helped in the difficult task of reforming his city. There were Sebastian Hofmeister in Schaffhausen, John Kessler in St. Gall, Francis Kolb in Berne, where he worked with Manuel and Musculus, Tschudi in Glarus, and many others. These men and their successors gave to the Swiss Reformation its special mark which it has retained to this day.

IX.

English Friends and Foes

At the conference of Calais where the English and French kings were meeting in July 1520 King Henry VIII walked up to Erasmus and patting him on the shoulder asked him: "Erasmus, why don't you defend that good Luther?" whereupon "that scoundrel Erasmus" answered: "Because I am not enough of a theologian; now that the professors of Louvain have put me down as a grammarian I don't touch such things." The English king was so pleased by that answer that he dismissed the wily humanist with a gift of fifty ducats.[1]

This incident, reported in a letter of Oswald Myconius to Rudolph Clivanus in Milan, indicated the early preoccupation of King Henry VIII with the theological aspects of the Lutheran Reformation. The following year he wrote his famous "Assertion of the Seven Sacraments" for which he earned the title "Defender of the Faith" from the grateful Leo X, a title, incidentally, which his Protestant successors still bear with pride. "As nothing is more the duty of a Christian prince," Henry wrote to Leo X, "than to preserve the Christian religion against its enemies, ever since I knew of Luther's heresy, I have made a study to extirpate it."[2] Sir Richard Wingfield was able to report shortly thereafter from the court of the emperor: "As to the matter of Luther, the Emperor sayde to be ryght glad to know that the Kynge hys broder [Henry VIII] had

244

wele takyn the manner of his proceedings in that behalf, sayenge that wher the sayde Luther had as well prechyd as also wryttyn moche false doctryne to the abusion of the grosse and unlernyd people, that it was the parte and office of the princes to do their best . . . that the said people might be reduced fro suche error as the said Luther may have set them in, and thanked the king most highly for his exhortation and his offered aid."[3] Luther, however, did not take this attack lying down. He answered the king in a sharply-worded treatise, "Against Henry, King of England." When a friend asked him why he had written so sharply, he replied on August 28, 1522: "You ask why I have answered the King of England so sharply. . . . I would have you to know that I did it on purpose, and will henceforth show no more gentleness to blasphemers and liars. . . . You know that Christ and Peter and Paul were not always gentle. How often does Christ call the Jews 'a generation of vipers,' 'murderers,' 'children of the devil,' and 'fools'? . . . And as for Paul, how sharply he reproves! He calls them dogs, apostles of the devil, liars, deceivers, falsifiers, seducers, children of the devil. I shall say nothing of the prophets. . . . My work is not that of one who can take a middle course, and yield this or give up that, as I have done hitherto, fool that I was."[4]

Thus the stage was set for the relationship between Henry VIII and Luther. Besides Henry many other Englishmen opposed the Reformation: Sir Thomas More despised Luther; Charles Booth, Bishop of Hereford, confiscated Luther's books; John Fisher, Bishop of Rochester, wrote two learned treatises against the Wittenberg Reformer; Edward Lee, Archbishop of York, forbade the reading of the Greek New Testament because it led people to believe in Lutheran errors. Other fervent opponents of Luther were John Longland, Bishop of Lincoln; Henry Standish, court chaplain of Henry VIII; William Warham, Archbishop of Canterbury; the theologian Nicholas Wilson; and Thomas Cardinal Wolsey. When Henry VIII later forsook Rome some of these Catholic prelates suffered persecution and martyrdom. When Cardinal Wolsey was unable to obtain permission for the divorce of Henry from Catherine of Aragon so that he might marry Anne Boleyn, he was removed from office and the English clergy was forced to recognize the king as supreme head of the Church. In 1533 Henry VIII divorced Catherine and married Anne whom, however, he sent to her death three years later. After that he married four more times. In 1534 Parliament recognized the king as "Supreme Head in earth of the Church of England." His chief advisor became Thomas Cromwell, a ruthless politician who secretly favored the Lutheran Reformation. Henry had him beheaded in 1540. All evangelical movements within the Church were thereafter suppressed with fire and sword. The "Bloody Statute" of 1539 retained under threat of severe penalty most Catholic doctrines, including those of transubstantiation, lay cup, celibacy, private masses, and auricular confession.

Lutheran Influences

In spite of Henry's aversion to Luther the influence of Lutheranism in England was strong. Tyndale, Constantine and Joy were Lutherans at heart. Tyndale had visited Luther and never renounced his Lutheran convictions. He died a martyr's death. In the summer of 1531 Robert Barnes, the famous English theologian, asked Luther for his opinion in the matter of the king's divorce. Luther strongly opposed it. In 1533 both Dr. Barnes and the Scottish theologian Alexander Alesius matriculated at the University of Wittenberg. When Henry VIII, after his final break with Rome and the execution of many Catholic partisans, sought a *modus vivendi* with Wittenberg he used the good offices of Barnes and Alesius. Barnes later returned to England and became personal chaplain of Henry, a position which Henry Standish had occupied years before. In March 1535 Barnes was sent to Wittenberg to begin negotiations with the Lutherans for a closer alliance between Canterbury and Wittenberg. The king's intentions were purely political: To keep the pope from having his council so that no one could be forced to "return under the yoke of Rome." Bishop Fox of Hereford and Archdeacon Heyth were sent as special ambassadors to the Saxon court. The king requested the Elector John Frederick to send Melanchthon to England that he may help reform the Church. John Frederick who had denied a similar request by Francis I of France now postponed a decision until after his return from Vienna where he had travelled, then again refused to make a decision until after he had conferred with his fellow-princes of the Smalcald League. After the meeting the theologians met at Wittenberg with Luther, Melanchthon, Jonas, Cruciger and Bugenhagen. Luther outlined the points on the basis of which a fellowship could be established between Wittenberg and Canterbury. In these points he insisted on the abolition of many Roman practices which were dear to the heart of Henry VIII, who had defended these practices publicly in his "Assertion of the Seven Sacraments" and elsewhere. The Englishmen disputed the points stubbornly until April 1536, but Luther had already in January grown tired of all discussions which he considered to be fruitless. On April 10, 1536, the embassy left Wittenberg after Barnes had published his book on the "Lives of the Popes" to which Luther had written a friendly word of introduction.

Henry VIII was ill pleased with the result of the lengthy negotiations. However, he did not immediately break with Wittenberg, but asked again for an advisor. This time the elector sent Frederick Myconius to London to whom Luther entrusted a letter to Bishop Fox in which the Reformer expressed the hope that the two movements may yet come to an understanding. But privately he said that Henry VIII wanted to kill the pope and papacy only bodily, not in their soul and essence. In fact Henry, although he dismissed the Wittenberg embassy very politely and sent them home with his best wishes to Luther and the elector, did not budge from his previously announced doctrinal position. Luther remarked: "The papists will laugh up their sleeves. . . . But let it go the way he wants it. He is still the same King Hank whom I have painted in my first little book. He will find his judge."[5] He thanked God, on July 10, 1539, that He had saved the Lutheran Church "from this obnoxious king who with great desire had sought an alliance with us. Without doubt God has done this in His wisdom. I am happy that we are rid of the blasphemer."[6] When Bucer tried to bring about peace, Luther strongly discouraged his elector. Henry, he said, was a sophist and a tyrant who knows the truth but acts against his own conscience. Many Lutheran sympathizers, including Robert Barnes, suffered martyrdom during the next year. Luther published

Barnes' Confession of Faith and wrote a preface to it. Few "Lutherans" survived this second bloodbath—the first had been against the Catholics—but they continued underground until the death of Henry VIII, in 1547, created better conditions for the Reformation of the Church. Among them was Thomas Cranmer, Archbishop of Canterbury, who had married a Lutheran wife from Augsburg. The influence of Lutheranism grew stronger until, in 1554, Bloody Mary restored the jurisdiction of the pope. Cranmer and over 300 other "Evangelicals" were martyred. Under Elizabeth I the Church of England was restored in 1559.

William Tyndale (about 1492-1536)

William Tyndale, best known as the translator of the English New Testament and Pentateuch, was born near the border between England and Wales, probably in 1492. In 1510 he enrolled at Oxford where he received his master's degree in 1515. Later he moved to Cambridge, was ordained to the priesthood in 1521 and entered the household of Sir John Welsh where he lived for two years. Suspected of heresy he was dismissed, but allowed to depart in peace. During these years he had been working on his translation of the New Testament. Now, since the publication of the work was impossible in England he embarked for Hamburg from where he proceeded to Wittenberg. Here he became acquainted with Luther who encouraged him to proceed with his plans. He had his New Testament printed in Cologne. However, Cochlaeus, watchdog for Catholic supremacy, obtained an injunction against the publication. Tyndale and his printer were able to escape from the Inquisition and went to Worms where the publication was completed in 1526. From Worms copies of the New Testament were smuggled into England. Attempts were made several times to seize Tyndale, but he fled from Worms to Hesse where Landgrave Philip protected him. While he was still considered a Lutheran heretic by the Church officials in England and Germany, his writings, especially the "Parable of the Wicked Mammon," written in 1528, and the "Obedience of a Christian Man," published a few months later, put forth the principles of the English Reformation which Henry VIII adopted a few years later. Thus it can be said that Tyndale's activities on the continent strongly influenced the course of the English Reformation.

After Henry's break with Rome Tyndale was invited to return to his native land. He did not trust the amnesty which the king offered him and preferred to remain on the continent. In May 1535 he was betrayed at Antwerp by a former friend for whom he had done much, was put into prison, tried and condemned for heresy in spite of the efforts of his English friends. On October 6, 1536, the valiant man was strangled at the stake and his body burned.

Though he had been absent from England for more than a decade, Tyndale was one of the great forces in shaping the English Reformation. He was one of the greatest Bible translators, having published the New Testament and finished the five books of Moses during his lifetime. It is also believed that he translated the Old Testament from Joshua to Chronicles while in prison. Like Luther he was the first to translate the Word of God for his people from the original tongues, Greek and Hebrew, and thus has been truly called the Father of the English Bible.

Edward Lee, Archbishop of York after 1531, had written to Cardinal Wolsey on December 2, 1525, that he had advised the king not to permit Tyndale's translation of the New Testament "to enter the realm. . . . We have cause to thank God for sending such a Christian spirit to the king that the realm is hitherto preserved in integrity."[7] And almost two years later John Hackett, the English minister at the court of Margaret, Regent of the Netherlands, who had requested the suppression of the English Lutherans at Antwerp, but had been refused, reported angrily to Wolsey: "Was told at Machlyng, on the 21st, that, notwithstanding the corrections that have been done, some Antwerp printers have brought here to the market divers English books, entitled the Nywe Testament. I have come hither to see the punishment executed. Have found twenty-four in mannys hand. Am seeking for more and trust shortly to see them burned."[8] But he reported that Nicholas van Liere, "the marquis of Antwerp," and Roland van Berchem, "the drossart" (or bailiff), were asking daily for a certification from England of particular articles of heresy without which they can make no corporal punishment on the printers. Hackett had also heard that at the Frankfurt Book Fair "there were more than 2,000 such English books; but there they favor Luther and leave all good old customs. I hear that some English disciples of Luther are beginning to translate the Bible into English. The King or Wolsey had better write my Lady [the Regent Margaret] about it." The conclusion of his letter is quite pessimistic: "There is great danger in these Low Countries. Two out of three keep Luther's opinions. I am told there are many in England, but they dare not declare themselves . . . ."[9]

Among the men who assisted Tyndale in Antwerp were George Constantine, Bachelor of Canon Law, who after being seized, in 1530, for distributing the forbidden books, escaped and returned to England and became a clergyman of the Church of England. Another helper was Joy, otherwise unknown, who with Constantine was at Antwerp while the New Testament was being printed. Simon Fish, the author of "The Supplication of Beggars," a former Oxford student who had fled to Antwerp in 1525 and died in 1531. And Thomas Bilney, who had studied at Cambridge, where he became Bachelor of Laws. In 1525 he began preaching, was arrested in 1527, recanted and released in 1529, but was rearrested and burned in 1531. These men "and others whom" a repentant Francis Dynamis, otherwise unknown to us, "abhors as pestiferous followers of Luther" were working on the continent and waiting for the dawn of the Reformation in their homeland. The books which they read are listed in the confession of June 1528 of the above named Dynamis to Wolsey: Luther's "On the Bondage of the Will" and "On the Babylonian Captivity," Francis Lambert's "Commentaries," St. Augustine's "On the Letter and the Spirit" (presumably Carlstadt's edition), Luther's "Magnificat" and "On the Appointing of Ministers," Savonarola's "On the Psalm Miserere," Schwenkfeld's "The Course of God's Word" (cannot be identified), Luther's "Letter to Henry, King of England," and "a little book of an author unknown against Natalis Beda." In French they read "The Book of Deuteronomy" (cannot be identified), Farel's "The Sermon of the Lord with Exposition," and the following books no longer known to us: "On the One Mediator Christ," "On Images," "On the Fundamentals of Christian Doctrine," and "The Epistles and Gospels for 52 Weeks." Finally Tyndale's New Testament in English, with an Introduction

to the Epistle of St. Paul to the Romans. Truly a cross-section of
heretical literature! These books were found in the possession of
Dynamis as he was brought before the English ambassador at St.
Germain, Bishop Clerk of Bath. He ends by "bespeaking the usual
clemency of the Cardinal."[10]

These details which were reported to the all-powerful Cardinal
who was soon to share the fate of his victims serve to give us a
picture of the life of the English exiles and perhaps of Tyndale who
lived among them.

Thomas Cranmer (1489-1556)

The influence of Luther upon Thomas Cranmer was indirect,
but it was strong. There is evidence that Cranmer considered himself a "Lutheran" before he was suddenly and unexpectedly appointed Archbishop of Canterbury and that he secretly continued
to hold Lutheran views during the lifetime of the temperamental
"Supreme Head of the Church of England," King Henry VIII. In
any case after Henry's death he began to act more and more like
a Protestant and finally suffered martyrdom for his faith.

Born at Aslacton, Nottinghamshire, on July 2, 1489, Thomas
Cranmer followed the usual path of well-to-do English youths. Later
he complained that he had "marvellously severe and cruel school-
masters," but they did not keep him from his favorite sports into
which his father had initiated him. He liked especially hunting and
hawking. After the death of his father his mother sent him to
Cambridge where he eventually became a Fellow at Jesus College.
For some unknown reason there was a break in his promising career.
It has been surmised that he had married "Black Joan," the daughter
of a local innkeeper, a love-match which severely handicapped his
advancement. However, Joan died soon after the marriage and
Cranmer had the opportunity to rehabilitate himself. He was reinstated as a Fellow, ordained to the priesthood in 1523 and made
a Doctor of Theology.

During the following years Cranmer was considered one of the
most promising young professors at the University. But on a trip
he met Henry VIII who was very much impressed by his sharp wit.

The king, in those days, had only one passion: To be divorced from his unloved wife. Cranmer was asked by the councillors of the king to give his opinion as a theologian and seeing his chance, he said what the king wanted to hear and what was correct according to canon law: That the marriage of Henry VIII and Catherine of Aragon was null and void because Catherine had been married to Henry's brother before the latter's death. Furthermore, Cranmer reasoned that since it could be proven that the marriage between Catherine and Prince Arthur, Henry's older brother, had been consummated before the latter's demise, Henry was now living in adultery and should be freed from this burden upon his conscience by a simple declaration of the universities without waiting for a decision from Rome.

The overjoyed king now immediately employed Cranmer, commanded him to forget about all scholarly pursuits and to devote himself exclusively to the pursuit of the happiness of his king. Cranmer was sent to Germany where he sounded out the Lutheran princes and Free Cities and even the Emperor Charles. Although his mission was less than a success he found one theologian, Andrew Osiander at Nuremberg, who favored the scheme. In return Cranmer fell in love with Osiander's niece, a second love match which almost ended his career, married her in 1532 and returned to England.

How surprised he was at the next move of the unpredictable king! Henry cast all ecclesiastic rules to the wind and appointed Thomas Cranmer Archbishop of Canterbury, a truly embarrassing situation for a newly-wed, devoted husband who now sought confirmation for his office from the pope. Although the archbishop remained always faithful to his Lutheran wife, he was forced to hide her before the eyes of the world. The pope who was not informed of the new archbishop's marital status approved the nomination and Cranmer was consecrated last Roman Catholic Archbishop of Canterbury on March 30, 1533. Within a year, as he was expected to do he had led the king out of wedlock and the Church of England out of the Church of Rome. Speed was necessary, since Anne Boleyn, the next chosen queen, was already "great with child." In June 1533 Cranmer married the king and Anne. On September 10 he stood as god-father to the happy couple's daughter, the future

Queen Elizabeth. From that time forward, Cranmer's rise continued, nobly and ignobly. He was forced to acquiesce when Henry tired of Ann Boleyn and sent her to her death. He saw his king married four more times. He made no visible effort to reform the wayward monarch, but after Henry's death he tried to reform the Church and cleanse her from Roman superstitions and impurities. He was so thorough in his Lutheranism that he earned the undying hatred of Bloody Mary who after the brief reign of Edward VI restored the Catholic religion in England. Cranmer was deposed as archbishop, brought into court, excommunicated, and forced to recant. In the end he had a change of heart and did what he had never done before: He stubbornly refused to compromise his faith, renounced all his former recantations together with his wicked past, and asked to be permitted to die as a martyr. His stand at the end was somewhat reminiscent of the stand taken by another great archbishop of Canterbury who like Cranmer had served his king well and his fellow-men badly, Thomas á Becket, whose martyrdom a few centuries before the Reformation may have inspired his successor. When he was led to the fire he let his hand be burned first, without batting an eye, because it had offended God by signing confessions and decrees which were not true. The calm cheerfulness and resolute faith with which the archbishop suffered martyrdom showed clearly that he had reconciled his conscience with God, and it inspired many others to do likewise.

Robert Barnes (1495-1540)

Born in 1495 Robert Barnes was educated at Cambridge where he joined the Austin Friars and later became their prior. After obtaining his doctorate Barnes became a well-known preacher, but was soon suspected of heresy. In 1526 he was brought before Cardinal Wolsey and four other Catholic bishops accused of "Lutheranism." Condemned to death by the bishops if he would not recant, he readily abjured his faith, was committed first to Fleet Prison in London and later in care of the Austin Friars. In 1528 he escaped to Antwerp and from there made his way to Wittenberg where he became a friend of Luther and the other Reformers. After his return to England in 1531 he was used as one of the chief intermediaries between Henry VIII and the Lutherans of the continent, as we have seen above. It is doubtful that the king was sincere in his desire to reform his Church, but he thought he needed the support of the German princes against the pope. Thus Barnes was sent to Germany several times, but his negotiations were fruitless. He became the most thorough Lutheran among the English Reformers and did not deny his faith. Henry VIII who had early in life taken a dislike to Luther and had never forgiven him the blast which the Reformer had issued in 1522 "Against Henry, King of England" finally broke off negotiations with the Lutherans, after the Lutherans and especially Luther had balked at the king's request for a sanction of his divorce. Added to this was the fact that Barnes had negotiated the marriage between Henry and the extremely homely princess, Anne of Cleve, a Lutheran, whom he had married for political reasons. When Henry repudiated this wife who looked to him "like a horse" he also turned against Barnes and his other Lutheran advisors. Over 300 of them suffered martyrdom, among them Barnes who was put to death on July 30, 1540.

When, in the summer of 1531, Robert Barnes made his first overtures in Wittenberg Luther recognized at once that he was acting at the behest of Henry VIII who, however, did not want to appeal directly to Luther. On September 3, 1531, Luther declared that the marriage between Henry VIII and Catherine of Aragon was valid. The hope voiced by Barnes that the powerful English king may become a good ally of the Wittenbergers did not influence him in the least. He did not care to have "that cruel fellow" as an ally in the cause of the Gospel. But on the other hand Luther did not try to win the favor of the emperor by protecting Catherine of Aragon, the emperor's kin. It was with him a matter of principle. Simply, sincerely and conscientiously he stated: "The marriage with the widow of a deceased brother is not forbidden by natural or divine law, but by human, ecclesiastic, and civil law; Moses had forbidden merely that someone could marry the wife of a living brother; divine law, on the other hand, prohibits divorce of a marriage which is valid according to divine law, and divine law takes precedence over human law."[11] In this point Luther agreed with the theologians of Louvain, while the theologians of Paris had favored the annulment of Henry's marriage. Luther stated that he wished to keep the king and the queen, for whom he felt sorry, from the sin of adultery. He added a significant sentence which later brought great heartache to him and his friends in the affair of Philip of Hesse: "I would rather permit the king to take a second wife simultaneously and to have two wives according to the example of the old Fathers and Kings," for polygamy, he thought, was not forbidden by divine law. Luther was not alone in this strange doctrine. The pope had given the same advice to Henry VIII.[12]

Barnes was again in Wittenberg when the first doctorates were conferred on June 16 and 17, 1533, on Bugenhagen, Cruciger and Aepinus. At the same time Magister Nicholas Glossenius, the new superintendent of Reval, was given the master's degree. Barnes attended the disputations which were held under Luther's presidency. Present were also the Elector John Frederick, his brother John Ernest, the Dukes Francis of Lueneburg and Magnus of Mecklenburg and many other distinguished guests. At that time Barnes and the Scotchman Alexander Alesius had enrolled at the university as students, although both of them were already well-known theologians in their own right. At the end of the lengthy disputation the elector gave a splendid banquet for the new doctors and all who had participated in the lengthy proceedings. Luther renewed his friendship with Barnes and the Englishman became Luther's "Table- and House-Companion." While Alesius was still banned from his native Scotland, Barnes was soon allowed to return to England, was appointed chaplain to the king and was soon back in Wittenberg with the king's request to stop the movement for a General Christian Council. Upon the request of Barnes Melanchthon now wrote to the king and dedicated to him the new edition of his *Loci*. It is possible that both Barnes and Alesius believed in the sincerity of the king when he professed that he was ready to learn from the moderate Lutherans, that he was not opposed to them but only to the radical Anabaptists. This trust of Barnes in his perfidious king influenced for a time even Luther who now approached the elector with the request to permit Melanchthon to go to England. As we have seen, the elector postponed the decision until the issue was settled by Henry's growing irritation with the Lutherans and his withdrawal from negotiations. Furthermore Luther was not willing to give up for the sake of policy any of his doctrinal points as the king had expected. There was no room for compromise. This applied especially to one of the most burning questions raised by the English monarch, the question of synergism, of co-operation between man and God, of good works and their reward in heaven. Here Luther issued one of his sharpest definitions: He emphasized the difference in the theology of St. Augustine, whom the Wittenbergers acknowledged as the greatest authority of the Church, and that of the New Testament. We are not justified before God through our ethical behavior or through virtues which we have received by the grace of God, but through faith which is accepted for the sake of Christ. "Who has been reborn of such faith will bring forth by necessity good works, as the sun shines of necessity according to her nature, and the believer is called 'righteous' also on account of these fruits; but with this righteousness which here on earth can never be pure nor take away sin and death, he cannot stand before God; and such works and virtues are 'righteous' before God only to the degree in which the person practicing them has become righteous through faith . . . ."[13]

After the death of Robert Barnes Luther published his "Confession of Faith" with a preface of his own in which he mentioned that Barnes had often told him confidentially that Henry was not concerned about religion. He excused the martyred Reformer for having served such an un-Christian monarch because his love for king and fatherland had blinded him. He was now through with King Henry, adding quietly—without rancor—: "We let Henry go with all his Henrys where they belong; we thank God, the Father of all mercy, that He can use such devils and devilish actors for our salvation and the salvation of all Christians and for the punishment of those who do not recognize God. This has been God's way of dealing with tyrants from time immemorial."[14]

X.

Other Movements

The Reformation of Martin Luther did not only give direction to the development of Lutheranism, Zwinglianism, Calvinism, and Episcopalianism, but also influenced a great number of other non-Roman movements which had either existed before the Reformation or had sprung up immediately after Luther's liberating action.

Pre-Reformation Movements

The oldest non-Roman movement existing in the Western Church at the dawn of the Reformation was that of the Waldensians who in spite of terrible persecutions had survived in Italy and southern France. They had retained much more of the Catholic substance than the Churches of the Reformation were willing to accept. From Strassburg these fighting remnants of the first revolt against Roman tyranny received doctrinal inspiration which led to important Protestant reforms within the movement. At the Synod of Chanforans in Savoy, in 1532, the Waldensian Church reformed itself. The immediate results were renewed cruel persecutions, especially under the "most Christian king," Francis I, who had posed during the 1530's as a reform-friendly monarch. The Waldensians were all but wiped out in southern France, but managed to survive to this day in the valleys of Savoy and as the strongest Protestant movement of Italy.

The work of John Huss had led to the establishment of strong centers of resistance against Roman exploitation among the Bohemians. Almost from the beginning of the Reformation the Bohemian Brethren and the Utraquists whose history during the century before Luther had been one of suffering and persecution were influenced by Lutheran doctrines. Not only did the Lutheran movement spill over from Saxony into neighboring Sudentenland where a large number of Lutheran congregations flourished, but a definite effort was made by the Wittenberg Reformers to lead the Bohemian Brethren into union with the Lutherans. The correspondence between Luther and the leaders of the Bohemians is extensive. The Bohemians visited Wittenberg at various times and emissaries of Luther worked among them until after the Reformer's death. The most important leaders among the Bohemians who were in contact with Wittenberg were the Seniors Lucas and Augusta, Poduska and Rodzalowsky, and the man who was most closely associated with Luther, the Senior John Horn.

John Horn, whose Bohemian name was Roh, was the foremost leader of the movement during the first part of the sixteenth century. With little formal schooling he taught himself and became one of the most learned men of his Church. In 1518, when he was pastor at Weisswasser, he met Michael Weisse, a convinced Lutheran, who had come from Breslau to Bohemia. Weisse prevailed upon Horn to go to Wittenberg.

At the beginning of 1522 we find him with Luther. Several times he returned to Bohemia, but always came back to Luther for new inspiration. At the time of the death of the Senior Lucas in 1528, John Horn and the new Senior John Augusta worked steadfastly for an organic union with the Lutheran movement. In 1533 Luther wrote a preface to their Confession of Faith. Weisse in the meantime had published the first Bohemian hymn book which, however, met with objections by the Bohemian leaders because it contained translations of Lutheran hymns whose texts were at variance with Bohemian doctrines, especially concerning the Lord's Supper. In 1532 Horn became Senior of the Bohemian Brethren. One of his first acts was to abolish the practice of Anabaptism, a practice which had a different origin than that of the Anabaptists of the Reformation period, but which nevertheless was unacceptable to Luther. He also restated the Bohemian doctrine of justification to bring it into line with the Lutheran doctrine. But in spite of all these efforts true union between Bohemians and Lutherans was never achieved. The Bohemians never forsook completely their Romanizing ways.

Shortly after Luther's death Horn confessed, at the Synod of Bunzlau, that the Bohemian Brethren had a great and precious heritage of their own "which does not make it necessary to look around for treasures elsewhere." Since then the Bohemian Brethren have led their own existence, but were again and again influenced by Lutherans, foremost by Count Zinzendorf.[1]

The New Movements

Among the new movements of the Reformation era the larger number was in existence in embryo form even before Luther nailed the Ninety-Five Theses to the Castle Church door. But his work brought them forth into the open, his ideas inspired and often inflamed them, his theology was at the same time their starting point and their stumbling block.

Among the numerous movements which were born during the age of the Reformation we may distinguish three main types: the almost countless numbers of Anabaptists, the great mystical-speculative thinkers, and the anti-Trinitarians. Between themselves these movements show many similarities, but also sharp contrasts. They are a colorful mixture of mysticism, chiliasm, pantheism, social revolution, scholasticism, and scepticism with Lutheran and Zwinglian ingredients. They are almost all agreed in their opposition to the organized Church which in the later years included also the Lutheran Church. Almost all of them suffered persecution at the hands of the state and the Churches. Some of them rejected all doctrine, others re-interpreted dogmas in unbiblical ways, while still others accepted the existing dogmas without question. Some subordinated Holy Scriptures to a force which they called the

"Inner Light," others abused it by making of it a law book. The enthusiasm of some of them ended in religious madness, as the "Muenster Madness," while others lived their own peculiar lives quietly and unnoticed by the world, as the "Quiet in the Land." They were independent and resembled in some respects certain modern sects, but it would be dangerous and unfair to compare them to modern Protestantism.

The Anabaptists

The roots of the Anabaptist movement go back to the Middle Ages, but its first appearance was in 1520 when radical *"schwaermerische"* enthusiasts began to proclaim a supernatural revelation. Carlstadt and Muenzer, although not Anabaptists in the real sense, were the fathers of the movement: Carlstadt at Wittenberg during Luther's absence and later at Orlamuende and elsewhere, Muenzer at Zwickau, Alstedt, Muehlhausen, and during the Peasant War. Especially Muenzer, who like Carlstadt had come from the Lutheran movement and had been pastor in Zwickau—among the Heavenly Prophets Stuebner and Storch—had fantastic ideas. The Cross to him was the experience of hellish pain from which the believer may be freed in mystical union with God; the Word of God was the inner voice which was proclaimed in visions. His fanaticism which had first attacked only the Catholic Church soon turned against Luther and Lutheranism and every form of secular government. He advocated the merciless killing of the "unbelievers" and then proclaimed the establishment of the Heavenly Kingdom.

But it was not until after the debacle of the Peasant War in which Muenzer and many early fanatics had been killed that the Anabaptist movement developed its historical form. The beginnings of the organized movement were in Zurich, the capital of Zwingli's Reformation, where Conrad Grebel, Felix Manz and Balthasar Hubmaier became the leaders of the group. Here already in 1524 William Roeubli had demanded that converted Christians should be rebaptized. The first anabaptism was that of Hubmaier by Roeubli. Hubmaier had been Lutheran pastor and Lutheran influences remained strong in his life until his death at the stake in 1528. Soon the movement spread to Upper Germany where the most important leaders became John Denk, a highly educated man, former rector of the famous St. Sebald School in Nuremberg, who after his expulsion from Nuremberg led a wandering life, dying in 1527 in Basel; Louis Haetzer, formerly chaplain in Zurich, who spread the Anabaptist doctrines in Augsburg, Strassburg and the Palatinate until he was beheaded, for adultery, in Constance in 1529; Hans Hut, popular preacher in Franconia, who burned down the prison in which he was kept and died from the burns in 1527; and Melchior Hoffmann, former Lutheran of Schwaebish-Hall, who worked in Livonia, Sweden, East Frisia and Strassburg where he was imprisoned during the Muenster Madness and languished in prison until his death in 1543.

Early the Anabaptists had preached against the state. Muenzer's sermons had inflamed the countryside of Thuringia. To a greater or lesser extent Hubmaier, Denk, Haetzer, Hut, and Hoffmann were also opposed to government. They established the law of the Bible, by which they were thinking especially of the fulfillment of the Sermon on the Mount. They suffered patiently all persecution, trusting that such suffering would lead to a better life for them and that the wicked authorities would be punished. They followed the "Inner Light" which led to confusion and dissension among them. They believed that they were a congregation of Saints, without sin, and thus their approach to life was strictly legalistic. They all agreed on the necessity of Adult Baptism or Anabaptism in case a person had been baptized in infancy. It can be seen from this brief tabulation of the tenets of their faith that the Anabaptists clashed with all existing Christian communities, especially in their insistence on the Inner Light and the false understanding of the communion of saints.

Besides these strong doctrinal deviations the Anabaptists showed economic and political tendencies which made them obnoxious to their fellowmen. Christian communism was widely practiced, their fantastic expectations of the approaching end of the world, finally the religious fanaticism which compelled a large part of the movement to take up arms against the godless, were at first annoying, later menacing. The results were unspeakable cruelties which were meted out to the patient sufferers who coveted martyrdom for its heavenly reward. After the Muenster Madness a bloodbath began which extended even to the Lutherlands of Saxony where a great number of guilty and innocent people were executed and imprisoned. Even Luther had by then changed his former benevolent attitude of tolerance and had assented to a harsh opinion of Melanchthon which condoned the execution of "heretics" for the sake of the common welfare.

The Muenster Madness.

The Anabaptist movement had spread from East Frisia where Melchior Hoffmann had preached his revolutionary gospel to the Netherlands and had found a leader in Jan Matthys, a baker from Haarlem. The center of the movement became Amsterdam. From here the "Apostles" of Jan Matthys preached the gospel of Anabaptism and soon all of Holland was aflame with the apocalyptic stirrings of the "Kingdom of God." From Holland the increasing fanaticism of the movement found its way back to Germany and found fertile soil especially in Muenster where Bernard Rothmann had introduced the Lutheran Reformation in 1533. Now Rothmann himself came under the spell of Jan Matthys. In 1534 the "Prophets" John Bokelson from Leyden and Jan Matthys came to Muenster, won the majority of the city council for their wild ideas and established their kingdom. The Muenster weaver Bernard Knipperdolling became mayor. Communism and obligatory Anabaptism were decreed. The Bishop of Muenster, Francis von Waldeck, was driven out and began to besiege the city. When Matthys was killed in a skirmish the crazened Anabaptists began a reign of cruel abandon and unspeakable immorality, establishing the "Kingdom of Zion," with John Bokelson as their king and bloody persecution of all who disagreed with them. Polygamy was introduced and wild orgies were celebrated until on June 25, 1535, Muenster was betrayed and captured and Anabaptism rooted out. The catastrophe of the movement at Muenster gave the signal to persecutions everywhere and the innocent suffered with the guilty. After this Anabaptism never tried again to win the world by force.

Anabaptism on the Eve of Luther's Life

The catastrophe of Muenster was decisive for the future course of the movement. The Anabaptists began now to organize their remnants into quiet, unobtrusive groups. Their greatest leader became the Frisian Menno Simons, a former Catholic priest and Lutheran pastor. Although he was not the founder he soon became the acknowledged leader of the sect which is named after him. The Mennonites established themselves in western and eastern Frisia, along the Lower Rhine, near the Baltic Sea and in Holstein. They rejected Infant Baptism and the taking of an oath, lived in retirement from the "wicked world," hard working and strait-laced folk. In their doctrines they accepted Calvinism in almost everything except Infant Baptism. They won toleration in Holland, Switzerland, the Palatinate, and a number of cities which included Emden, Hamburg, Danzig, and Elbing.

The Mennonites, split into groups from the very beginning, did not absorb all the remnants of the Anabaptist movement. A large group gathered around the Delft glazier David Joris who proclaimed that he was the Messiah. After an adventurous life he spent the last years of his life under an assumed name, John von Bruegge, in Basel where he lived outwardly as a Zwinglian but continued to write his radical Anabaptist books. He died in 1556, ten years after Luther.

Other groups veered away from strict Anabaptism and later became absorbed by the Arminians and Socinians. In Moravia Jacob Huter, a native of the Tyrol, established the sect of the Hutterites which after his martyrdom in 1536 experienced a long period of peaceful development until the Jesuit persecution of 1622 drove them out.

The Mystics

The mystics did not at first attempt to form groups and congregations. Most of them were lone prophets who followed their spiritualist inclinations and tried to attract as little attention as possible. They were pantheists who exalted the "Spirit" and abased the "Letter," who—like the Anabaptists—believed in the "Inner Light" and accepted personal revelation as the only source of Christian life. They concentrated on self-examination, psychological exercises and wild speculations. Their most important representative was Sebastian Franck.

Franck, a former Catholic priest and Lutheran pastor near Nuremberg, demitted the ministry in 1528 and resided as free writer in Nuremberg and Strassburg, later became soapmaker in Esslingen, printer in Ulm, and finally retired to Basel. He was opposed to pope, Luther, and legalistic Anabaptism. He advocated a Christian individualism which did not need Church organization and dogma. "Spirit" was to him the Word of God. Christology and Trinity were denied. His ethics were strictly mystical, lacking any clear connection to this world.

Among the mystics we also find Theobald Thamer, the personal student and great admirer of Luther who served for a while as professor at the Lutheran University of Marburg and later joined the Catholic Church, Valentin Weigel, who was pastor at Zschopau, the former Dominican Giordano Bruno and the Goerlitz shoemaker Jacob Boehme. Scholarly freaks like Agrippa von Nettesheim and Bombastus Paracelsus von Hohenheim were also numbered among them. Only two of them became founders of organized movements: Henry Niclaes and Caspar von Schwenkfeld. The former founded the *Familia Charitatis* which was called in England the "House of Love" or Familist movement. The movement was never very strong on the continent, but existed for a long time in England where the "Ranters" formed a continuation of it. Schwenkfeld's sect, however, has survived to the present day and is especially strong and vigorous in America. The Silesian nobleman and early follower of Luther soon differed from Lutheranism in his peculiar Christology and in his doctrine of Holy Communion and found followers throughout Germany where his sect became strong in Swabia and Silesia. Driven from Silesia by the Jesuit terror the remnant settled in Pennsylvania during the 18th century.

The Anti-Trinitarians

The most dangerous attack against the Christian dogma came from those who denied the Trinity of Father, Son, and Holy Ghost. During the Reformation era they were called anti-Trinitarians while today they refer to themselves as Unitarians. The greatest anti-Trinitarian leader of the sixteenth century was Michael Servetus who was burned by Calvin in 1553. Strongly influenced by Renaissance and humanism Servetus preached a type of pantheistic Neo-Platonism which has remained part and parcel of Unitarian philosophy to this day. He was a highly educated, gifted man. His books, "On the Errors of the Trinity" and "On the Restitution of Christianity," belong to the best scholarly works of the period, but are devoid of Biblical theology. His work influenced later generations, gave a foundation to rationalism, and led even in the sixteenth century many theologians away from historical Christian beliefs. Among the men who were influenced by Servetus were especially the Calvinist Castellio who forsook Calvin after Servetus' death, and the great Acontius, a native of Trent, whose "Stratagemes of Satan" influenced wide circles in Switzerland, Strassburg and London to join the anti-Trinitarian movement.

Besides these centers of anti-Trinitarianism there were large pockets of the movement in Italy, Poland, and Transylvania. In Italy the leaders were Camillo Renato, Matthias Gribaldo, George Blandrata, Valentine Gentilis, and Lelio Sozzini, the uncle of Fausto Sozzini, founder of the Socinian sect. These men merged their movement with the Anabaptists, organized an anti-Trinitarian-Anabaptist Council of Venice in 1550 which was attended by 60 delegates, but driven from Italy by the Catholic Counter-Reformation were forced to resettle in Switzerland. After the execution of Servetus many anti-Trinitarians fled from Switzerland and found a temporary haven in Poland and Transylvania. Blandrata became the leader of the Transylvanian group, while Fausto Sozzini (1539-1604) became the father of the Socinians whose center was at Racov in Poland. Here in Poland the anti-Trinitarian movement found its greatest development in the century after Luther until it was driven from Poland by the Jesuits. The remnants of the "Arian heresy" fled to the Netherlands, Transylvania, and later to America.

Andrew Carlstadt (1480-1541)

Andrew Bodenstein was born at Carlstadt, Franconia, probably in 1480. From his hometown he took the name by which he is known in history. After having been educated at home he went to Rome where he studied theology and canon law. In 1504 he came to Wittenberg where he soon played an important role among the professors of the little university. In 1510 he was awarded the degree of Doctor of Theology.

CARLSTADT

Carlstadt was a restlessly-active man. He was an energetic promoter, first of himself, and incidentally of the doctrines in which he believed at the time. In his dealings with friend and foe he showed a regrettable lack of truthfulness and integrity. Vain and often proven to be wrong he forsook former friends and associates with the greatest of ease and changed his convictions almost overnight. Originally a Thomist, a follower of the theology of St. Thomas Aquinas, he adopted Scotism, the "New Way" of Duns Scotus, when the latter became fashionable at the University of Wittenberg. After Luther's arrival in Wittenberg he felt pushed into the background and went to Rome to realize his ambition to be recognized as one of the great theologians of his time. Apparently the Romans did not receive him with open arms, for he soon returned to Wittenberg where he now joined Luther whom he could not successfully oppose, became his avowed friend and open champion while continuing secretly in his efforts to scuttle him. When Augustine became the fashion of the day, Carlstadt posed as an Augustinian, trying feverishly to hold on to his position as the theological leader of Wittenberg, but with little success. On April 26, 1517, he disputed in 152 theses "Against Scholasticism." Two years later he arranged a disputation with Eck, still trying to take the initiative away from Luther, but was frustrated when his disputation with the Ingolstadt theologian bogged down and when Luther had to come to his rescue.

Carlstadt had no loyalties and few friends. In November 1517 he complained bitterly that Luther had gone too far, but a few years later he criticized the Reformer severely for his "compromises." When Luther voiced some doubt about the canonicity of the Epistle of James, Carlstadt thundered against him in his "Booklet on the Canonical Scriptures," but later rebuked Luther for insisting that the "dead letter" of Holy Writ should be the guide and rule for the Church.

When Luther was at the Wartburg in 1521 and 1522 Carlstadt appointed himself leader of the "orphaned" Reformation. He was always a man in a hurry as if he had premonitions that his plans would be frustrated by outside interference. He proclaimed a German order of service for the congregation in Wittenberg, changed the contents of the liturgy, insisted on the lay cup, wrote a treatise against celibacy, and distributed the Lord's Supper in both kinds. Large numbers of monks left the monastery, the Black Cloisters was all but deserted and the Augustinians of Germany decided to disband. But Carlstadt's reforms met with great opposition and Luther was forced to make a hurried trip to Wittenberg in December 1521 to pacify the confused Wittenberg theologians. As soon as Luther had left Carlstadt again caused new trouble. On Christmas Day 1521 he distributed the Lord's Supper under both kinds, preached in his street clothing, and got married on January 20, 1522.

While Wittenberg was thus in great turmoil Carlstadt received

sudden help from the Heavenly Prophets of Zwickau, Storch and
Stuebner, who not only urged him on to ever more radical reforms,
but also silenced the opposition of the theologians, from Melanchthon down, whom they hypnotized with their weird ideas. Order
was not restored until Luther returned from the Wartburg in March
1522. In eight great sermons, the so-called "Invocavit Sermons," the
Reformer re-established Christian order in Wittenberg. Carlstadt
took the reproof ungraciously. Later in the year, in December 1522,
he met and formed an alliance with Thomas Muenzer, the revolutionary preacher from Upper Saxony.

In 1523, under the influence of Muenzer and the Heavenly Prophets Carlstadt renounced his academic honors as "temptations of
the devil," bought a farm and let it be known that henceforth he
wanted to be known as "just neighbor Andrew." But he soon tired
of this experience of humility. In March 1523 he wrote against
Luther, went to Orlamuende in Thuringia where he had himself
elected pastor and from where, on December 29, 1523, he sent
out a vituperative missive against the Wittenberg Reformer, "On
the Priesthood and the Sacrifice of Christ," in which he opposed not
only the Mass, but also Infant Baptism.

After that there was no turning back from his fanaticism. He declared: "Where Christians rule no secular authority should be acknowledged, but everyone should be permitted to hack to pieces
and to overthrow what is against God's order."[2] In 1524 he openly
espoused the practice of bigamy among his parishioners. After
some turbulent months in Orlamuende Carlstadt was expelled from
the Electorate in September 1524. He fled to Strassburg and Basel
where in spite of Luther's opposition he was given asylum. But he
could not keep quiet and was forced to leave both cities and went
to Bavaria where he incited the peasants to revolt. He was also present at the Peasant Assembly of Schweinfurt. When the Peasant War
was drowned in the blood of the poor misguided hordes Carlstadt,
now an outlaw, knocked at Luther's door in Wittenberg. The kindly Reformer forgave him and took him into his house hiding him
from the vengeance of the elector. Finally Carlstadt was amnestied
and allowed to live at Kemberg near Wittenberg where he eked
out a meager living selling brandy, beer and "Pfefferkuchen." In

1526 an apparently reformed Carlstadt asked Luther to be sponsor at the baptism of his infant son.

But the peace between the two men did not last. When Carlstadt heard about Luther's controversy with Zwingli he was quick in taking the side of the Swiss Reformer against the man who had just saved his life. In spite of the strict order by the elector not to publish any more treatises, Carlstadt wrote against the doctrine of the Real Presence. He escaped to East Frisia, sold Bibles and associated with Anabaptists and Schwenkfeldians. He also incited the people to disregard the Holy Day and to live in matrimony without churchly sanction. Again he was expelled and wandered aimlessly on the highways with wife and children until he found refuge in Zurich where he was allowed to live under the protection of Zwingli. After the death of Zwingli and Oecolampadius the Swiss began to look upon Carlstadt as a great theologian and called him to the University of Basel where he lived from 1534 until his death. Here Carlstadt who had once affected disdain for academic degrees became the champion of academic stuffiness and violently opposed poor Myconius because he was of a humbler bend of mind. Incidentally, Myconius had been instrumental in getting the position of professor for Carlstadt.

After a life, ingloriously lived, this highly gifted, but unscrupulous, vain, ambitious, insincere opportunist who had nearly succeeded in wrecking the Reformation and who had made life miserable for himself as well as for those around him, died on Christmas Day 1541.

Luther's first open clash with Carlstadt occurred in 1516—one year before the start of the Reformation—when he denied the authenticity of a book attributed to Augustine. At that time he wrote to John Lang: "I offended . . . Dr. Carlstadt, because . . . I dared to deny the authenticity of the book. Therefore, tell these wondering, or rather wonderful theologians, that they need not dispute with me what Gabriel said, or what Raphael said, or what Michael said. . . ."[3] On February 15, 1518, he wrote to Spalatin: "Indulgences now seem to me to be nothing but a snare for souls, and are worth absolutely nothing except to those who slumber and idle in the way of Christ. Even if our Carlstadt does not share this opinion, yet I am certain that there is almost nothing in them. . . ."[4] And there were many other disagreements. But in spite of these disagreements the names of the two men were always mentioned in one breath during the early years of the Reformation. Eck wrote to Carlstadt on May 28, 1518: "Most famous Carlstadt, I have heard that you and your Wittenbergers are moved against Eck because I wrote something private for my bishop against the opinion of our common friend Martin Luther." Carlstadt answered on June 11, 1518: "I answer briefly to let you know that I am greatly displeased with the taunts with which you have assailed my most learned friend, Martin Luther. . . . I weep for the wound your humanity received in forcing on us the necessity of fighting you."[5] On July 1, 1519, Eck reported to his friends George Hauen and Francis Burckhardt: "At Leipzig the beer was bad for me, so I stopped drinking it for six days, and feel better. . . . Luther and Carlstadt entered in great state, with two hundred Wittenberg students, four doctors, three licentiates, many professors and many Lutherans."[6] After it was all over Amsdorf stated to Spalatin: "Eck surpassed Dr. Carlstadt by far in memory and delivery." Luther saved the day.[7]

It seems that from this day Carlstadt tried to erase the memory of this defeat. As long as Luther was in Wittenberg he dared not come out into the open. In 1520 he was included in the bull of excommunication which the pope issued against Luther. The following year he thought that his opportunity had come. On August 1, 1521, Luther helpless in exile at the Wartburg—cautioned Melanchthon against the rashness of "that excellent man, Carlstadt" who misquotes Scripture. On August 15 he wrote to Spalatin: "I wish that Carlstadt had relied on more appropriate passages of Scripture. . . . He has made a good attempt; I only wish it were great and skillful and successful too."[8] Matters deteriorated quickly during the next few months. Luther admonished Carlstadt once, rebuked him the second time. Shortly after his hurried return from the Wartburg, he reported to Spalatin: "Do pray for me, and help me tread underfoot that Satan who, in the name of the Gospel, has set himself up here in Wittenberg against the Gospel. . . . It will be hard for Carlstadt to give up his views, but Christ will force him to do so if he does not yield of his own accord."[9] To Linck at Nuremberg he wrote a few days later: "Carlstadt and Gabriel Zwilling were the authors of these monstrous teachings, though Gabriel has come to himself and has become a different man; what will become of the other I do not know. It is certain that he will be forbidden to enter the pulpit."[10] Carlstadt did not take his defeat lying down. He wrote an accusation against Luther, although "he almost took an oath that he is not writing against me," as Luther wrote to Spalatin late in April. By the end of the year we hear that "Carlstadt's lectures are irregularly given." In April 1523 when the nine nuns from Nimbschen arrived in Wittenberg Luther remarked: "Carlstadt is away from home." He had left and was now coming out into the open against Luther. "Carlstadt keeps on as is his wont," Luther told Spalatin on January 14, 1524. "A book of his has been published by a new printer in Jena, [Michael Buchfuehrer], and he will publish eighteen more books, so it is said."[11]

After the disaster of the Peasant War Carlstadt had written a humble apology to Luther begging him to allow him to return to Saxony. At the same time he had sent his wife to Saxony. About July 1, 1525, he himself returned to Wittenberg, terrified by the fate of Muenzer, and found refuge in Luther's home for three months. As a price of his protection Luther forced Carlstadt to publish a recantation of his errors. This he did on July 25 in the following intentionally ambiguous language: "I recognize before God, without jest and from the heart, that all that I wrote, spoke or taught from my own brain or discovered for myself, is human, false, unpraiseworthy, deceitful, satanic, to be shunned and avoided."[12] On September 12, 1525, Luther interceded for him with the elector. "Serene, highborn Prince, gracious Lord!" he wrote, "I come again with trouble and vexation before your Grace, who hold your office from God. Carlstadt begs for a trial to excuse himself from the charge of sedition, and has sent me a retraction of his errors which I shall publish. . . . Your Grace might permit him to reside at Kemberg, or some village near by, on condition that he should never preach nor write any more, but should keep still and support himself by manual labor. . . ."[13] For the next three years Carlstadt lived on a farm at Kemberg, grumbling that he would have been better treated in Turkey than in Saxony. Then he escaped and went to Frisia. On June 15, 1529, Luther reported to Justus Jonas: "Carlstadt has for some time settled in Frisia. He is joyful and triumphant. In two boastful letters he has summoned his wife to him. That is to say, Satan will make new portents for us there."[14] After that Luther had no more dealings with his former friend. When he heard that Carlstadt had died on Christmas Day 1541 Luther desired to know whether he had repented before his death, for he had always wished that Carlstadt should be saved. But when he heard about a terrible ghost that Carlstadt had seen shortly before his death, he readily believed the story and was convinced that his former friend was now paying for his sins in hell. Carlstadt's wife and children, however, he commended to the care of the city council of Basel.

Thomas Muenzer (about 1490-1525)

On May 23, 1525, Luther wrote to his kinsman John Ruehel at Mansfeld: "I thank you, honored and dear sir, for your recent news, all of which I was glad to have, especially about Thomas Muenzer. Please let me have further details about his capture and of how he acted, for it is profitable to know how that proud spirit bore itself.[15] A week later he added in another letter to the same person: "Anyone who has seen Muenzer can say that he has seen the very devil, and at his worst."[16] In the meantime Muenzer had been captured on May 25 at Muehlhausen and had been put to death with Pfeifer and other leaders of the Peasant Revolt. Muenzer who had hidden under a bed was completely broken in spirit. Before his death he made a humble confession of his errors and received Holy Communion. He was so terrified that he was unable to recite the Apostles' Creed as he was being led to his death. Thus ended the life of the most defiant man of the Reformation period.

Thomas Muenzer was born at Stolberg in the Harz Mountains. His birthdate is not known and we know little of his early life except that even as a youth he was influenced by the great mystics of the fourteenth century and studied them thoroughly. He led an unstable life, journeying from place to place. In 1515 he was provost of a convent in Frohna, Saxony, but soon we find him in Brunswick, then in Leipzig, then in Weissenfels where he served for some time as father confessor of the nuns of St. Bernard, and finally in Zwickau, traditional hotbed of religious fanaticism. Here he came into contact with the "Heavenly Prophets." Here he also left the Catholic Church and turned to Luther's teaching.

On account of his association with the "Heavenly Prophets" Muenzer was forced to leave Zwickau. He now turned to Bohemia where he preached the imminent advent of the Kingdom of God, but found no response among the people. He was arrested in November 1521, escaped to Saxony and continued to Thuringia. At Nordhausen and later at Alstedt he continued his preaching which now took the form of revolutionary activity. In 1523 he married a former nun. Yet even in Alstedt he considered himself a Lutheran, introduced an excellent order of service, one of the best liturgies of the fifteen-twenties. But Luther who by this time had formed a great aversion to the "Satan of Alstedt" did not accept Muenzer's contribution to the Church.

In December 1522 Carlstadt and Muenzer had met secretly to map out common strategy to save the Reformation from the "lazy flesh of Wittenberg." During the next years until Muenzer's death they worked together closely. Both men were dissatisfied with the conservatism of Luther and surrendering to communistic ideals began to preach revolt against the authorities. On March 24, 1524, Muenzer and his band of fanatics burned down St. Mary's Chapel at Mellerbach and in July of the same year Muenzer threatened Duke George of Saxony openly with rebellion. At the same time he preached before George's cousins, the Elector Frederick the Wise and Duke John the Constant, who for some strange reason had been desirous to hear the fiery crusader. In this famous sermon Muenzer admonished the two princes to kill the "godless" with fire and sword. Forced to flee after his stubborn refusal to discuss his difficulties with the Wittenberg theologians, he first found refuge in Muehlhausen from where he was expelled at Luther's behest, then at Nuremberg from where he issued his abusive blast against Luther, "Against the Rotten Flesh of Wittenberg." In it he exhorted the people "to take up arms against the tyrants who strive against the Gospel." He proclaimed that one faithful Christian could slay and strangle one thousand, nay, twenty thousand enemies. "The time has come," he stated, "that a bloodbath will be brought down upon the hard-hearted world for the punishment of its unbelief. Then all goods will be taken away from those who for the sake of the devil did not dare to come out openly for God." Luther he called "Dr. Liar, the archdevil, the Wittenberg pope" and urged all Christians to take up "knives and spears," for by force alone "the people will be freed and the Lord will rule over them."[17]

After having made contact with Anabaptists in Upper Germany and at Zurich Muenzer returned to Muehlhausen on December 13, 1524, overthrew the city council, destroyed all altars and pictures in the Churches, plundered all monasteries within reach, and began a reign of terror which was intensified after he had had a dream in which he was commanded to kill all the mice. The end came with lightning speed. Within five months the dream of the Heavenly Kingdom had collapsed, its author had repented and died. The heads of Muenzer and his lieutenants were put on posts as a warning to future troublemakers.

Balthasar Hubmaier (died 1528)

The father of the modern Baptist movement and one of the finest leaders of the Anabaptists of the Reformation era came from Friedberg near Augsburg. In 1503 we find him as a student of John Eck at Freiburg who later became the foremost spokesman for Catholicism and one of the persecutors of heretics. After the completion of his studies Hubmaier was, for a time at least, school teacher at Schaffhausen in neighboring Switzerland, but soon he returned to Freiburg where, in 1510, he received his bachelor's degree and, in 1512, became Doctor of Theology. He was called to Ingolstadt as professor and canon. There he met his former teacher Eck who during these years had moved from Freiburg to the famous Catholic school in Bavaria. In those days Hubmaier was a "fanatical Catholic," a follower of Eck and Hoogstraten, participating in the cruel expulsion of the Jews from Regensburg. Even then he was known as an eloquent orator who could hold his audience spellbound. When he accepted some of Luther's doctrines he was forced to leave Regensburg and settled at Waldshut, near Basel, where he became a "Lutheran" pastor. Zwingli soon noticed the presence of the able preacher, made contact with him and for several years Hubmaier was active in the Zwinglian movement. After the Second Zurich Disputation of October 1523 Hubmaier wrote a treatise, "Eighteen Talks on the Christian Life," which was published early in 1524 and forced him to flee after the Austrian authorities had demanded his extradition. He went to Schaffhausen wrote the challenging treatise "Of Heretics and Their Burning" in which he demanded instruction rather than fire and sword for those who disagreed with the official doctrines of the Church.

For some time now Hubmaier had come under the influence of the revolutionary preaching and teaching of Thomas Muenzer. He had himself rebaptized defending his decision with another important book, "On the Baptism of Believers." The debacle of the Peasant War forced him to take to the road. First he went to Zurich to see his old friend Zwingli, where he disputed on Infant Baptism, then to Constance, and finally to Nickolsburg in Moravia where he was protected from Austrian revenge by the noble Lord of Lichtenstein. There Hubmaier took up his Anabaptist activities in earnest, writing several scholarly treatises on Infant Baptism, Holy Communion, and human freedom. Although he was a moderate and had discarded Muenzer's communistic ideas and accepted temporal government as divinely ordained the Austrians were still anxious to lay their hands on him. When Ferdinand of Austria annexed Moravia in 1527 Balthasar Hubmaier was caught in the net. He was immediately imprisoned. He was burned at the stake on March 10, 1528, while his devoted wife received the more clement sentence of drowning. He remained firm in his faith to the end and died with quiet dignity.

In one of his last treatises Hubmaier had appealed to Luther. At the beginning of February 1528 Luther answered indirectly by publishing his Open Letter to two unnamed pastors who were then working in Catholic Bohemia. This Open Letter, "On Anabaptism," was meant for instruction and the strengthening of "simple, pious Christians." On the question of Anabaptism Luther asked for positive proof that Infant Baptism was against God's Word. Here as so often in Luther's theology the maxim that, wnat is not forbidden by God's Word is permissible, is upheld while the Reformed and with them the Anabaptists always asked for proof that something was expressly commanded before they permitted it. In the matter of abolishing monasteries and abrogating the sacrifice of the Mass Luther agreed with Hubmaier because such things were clearly against the Word of God. But the claim of the Anabaptists that children could not believe and therefore should not be baptized, was a human assumption and nowhere found in Scripture. John the Baptist believed already in his mother's womb (Luke 1:41). Furthermore the Apostles baptized whole households. If they had been wrong God would have seen to it long ago that Infant Baptism would have been discarded in the Church. The insistence of Hubmaier that only believers should be baptized Luther answered with the question: "How do you know that a person believes? Can you look into his heart?" In conclusion Luther openly criticized the persecution of the Anabaptists by the authorities. "It is not right," he stated, "and I am truly vexed that these poor people are so miserably burned and cruelly strangled; one should let every one believe what he wants. If his faith is wrong he will suffer eternal punishment. Why do you want to torture them here in time, if they merely err in doctrine and do not start a rebellion? Good Lord, how quickly it can happen that someone errs and falls into the snares of the devil! We should defend ourselves and resist them with God's Word. With fire and sword we won't get anywhere!"[18]

Caspar von Schwenkfeld (1490-1561)

At first Caspar von Schwenkfeld was one of the most fervent Lutherans and the most active Reformer of Silesia. But soon he came under the spell of Carlstadt and Muenzer, warning Luther as early as 1525 against the danger of the doctrine of justification by faith. He felt that active Christian life was immobilized by this doctrine. He also disagreed with Luther on the question of the Sacrament of the Altar. With the Strassburgers and others Schwenkfeld tried to find a middle road between Luther and Zwingli. He con-

stantly admonished Luther to be more charitable and to insist on
a stricter Church discipline, after the manner of the Bohemian
Brethren. For a while Luther humored the Silesian nobleman, but
soon growing suspicious of his doctrines he also became suspicious
of his motives. Thus when Schwenkfeld became involved in Anabaptist disturbances in Silesia—he had protected the persecuted
sect—both Catholics and Lutherans prevailed upon his prince, the
Duke of Liegnitz, to dismiss the worthy servant. In 1529 Schwenk-

SCHWENKFELD

feld secretly left Silesia. He was kindly received at Strassburg
where he had taken refuge and lived there for five years. Driven
from Strassburg by the renaissance of stricter Lutheranism in the
fifteen-thirties he went to Ulm, where again he was expelled. After
a long wandering life he returned to Ulm where he died, un-
broken in spirit, on December 10, 1561.

In 1539 Schwenkfeld had published his most important treatise
in which he taught a doctrine on the person of Christ which
brought him into sharp conflict with Luther. Yet he never tried to
win Luther to his side. In 1543 he sent some of his books to Luther

which the Reformer received, but refused to keep in his library. Schwenkfeld who had written a treatise on the difference between Lutherans and Zwinglians at a time when both Zurich and Wittenberg were anxious to come to an agreement was considered a meddler and outcast by both of them. After Smalcald he went into hiding and withdrew completely from membership in the Church, declining to receive the Sacrament. Wherever he went he formed small societies of people who held opinions like his own. They called themselves "Confessors of the Glory of Christ," but were commonly referred to as Schwenkfeldians.

Schwenkfeld's works were collected after his death and published in 1564. In the seventeenth century his descendants were closely associated with the mysticism of Jacob Boehme. In 1720 a commission of Jesuits was dispatched to Silesia to convert them by force. Those who survived fled to Holland, England and North America. Only a small number remained in Silesia where they gained tolerance under Frederick the Great who had conquered the province from the Austrians. Later some of these Schwenkfeldians emigrated to Russia.

Schwenkfeld made a clear distinction between the so-called Inner Word and External Word, the latter being perishable as a written record while the former is written in the hearts. In his Christology he discarded completely the human nature of Christ and made Him one-sidedly divine.

Luther who in his later years liked to call the worthy Silesian nobleman a "Stinker" *(Stenkefeld)* numbered him, in a letter to Spalatin which he wrote on March 27, 1526, among the five great troublemakers of the evangelical movement, the others being Carlstadt, Zwingli, Oecolampadius, and Cellarius. "They vex us wonderfully with their writings and are troublesome babblers; I wish that they who think they are so strong had my suffering from the stone."[19] To Schwenkfeld himself he wrote the following month: "Dear Sir and Friend. We have put off answering you for a long time so that you may know we did not read your matter in a hurry. . . . What shall I say? Perhaps it is God's will that you have fallen like this. . . . We cannot believe you and build our souls on your words; therefore I ask you very kindly to desist from this public error and not put yourself in the number of those who are wretchedly deceiving the world. If you will not do this—well, God's will be done! I am heartily sorry, but I am free from your blood and that of all whom you lead astray. May God instruct you! Amen." Luther never changed his mind. When Schwenkfeld sent him his books in 1543 Luther sent back word by messenger: "If Schwenkfeld, the mad fool, does not want to stop, he can at least leave me alone with these books which have been spewn out by the devil."[20]

John Bokelson (1509-1536)

The young man whose execution took place on January 22, 1536, had been known during the last two years of his life as the "King of the Heavenly Kingdom," called by some the Muenster Madness. His name was John Bokelson or John of Leyden, because he was born near Leyden in Holland in 1509. His father was the village mayor and John came thus from a respectable, conservative home. Not much is known of his youth, except that he married before he was 24 years old.

In 1533 John went secretly to Muenster in Westphalia where he was converted to violent Anabaptism by Melchior Hoffmann, the "Prophet," who had predicted the end of the world for that year. He left behind his wife and family who had objected to his journey. Soon, however, Bokelson returned to Leyden where Jan Matthys, another fanatic, rebaptized him. Then both men returned to Muenster as "Prophets of Doom."

The next year and a half were probably the most amazing period in the whole history of the Reformation. Bokelson, at first second-in-command to Matthys, assumed the title "King of the Heavenly Kingdom" after his friend's death in battle, at Eastertime 1534. He abolished monogamy and lived a life "worse than a heathen," unequalled in the revolutionary and bloodthirsty sixteenth century. Finally, on June 24, 1535, he was defeated when the armies of the Bishop of Muenster entered the city. His punishment was as cruel as the penalties which he had meted out during his reign of terror. Before the end he made his peace with God, refusing, however, to renounce his Anabaptist views. Strengthened in his faith Bokelson showed singular courage and great humility at his execution which took place on January 22, 1536.

Luther had disregarded the Muenster disturbances which had been building up for some time until Bernard Rothmann, who since 1531 had been pastor in Muenster, had joined the madness. Luther had warned Rothmann repeatedly against the false doctrines of the Anabaptists. He had assured him of his high esteem and love and had praised the work which he was doing among the people of Muenster. To the city council in Muenster he had written: "God has given you fine preachers, especially Bernard Rothmann; yet they need to be admonished, for the devil is a rascal who can lead astray good, pious and scholarly preachers."[21] A few weeks later Rothmann, a highly gifted speaker and well educated man, had joined the madness. Now Luther's anger knew no bounds. He saw in the Muenster affair the logical continuation of Carlstadt's and Muenzer's former activities. Muenster was reaping the whirlwind of all the storm which the older fanatics had unleashed. Like Carlstadt and Muenzer a decade before the Muenster fanatics were now attacking the pope and Luther in one breath as the "Twin Prophets of Wickedness." Luther wrote two missives against them in the form of two prefaces, one to Rhegius' "Confutation of the Muenster Confession" and one to "News from Muenster." He did not waste many words on Bokelson and the other miserable creatures involved in the madness. For everyone could see clearly that the devil in person was keeping house in Muenster. Only the strange doctrine of the Anabaptists that the flesh of Christ did not come from Mary, but directly from heaven did he oppose. Their attacks against him he wanted to suffer patiently since they had attacked the Holy Word of God much more than him. Moreover, he was confident that the devil would soon be defeated since he was carrying on so stupidly and rashly in Muenster. He never referred to the matter again.

Simons Menno (1492-1559)

One of the most lovable persons of the Anabaptist movement was the venerable Simons Menno, father of the Mennonite movement who led the remnants of the Anabaptists back into the quiet harbor of Christian life and work after the excesses of Muenster and the catastrophe which had followed its end.

Simons Menno was probably born at Witmarsum, Frisia, in 1492. His father was a peasant. Menno was educated at monastery schools, learning Latin and Greek and receiving a better than average education. In 1515 or 1516 he was ordained to the priesthood and served for a time as vicar of Pingjum.

Early in his career Menno began to doubt the Roman doctrine of transubstantiation and turned in earnest to the study of God's Word which he had neglected till then. He also read Luther's Reformation writings of 1518-1520 and learned from them that there are many man-made laws in the Church which have no biblical foundation. From a Catholic priest he slowly turned into an evangelical preacher and for ten years considered himself a Lutheran.

In 1531 Menno attended the execution of an Anabaptist. This event was to change the course of his life. Seeing the faith of the dying man he made a study of the doctrine of Infant Baptism and began to doubt it. But being a cautious and a charitable man he did not take a fanatical attitude, but continued as pastor in his native Witmarsum. Later he associated more freely with Anabaptists who confirmed him in his views. But he stayed away from the excitement of the Muenster Rebellion which was then gripping the whole countryside.

The disaster of the Heavenly Kingdom led Menno to his second great doctrine: His teaching of non-resistance. He laid down his office as Lutheran pastor and had himself rebaptized. At that time the Anabaptist movement was badly disorganized and the remaining splinter groups were fighting each other, often viciously. One of these groups almost immediately elected Menno as "Elder." After much persuasion he finally consented to accept this office, and, beginning in 1537, he administered it with great conscientiousness and strictness. The movement spread rapidly. His followers were soon called Mennonites, after their leader.

Menno who had in the meantime married in Groningen, Holland, fled his adopted city after the proscription of the Anabaptist movement by Charles V. He first went to Amsterdam, but no longer safe in the domains of Charles, he finally went to Holstein where he found a haven at Wuestenfeld near Oldesloe under the protection of the kindly Count Bartholomew von Ahlfeldt. There he became the revered patriarch of the Mennonite movement, visited and consulted by many, including even Lutherans. He died on January 13, 1559.

Michael Servetus (1511-1553)

Luther's first brush with anti-Trinitarianism was with John Campanus, from Maeseyck in Belgium, who enrolled at Wittenberg in 1528. Campanus had spent some time with George Witzel at Niemegk and later appeared in Marburg where he vainly tried to suggest a new interpretation of the Words of Institution. But the Reformers paid no attention to him. Now in 1530 he had submitted to the Elector John of Saxony a whole list of "godless, monstrous dogmas," as Luther and Melanchthon called them. He taught that the Holy Spirit was not a person and that the Son was not of the essence of the Father and was not eternal. He also attacked the Lutheran doctrines of justification, repentance, and the Means of Grace, had strange ideas about the Christian Church and boasted that he was the first who since the times of the Apostles had rediscovered the truth. On the title page of his book which he sent out in manuscript form he wrote: "Against the whole world after the Apostles!" He later published this work in 1532. Since the Wittenberg Reformers rejected him he had to leave Wittenberg. He called Luther "a satanic liar" to which the Reformer retorted that Campanus was "an enemy of the Son of God, a blasphemer, a son of Satan."[22] Bugenhagen published a book allegedly written by Athanasius, the great enemy of Arius and defender of the Trinity.

We do not know whether Luther had heard at this time about the Spaniard Servetus who had published an attack against the Trinity in Strassburg in 1531. He mentions him much later when he published his series of theses on the Trinity in 1544. In these theses of December 12, 1544, Luther stated that the mystery of incarnation can not be grasped by the human mind and that blaspheming heretics who deny it must be silenced. He mentioned Campanus and Servetus, but stated that there will be many more in the future who will deny the divinity of Christ. Another set of Trinitarian theses was discussed on July 3, 1545. Thus we see that Luther's concern with the anti-Trinitarian movement came towards the end of his life. The thought that people could deny the Godhead of Christ was so strange to him that at first he did not take these rumblings seriously. The greatest anti-Trinitarian, Michael Servetus, was almost unknown to him.

Miguel Serveto was a Spanish physician, born at Tudela in Navarra in 1511. He came of a good family, studied law at Toulouse in Southern France where he also became familiar with the Bible. His patron since 1525 had been Juan de Quintana, father confessor of the Emperor Charles V. With Quintana Servetus attended the coronation of the emperor at Bologna in February 1530. There he turned sharply against popery having witnessed the spectacle of human adoration. In 1531 he wrote "On the Errors of the Trinity" which forced him to leave the imperial court. At Lyons, France, he found a new patron and continued to Paris to study medicine. In 1536 he also met Calvin who proposed to correct the doctrinal errors of Servetus. But Servetus would not listen. In 1539 he left France to study Hebrew and theology at Louvain, but in 1540 he returned, this time to Montpellier, to continue his medical studies.

During the following years Servetus became private physician of the Archbishop of Vienne. Secretly he had himself rebaptized, for he maintained that it was necessary to rebaptize adults at the age of thirty. In 1545 and 1546 he once more got in touch with Calvin, this time with fatal results to him. He went to Geneva on his own peril believing that his one-time friend would not harm him. But Calvin had read the manuscript of the book. "The Restitution of Christianity" and Servetus found himself in trouble. He was arrested and brought to court. His trial lasted from August 14 to October 26, 1553. Although friends prevailed upon Calvin not to carry out the death sentence which the court had passed, Calvin ordered the burning of Servetus which took place on October 27, 1553. Servetus died firmly confessing the faith for which he had fought.

XI

Emperors, Kings, and Princes

Maximilian of Hapsburg, "the Last Knight," occupied the throne of the Holy Roman Empire when the Reformation began. Born at Wiener-Neustadt on March 22, 1459, the son of the Emperor Frederick III, the most undecided and ineffectual ruler in the empire's history, Maximilian had inherited from his father a certain indecisiveness and from his mother, Leonora of Portugal, the ambition to enlarge his domains. On August 18, 1477, he had married Mary of Burgundy, the daughter of Charles the Bold, and had become embroiled in a rivalry with the French kings which was to haunt his descendants for centuries to come. After the early death of his wife he had transferred the Burgundian holdings to their son, Philip the Handsome, who later married Joan, the daughter of Ferdinand and Isabella of Spain. Thus the grandson of Maximilian fell heir not only to the Austrian realm of the Hapsburgs, but also to the Netherlands and Burgundy as well as to the empire of the two Spanish monarchs.

When Maximilian tried to marry Anne of Brittany King Charles VIII of France intervened personally and frustrated the marriage.

In consequence Maximilian married Bianca Maria of Milan, daughter of the Duke of Milan whom the French were soon to drive from his duchy. Thus the aging emperor became involved in yet another war with France, the war with Charles VIII which ended disastrously at first for the French, but which was to keep Maximilian's successors busy for the next fifty years. Especially Charles V had to bear the brunt of his grandfather's folly and was not able to curb the Reformation as he would have liked to do. In this way did the often foolhardy policy of Maximilian I favor Luther and the spread of Lutheranism many years later.

Now, in 1517, Maximilian was old and his powers were spent. While he had been a better emperor than his long-reigning father Frederick III, he had been unable to curb the independent behavior of the princes and cities of the empire. During his reign the first rumblings of social upheaval had been heard, the first uprisings of peasants had been put down. He yet presided at the Diet of Augsburg in 1518 where he insisted that the Wittenberg monk should not be given up to the Romans but should be heard on German soil. He died shortly thereafter, on January 12, 1519, at Wels, Austria. It is difficult to say what would have happened to the Reformation and to the religious conditions in Europe in general had Maximilian ruled ten or fifteen years longer.

As it were, rivalry broke out immediately between the Hapsburgs and the king of France about the succession. In the end Charles V won, but not until the pope, who wanted the French king on the German throne had made many concessions to the German princes, including Frederick the Wise of Saxony, protector of Martin Luther. When Charles was crowned in late 1520 it was too late to turn back the clock of history.

Charles and Ferdinand, Luther's Two Kings

"Emperador y Rey Nuestro Señor Don Carlos Primero de España y Quinto de Alemaña" reads the inscription on the little sarcophagus in the monastery of San Juste in Central Spain where Charles died in 1558. In a sense he had always been more Charles I of Spain than Charles V of Germany. Born at Ghent, capital of Philip the

Handsome and Joan of Spain, on February 20, 1500, he inherited his
Burgundian realm as a child when his father passed away and his
mother went mad. At first Ferdinand and Isabella had no intention
to add the Spanish realm to his inheritance, but preferred his
younger brother Ferdinand, who was brought up at the Spanish
court. But after the death of Isabella and years later of Ferdinand,
Charles, seventeen years old, appeared with a retinue of Flemish
nobles to claim his paternal and maternal inheritance. Soon Maximilian died too, and Charles had the greatest empire ever seen

CHARLES V

in the history of mankind. America was discovered and conquered,
India and parts of Africa added to his realm, and at the end of his
rule Charles could truly say that the sun never set on his realm.

Ferdinand, the younger brother, was shifted to Austria, far away
from Spain where he could have made serious trouble. For no
sooner had Charles left for Germany to be crowned emperor and
to preside at the Diet of Worms, than there was a violent outbreak
of Spanish rebellion against the Flemish rulers who had been imported by the young king. The rebellion was crushed in the blood
of the grandees.

Charles, the timid youth, developed into a self-possessed and strong ruler. Although he did not like war, he was forced to wage wars until his end. Francis I, his rival at the imperial election, challenged him again and again. As a matter of fact Charles was so busy fighting the French and the Turks that he had no time for the heresy which he would have liked to stamp out at the very beginning. To make things worse the pope of Rome concluded an alliance against him and had to be defeated by the most faithful son of the Church. The sack of Rome in 1527 left the Roman Church immobilized for many years.

During this fateful decade Ferdinand of Austria ruled in his brother's stead in Germany. Although of a milder disposition toward the Lutherans whose support he needed against the Turks in Hungary, he was carrying out his brother's commands to the best of his ability. Sporadic persecutions of Lutherans, Zwinglians and Anabaptists took place again and again. The toleration which had been promised at Speier in 1526 was rescinded at Speier in 1529. This led to the famous Protest of Speier from which the evangelicals received the name Protestants. Again in 1530, at the first Diet which Charles could attend in person, the Lutherans were told—immediately after they had presented the Augsburg Confession—that they must give up their separate ways and return to the fold by next spring. But events forced the emperor to rescind this action. The Turks were once more at the gates of Vienna and the French king was making common cause with the German Lutherans, while at home he was persecuting the Protestant dissenters. It was not until the fifteen-forties that the emperor found time to settle his score with the Lutherans. By that time Luther was dead, and the victorious emperor, standing on the grave of the Reformer, could only declare to the Duke of Alba: "I wage war against the living, not against the dead."[1] Eight years later he retired to the monastery of San Juste after having abdicated the imperial crown in favor of his brother, Ferdinand I, and the royal crown of Spain in favor of his son, Philip II.

Ferdinand, more human than his famous brother, happier in his personal life, ruled only a short while. He died at Vienna on July 25, 1564.

Luther's Princes

The number of princes who took Luther's side and who opposed him is as large as the number of principalities and little realms which split Germany into hundreds of atoms. But there are a few princes who stand out in the history of the Reformation.

First of all, Frederick the Wise. Without Frederick the Wise to protect him, a historian has said, Luther would have burned. Even though Frederick did not officially embrace Lutheranism until the day before his death—when he took Holy Communion in both kinds —he was the most powerful stumbling block against the designs of emperor and pope. He protected Luther in 1518, when Luther faced Cajetan at Augsburg, he refused to surrender Luther in 1519 and 1520, he saw to it that Luther received a safe-conduct to Worms, and he spirited Luther away after he had been declared an outlaw by the Diet of Worms. He steadfastly refused to give up the professor, whom he probably had seen only once in his life—at the Diet of Worms—and with whom he had never so much as exchanged a word. He helped the man who destroyed his favorite hobby of collecting relics—the most famous relic collection in Germany was found in Wittenberg—and who wrote to him proud and almost rebellious letters. But when Frederick died in 1525 his realm was solidly Lutheran, in spite of the fact that his cousin George, Duke of Albertine Saxony, and his kinsman, Joachim, Elector of Brandenburg, were sternly persecuting all Lutherans on the northern, western, southern, and eastern fringes of his electorate. It was almost completely surrounded by inimical princes.

Frederick's successor, John the Constant, did not possess the sagacity of his brother, but he was more determined than his predecessor to make his Lutheran convictions known. History has given him the name: the Constant. Somewhat bungling, he often realized his limitations and called on the Wittenberg theologians to straighten him out. Under him the Articles of Schwabach, the first Lutheran Confession, and the Augsburg Confession and its Apology were written. In his lifetime the churches were visited and reorganized, Luther's two Catechisms serving as text-books for all instruction. He was opposed to compromise and did not mind that the reformers did not get together in Marburg. He backed Luther to the hilt in the Communion controversy, although it put him into a difficult position vis-à-vis his new ally, Philip of Hesse, the great mediator of the Reformation period. Unfortunately, John the Constant fell off his horse and died a few years after Augsburg, before the Lutheran Church was strong enough to weather future storms.

John Frederick his son and successor, the last elector of the Ernestine line of Saxony, was also the first prince who had received a completely Lutheran education. Spalatin had been his tutor. To Spalatin he turned in many trials. He is called: The Magnanimous. He truly was. But on the other side of the ledger were serious difficulties which made his reign hard and disappointing. He was a heavy drinker—Luther called him a "guzzler"[2]—he was proud and arrogant against his relatives, especially his Saxon cousins, one of whom, Maurice of Albertine Saxony, never forgave him and took the electoral dignity away from him at the first opportunity. He did not have the humility of his father nor the wisdom of his uncle. He often decided things for himself. Yet Luther loved this prince who was often so hard to handle. Even before Luther's death John Frederick had almost succeeded in bringing war to Saxony, but was prevented by the timely intervention of Philip of Hesse. Immediately after Luther's death he reaped the harvest of his foolish acts when both the emperor and the turn-coat prince Maurice of Saxony attacked him on two fronts. Made a prisoner by the Hapsburgs he had to resign his electoral office, which Maurice received as a Judas-award. He spent most of his remaining years in prison, until he was freed by the downfall of Charles V and reunited with his family. He died shortly thereafter, two weeks after his faithful wife, on March 3, 1554, "of a broken heart."

There were other Saxon princes whom history had placed on the other side of the fence. Saxony had been divided by the generation preceding Luther, the sons of Duke Ernest receiving the larger portion and the electoral dignity, while the sons of Albert became dukes of Saxony and received the more advanced regions of the realm. Thus it happened that at the outbreak of the Reformation,

Frederick, the son of Ernest, was ruling over Wittenberg, Torgau and the rest of the "sandbox of the Holy Empire," while Duke George, the son of Albert, was ruling in Leipzig, Meissen and Dresden. The domain of Thuringia was divided between the two in such a way that both realms overlapped like the squares on a checkerboard. Luther, returning from the Wartburg to Wittenberg had to travel—incognito, of course—through the realm of his fierce enemy, Duke George.

Of all the Saxon princes, including Frederick the Wise, Duke George was perhaps the ablest administrator. Luther had a high regard for him, regretting only that such a fine prince could be so mistaken in his religious beliefs. Duke George, who had been originally destined for a religious career, had a fine understanding of theological issues. This and the fact that his vanity was often hurt by Luther's outbursts may have accounted for his undying hatred of the Wittenberg Reformer. Furthermore he was married —very happily—to a Polish princess who was a strict Catholic. Even after she died he kept faithful to her, letting his beard grow, so that he is known to us today as George the Bearded. On the eve of his life he saw practically his whole domain turn Lutheran. His heirs had died out. His brother, Duke Henry, a man of limited talent, but great piety, had already introduced the Reformation in his part of Saxony. After George's death, in 1539, all of Saxony was Lutheran at one stroke, and although Henry the Pious died after two years and Maurice of Saxony subsequently turned against his Wittenberg uncle and defeated him in the Smalcald War, he had to respect the faith of his subjects who called him "Judas," but who accepted him as a ruler. Under Maurice, Wittenberg faded away. The strict Lutherans did not only mistrust him but also those who worked with him, like Melanchthon, and Wittenberg soon became the center of compromise and was read out of the Lutheran Church. The faithful Lutherans had either followed the imprisoned Elector John Frederick to his new residence at Weimar, had helped him establish the strictly Lutheran University of Jena, or had migrated to neighboring territories and towns where they spread the Lutheran gospel.

Two others must be numbered among Luther's princes: Philip of Hesse, the unpredictable, uncontrolled, but brilliant defender of the Reformation, and Count Albert of Mansfeld, the humble prince of Luther's home town. Philip, married to a woman whom he loathed, was one of the most unfortunate rulers of the Reformation period. He ended as a bigamist and a millstone around the neck of the Lutheran Church. Yet he was the most enthusiastic admirer of Luther. He did not forsake him, even when Luther's "stubbornness"—others call it Luther's faithfulness—made it impossible for him to carry out his favorite plan of reuniting all Protestants into one movement. Philip convened the Colloquy of Marburg, he tried to form a common front at Augsburg and later in the Smalcald League, he was the driving force behind the Wittenberg Concord, but when at the end of the fifteen-thirties he committed the unforgivable sin of contracting a bigamous marriage with Margaret von der Saal—with Luther's and Melanchthon's connivance—he became the lame-duck prince among the Lutheran princes. Obeying more the call of the flesh than the call to duty, Philip became indirectly responsible for the first great defeats of Lutheranism in the fifteen-forties, at Cologne and during the Smalcald War. He was also the father of the pernicious tendencies of princes and theologians to compromise their faith for the sake of expedience. Hesse, once a stronghold of Lutheranism, was soon to become a land where all Protestants could meet on common ground.

The other prince, Albert of Mansfeld, born three years before Luther, was perhaps the closest personal "friend" among the princes. He bore the brunt of the Peasant Revolt of 1525, but tried to remain humane even in this great tragedy. With his brother, Count Gebhart, he joined the first league of Lutherans which was being formed as early as 1526 by the Elector John and the Landgrave Philip of Hesse. He protested at Speier and confessed at Augsburg. But his relationship to his relatives caused Luther much trouble. They were always bickering with each other. Luther died on February 18, 1546, on the day after he had accomplished his last mission of mercy—to bring peace between the Mansfeld counts.

These were the princes whose life was closely tied up with Luther's. But there were others.

Other Princes

There were three kings of Denmark and Norway, Christian II, Frederick I and Christian III. Perhaps the unfortunate Christian II was closest to Luther among all the Scandinavians who from time to time came to Wittenberg. After his expulsion from Denmark Christian II lived for several years in Wittenberg, humbling himself to the extent that he was even serving as a deacon of the Wittenberg Church. In those years he was the most faithful, but also the most miserable among the Lutheran princes. Soon ambition got the better of him, he withdrew from Wittenberg, reconverted to Catholicism and with the help of the dissatisfied Norwegian bishops tried to regain his realm from Frederick I who had replaced him. His life ended in tragedy. He lived on for a long time, a prisoner of two kings.

Frederick I, as we have seen, introduced the Reformation—at least unofficially—in Denmark, but it was not until the rule of his son, Christian III, that the Lutheran religion became the religion of Denmark, Norway and Iceland.

Turning east we have seen the work which Gustavus Vasa did among the Swedes and Finns. Although he was not close to Luther, neither in spirit nor in person, Gustavus Vasa established what in the sixteenth century might have been considered the most conservative of Lutheran churches. His church, like the other Scandinavian churches, was strictly a state church, but it was also a church where the break between Roman tradition and Lutheran substance was least noticeable.

South and East of Scandinavia were the Teutonic Knights of the Baltic States who, however, either preceded or followed their East Prussian Grandmaster, Albert of Hohenzollern, into the Lutheran fold. Albert, kinsman of the famous Albert of Mainz, whose monetary schemes he detested, secularized his realm in the mid-twenties and ruled the rest of his life as a faithful Lutheran prince —although not always strictly orthodox. He defied all pressures put on him by his suzerain King Sigismund of Poland, who remained fanatically Catholic. Of Russia and her Czar we hear little during the Reformation period.

Among the scores of princes of Germany outside of the heart-land of the Reformation only two need to be mentioned: Joachim I of Brandenburg and Ulrich of Wuerttemberg.

Joachim was by far the worst of the five Hohenzollerns in Luther's life. He was cruel, immoral, self-centered and one of the worst rulers of Brandenburg. When he died on July 11, 1535, at Stendal there were very few who mourned his passing. His rela-

CHRISTIAN III

tionship to Luther was poisoned from the beginning by the other Hohenzollern, Albert of Mainz, in whose fortunes Joachim I was vitally interested. Unfaithful to his wife Elizabeth, he expelled her from his realm when he discovered her Lutheran leanings. Luther repeatedly rebuked the elector for his unfaithfulness, but to no avail. But before his death Joachim, like George of Saxony, had to realize that the majority of his subjects were fervently Lutheran. His son, Joachim II, officially introduced the Reformation in Brandenburg.

Ulrich of Wuerttemberg whose life before the Reformation was anything but exemplary—he had killed and thrown down the stairs a rival for his mistress—was restored in the fifteen-thirties to his throne by the efforts of Philip of Hesse. Thus Austria which had taken over from Ulrich at the expulsion of the duke was dispossessed and Wuerttemberg became a fortress of the Lutherans from which they could not be dislodged in future years. Ulrich became a devoted and able protector of the faithful and assembled in his domain a great number of outstanding Lutheran theologians. He died on November 6, 1550.

There were other princes who played an important part in the Reformation history, but their parts were played in the wings. They set the stage for the persecution, like the dukes of Bavaria, and especially Ernest of Bavaria, the father of the counter-reformation in Germany. There was the pious George of Anhalt whom even his enemy Charles V had to praise as one of the most faithful men of his empire. There were the dukes of Mecklenburg and of Pomerania who helped introduce the Reformation. There was the mean Henry of Brunswick-Wolfenbuettel, Luther's "Jack Sausage," and many others. They were important to thousands and tens of thousands of people. Luther dealt with them at various times. But to deal with them here would be an impossibility.

A King of England and a King of France

Henry VIII, husband of Catherine of Aragon, Anne Boleyn, Jane Seymour, Anne of Cleve, Catherine Howard and Catherine Parr—he must have loved the name Catherine!—was perhaps the one prince who was attacked by Luther and who tried again and again to establish friendly relations with the Wittenbergers. But Luther saw through him and despised him. After the king did no longer need the support of the Wittenbergers he withdrew completely from them and murdered all his councillors whom he suspected of Lutheran leanings. He was callous and unscrupulous, surpassing even Machiavelli's famous "Prince" in the way in which he dispatched not only religious antagonists—Roman Catholics and Lutherans alike—but also his wives. Yet he was the godfather of the Anglican Church and received theological insights from the

Lutheran movement which gave to the Anglican theology the strange intermediary position between Catholicism and Protestantism.

Francis I, a slightly better person and a better ruler than Henry, criss-crossed the history of Lutheranism directly and indirectly during his long and prosperous reign. Sworn enemy of Charles V and yet a good Catholic, he kept the emperor away from

HENRY VIII

Germany during the fifteen-twenties, thus giving the Lutheran movement a breathing spell which it needed to consolidate its gains. In the fifteen-thirties he often made overtures to the Lutheran princes, shamelessly denying his own persecutions against the Protestants of France, a fact which aroused the wrath of Calvin to such an extent that he dedicated his Institutes of Christion Religion to the king whom he accused of lying. Francis died in 1547, a year after Luther, two months after Henry VIII.

Frederick the Wise (1463-1525)

"I am under a higher Protector than your Electoral Grace,"[3] Luther wrote to Frederick from Borna, after he had defied the elector's orders to stay at the Wartburg. Yet he appreciated the protection which this faithful prince gave him throughout his life.

Frederick was born on January 17th, 1463, the oldest son of Duke Ernest, who with Albert had divided the Saxon lands. After the death of his father he ruled his part of the domain together

FREDERICK III, THE WISE

with his brother and later successor, John. The princes lived in concord, enjoying the respect of their fellow princes and the esteem and jealousy of the emperor. Although Frederick did not openly confess his Lutheran leanings, his protection of the Reformer was a most remarkable feat of political maneuvering. He succeeded partly because the Hapsburgs had often wronged him. This had endeared him to the rest of the German princes, especially his steadfast refusal, at the Diet of Augsburg in 1518, to have Maximilian's grandson Charles declared emperor in case of the old emperor's death. But when the final vote was cast, Frederick rejected the bribe offered by Francis I and cast his lot with Charles V. The young emperor showed his gratitude to the Saxon prince by following his suggestion to have Luther appear and defend himself before the Diet of Worms, a promise to which he remained faithful even against the machinations of the nuncio Aleander and Glapion, his father-confessor. But soon the relationship between the Hapsburgs and the House of Saxony cooled off again, especially when Frederick refused to carry out the Edict of Worms. Francis I, quick to grasp a hand when he saw it, wanted to make an alliance with the Saxon prince, but Frederick refused, because he looked through the wily French king's ulterior motives.

Throughout his life Frederick was a devout, if sometimes misled, Christian. In 1493 he had made a pilgrimage to the Holy Land. From that time stemmed his great hobby, the relic collection of Wittenberg. Men like Staupitz supported him in his harmless pastime, although Luther did by no means approve of it. He attacked, however, the indulgence traffic, partly for religious reasons, partly because it was a heavy financial drain on his economy, partly because it turned away the hearts of his people from his beloved relics. He also withheld the moneys which he had collected for the Turkish war, but which the pope was using for the rebuilding of St. Peter, and used part of these moneys to build the University of Wittenberg which was opened in 1502. Still the indulgence traffic, on account of the proximity of Brandenburg where Tetzel sold his indulgences, was a continuous annoyance. Therefore, Frederick was happy when Luther put an end to it and thereafter was ever the champion of the Reformer. He fought valiantly for him, hovering over him like a hen before and after Worms. But while he protected Luther, the introduction of the Reformation in Saxony was largely left to the men at his court. He did not want to be put into an embarrassing situation opposite the other princes and the pope. Even at that time Duke George had his eyes on the electoral dignity which the emperor might have bestowed upon him if Frederick the Wise would have stumbled into the trap.

Frederick died on May 5, 1525, at Lochau and was buried in the Castle Church in Wittenberg. He had never married. Only once had he been deeply in love, with a commoner whom he could not marry, Anna Weller. To her he remained faithful throughout his life. From her he had two sons and a daughter. After his death the electoral dignity passed on to his faithful brother and co-regent, John the Constant.

John the Constant (1468-1532)

Born at Meissen on June 30, 1468, John was the fourth son of Duke Ernest and a younger brother of Frederick. He received an excellent education at the court of Frederick III, great-grandfather of Charles V and his great-uncle. Later he accompanied the aging emperor on his travels and also remained for a while with Maximilian I during the campaigns against Venice and Hungary. After the death of his brother, in 1525, he became the sole ruler of Electoral Saxony, at the age of fifty-seven. The first few months of his reign were spent putting down the bloody Peasant Revolt.

After the defeat of the peasants and the execution of their leaders—among them Muenzer and Pfeifer—John showed marked clemency toward his defeated subjects. He also intervened on behalf of the peasants with his bloodthirsty fellow-princes. When George of Saxony, in a rage, tried to put the blame for the revolt at the doorsteps of Luther, John defended the Reformer's integrity vigorously and came out openly for the Lutheran religion. From then on he never swerved in his support for the cause of Lutheranism, but took an active part in the establishment of the Lutheran Church in Saxony. In Weimar, in August 1525, he advised the clergy to preach the pure Gospel. He also gave Luther greater influence in public affairs and favored him in many ways. In 1530 he defied the emperor at Augsburg when he declared that he was willing to lay down his life for the cause of the Reformation. For this history has given him the name: "the Constant."

Like his brother Frederick John the Constant was often threatened not only with the loss of his electoral dignity, but with the loss of his land. To counteract Catholic plots against Saxony he early in his reign formed the league of Lutheran princes against the Catholic league of Dessau. This first Lutheran League of Torgau was later followed by the more inclusive Smalcald League.

Perhaps the most important event in his life occurred on June 25, 1530, when his two chancellors, Brueck and Beyer, read the Augsburg Confession to the Emperor and the estates assembled at Augsburg. But there were other important events that took place during his brief rule: The church visitations, the adoption of church constitutions, and the writing of Luther's Catechisms. Leopold von Ranke had said to him: "There has been no prince who has done a greater service for the establishment of the Lutheran Church."[4]

John entered into defensive alliances with Philip of Hesse and others, but always restrained his impetuous partners from rash actions. He even came to an understanding with the Archbishop Albert of Mainz that they would respect each others' rights. He endeavored, and partly succeeded, in establishing better relations with his strongly anti-Lutheran cousin, Duke George.

At the second Diet of Speier John the Constant was the rallying point for all Lutherans. He had his motto "Verbum Dei manet in aeternum" put over his door and also on the uniforms of his servants. As a result he was cold-shouldered by many of his fellow-princes. He knew of Charles' threat to confer the electoral dignity on George of Saxony, yet he did not go along with Philip of Hesse when the impetuous landgrave advocated a preventive war against the emperor.

Again in 1530 John showed his courage. After arriving in Augsburg with his heir-apparent, John Frederick, and his theologians he refused to heed an imperial summons to come to Innsbruck. The emperor finally arrived in Augsburg and rebuked John in the presence of the other princes. In retaliation and at the risk of his life, John refused to participate in the Corpus Christi celebration which the emperor had ordered. When Charles V and Joachim I of Brandenburg openly threatened him with execution, John quietly replied: "I want to confess my Christ. . . . I must either deny God or the world. Who can be in doubt what is the best course?"[5]

At the end of the Diet John took leave of the emperor and went to Smalcald where, in December 1530, he formed the Smalcald League. The emperor who needed the support of the Lutherans in his fight against the Turk postponed the enforcement of the Speier and Augsburg edicts forbidding the Lutheran religion, until a later date. The Nuremberg Truce of July 28, 1532, was the last political triumph of John. He died soon after in a hunting accident at Schweinitz, on August 16, 1532. "With him," Luther said, "integrity has died, while with his brother Frederick wisdom was buried."[6]

John Frederick the Magnanimous (1503-1554)

The Elector John Frederick lacked the wisdom of his uncle and the constancy of his father, the two predecessors after whom he had been named. Although he had been trained from his youth for his future office and had often accompanied his father on important missions, he was inclined to be lazy and indecisive once he became ruler of Saxony in his own right. He was terribly fat and often drank too much for his own good. He was proud and tactless, making many enemies throughout his unhappy reign. Yet he has been named the Magnanimous by a grateful posterity, because in spite of all these shortcomings John Frederick was a deeply pious soul who had the interest of the church at heart.

The elector took great care to give to his country a well-educated clergy, he established consistories and revived the custom of periodical visitations. He took a special liking to Luther for whom he provided amply, making the last fifteen years of the Reformer's life as pleasant as possible. But Luther recognized the limitations of his prince. John Frederick was no match to the ever active Philip of Hesse and the determined George of Saxony, neither did he understand the scheming Emperor Charles and the betrayal of Maurice of Saxony until it was too late. His childlike faith and deep piety often served as an excuse for his lack of action. Yet once his sluggishness was cast off the elector could take drastic action which, however, did not always prove sound, as in the case of the city of Wurzen when he almost clashed with his relative Maurice.

His disdain for Maurice, although it may have been founded on the recognition that Maurice was not a true Christian, but an opportunist, nevertheless led to the disaster of John Frederick's downfall. Maurice, resentful and hurt, was plotting for his uncle's downfall even while appearing peaceful to him. He laid his plans carefully, enlisting the aid of the emperor whose hands were now freed after the final defeat of Francis I of France. John Frederick was utterly surprised when shortly after Luther's death, in 1546, he was attacked, first orally, then by the force of arms. Even at the last minute he could not make up his mind to take up arms against the emperor and he made no effort to co-ordinate his moves with those of Philip of Hesse. He did not help his fellow-elector Hermann of Cologne when the latter tried to introduce the Reformation in his land. All he did was to stay away from the Diet which was then meeting at Regensburg, asking his pastors to invoke divine mercy upon Saxony. Thus he lost all the advantage of a strong leader who could not only have defeated his enemies, but also could have advanced the cause of Lutheranism throughout western Germany.

While the emperor was attacking John Frederick his turn-coat relative, Maurice, turned on him from the back. The electoral armies were soon ground to small segments between the two millstones of double attack. The infamous Duke of Alba led his prisoner personally to the emperor and had the effrontery to ask Charles V for the execution of the heretic. But Maurice, who must have had a slight change of heart, pleaded for his kinsman and John Frederick was imprisoned. On May 19, 1547, he resigned the electoral dignity. Thus ended the dynasty which had given strength and comfort to the Lutheran movement during its formative years.

In captivity the former elector showed traits which had been lacking in happier days. He deported himself admirably. He refused steadfastly to sign the Interim, even though it meant that his captivity would be prolonged interminably. Paradoxically, however, he was freed from prison by the same man who had betrayed him: Maurice of Saxony. Returning to the rump of his former realm he was greeted at the border by his faithful wife, Constance, who had mourned for him during all these years. Now she exchanged her mourning dress for the first time in five years. But their happiness did not last long. Less than two years later Constance died, and John Frederick, heartbroken, followed her into the grave two weeks later, on March 3, 1554.

The University of Jena which was founded according to his plans became a stronghold of sixteenth century Lutheranism, a refuge for all faithful Lutheran theologians from where Melanchthonian and Crypto-Calvinist theology was valiantly attacked.

Philip of Hesse (1504-1567)

Philip of Hesse was the most energetic and perhaps the most gifted of the Lutheran princes, and yet he caused more trouble to the Lutheran cause than all the others. Born in Marburg on November 13, 1504, Philip became Landgrave of Hesse at the tender age of five. When he was 14 years old, in 1518, he began to rule his realm in his own right, an impetuous, immature youth. At the age of 19, in 1523, he married Christina of Saxony, daughter of Duke George, a purely political match without love and consideration which he soon regretted. Always ready for a fight Philip fought against Lutherans as well as Catholics. He was one of the chief enemies of the valiant knight, Francis von Sickingen, and contributed to his downfall. His behavior toward the defeated peasants in 1525 is one of the black marks in the Reformation history. By this time, in 1525, Philip had become a follower of Luther.

Almost from the beginning Philip had been interested in mediating the differences between Luther and Zwingli. The Marburg Colloquy of 1529 was held under his patronage. In spite of his personal disappointment with Luther's "stubbornness," Philip remained true to the Lutheran doctrine and signed the Augsburg Confession. But during the next decades Hesse remained one of the centers of mediation between Zurich and Wittenberg.

Philip was the prime mover behind the Lutheran defensive

alliances which would have turned into offensive alliances if he had had his way. He was ready to fight against his father-in-law, Duke George, during the notorious Pack Affair (he may have forged the incriminating documents against the Catholic princes himself). He was restrained only by the hand of his powerful ally, the Elector of Saxony. Again, after Augsburg and before the Smalcald War, Philip was ready to settle the religious issues by a preventive war against the Catholic princes. He offended the Hapsburgs by restoring Ulrich of Wuerttemberg to this throne. But he also prevented a war between the two Lutheran Saxon princes, John Frederick and Maurice, in the early fifteen-forties. At that time, however, Philip was the lame duck among the Lutheran princes, having incurred the censure of the empire by his odious bigamous marriage to Margaret von der Saal.

After the Smalcald War Philip was captured and put into prison. Ironically he was saved, like John Frederick, by his betrayer who also was his son-in-law, the "Judas" Maurice of Saxony. After his release he ruled for another decade and a half, trying to the end to bring about not only a reconciliation between Wittenberg and Zurich or Geneva, but also to stop the squabbling among the Lutheran theologians. He died at Cassel on March 31, 1567.

Ulrich of Wuerttemberg (1487-1550)

The man who helped establish the strongest, and in many respects healthiest, Lutheran Church outside Saxony was the Duke of Wuerttemberg who had been restored to his throne in 1534 by Landgrave Philip of Hesse.

Ulrich, like Philip, succeeded early in life to the throne. Also like Philip he was of an impetuous nature, inconsiderate to his friends of whom he had few, irresponsible to his subjects, pleasure-loving and violent. His ruthless taxation of the peasants—to defray the expenses of his pleasures—led to the "Poor Conrad" rebellion, the first major peasant revolt. When Ulrich broke the peace of the empire by occupying the Free City of Reutlingen he was expelled by the armies of the Emperor Maximilian. After that Wuerttemberg was an Austrian mandate for about 15 years, until it was taken away again from the Hapsburgs by the action of Philip of Hesse.

The Duke who returned to Wuerttemberg in 1534 was a changed man. He became one of the best rulers of the period and a fervently religious man. Under his protection the Swabian reformers were able to establish the strong Lutheran tradition which was to be a blessing to his land for centuries to come.

And So On

There were many other worthy princes who accepted Luther's doctrines and established them in their realm. Many of them were in touch with the Wittenberg Reformer to the end of his life. They are too numerous to be mentioned here, let alone to have their biographies recorded. Those whom we have introduced in this chapter were the most representative of them.

XII.

The Roman Camp

The publication of the Ninety-Five Theses on October 31, 1517, brought fame and also defamation to Martin Luther. From that date stemmed the fight against him by the Roman camp which was to continue until the end of his life. Yet at the beginning, Rome was slow to take up the gauntlet which the intrepid Wittenberg professor had flung in its direction.

If we begin at the top of the hierarchy we see Leo X, a Medici and a patron of arts, who would have preferred to stay out of the whole controversy—"the squabble of a drunken German monk" he called it—if only Luther's attack would not have hurt his financial interests. It is doubtful that Leo ever fully understood the full impact of Luther's attack. He finally issued the bull "Exsurge Domine," but only after Eck had lobbied for it in Rome for at least half a year. Leo's successor, a sincere, but narrow-minded reform pope ruled only for a short time. Furthermore, Adrian VI, was too closely connected with the University of Louvain and its "execrable" theologians—he had been professor there—to be able to serve as an arbiter in the dispute. His successor Clement VII was another Medici who loved his scheming better than his religion. He allied himself against Charles V, the most powerful defender of the faith, and suffered the misfortune of the Sack of Rome. Finally, the last pope to rule in Luther's lifetime, Paul III, was also the last of the "Renaissance Popes." He had to be pushed by the Jesuits into the Counter-Reformation. With the greatest reluctance he called the long-overdue Council of Trent, but did nothing to expedite its business.

There were, however, even before 1520 and 1521 scholars and churchmen in Rome who recognized the seriousness of the situation which had been created by Luther's attack. The foremost of these men was Sylvester Prierias, a Dominican, and thus a natural ally of Tetzel who was also a Dominican. Prierias attacked Luther very ably within a year after the publication of the Ninety-Five Theses. There were the emissaries of Pope Leo, Cardinal Cajetan who tried to force Luther to recant in October 1518, and the Chamberlain Charles von Miltitz who by various means tried to buy Luther's silence in 1519 and 1520. Finally, there was the able, wily Aleander, papal nuncio at the Diet of Worms. Later Campeggio, Chieregati, Vergerio, Castiglione, Carraciolo and many others tried their best to stop the rolling stone of the Reformation.

In Germany the Romanists were not without champions. Among the princes, the fiery Duke George of Saxony and the profligate Elector Joachim I of Brandenburg formed a pincers around electoral Saxony. But Frederick the Wise stood firm, although he did not come out openly for the Reformation until the day before his death in 1525. Under the protection of Joachim I Tetzel and Wimpina, professor at Frankfurt-Oder, were able to launch their first, ineffective counter-attack against Luther. At Frankfurt Tetzel was made an honorary Doctor of Theology. George of Saxony not only made it possible for Eck to challenge Luther at Leipzig, but also harbored a whole nest of anti-Lutheran theologians and mischievous laymen. Here we find Emser, the Leipzig Goat, who wrote one missive after another against Luther and later plagiarized Luther's Bible translation; here were Alveld, whom Luther called an ass; Breitenbach, the "devilish lawyer"; later Cochlaeus, the most abusive of all of Luther's opponents (with the possible exception of Thomas Murner); Dungersheim, Hennigk, John of Meissen, Ochsenfart, Weissestadt, Heyden, Hasenberg, and all the vermin who spread their poison against Luther and the Reformation of the Church. It has been said, that even Ingolstadt, the university town of Eck, was not as safe for the Romanists as Leipzig. When Eck tried to burn Luther's books in his own bailiwick he was hindered by enlightened Catholics which included Reuchlin, Melanchthon's great-uncle.

The bishops of Germany were divided. John of Meissen has been mentioned. He belonged to the fanatical enemies of Luther. Furthermore he lived too close to George of Saxony to be unprejudiced. On the other hand Luther's own bishop, Jerome Scultetus of Brandenburg, to whose diocese Wittenberg belonged, was friendly and understanding towards the Reformer, in spite of the fact that he was living under the nose of Joachim I. He even permitted Luther—implicitly—to publish his defense and explanation of the Ninety-Five Theses. The successor of Scultetus, Dietrich von Hardenberg, did not come out openly against Lutheranism until his hand was forced by the irate elector, Joachim I. This attitude of Luther's own bishops is not surprising, in view of the fact that even Albert of Mainz who had been attacked by Luther directly tried for years to keep on good terms with the Reformer. He wrote apologetic letters to Luther, sent him a wedding gift in 1525—disregarding completely the canon law which prohibits marriage between monks and nuns—and until 1530 led Luther to believe that he would eventually become a Lutheran.

In spite of the friendliness which many bishops showed to the Wittenberg professor—the Bishop of Wuerzburg, Lawrence von Bibra, took Luther into his home when the Reformer passed through Wuerzburg and a later bishop, Conrad von Thuengen tried to conciliate between Lutherans and Catholics for many years—there were only a few who joined the Reformation outright. Polentz in East Prussia made the switch and succeeded, because he was backed by Albert of Prussia who at that time accepted Lutheranism and secularized his country. Hermann of Cologne who tried to do the same in Western Germany, was deposed and died as a Lutheran layman. But even so, there was no wholesale persecution of Lutherans in Germany during Luther's lifetime, as there was in the Romance countries and in the Netherlands and in England. Dantiscus, also in East Prussia, managed to remain a Catholic bishop under a Lutheran prince and was a life-long friend of both Lutherans and Catholics at his court. Richard of Trier and his chancellor, John von der Ecken, who questioned Luther at Worms, were working for a compromise long after their neighbors to the west had embarked on bloody persecution. Matthew Lang, Archbishop of Salzburg and faithful friend of Staupitz to whom he gave asylum, was at first a moderate. His cruelty became evident much later. Thus we have, apart from the Dominicans and a few Franciscans, mostly in Leipzig and Cologne—home of the notorious Inquisitor Hoogstraten—no fanatical anti-Lutherans in Germany, until at last the Peasant War and Luther's separation from the humanists led to an alignment of forces.

There are various reasons for this strange state of affairs. The death of the Emperor Maximilian I and the uncertainty of the succession has often been cited. Leo X was opposed to the candidacy of Charles V, favoring—for political reasons—Francis I of France. Many bishops who held no brief for the Hapsburg pretender, but did not like the interference in internal German affairs from across the Alps, made no effort to silence the monk who had "touched the crown of the pope." Moreover, some of the electors actually chose Frederick the Wise to succeed Maximilian, and Frederick was very touchy on the subject of Luther's alleged heresy. But there were other reasons. Most German bishops were dissatisfied with the financial policy of the Roman See. They felt that Germany and "the dumb Germans"—as Luther called them—were being exploited. They had drawn up a list of grievances again and again, and even evoked from Pope Adrian VI a humble apology for past mistakes. John von Thurzo, Bishop of Breslau, welcomed Luther's attack against Rome. Weigand von Redwitz, Bishop of Bamberg, openly opposed papal collections in Germany. Even Albert of Mainz, whose rapacious money deals had caused the furor in the first place, had to admit that there was room for reforms. He assured Luther by letter that he would change his ways of raising funds. Is it not strange that at the court of Albert of Mainz we find many outstanding Lutherans during the years after 1517?

But perhaps the most cogent reason why the German episcopate did not oppose Luther until the mid-twenties was that almost all the elite of the humanists and scholars were on Luther's side. The influence of a Hutten cannot be underestimated. He was at once respected and feared. Bishops wanted to be openminded and liberal, especially after the publication of the "Epistles of the Obscure Men" which had held up the whole Roman system to ridicule, Erasmus again and again postponed his attack against Luther, and when it finally came it was a weak "Diatribe on the Free Will," a topic to which neither Catholics nor Lutherans could rally with any show of enthusiasm. Until then all the great humanists of Germany had been non-committal or friendly to Luther. These humanists were the teachers at the schools of Germany and the companions of the bishops at whose courts they spent much of their time. After Luther's "Bondage of the Will" all this changed. Soon Erasmus was moving away, not only spiritually, but also physically, from liberal Basel to reactionary Freiburg, and in their own ways most of the humanist band followed him. After that the opposition in the Catholic camp became more determined.

Yet it would be missing the point if we were to assume that the opposition to Luther sprang up all of a sudden and was due to his involvement in historical events like the Peasant War or to his controversy with Erasmus. As a matter of fact, defections from the Lutheran camp started as soon as the Reformation had begun. On the other hand, defections from the Catholic camp did not all take place in the early years of the Reformation but continued throughout the lifetime of Luther, as we have seen in the case of Hermann von Wied, Archbishop-Elector of Cologne, and Peter Paul Vergerio, Papal nuncio who visited Luther in the mid-thirties. Among those who first jubilantly hailed Luther as the liberator and later forsook, him, was Staupitz, Luther's mentor during the formative years. He and his friends Bessler and Mayr retired from the Lutheran movement early. Staupitz even left the Augustinian Order because its escutcheon was tarnished. Paul Lange, the chronicler, who had first forgotten to include Luther in his "Who's Who" and later made up for the omission

by overly praising him, soon returned to the Catholic fold. Among
the defectors were several South Germans like Adelmann, the
canon at Augsburg, and Guy Bild, an enthusiastic monk in that
same city; some Wittenbergers like Oldecop, Boeschenstein, and
Conrad Helt; the liberal-minded Leipzigers (but not all of them,
e.g., the Lotthers) who renounced their Lutheranism under duress:
Auerbach of the famous Auerbach cellar, who was a scholar and
professor at the University of Leipzig, and Andrew Franck who
was forced by Emser to break with Luther. There was Pirckheimer,
Duerer's protector, who abjured all Reformation ideas when Eck
returned with the bull from Rome and threatened to include the
name of the famous Nuremberg art-lover; there was also Henry
Cornelius Agrippa, the occultist of Cologne, who could not stand up
against the pressure of Hoogstraten; Otto Beckmann who went all
the way and became a Catholic priest, appearing as a Catholic delegate at the Diet of Augsburg; Billicanus, Charles von Muensterberg,
Thomas von Fuchs, Langenmantel, Miritsch, the two Schwarzen-
bergs, Stehelin, Symler, Wimpfeling, and others. Most of these
names were in good repute in the early years of the Lutheran
Reformation. One of the apostates, George Witzel, who had served
as Lutheran pastor in Niemegk near Wittenberg returned to Luther's hometown of Eisleben as a Catholic priest trying to reconvert
the realm of the Counts of Mansfeld, Luther's counts. In spite of
these defectors the outspoken enemies of Luther in Germany,
whose efforts amounted to something, can be counted on the
fingers of two hands. Most of the attack, and practically the whole
Counter-Reformation was imported from the outside. At the time
of Luther's death nine-tenths of Germany's population was no
longer Catholic and only the fact that there were no strong
Lutheran rulers for all of Germany—as there were two in Scandinavia, Christian III and Gustavus Vasa—saved the day for the
Catholic Church. The remaining bishops merely sat and waited
for the Jesuits to move in.

As we survey the Roman camp we shall divide it into four
sections: First, the humanists and scholars who never fully broke
with Rome and were led back into the camp by lack of conviction, fear, or annoyance with Luther; secondly, the faltering

friends of the Reformer who later became either neutral onlookers or reconverted foes; thirdly, the outspoken enemies, the professional warriors of the Roman camp; and finally, the officials, bishops and popes of the Roman Church.

Humanists and Scholars

The tremendous influence of the humanists during the era of Martin Luther has been described in the first part of the book. The greatest of them was Desiderius Erasmus whose biography is given below. But there were many others, and their influence upon Luther should not be underestimated. Rubeanus Crotus at Erfurt, whose "Epistles of the Obscure Men" deeply moved Luther as is evident from his early letters; Lawrence Corvinus, the Silesian poet and geographer, highly esteemed by the Reformer for his erudition; Nicholas Copernicus, whose epochal book "On the Revolution of the Celestial Bodies" was prefaced both by a Catholic bishop and a Lutheran theologian and whose implications Luther never fully grasped; John Reuchlin, the great-uncle of Melanchthon, without whose Hebrew Grammar Luther would not have been able to master the language of the Old Testament; Beatus Rhenanus, the scholarly friend of Erasmus, editor of many important documents; Willibald Pirckheimer who first wrote an attack against Eck "The Unplaned Eck," but later apologized when Eck waved the bull under his nose; Conrad Peutinger, the best known antiquarian of the period; Theophrastus Bombastus Paracelsus, mystic, quack, or scholar; the brilliant conversationist Conrad Mutianus who never wrote a book, but is said to have had greater influence upon his fellow-humanists than most of the great authors; Peter Mosellanus, who gave the opening address at Leipzig; Bartholomew Latomus of Trier, who was present at many colloquies; Henry Cornelius Agrippa, the occultist; Louis Ber, who moved with Erasmus from Basel to Freiburg and was active at many disputations; James Montanus, Erasmus' old schoolmate, who first corresponded with Luther; Michael Maeurer, philosopher, theologian, musician; Michael Hummelberg, the Greek scholar and friend of Reuchlin; and many others.

Desiderius Erasmus of Rotterdam, the greatest humanist of all times, had a tremendous influence upon both the Lutheran and Catholic theology. Although Luther early recognized the limitations of Erasmus' leadership—he could show the way to reform, but could not and would not lead the movement—he also felt deeply indebted to him.

By the time the Reformation began Erasmus was already the most famous scholar of Europe, a friend of emperors, kings, popes and bishops. He had lived in Holland, France, England, Switzerland, had published numerous works, including the "Praise of Folly," the "Enchiridion of a Christian Soldier," and the Greek New Testament. He had come a long way from Gouda, where he was born in 1466 as the son of a priest and his mistress.

When the newly elected Emperor Charles V arrived in the Netherlands, Erasmus attached himself to his court. During these early days of the Reformation he often defended Luther, in letters to his friends, as for example to Eobanus Hess, or his patrons, including Albert of Mainz, or in witty statements which did not commit him, however. Thus he told Frederick the Wise not to worry about Luther. Luther had made only two mistakes: He had attacked the bellies of the monks and he had touched the crown of the pope. Luther was so thankful for this patronizing defense of Erasmus—who had just been appointed imperial councillor—that he wrote to him on March 29, 1519, calling him his brother in Jesus. Erasmus replied in kind.

But Erasmus was not impervious to flattery and other types of pressure which the Roman camp began to apply to him. One of his weaknesses was the feeling of jealousy, another his desire to be considered always the greatest among the great. From his Roman friends he received many presents. Due to their generosity he lived a comfortable life. He was no hardy crusader. Beer he could not drink, nor did he like white wines. He drank Burgundy, but sparingly. He had an allergy against the smell of fish. Thus this pampered man—some have called him a hypochondriac—was no made-to-order reformer. He said jokingly that his stomach was Lutheran, but his heart was Catholic.

Throughout his life Erasmus tried to avoid issues. When the

Emperor Charles invited him to reside at his court in Louvain, he refused because the bleak atmosphere of Catholic reaction and of the Belgian countryside did not agree with his delicate health. He preferred to stay in Basel, in spite of the Zwinglian reformers, editing with great industry his monumental edition of the Church Fathers for Froben and writing a book on "The Institution of Christian Marriage." People from all over Europe made pilgrimages to Basel to see the famous scholar, to have their books

ERASMUS

prefaced by him, and to bathe in the light which was emanating from the delicate lips of the smallish man.

For several years Erasmus had steadfastly refused to take sides in the Reformation controversy. Again and again he used the excuse that he had not had time to read Luther's books, a weak excuse from a man who had a keen intellectual curiosity. Finally he consented to write his "Diatribe on the Freedom of the Will" which fifteen months later, in December 1525, was answered by Luther's "The Bondage of the Will." After this the break between the two men, not only on theological grounds, but on a purely personal basis, was irreparable, although Erasmus continued to remain on friendly terms with many Lutheran theologians, including Luther's best friend, Melanchthon. Shortly after his break with the Reformation movement, after the death of Froben, Erasmus left Basel and moved to Freiburg where he lived for the next six years in lonely splendor, occupying a palace which had been built for the Emperor Maximilian. Finally he returned to Basel and, surrounded by Protestant and Catholic admirers, passed away at the age of seventy, on July 11, 1536.

Erasmus was a prototype for all humanists. He was more a philosopher than a theologian. He was appalled by the abuses of Rome, but was not ready to take action. He was not particularly interested in dogma. Thus it was easy for him to accept the doctrines of Rome because it was convenient to him and "because the Fathers had accepted them."

Like Erasmus, John Reuchlin whose ties to the Reformation were even closer on account of his great-nephew Melanchthon, returned to the Catholic fold. Erasmus had had his detractors among the fanatical theologians of Louvain. Reuchlin had his enemies in Cologne, Hoogstraten and Pfefferkorn, who tried for years to undo his Hebrew research. Reuchlin, about a decade older than Erasmus, had written, a decade before his colleague published the Greek New Testament, the Hebrew Grammar which established his fame. Thus Luther was indebted to both Reuchlin for his Hebrew scholarship and to Erasmus for his Greek New Testament.

But Reuchlin was a more complicated person than the famous Basel professor. Under the influence of Pico della Mirandola he had taken up cabbalistic studies, had lived in the Ghetto to learn Hebrew, and had been active in many affairs, including the Swabian League. Finally, in 1512 he had retired to a small estate in his beloved Stuttgart. But there was no peace for him. The greatest controversy to shake the Church during the decade before the Reformation—the burning of Reuchlin's books and all his Hebrew collections—caused the writing of the "Epistles of the Obscure Men" which deeply influenced Luther shortly before the start of the indulgence controversy. Although the injustice done to Reuchlin was finally settled by Rome—where the heresy trial

was squashed—the damage had been done. However, when the
Reformation of the Church began, Reuchlin, after recommending
his great-nephew Melanchthon to the University of Wittenberg,
soon withdrew and moved to the arch-Catholic University of Ingolstadt where he became a colleague of Eck. Yet even then he opposed Eck's scheme to have Luther's books burned. He died a year
after the Diet of Worms, at Bad Liebenzell, where he was vaca-
tioning.

There were humanists who tried to heal the breach between the
two movements, humanism and Reformation. Among them was
Rhenanus, one of the closest friends of Erasmus. Although he came
of a very humble background—his father had been the village
butcher at Schlettstadt—he attained great stature at the Sorbonne
and at Basel. In spite of the fact that he was twenty years younger
than Erasmus, Rhenanus soon became his closest friend. When after
1525 Zwingli asked Rhenanus to heal the wounds which Luther's
answer had struck in the heart of Erasmus, Rhenanus enlisted the
efforts of Melanchthon—who was trying to do the same for his friend
Luther—but their efforts were in vain. Erasmus and Rhenanus both
moved away from Basel, the one to Freiburg, the other to Schlettstadt, but both died surrounded by Lutheran and Zwinglian divines
who brought comfort to them in their last hours. Rhenanus died in
Strassburg, in 1547. Hedio, one of his Strassburg friends, summed
up his character when he said: "Rhenanus undoubtedly loved
the pure Gospel, the true religion, although he accepted the Catholic
ceremonies of his native city following the advice of Erasmus."
Unlike Erasmus, however, Rhenanus was married to a widow, Anna
Braun, but lived in a separate house "in order to be able to pursue his studies without interference."

Pirckheimer of Nuremberg and Peutinger of Augsburg were
two humanists who never found their way through the maze of
religious controversy. Willibald Pirckheimer, the patron of the
fervent Lutheran Duerer, had imitated the Reformer in the early
years of the Reformation, writing attacks against Rome and an
attack against Eck which, however, he hastily withdrew when
Eck returned from Rome with the bull. The last ten years of his
life he continued to live in Nuremberg, more and more isolated

and confused, trying to forget theology by keeping busy with the affairs of his city. He wrote only one more book which may be considered theological, "On the Second Marriage of Priests." But the book was a failure.

Conrad Peutinger, about as old as Erasmus and Pirckheimer, had been a friend of the Emperor Maximilian and was the foremost coin collector of his times. When Luther came to Augsburg for his colloquy with Cajetan, Peutinger looked after his wellbeing. At the Diet of Worms he played an important part in the negotiations which followed after Luther's two public appearances. When Luther was declared an outlaw a month later, Peutinger suddenly and inexplicably withdrew from the Reformation movement. The rest of his days he lived in obscurity.

Closer to Luther geographically was Conrad Mutianus, the brilliant conversationist, who taught only a short time and never published a line. Yet he is considered the third greatest German humanist, after Erasmus and Reuchlin. But he died lonely and forgotten nine years after the dawn of the Reformation.

Mutianus who had travelled much and was known by and knew almost every scholar of note, found a home in Erfurt where he became the center of a circle of scholars to which belonged Rhegius, Spalatin, Hess, Eberbach, Rubeanus, Jonas, and others. In spite of these contacts with many of Luther's supporters and the Reformer himself, he was frightened, like Staupitz, by the violence of the Reformation. The man who had inspired during his active years at Erfurt a hatred of ecclesiastic abuses, ceremonies, fasting, immorality died a lonely man at Gotha, on March 30, 1526.

Mosellanus, who gave the opening speech at Leipzig in 1519 and who wrote an enthusiastic description of Luther and the other disputants, was another great humanist who could not make up his mind. Very much younger than the other humanists, he died at the age of thirty-one, mourned by both sides. Melanchthon said of him: "His death is a heavy loss for scholarship, for he had many fine gifts."[1]

These men are representative of the scholars of the age. While it is true that some of the outstanding fighters on both sides were humanists, most of the humanists remained on the sidelines slowly returning into the Catholic camp, whether by fear or indifference toward religious issues is often hard to tell. Quite a number were jealous of Luther or were annoyed by his methods.

The Faltering Friends

When we think of the faltering friends of Luther, there comes to our mind immediately the name of John von Staupitz, the man who had a greater influence upon the young Luther, both personally and theologically, than any other man. Yet he was one of the first to forsake him.

The man who led Luther from "utter despair" to the knowledge that he had a gracious Savior, who brought him to Wittenberg and who has been called "the godfather of the Reformation," was born in Meissen of an old noble family. The year of his birth as well as his early years are shrouded in darkness. Born about 1470, Staupitz studied at the University of Tuebingen where, in 1497, he received his master's degree. Two years later he was created a doctor of theology.

From Tuebingen Staupitz' way led him to Munich and hence to Wittenberg where he became a charter member of the faculty of the newly established university. Soon he was vicar general of the Augustinian Order.

On one of his official visits to Erfurt Staupitz met a young 23-year-old monk to whom he took a special liking. Thus Luther came under the special protection of the powerful vicar general who healed him from the fever of unhealthy religious doubts and led him to the Word of God. In 1508 Staupitz called Luther to Wittenberg to substitute as a teacher.

In those years the vicar general was often absent from the classroom, visiting monasteries throughout Germany and settling disputes. Luther returned to Erfurt in 1509, was sent to Rome in 1510, but soon after his return from the Eternal City was called back to Wittenberg. Due to his partiality for the vicar general his stay in Erfurt had become unpleasant. The monks in Erfurt had opposed Staupitz' leadership, while Luther, after his return from Rome, had accepted it. Therefore, when Staupitz called him back to Wittenberg, he accepted the summons after some initial hesitation.

During the next seven years—from 1512 to 1519—Luther and Staupitz were close friends. In 1515 Luther was elected district vicar for the Saxon monasteries. But when the Reformation which the theology of Staupitz had prepared became a reality, the cautious vicar general gradually withdrew from Luther. In the spring of 1518 he still supported Luther at the Heidelberg Convention, but

STAUPITZ

in the fall of the year, after the colloquy with Cajetan, Staupitz suddenly absolved Luther from the monastic vow of obedience and left Augsburg. He went to Salzburg where his friend, the Archbishop Lang, appointed him as abbot over a Benedictine monastery. Staupitz had left the tarnished Augustinian Order. But his interest in Luther continued, as is evident from his letters to his successor in the office of vicar general, Wenceslas Linck. He inquired again and again about Luther, showing great anxiety and fear for his safety. The Reformer, on his part, reminded him in 1521 that Staupitz had told him in 1518: "Remember, brother, that you have begun this in the name of our Lord Jesus Christ" and rebuked him "with your own saying. Remember," he wrote to Staupitz, "that you said this to me. All hitherto has been child's play; now it begins to be serious . . . ."[2] Several times during the next few years the two men corresponded, Luther rebuking Staupitz, Staupitz excusing his weakness. In his last letter to the Reformer, sent to Luther through George Fuehrer on April 1, 1524, the former vicar general wrote: "You write me often, dear Martin, and suspect my constancy. To which I reply: My faith in Christ and the Gospel keeps whole, even if I need prayer that Christ may help my unbelief. . . . My love for you is most constant. . . . Spare me if, on account of the slowness of my mind, I do not grasp all your ideas and so keep silent about them. . . . We owe you much, Martin, for having led us from the husks of swine back to the pastures of life and the words of salvation."[3] He died on December 28, 1524, at Salzburg.

Like Staupitz, there were others who left Luther: Lange, Oldecop, Scheurl, Trutvetter, Usingen, Wimpfeling, Zasius, and so forth. Trutvetter and Usingen had been Luther's teachers in Erfurt, and like Staupitz, they had contributed to the development of his theology. But when Luther wrote the Ninety-Five Theses, Trutvetter and Usingen drew away from him. In the spring of 1518 Luther visited his old teacher Trutvetter at Erfurt, but the interview was a frosty affair, and a month later Trutvetter accused the Reformer of ignorance and vented his anger on him because he had started so much trouble within the Church. In spite of these attacks Luther continued to show great respect to his old teacher. "You have taught me to fight against the sale of indulgences," he wrote him, "and to rely on Scripture alone."[4] But Trutvetter remained unreconciled. On December 7, 1519, Luther received the news that his old teacher had died.

Usingen, on the other hand, continued to live until 1532. Like Staupitz he was kindhearted and had a simple faith in Christ, but he recoiled from attacking the Mother Church. When Erfurt became Lutheran the old teacher retired for a time from the city, where he had taught 30 years, to Catholic Wuerzburg. But in the end he returned to Erfurt where he passed away in the Augustinian monastery on September 9, 1532.

Christopher Scheurl who played an important part in the early years of the Reformation as a go-between between Luther and Eck, was another faltering friend who had known Luther since 1508, when he (Scheurl) had been rector of the University of Wittenberg. Born in 1481 at Nuremberg, he returned to his native city during the crucial years of the Reformation. Scheurl, who was not a theologian, but a lawyer, worked for the Reformation in Nuremberg, declaring, "I would gladly die, if someone would first preach Christ to us."[5] But after 1519 the speed with which the Reformation was spreading was beginning to frighten him. Like the humanist Pirckheimer and other Nuremberg leaders Scheurl became increasingly critical. Soon Luther and Melanchthon accused him of playing both sides. When Scheurl came to Wittenberg on official business he would no longer visit Luther, stating that he hated to go to Wittenberg, "the center of errors and the hell of all heretics."[6] In 1536—six years before his death—after Nuremberg had become Lutheran, Scheurl wrote: "By the grace of God I shall remain faithful to the Catholic Church to my last breath."[7] He did. When, in 1528, Scheurl had betrayed a letter to Duke George, in which Luther had called the Saxon duke "the worst of fools, who, like Moab, is bold beyond his power and proud beyond his strength," Luther wrote to Linck in Nuremberg, "I have no fear whatever of that Satan, Duke George, though I am surprised at Scheurl . . . because he is so intimate with our worst enemies . . . ."[8]

Outspoken Enemies

While Luther was hurt by the defection of his former friends, but continued to show them generally some consideration, he had no such qualms in dealing with his outspoken enemies, although at times he could relent, as in the case of Tetzel to whom he wrote a beautiful letter of comfort shortly before the former indulgence peddler died in the Leipzig convent of the Dominican Order. But on the whole Luther's dealings with the "hirelings of Rome" were harsh and often abusive. It must be borne in mind, however, that their attacks against Luther were even more abusive. The sixteenth century was a rough century.

There were a great number of enemies of the Reformer, but most of them bore non-German names. Aquensis, Baechem, Beda, Carjaval, Clichthove, Gramaye, Isolani, Jacobacci, Nijs, Quercu, Catherinus, and so on, carried on their attacks from across the Alps and across the Rhine. In Germany the chief opponents of Luther, besides such annoying nonentities like the poison letter writers Heyden and Hasenberg, were Alveld, Cochlaeus, Eck, Emser, and Murner. Others like Weissestadt, Dungersheim, Hoogstraten, Pfefferkorn, Vehe, Wimpina, and the notorious Tetzel could do little or nothing to sway the opinions of the Christian believers in spite of their determined offorts.

Augustine Alveld appeared on the stage of history in 1520 when he wrote against Luther the treatise, "On the Apostolic See." Nothing is known of his earlier life and soon after 1520 he disappeared in Halle. Alveld's treatise grew out of his resentment of Luther's attack against the supremacy of the pope. He had attended the Leipzig debate as a member of the Franciscan Order. He was determined, courageous, well versed in theology, and of a quick wit. He was highly regarded by his fellow-monks who said of him that he had built a high wall around the true Israel. However, under the trumpet blows of Luther's answer his walls came tumbling down like the walls of Jericho. His adversaries called Alveld a noisy old donkey. Lutheran satire against him was most unkind. Yet in spite of all threats he was not intimidated. He even appeared at a disputation, on January 20, 1522, when he confronted John Lang on the question of the validity of monastic vows.

While Alveld had one of the finest personalities among the enemies of Luther, John Cochlaeus was one of the worst agitators of the age. Yet this man, born in 1479 at Wendelstein near Nuremberg, had been one of the partisans of Reuchlin against the Cologne inquisitors. He was a friend of Pirckheimer, and a patron of arts. During the early years of the Reformation he went to Italy where he studied theology and secretly associated with Luther's enemies there. At that time a friend reported, "I am afraid our friend Cochlaeus has gotten into the sheep's stable. I know the people with whom he has associated in Rome."[9] A year later he reappeared as advisor to the wily papal nuncio Aleander.

From the days of the Diet of Worms until his death in 1552

Cochlaeus fought viciously against Luther and Lutheranism. He wrote numerous books, "On the Efficacy of the Sacraments," "The Seven-Headed Luther," "The Billy Goat Play of Martin Luther," and so forth. Luther, on his part, did not mince words in dealing with his opponent, as is evidenced from the title of his best known treatise against the vicious enemy, "Against the Armed Man Cochlaeus."

Cochlaeus tried in vain to drive the Lutherans from Frankfurt, Regensburg and Nuremberg. He had to flee from their wrath to the court of Albert of Mainz, then to Cologne. Finally he found a refuge at the court of Duke George who had been collecting enemies of Luther for several years. He was at Augsburg, trying to help Eck write the Confutation, but Eck refused to recognize the vitriolic Leipzig theologian as a Catholic scholar. In spite of rebuffs he continued to attend colloquies. After the death of Duke George in 1539 Cochlaeus had to witness the quick disintegration of the walls which he had built around Leipzig. He died frustrated, but still fighting, in 1552.

Jerome Emser (1477-1527) the "Leipzig Goat" (his coat-of-arms showed a goat's head) had come to Leipzig from southern Germany. He was born in Ulm, had studied at Tuebingen, had taught for a time at Erfurt (he later claimed that he had been Luther's teacher), and had finally become professor at Leipzig in 1510. Duke George enlisted the services of the gifted writer in order to advance his pet project which was the canonization of Bishop Benno of Meissen, a "scoundrel and a traitor" as Luther called him. Although Emser's literary efforts on behalf of Benno were not crowned with success, Duke George continued to show him many favors. Thus Emser lived a carefree, rather immoral life when he first became acquainted with Luther.

Very slyly he posed as a friend of the Reformer. On July 25, 1518, Luther preached at Dresden. After the sermon which had aroused the first antagonism of Duke George, Emser invited the Wittenberg colleague to a banquet at which they freely discussed issues and personalities. Luther, who trusted Emser, made several uncautious remarks which were promptly taken down by a secretary of Duke George who had been hidden behind drapes. These statements of

Luther were later used against him. But Luther was slow to break with the Leipzig professor. As late as 1519 he called him "our friend Emser."[10]

The break between the two men came at the Leipzig Debate. At the beginning of the debate Emser had sanctimoniously admonished Luther, Carlstadt and Eck "to use moderation," but all along he continued to insinuate that Luther was not really as dangerous as he seemed. Luther was especially enraged when Emser stated that Luther could not possibly take the side of John Huss, because that would not only be heresy, but also treason in Saxony which had suffered so much during the Hussite Wars. Thus Emser succeeded in turning Duke George and many other Saxons against Luther.

After that there was an exchange of the unpleasant treatises which were sent back and forth between Wittenberg and Leipzig. On New Year's Day, 1521, as he was ascending the pulpit, Emser found a derogatory note which moved him to attack Luther. On January 20, 1521, his attack against Luther's treatise "To the Christian Nobility" appeared which he called an "Unchristian Book to the Christian Nobility." Luther shot back with "To the Leipzig Goat" whereupon Emser wrote "Against the Steer of Wittenberg." Again Luther answered "Against the Answer of the Leipzig Goat" and Emser retorted "Against the Steer's Raging Reply." Luther answered once more "Against the Superchristian, Superspiritual, Superartificial Book of Goat Emser," but then let the controversy rest, although Emser continued to write furiously against him, publishing no less than eight treatises against the Reformer. After Luther had published his New Testament translation, Emser found over one thousand mistakes in it and set out to give a Catholic translation of his own. But he soon grew tired of the work and plagiarized Luther's translation outrageously, publishing it under his name and the title "The New Testament According to the Text Preserved in the Christian Church." Luther at first was angry, but then laughed it off, because now the Catholics would have to read his (Luther's) translation when they opened Emser's New Testament. Soon after that event, Emser died, on November 8, 1527. Charity Pirckheimer had called him charitably "The pillar of the

Church, the jewel among the clergy." But today this estimate has changed considerably."[11]

We may pass Hoogstraten, who died discredited in 1527 (even the archbishops of Mainz and Trier had evicted him from their dioceses), and the converted Jew Pfefferkorn, who faded away in 1521. There is not much to be said about Murner who wrote "The Great Lutheran Fool," except that he was loved by no one and that he died in 1537 unmourned even by his co-religionists. John Tetzel, who died during the Leipzig Debate of 1519, has historical significance merely because his work triggered the first shot of the Reformation. His theses against Luther, drawn up with the help of Wimpina (died 1531), are insignificant. Witzel was a noble figure who sincerely, but ineffectually, tried to stem the tide of Lutheranism in Saxony, including Luther's hometown of Eisleben, where he was a thorn in the flesh of Luther and his co-workers. He died forgotten in 1573. With Vehe he had written a good Catholic hymnbook with which he tried to counteract the appeal of the Lutheran hymns. Vehe, of Halle, one of the most energetic Catholic opponents of Luther, attended many colloquies and, besides his hymnbook, wrote many books: "A Refutation of Melanchthon's Theology," "On Celebrating Holy Communion in One Kind," "Against the Bugenhagen Gallows," "How Christ Wants to be Venerated in His Saints," "On Different Doctrines," and so forth. He died in 1539, just before Halle became officially Lutheran.

This leaves John Maier of Eck in Swabia, the man whose name is usually mentioned on the same level with Luther's. What Luther was to Wittenberg and the Protestant movement, so the reasoning goes, Eck was to Ingolstadt and the Catholic Church. This is deceptive. For Eck was no Luther.

He was born on November 13, 1486, at Eck in Swabia and like Luther he came of peasant stock. He studied at Heidelberg and other universities. At the age of 24 Eck was a doctor of theology and a professor. In 1510 he was called to Ingolstadt, the Bavarian university which was later moved to Munich, and there he established his fame.

Eck was an ambitious and able scholar. He had imbibed the spirit of humanism, but he had no intention to reform the Church.

Nevertheless, he disputed fearlessly about the abuses rampant in the Church and won his laurels at Augsburg, Bologna, Vienna, and elsewhere. He became a friend of the powerful Augsburg banker, Jacob Fugger. His advice was sought by emperors, popes, and princes.

When Eck received a copy of the Ninety-Five Theses of Luther, probably through Scheurl, he did not make a public reply, but drew up for private circulation a number of criticisms of the Theses

ECK

which he called Obelisks, or dagger points. During Luther's absence in Heidelberg, Carlstadt who then considered himself the primary champion of the Reformer, received these Obelisks and immediately wrote some 400 clumsy Counter-Theses. Although Luther was able to quash the controversy before it got under way, Eck's pride had been deeply hurt and his suspicions aroused. He was now ready to challenge the Wittenbergers and to establish the superiority of Ingolstadt and Eck over Wittenberg and Luther. At Augsburg, in October 1518, he met with Luther and arranged a colloquy which was to be held the next year in Leipzig. Duke George readily consented, although the faculty of the University of Leipzig and the Catholic bishop had objected. Strangely the debate was to be between Eck and Carlstadt, but Luther was invited as a visitor and admitted to the debate on the day before it began. When Carlstadt's cumbersome method collapsed before the brilliant oratory of Eck, Luther took over. Luther insisted on quoting the Scripture, while Eck constantly quoted from the Church Fathers. Outwardly, Eck was victorious because he induced Luther to admit that certain heresies, including those of Huss, had been justified. There was no doubt on whose side Duke George was. When Luther defended Huss he stomped angrily out of the hall. After the disputation he feasted Eck, while dismissing Luther with the barest of courtesies. The minutes of the debate were submitted to two universities who were slow in condemning Luther. Eck, therefore, took his case to Rome where he spent the winter of 1519 to 1520, forced the drafting of a bull against Luther and had it signed by a reluctant Pope Leo X. He brought the bull personally to Germany, published it with great difficulties, sent a copy to Luther which the Wittenberg professor promptly burned, and appealed to the Emperor Charles V to use force against Luther.

In spite of all these activities Eck was constantly frustrated. He was unable to check the spread of Lutheranism in Bavaria, even though he appeared as prosecutor in several cases. Since Luther steadfastly refused to get involved with Eck again, he now turned to the Swiss Reformers. He disputed with Oecolampadius and others, but his success was tenuous. His greatest hour came at Augsburg, when he was entrusted by the Emperor Charles V to refute the Augsburg Confession. The Confutation of the Catholic Church is Eck's work; but it was so hastily written that even Catholic scholars found it weak and some opposed it outright. After that Eck continued his restless work against the Reformation. He was present at many colloquies. The presence of the quarrelsome champion of the Old Church helped nothing to bring these discussions to a fruitful end. He died at Ingolstadt three years before Luther. His works, *Opera Contra Lutherum*, were published in four volumes.

Roman Officials and Bishops

Finally, there were the officials, bishops, and popes. As has been stated before, the officials who attacked Luther were mostly non-Germans, the German episcopate was divided during the early years of the struggle, and the popes were interested more in power politics than in settling the issue.

Among the officials we have Cajetan, the nuncio at the First Diet of Augsburg (1518) who colloquized Luther; Miltitz who tried to silence him in 1519; Prierias who wrote against him; Gabriel della Volta, the general of his order, who made halfhearted attempts to solve the controversy; Aleander, Chieregati, Campeggio, Vergerio, Caracciolo, Castiglione, and other nuncios, and various officials of the curia who worked against Luther from Rome.

Prierias was the first Roman to take on Luther. Silvester Prierias, born at Priero in Piedmont in 1460, had been appointed to office by Pope Julius II after a brilliant career as theologian in Bologna, Pavia and Rome. Leo X made him Master of the Sacred Palace, an office which he held until his death in 1523.

Prierias, like Tetzel, was a Dominican, and it may have been that he regarded the controversy an affair between Augustinians and Dominicans. The Dominicans were still smarting under the attacks which the order had suffered on the part of the Augustinians at the time of Savonarola's trial. Now there was the time for revenge. After Prierias had seen Tetzel's ineffective counter-theses—the Romans called them "scattered pages"—he felt moved to write a treatise "Concerning the Powers of the Pope." Relying on the weight of his official position he expected the Wittenberg monk to accept his arguments in silence. Luther received the treatise together with a citation to come to Rome on August 7, 1518. On August 8 he informed Spalatin that he would answer Prierias. Within two weeks the answer was printed by Melchior Lotther in Leipzig. It was a disrespectful treatise. Luther called his adversary's literary efforts "trifles." "If you want to hit back," he told Prierias, "come better armed."[12] Luther's answer is important because here for the first time appears a distinction between the Holy Catholic Church and the Roman Church. Prierias answered back. Luther did not keep silent. Finally Luther broke off the discussion—after Leipzig—by publishing Prierias' third treatise against him with his own preface.

In the meantime Luther had been busy talking with Cajetan and Miltitz and passed his most severe test with Eck. Thomas de Vio, called Cajetanus, was probably the most distinguished Roman to talk to Luther. He was an excellent man, a great scholar (the greatest authority on Thomas Aquinas), and—like Prierias—a Dominican. As a matter of fact, he was the general of the Dominican order. Yet in spite of his exalted position he was later viciously attacked by some overzealous Romans and died, almost forgotten, in 1534.

Julius II had appointed him general of the Dominicans (in 1508) and later had intrusted him with a confutation of the claims of the Council of Pisa, meeting on the eve of the Reformation against the will of the pope. In recognition Cajetan had been created a cardinal.

When the efforts of other Roman officials failed to quiet Luther, and when Frederick the Wise and the German bishops did not cooperate, Cajetan was sent to Germany to negotiate with Luther directly. By sending a Dominican to Germany to do this task Leo X had shown that he did not understand the issues involved. Yet Cajetan discharged his duty with great dignity, discussing in a fatherly way with Luther the necessity for a recantation. He lost his temper only when the monk did not accede to his fatherly exhortation. When Luther found out that Cajetan had received a secret breve from the pope to bring him to Rome, he secretly escaped from Augsburg at night. The Augsburg Acts, published by Luther after his return from the colloquy with Cajetan, drew the battle lines more sharply than ever before.

Nevertheless Cajetan continued his efforts for a reasonable reform of the Church, or what he considered to be a reasonable reform. He helped elect the reform Pope Adrian VI, he favored strictness, recommended to Adrian's easygoing successor, Clement VII, a number of far-reaching concessions to the Lutherans which were based on earlier decisions made before the Reformation by the Reform Council of Basel, and in return incurred the suspicion and the wrath of his Roman colleagues.

Carl von Miltitz, the vain Saxon nobleman at the court of Leo X, was an unworthy successor to Cajetan. Yet, perhaps because he was a Saxon by birth, he made with his simulated tears ("Crocodile tears") the greatest impression on the Reformer. Luther made concessions to Miltitz which he was not ready to make to Cajetan or the pope himself. He promised to keep quiet from now on, unless provoked. Fortunately, he was soon provoked by Eck. The meeting of Miltitz with Luther at Altenburg (January 1519) and two later meetings thus were abortive, and Miltitz never recovered from the failure of his mission. He became a heavy drinker and fell overboard while crossing the Main River in a boat, in 1529.

As to Gabriel della Volta, Luther's general, he was mostly concerned about the good name of the Augustinian Order. "Enormous evils threaten our whole order unless Martin ceases from speaking," he wrote to Staupitz, "the habit and name of the Augustinians are so hateful, that we are, as it were, insulted as worthless by the apostolic see. We must appear to the public the more slack, in that having been the only mendicant order never accused and suspected of heresy, we are now, like heretics, forced to flee the face of men. . . . In the face of the innumerable benefits which [the pope] has conferred on us it is to our interest not to cross him, but to please him and to be humble . . . ."[13] That is as far as the Augustinian general would go in carrying out the strict command of Pope Leo X to bring Luther to justice.

Jerome Aleander, whose name is connected with the events leading to Luther's appearance at the Diet of Worms, was like Cajetan, a great scholar, but unlike Cajetan, a wily diplomatist. He did everything in his power to make the appearance of Luther before the Diet impossible, but was defeated by Charles V and his German advisors. When he realized that he had failed he tried to enlist Sickingen's services by painting a bleak picture of Luther's chances for survival in Worms. Sickingen almost fell for the ruse, but Luther refused to be detained and went straight to Worms where he made his famous profession of faith. Immediately after Luther and his most important supporters among the princes had left Worms, Aleander saw to it that the Edict of Worms was issued by the emperor which declared Luther an outlaw. Later Aleander became notorious as a persecutor of Lutherans in the Netherlands. He was largely responsible for the burning of the first two Lutheran martyrs at Antwerp. He also served in France, where he was captured with King Francis I, and at different other diplomatic posts. In 1536 he was created a cardinal, but died before the slovenly Pope Paul III inaugurated the Counter-Reformation.

The letters which Aleander wrote from Worms in the spring of 1521 belong to the best documents of the times. On April 16, 1521, he reported: "I had just closed my last letter when I learned from several reports and from the running of the people that the great heresiarch was entering the city. I sent one of my people out, who informed me that about a hundred horsemen, presumably Sickingen's, escorted him to the gate. Sitting in a wagon with three companions he entered the town, surrounded by about eight riders. . . . As he left the wagon a priest threw his arms around him and touched his gown three times. . . . I expect they will soon say he works miracles. As this Luther alighted, he looked around with demoniac eyes and said: God will be with me. . . . This is the present state of affairs, and it will get worse daily . . . ."[14] And after the final hearing of Luther he reported: "As Martin left the hall he stretched forth his hand as the German soldiers do when in jousting they exult over a telling blow."[15]

Caracciolo was with Aleander in Worms, helping him draft his reports. After the conclusion of the negotiations with Luther he reported his departure from Worms: "So the scoundrel left yesterday morning at nine o'clock with two wagons. . . . At the gate twenty horsemen received him, presumably sent by Sickingen at Hutten's behest. Some think that at the expiration of his safe-conduct he will go to Bohemia, others that he will go to Denmark. . . . As this scoundrel won't even accept reason, may God at least keep princes (including the emperor) on the right path of the faith."[16] Marino Caracciolo, who died in 1538, never was able to grasp the importance of the meeting at Worms.

Similarly Francis Chieregati who followed him as legate in Nuremberg in 1522 and Lawrence Campeggio, the legate in 1524, never understood the concern of the Reformation. They were convinced that a few minor concessions would end the whole commotion caused by the Wittenberg monk. Only Vergerio, the last papal

nuncio to contact the Lutherans—and incidentally Luther directly—
saw the greatness of the cause and was converted to Lutheranism.

Peter Paul Vergerio, born at Capo d'Istria in 1498, had entered
the service of the papacy late, after the death of his wife Diana
Contarini, but had risen fast in the ranks of Roman officials. He was
papal nuncio at the Diet of Augsburg in 1530 where the Augsburg
Confession was read. Again, in 1534, Pope Paul III sent Vergerio to
Germany to sound out German princes on the prospects for a gen-

ALEANDER

eral council. Thus he came to Wittenberg where he met, rode in a
carriage with, and dined with Luther, the "German Pope." He
found Luther in good humor, teasing the ambassador of the Anti-
christ. He was so impressed by him that after his return to Rome
he resigned his nunciature and withdrew into the isolation of a
bishop's palace. The pope used his services once more: He sent
him to the colloquy of Regensburg where Vergerio was even more
convinced of the rightness of Lutheran doctrine than he had been
before. Accused of heretical leanings he tried to defend himself, in
1546—Luther's death year—before the Council of Trent, but being
appraised of his imminent capture and having witnessed the mar-

tyrdom of a close relative he fled into Switzerland. There he became
pastor of a Lutheran Church, later moving to the court of Duke
Christopher of Wuerttemberg, the successor of Ulrich. He taught
at the University of Tuebingen, translated many of Luther's writings into the Italian language, and was used for many diplomatic
missions. He visited with Melanchthon in Wittenberg, with Flacius
in Jena, with the Bohemian Brethren, and was even a welcome
guest at the court of the peaceloving, enlightened Emperor Maximilian II, the son of Ferdinand I, who had married Mary, the daughter
of Charles V. From all these travels he always returned to Tuebingen, his second home, where he died on October 4, 1565.

Among the bishops we have discussed the various attitudes which
the members of the German episcopate displayed towards Luther.
John VII of Schleinitz, Bishop of Meissen, was one of the few
fierce enemies of Luther. Adolph of Anhalt, Bishop of Merseburg,
burned Luther's books and forbade, without success, the reading of
Luther's translation of the New Testament. Both had the chagrin to
witness the spread of Lutheranism throughout their dioceses.

Jerome Scultetus, Luther's own bishop, son of a village mayor,
born about 1460, was hesitant to take action against his wayward
monk. The grateful Luther dedicated his "Resolutions" to the 95
Theses to the kind bishop. Jerome's successor, however, carried
out the wishes of the curia.

On the other hand, men like George Polentz and Hermann von
Wied joined the Reformation openly. Polentz, who died in 1550
at the age of 72, became such a staunch Lutheran that he even
refused to celebrate a mass for the wedding of his prince, Albert
of Prussia. "I shall never again celebrate mass." When Luther
heard of the firm stand of Polentz he exclaimed: "How wonderful Christ is! Even a bishop honors Him now. . . ."[17] Von Polentz
abolished a great number of Catholic saints' days and forbade fasting
in his diocese. In due time he was excommunicated. But this had
little effect on the courageous prince of the Church. He immediately set out to begin Church visitations, patterned after the
Wittenberg visitations, and reorganized education in East Prussia. Then he retired from his office, leaving Briesemann in charge
of his diocese with the title of administrator.

Hermann von Wied, archbishop-elector of Cologne, joined the Reformation on the eve of Luther's life. He had been elector since 1515, but did not begin to reform his diocese until 1536 and later. In 1542 he invited Lutheran theologians to help him in this task. Supported by the estates in his electorate and relying on the recess of the Diet of Regensburg, Hermann was confident that he would succeed. But Luther and the Saxons gave him only half-hearted support, the Emperor Charles V stepped in, and the Reformation was lost in Cologne and large parts of western Germany. Success of the Reformation in Cologne might have crowned the work of the Reformation in central Europe. As it was, Hermann's defeat (he was forced to retire) signaled the end of efforts by other princes of the Church who might have considered following the example of their Scandinavian and English colleagues.

Luther was directly involved in the defeat of another bishop, the staunch Catholic bishop of Naumburg-Zeitz, Julius von Pflug. Here John Frederick, following Luther's advice, was able to impose Amsdorf as bishop, which, however, was only a temporary success, since the end of the Smalcald War settled the issue in favor of Julius von Pflug.

Von Pflug, a man of noble and mild disposition, ruled his bishopric with great leniency, insisting on Catholic ceremonies only for his cathedral and permitting Lutheran pastors and services in all the other churches of his diocese. When, after 1555, Lutheran pastors driven out by the Interim returned to Naumburg-Zeitz von Pflug gradually lost his influence and retired more and more within the walls of his palace where he died, faithful to his Church, on September 3, 1564.

The best known representative of the German episcopate was, of course, Albert of Hohenzollern, Markgrave of Brandenburg, Archbishop of Mainz and Magdeburg, Bishop of Halberstadt, Elector, Cardinal, and a brother of Joachim I. In defiance of canon law he held more bishoprics than was permissible, and paid heavily for it. In order to collect the bribe which he had paid Leo X he sent out his indulgence peddler Tetzel and started the Reformation movement.

Albert of Mainz was not a churchman. He was more interested

in money and in the arts, including women, than in prayer. Luther rebuked him as late as 1539 for having a mistress carried into his palace in a relic box. Albert had many friends, from Erasmus and Hutten to Capito and Hedio. Even Luther liked the amiable Hohenzollern princeling. In 1525 he advised him to get married, but Albert demurred and sent Luther a wedding present instead. He promised again and again to stop the sale of indulgences,

ALBERT OF MAINZ

the exhibition of relics, and other abominations. A cardinal since 1518, Albert could also at times severely embarrass the pope. He was faithful to Charles V and against Pope Clement VII, the libertine Medici, who had defied the emperor and was held a prisoner during the Sack of Rome. As late as 1530 Luther dedicated one of his books to the archbishop.

As he grew older, Albert hardened his heart towards Lutheranism. At his suggestion, it is believed, one of the early Lutheran pastors in Halle, George Winkler, was murdered. He persecuted the valiant Lutheran knight, Hartmut von Kronberg. When in 1541 Justus Jonas became pastor in Halle, which until then had been Albert's favorite residence, the sick archbishop moved in chagrin to Mainz, where he died, after much painful suffering, in his fifty-fifth year, on September 24, 1545.

And the Popes

Luther never saw Julius II who ruled in Rome during Luther's journey to the eternal city. Julius who has often been acclaimed the greatest pope between Innocent III and Leo XIII, had become pope in 1503, at the age of sixty, but in spite of his age, he energetically set out to clean the Augean stables which he had inherited from his lax predecessors, especially Alexander VI, the notorious Borgia. Although not primarily a theologian, he ruled with a firm hand and changed some of the abuses. He pacified to a degree the restless Appenine peninsula, but when he died in 1513, the old disorder reappeared with the election of Leo X.

Leo X, Giovanni de'Medici, son of the great Lorenzo il Magnifico, was a typical pope of his time: He was tonsured at the age of seven, became a cardinal at the age of twelve, and lost his home at the age of 19, when the Medici were driven from Florence by the reforms of Savonarola. After that Leo was an arch-reactionary politically. At the death of Julius II he was chosen pope as the candidate of the "young cardinals." It was not until then that he received his ordination as a priest of the Church. On March 15th he became a priest, on March 16th a bishop and on March 17th a pope.

Leo was no match for the powerful adversaries which were threatening the domains of the Church. It was not surprising that he was unable to curb the activities of Luther. His chief interests were the fine arts and money which he needed to pursue these interests. His extreme family loyalty resulted in nepotism. He spent the money of the Church so freely that at his death not enough funds were in the coffers to buy new candles for his bier. Like his predecessors he obtained money by confiscating the wealth of cardinals and political rivals. Thus it is not surprising that Leo did not take an active interest in the affairs of "the drunken German monk." He told Gabriel della Volta to silence the monk, and failing this he sent Cajetan and Miltitz to Germany, and finally excommunicated the Reformer. He appreciated the valuable help which he received from Henry VIII who wrote a book on the seven sacraments and gave him and all his descendants on the English throne the title "Defender of the Faith." But when he died, on December 1, 1521, nothing had been solved, Luther was at the Wartburg, the emperor busy with Spain and Francis of France, and the Roman Church was in headlong retreat on all fronts.

Adrian VI (1459-1523) tried to change all this. A former professor at the arch-Catholic University of Louvain and a former tutor of Charles V, he at once instituted reforms which might have led to a reunification had his efforts not been scuttled by the reluctant cardinals of the curia and the brevity of his reign. At the Diet of Nuremberg in 1522, while demanding the execution of the Edict of Worms, Adrian also, through his nuncio Chieregati, confessed the past sins of the Church and advocated sweeping reforms. Yet he strongly opposed any doctrinal changes, except that he was willing to admit—like most popes at that time—that he was not infallible. A Catholic historian has said of Adrian's brief pontificate: "History presents no more pathetic figure than that of this noble pontiff, struggling singlehanded against insurmountable difficulties."[18]

After Adrian Clement VII, another Medici and a cousin of Leo X. Like his cousin, Giulio de'Medici (b. 1478) was completely unsuited for the office to which he was elected by the worldly-minded cardinals. His cousin Leo had made him archbishop by special dispensation because under canon law Giulio was not allowed to hold ecclesiastic office, being the illegitimate son of Giuliano de'Medici. In 1513 he received the red hat, and during the pontificate of his cousin, practically the whole papal policy was entrusted to his hands.

When Clement VII had been elected, he engaged in reckless politics, antagonizing the Emperor Charles V who took terrible vengeance on the faithless pope. With the Sack of Rome the prestige

of the papacy reached its nadir. Cardinals and bishops had to do
service as common laborers, and the proud pope had to pay 400,000
scudi as a ransom for himself. He also had to promise to convene
a general council, a promise which he never carried out. Under
his pontificate the Church of England broke away from Rome.

Paul III, the last pope to rule during Luther's life, was a clever
and scheming courtier, but not a churchman. Born in 1468, he

LEO X

belonged to the house of Farnese which was closely related to the
Medici. Paul made his first move towards the papacy when one of
his predecessors, the notorious Alexander VI chose his sister Giulia
for his mistress. As a reward for serving the old Borgia's lustful
desires the brother of the mistress received the red hat. From that
moment until his election in 1534 Paul never suffered need.

Paul III was no reform pope. Having served as panderer in his
youth, he showed no inclination to reform the morals of the Church.
It is ironic that circumstances and the Jesuits forced him to reform

the Church. After much hesitation and several postponements he finally convened the General Council, promised for so many years, to Trent, but died before it got well under way, in 1549.

Always procrastinating and irresolute, easy going and luxury loving, Paul's character has been described in these words by a Catholic scholar: "He had his faults, but they injured no one but himself. The fifteen years of his pontificate saw the complete restoration of Catholic faith and piety."[19]

These were the men around Luther who were fighting against him and the Gospel from the direction of the Roman camp. Some of them were good and noble, some of them villainous, some of them neutral and indifferent, but all of them had closed their minds to the new day that was dawning in Christendom—the restoration of the Church of Christ in the light of the Gospel.

Notes

PART ONE

I. Luther's World

1. The two Ferdinands are often confused, because both ruled over Naples, Ferdinand I (1458-1494) and Ferdinand of Aragon and Sicily (1509-1516). Durant. *Renaissance,* pp. 353 f.
2. Dittmar, *Weltgeschichte,* p. 510.
3. On the morals of the Borgia. Burckhardt, *Renaissance,* pp. 75-81.
4. Palmer, *Modern World,* p. 66.
5. "The brilliant but meaningless Battle of the Spurs." Tschan, *Western Civilization,* p. 678.
6. Louis had been married to Jeanne, a sister of Charles VIII. Upon his accession to the throne he had this marriage annulled (with the help of the Borgias) and married Anne of Brittany, Charles' widow. She died a year before him, in 1514. "He accepted Mary Tudor, the sixteen year old sister of Henry VIII. She led the ailing king a merry and exhausting life. . . . Louis died in the third month of his marriage." Durant, *Reformation,* pp. 95 f.
7. "Huge sums of money were borrowed. . . ." Tschan, *Western Civilization,* p. 673.

II. A Century in Ferment

1. On the torture and confessions of the Knights Templar, see Dittmar, *Weltgeschichte,* p. 29. Durant, *Renaissance,* p. 50, tries to vindicate Clement V, but historians generally condemn his base motives.
2. After spending several years in jail, John XXIII-A was allowed to go to Italy where he paid homage to the new pope, Martin V. He was rewarded with a cardinal's hat.

3. The Empress Barbara had conspired against her aging husband. Menzel, *Germany*, p. 821.

4. Durant, *Renaissance*, p. 142. Lorenzo was only 43 years old.

5. In the service of Frederick III since 1442, Piccolomini had accepted a bribe from Eugene IV (the promise of a cardinal's hat). Sixteen years later he was pope. Dittmar, *Weltgeschichte*, p. 156.

III. The Rebirth

1. "Here for the first time the foundation of a dynasty based on mass murder and endless abominations is attempted." Burckhardt, *Renaissance*, p. 3.

2. He trained the dogs "to eat human flesh, and joyfully watched them feed on live men." Durant, *Renaissance*, p. 181.

3. Burckhardt, *Renaissance*, p. 152.

4. "She made the mistake of outliving her charms; she died in a wretched hut near the Tiber." Durant, *Renaissance*, p. 578.

5. Durant, *Renaissance*, p. 571 ff. Bezold, *Reformation*, p. 83, and others.

6. "I have children, which is becoming to a layman, and I have a mistress, which is an old custom of the clergy." Durant, *Renaissance*, p. 83.

7. Burckhardt, *Baukunst*, p. 5.

8. Lucas, *Renaissance and the Reformation*, pp. 340 f.

IV. New Lands to Conquer

1. Ruge, *Entdeckungen*, pp. 3 ff.

2. Durant, *Reformation*, pp. 261 f.

3. "The Portuguese king resented the drawing of this demarcation line. . . . In the treaty of Tordesillas, 1494, these two countries agreed upon a line drawn 370 leagues west of the Cape Verde Islands, a line which permitted Portugal to retain Brazil." Tschan, *Western Civilization*, p. 547.

4. Ruge, *Entdeckungen*, p. 481, gives the number of survivors as 18.

5. The following account is based on Prescott's definitive history of the *Conquest of Mexico*.

V. The Holy Empire

1. " 'To go to Canossa' in later times became a byword for submission to the will of Rome." Palmer, *Modern World*, p. 36.

2. Dittmar, *Weltgeschichte*, pp. 16 ff.

3. "Henry VII died (1313) before he could make up his mind to be or not to be a Roman emperor." Durant, *Renaissance*, p. 4. Dittmar traces the rumor that the emperor was poisoned to a fabrication by the Ghibellines. *Weltgeschichte*, p. 43. But Menzel, *Germany*, p. 745, states categorically that "with his expiring breath he said to his murderer, 'You have given me death in the cup of life, but fly, ere my followers seize you!' "

4. "Contemporary accounts are undoubtedly exaggerated. Yet we have reasons to believe that in some cities more than half the population perished." Tschan, *Western Civilization*, p. 402.
5. A possible reason for his dethronement: "In a drunken frolic, he ceded Genoa to France and recognized the antipope at Avignon as pope, instead of Boniface IX, who then wore the tiara at Rome." The archbishop of Mainz "began to tremble for his miter, and urged the princes to depose him." Menzel, *Germany*, p. 784.
6. "One of the most uninteresting rulers in German history." Tschan, *Western Civilization*, p. 460. Frederick "felt no attraction for the new learning, preferring the study of astrology, alchemy, and chivalry, the care of his stables. . . ." Lucas, *Renaissance and the Reformation*, p. 369.
7. "Mary was thrown from horseback. . . . From a false feeling of delicacy, she concealed her state (pregnancy) until surgical aid was unavailing, and expired in the bloom of life." Menzel, *Germany*, p. 844. On Maximilian's troubles after Mary's death, see pp. 845 ff.

PART TWO

I. Luther and His Contemporaries

1. Koestlin, *Martin Luther: Sein Leben und seine Schriften*, I, 18.
2. Mackinnon, *Luther and the Reformation*. I, 14. Schwiebert, *Luther and His Times*, p. 123: "The final answer . . . may never be discovered."
3. Koestlin, *op. cit.*, I, 29.
4. Schwiebert, *op. cit.*, p. 134.
5. Koestlin, *op. cit.*, II, 584.

II. The Inner Circle

1. Koestlin, *op. cit.*, II, 607.
2. Rupp, *Luther's Progress to the Diet of Worms*, pp. 104-108.
3. *Allgemeine Deutsche Biographie*. Article on Amsdorf. (Quoted hereafter ADB). Also *Realenzyklopaedie fuer protestantische Theologie und Kirche*, I, 464 ff.
4. Smith-Jacobs, *Luther's Correspondence*, II, 461.
5. *Ibid.*, II, 141.
6. *Ibid.*, II, 154-156.
7. Schwiebert, *op. cit.*, p. 649.
8. *ADB*. Article on Cruciger.
9. Smith-Jacobs, *op. cit.*, I, 177.
10. *Ibid.*, I, 525.

11. *ADB*. Article on Jonas.
12. *Ibid.*
13. Smith-Jacobs, *op. cit.*, II, 404-407.
14. *Ibid.*, II, 429.
15. *Ibid.*, II, 497-499.
16. Schwiebert, *op. cit.*, p. 750.
17. *ADB*. Article on Melanchthon.
18. Smith-Jacobs, *op. cit.*, II, 325.
19. *Ibid.*, II, 483-484.
20. Koestlin, *op. cit.*, II, 527.
21. Smith-Jacobs, *op. cit.*, I, 32.
22. *Ibid.*, II, 152-153.

III. *The Larger Circle*

1. Complete list in Aland, *Hilfsbuch zum Lutherstudium,* 1957.
2. Schwiebert, *op. cit.*, pp. 603-12.
3. Koestlin, *op. cit.*, II, 549-551.
4. A century later Wittenberg for a short time experienced a resurgence of importance, but was rendered ineffective by the Hohenzollerns.
5. Marburg, although the first Lutheran University, soon came under Calvinist influence. A century later it was a center of "Syncretism."
6. Linck's great work for Lutheranism in South Germany has never been adequately recognized.
7. Among the greatest Tuebingen alumni were Melanchthon, the father of the Augsburg Confession and the Apology, and Andreae, the father of the Formula of Concord.
8. *ADB*. Article on Cordatus.
9. *Ibid.* For other opinions by Luther see *Realenzyklopaedie,* VII, 487.
10. Smith-Jacobs, *op. cit.*, II, 114.
11. *ADB*. Article on Major. See also *Realenzyklopaedie,* XII, 86-91.
12. Schwiebert, *op. cit.*, p. 536.

IV. *Lutheran Laymen*

1. "A Simple Way to Pray, For a Good Friend" (1535). The following year this barber killed his own son-in-law and was exiled from Saxony. Luther saved him from the hangman's noose.
2. Koestlin, *op. cit.*, II, 251.
3. *Ibid.*, II, 214.
4. Smith-Jacobs, *op. cit.*, II, 156 and 389.
5. *Ibid.*, II, 443.

6. *ADB.* Article on Lufft.
7. Smith-Jacobs, *op. cit.*, II, 399.
8. *Ibid.*, I, 524.

V. *Scandinavian Lutherans*

1. Muenter, *Kirchengeschichte von Dänemark und Norwegen*, III, 19-40.
2. After 1536 Helgesen fades away.
3. Muenter, *op. cit.*, III, 515-528.
4. *Ibid.*, III, 530 ff.
5. *Realenzyklopaedie*, XVIII, 27.
6. The Augsburg Confession was officially accepted at the end of the XVIth century.
7. *Realenzyklopaedie*, XIX, 460.
8. Durant, *The Reformation*, pp. 625-626.

VI. *The Martyrs and the Persecuted*

1. Smith-Jacobs, *op. cit.*, II, 193.
2. *Ibid.*, II, 195
3. *Ibid.*, II, 213-215.
4. *Ibid.*, II, 331.
5. Luther's relation to George is summarized in *Realenzyklopaedie*, VI, 529 ff.
6. Koestlin, *op. cit.*, I, 619.
7. *Ibid.*, II, 104.
8. Smith-Jacobs, *op. cit.*, II, 252.
9. *Ibid.*
10. *Ibid.*, II, 259-260.
11. Koestlin, *op. cit.*, II, 106.
12. *ADB.* Article on Wyck.

VII. *The Strassburgers*

1. On Melanchthon's attitude see: Smith-Jacobs, *op. cit.*, II, 477-478.
2. *Ibid.*, I, 82.
3. *Ibid.*, I, 112.
4. *Ibid.*, I, 369.
5. *Ibid.*, I, 276-77.
6. *Ibid.*, I, 285.
7. *Ibid.*, I, 510.
8. *Ibid.*, I, 513.
9. *Ibid.*, II, 41.

10. *Ibid.*, II, 346.
11. *Ibid.*, II, 377-78.
12. *Ibid.*, II, 450.
13. *Ibid.*, II, 499.
14. Koestlin, *op. cit.*, II, 616-17.
15. Smith, Jacobs, *op. cit.*, I, 111.
16. *Ibid.*, I, 129.
17. *Ibid.*, I, 408.
18. *Ibid.*, II, 56-57.
19. Luther rebuked Capito later for his lack of decision.
20. During the Communion controversy Capito showed clearly his lack of appreciation for the theological side of the question.
21. Smith-Jacobs, *op. cit.*, II, 31.
22. *Ibid.*, II, 188.
23. *Ibid.*, II, 302-303.
24. *Ibid.*, I, 368.
25. *Ibid.*, I, 430-431.
26. *Ibid.*, I, 477-478.

VIII. *The Swiss Reformers*

1. Smith-Jacobs, *op. cit.*, I, 304.
2. *Ibid.*, I, 524.
3. *Ibid.*, II, 455 and 346-350.
4. Schwiebert, *op. cit.*, p. 708-709.
5. *Realenzyklopaedie*, XXI, 810.
6. Koestlin, *op. cit.*, II, 352-353.
7. *Ibid.*, II, 354.
8. *Ibid.*
9. Smith-Jacobs, *op. cit.*, I, 202.
10. *Ibid.*, II, 190.
11. *Ibid.*, II, 198.
12. *Ibid.*, II, 282.
13. *Ibid.*, II, 340.
14. *Ibid.*, II, 346.
15. *Ibid.*, II, 377.
16. *Ibid.*, II, 393.
17. *Ibid.*, II, 496.
18. *Ibid.*, II, 495-496.
19. Koestlin, *op. cit.*, II, 577.
20. *Ibid.*, II, 603-604.

IX. English Friends and Foes

1. Smith-Jacobs, *op. cit.*, I, 396.
2. *Ibid.*, II, 33.
3. *Ibid.*, II, 41.
4. *Ibid.*, II, 133.
5. Koestlin, *op. cit.*, II, 400.
6. *Ibid.*, II, 400.
7. Smith-Jacobs, *op. cit.*, II, 354-355.
8. *Ibid.*, II, 400.
9. *Ibid.*, II, 400.
10. *Ibid.*, II, 445-446.
11. Koestlin, *op. cit.*, II, 256.
12. Durant, *op. cit.*, p. 539. Letter by Giovanni Casale, September 18, 1530: "A few days ago the pope secretly proposed to me that your Majesty might be allowed two wives."
13. Koestlin, *op. cit.*, II, 368.
14. *Ibid.*, II, 400.

X. Other Movements

1. Zinzendorf reorganized the remnant of the Hussites at Herrnhut.
2. Durant, *op. cit.*, p. 396 and *ADB* article on Carlstadt.
3. Smith-Jacobs, *op. cit.*, I, 41-42.
4. *Ibid.*, I, 71.
5. *Ibid.*, I, 90 and 93-94.
6. *Ibid.*, I, 196-197.
7. *Ibid.*, I, 209-211.
8. *Ibid.*, II, 48 and 52.
9. *Ibid.*, II, 101-102.
10. *Ibid.*, II, 112.
11. *Ibid.*, II, 212.
12. *Ibid.*, II, 337.
13. *Ibid.*, II, 337.
14. *Ibid.*, II, 482-483.
15. *Ibid.*, II, 317-318.
16. *Ibid.*, II, 321.
17. Koestlin, *op. cit.*, I, 678.
18. *Ibid.*, II, 147-148.
19. Smith-Jacobs, *op. cit.*, II, 367.
20. *Ibid.*, II, 371.

21. Koestlin, *op. cit.*, II, 321.
22. *Ibid.*, II, 323.

XI. *Emperors, Kings and Princes*

1. Dittmar, *Weltgeschichte,* p. 510.
2. *Luther's Works, American Edition,* XIII, 216.
3. Schwiebert, *op. cit.,* p. 540.
4. *ADB.* Article on John the Constant.
5. *Ibid.*
6. *Ibid.*

XII. *The Roman Camp*

1. *ADB.* Article on Mosellanus.
2. Smith-Jacobs, *op. cit.,* I, 440-441.
3. *Ibid.*, II, 226.
4. *Ibid.*, I, 194.
5. *ADB.* Article on Scheurl.
6. *Ibid.*
7. *Ibid.*
8. Smith-Jacobs, *op. cit.,* II, 462.
9. *ADB.* Article on Cochlaeus.
10. Smith-Jacobs, *op. cit.,* I, 149-152.
11. *Realenzyklopaedie,* V, 342.
12. *Realenzyklopaedie,* XVI, 31.
13. Smith-Jacobs, *op. cit.,* I, 297.
14. *Ibid.*, I, 521-522.
15. *Ibid.*, I, 530.
16. *Ibid.*, I, 547.
17. *Realenzyklopaedie,* VI, 541.
18. *The Catholic Encyclopedia,* I, 160.
19. *Ibid.*, XI, 580.

Bibliography

Allgemeine deutsche Biographie, 56 volumes (1875-1912)

ARMSTRONG, EDWARD, *The Emperor Charles V* (1902)

ARMSTRONG, EDWARD, *Lorenzo de' Medici and Florence in the Fifteenth Century* (1896)

BAINTON, ROLAND, *Here I Stand: A Life of Martin Luther* (1950)

BAINTON, ROLAND, *The Reformation of the Sixteenth Century* (1953)

BATIFFOL, LOUIS, *The Century of the Renaissance* (1935)

BAUSLIN, DAVID, *The Lutheran Movement of the Sixteenth Century* (1919)

BERGER, ARNOLD, *Luther und die deutsche Kultur* (1919)

BEZOLD, FRIEDRICH VON, *Geschichte der deutschen Reformation* (in Wilhelm Oncken, *Allgemeine Geschichte* III, 1) (1890)

BOEHMER, HEINRICH, *Luther and the Reformation in the Light of Modern Research* (1930)

BOEHMER, HEINRICH, *Road to Reformation* (1946)

BORNKAMM, HEINRICH, *Luther's World of Thought* (1958)

BROCKHAUS, *Der neue Brockhaus,* 5 volumes (1937)

BROCKHAUS KONVERSATIONSLEXIKON, 17 volumes (n.d.)

BURCKHARDT, JACOB, *Die Baukunst der Renaissance in Italien* (1955)

BURCKHARDT, JACOB, *Die Kultur der Renaissance in Italien. Ein Versuch* (1955)

BURCKHARDT, JACOB, *Der Cicerone. Eine Anleitung zum Genuss der Kunstwerke Italiens* (1957)

BURDACH, K., *Reformation, Renaissance, Humanism* (1918)

Cambridge Medieval History, volume 7 (1932) and volume 8 (1936)

Cambridge Modern History, volumes 1 and 2 (1907)

Catholic Encyclopedia, 16 volumes (1913 ff.)

CHEYNEY, EDWARD, *European Background of American History* (1904)

CLARK, WILLIAM, *The Anglican Reformation* (1897)

DALLMANN, WILLIAM, *Robert Barnes* (n.d.)

DALLMANN, WILLIAM, *John Hus* (1915)

DALLMANN, WILLIAM, *William Tyndale* (n.d.)
DARMSTAETTER, J., *A History of the Reformation* (1916)
DAU, WILLIAM, *Four Hundred Years. Commemorative Essays on the Reformation* (1917)
DAU, WILLIAM, *The Leipzig Debate* (1919)
DAU, WILLIAM, *At the Tribunal of Caesar* (1921)
DEITZ, REGINALD, *Luther and the Reformation* (1953)
DITTMAR, HEINRICH, *Die Geschichte der Welt vor und nach Christus*. Vol. IV (1861)
DURANT, WILLIAM, *The Renaissance*. Part V of *The Story of Civilization* (1953)
DURANT, WILLIAM, *The Reformation*. Part VI of *The Story of Civilization* (1957)

EMERTON, EPHRAIM, *The Beginning of Modern Europe* (1917)
EMERTON, EPHRAIM, *Desiderius Erasmus of Rotterdam* (1899)
Encyclopedia Americana, 30 volumes (1950)
Encyclopedia Britannica, 24 volumes (1953)
Encyclopedia of Religion and Ethics, 13 volumes (1926 ff.)

FIFE, ROBERT, *The Revolt of Martin Luther* (1957)
FISHER, GEORGE, *The Reformation* (1873)
FISKE, JOHN, *The Discovery of America* (1902)
FOX, JOHN, *An Universal History of Christian Martyrdom* (1838)
FREY, AUGUST, *Geschichte der Reformation* (1880)
FROUDE, J. A., *Life and Letters of Erasmus* (1894)

GEIGER, LUDWIG, *Renaissance und Humanismus in Italien und Deutschland* (in Wilhelm Oncken. *Allgemeine Geschichte* II, 8) (1882)
GILMORE, MYRON, *The World of Humanism* (1952)
GOBINEAU, J. A., *The Renaissance* (n.d.)
GRIMM, HAROLD, *The Reformation Era* (1954)
GRISAR, HARTMANN, *Martin Luther, His Life and Work* (1953)

HAEUSSER, LUDWIG, *The Period of the Reformation* (n.d.)
HEARNSHAW, FOSSEY, *The Social and Political Ideas of Some Great Thinkers of the Renaissance and Reformation* (1925)
HELPS, ARTHUR, *Christopher Columbus* (n.d.)
HERTZ, FREDERICK, *The Development of the German Public Mind* (1957)
HEUSSI, KARL, *Kompendium der Kirchengeschichte* (1933)
HOLL, KARL, *Luther* (1923)
HOLLINGS, MARY, *Europe in Renaissance and Reformation* (1911)
HUDSON, W. H., *The Story of the Renaissance* (1912)
HULME, EDWARD, *The Renaissance, the Protestant Revolution and the Catholic Reformation* (1915)

JACKSON, SAMUEL, *Huldreich Zwingli, the Reformer of German Switzerland* (1900)

JANELLE, PIERRE, *The Catholic Reformation* (1949)
JANSSEN, J., *History of the German People at the Close of the Middle Ages,* 17 volumes (1896 f.)
Johnson's New Universal Encyclopedia, 4 volumes (1884)

Kirchliches Handlexikon, 7 volumes (1902)
KOEHLER, WALTHER, *Dokumente zum Ablassstreit von 1517* (1902)
KOEHLER, WALTHER, *Die Geisteswelt Ulrich Zwinglis* (1920)
KOEHLER, WALTHER, *Luther und die Kirchengeschichte* (1900)
KOEHLER, WALTHER, *Reformation und Ketzerprozess* (1901)
KOESTLIN, JULIUS, *Martin Luther. Sein Leben und seine Schriften* (1903)
KOLDE, THEODOR, *Martin Luther. Eine Biographie* (1884)
KOOIMAN, WILLEM J., *By Faith Alone. The Life of Martin Luther* (1955)

LAGARDE, ANDRE, *The Latin Church in the Middle Ages* (1915)
LAMARTINE, ALPHONSE, *Life of Christopher Columbus* (1860)
LANG, AUGUST, *Zwingli and Calvin* (1913)
LANGE, WILIAM, *An Encyclopedia of World History* (1948)
LEHMANN, EDVARD AND PETER PETERSEN, *Illustrierte Weltgeschichte,* 6 volumes (1928)
LILJE, HANNS, *Luther. Anbruch und Krise der Neuzeit* (1948)
LINDSAY, THOMAS, *A History of the Reformation* (1906)
LUCAS, J., *The Renaissance and the Reformation* (1934)
Lutheran Cyclopedia (1954)

MACKINNON, JAMES, *Luther and the Reformation,* 4 volumes (1925 ff.)
MATHER, F. J., *History of Italian Painting in the Renaissance* (1922)
MENZEL, WOLFGANG, *Germany from the Earliest Period,* vol. II (1900)
MERZ, GEORG, *Der Vorreformatorische Luther* (1926)
MERZ, GEORG, *Glaube und Politik* (1933)
Meyers Lexikon, 15 volumes (1924-1933)
MONNIER, P., *La Quattrocento* (1920)
MOSSE, GEORGE, *The Reformation* (1953)
MUENTER, FRIEDRICH, *Kirchengeschichte von Dänemark und Norwegen* (1823)

PALMER, R. R., *A History of the Modern World* (1950)
PATER, WALTER, *The Renaissance* (1919)
PERRY, GEORGE, *History of the Reformation in England* (1898)
PETER, P., *History of the Reformation* (1916)
PHILIPPS, MARGARET, *Erasmus and the Northern Renaissance* (1949)
POLLARD, ALBERT, *Henry VIII* (1905)
POLLARD, ALBERT, *Thomas Cranmer and the English Reformation* (1904)
PRESCOTT, WILLIAM, *History of the Conquest of Mexico* (1936)
PRESCOTT, WILLIAM, *History of the Conquest of Peru* (1874)
PRESCOTT, WILLIAM, *Mexico and the Life of the Conqueror Fernando Cortez* (1898)
PRESTAGE, EDGAR, *The Portuguese Pioneers* (1933)

RANKE, LEOPOLD VON, *History of the Popes, the Church and State* (1902)
RANKE, LEOPOLD VON, *History of the Reformation in Germany* (1845)

350 Bibliography

350   Bibliography

350 BIBLIOGRAPHY

Realenzyklopaedie fuer protestantische Theologie und Kirche, 24 volumes (1896 ff.)
Reformation Album, 24 Bilder (1885)
REU, JOHANN MICHAEL, *Luther's German Bible* (1934)
REU, JOHANN MICHAEL, *Life of Martin Luther* (1917)
REU, JOHANN MICHAEL, *The Augsburg Confession* (1930)
REU, JOHANN MICHAEL, *Thirty Years of Luther Research* (1917)
RICHARD, JAMES, *Philip Melanchthon, Protestant Preceptor of Germany* (1898)
RUGE, SOPHUS, *Geschichte des Zeitalters der Entdeckungen* (in Wilhelm Oncken. *Allgemeine Geschichte* II, 9) (1881)
RUPP, E. GORDON, *Luther's Progress to the Diet of Worms* (1951)

Schaff-Herzog Encyclopedia of Religious Knowledge, The New, 12 volumes (1908 ff.)
SCHAFF, PHILIPP, *History of the Christian Church* (1915)
SCHRECKENBACH, PAUL, *Martin Luther* (1921)
SCHWIEBERT, ERNEST, *Luther and His Times* (1950)
SCOTT, G., *The Architecture of Humanism* (1924)
SECKENDORFF, VEIT LUDWIG VON, *Reformationsgeschichte* (1781)
SEEBOHM, FRED, *The Era of the Protestant Revolution* (1928)
SERGEANT, LEWIS, *John Wycliff* (1892)
SMETZ, WILHELM, *Kurze Geschichte der Paepste* (1829)
SMITH, PRESERVED, *The Age of the Reformation* (1920)
SMITH, PRESERVED, AND CHARLES M. JACOBS, *Luther's Correspondence*, 2 volumes (1913 ff.)
STEINHAEUSER, ALBERT, AND OTHERS, *Leaders of the Lutheran Reformation* (1917)
STICKELBERGER, EMANUEL, *Reformation. Ein Heldenbuch* (1928)
STUMP, JOSEPH, *Life of Melanchthon* (1897)
SWARZE, M. N., *John Hus* (1915)
SYMONDS, J. A., *The Renaissance in Italy* (1875)

TAYLOR, HENRY O., *Thought and Expression in the Sixteenth Century* (1920)
THOMPSON, JAMES, *The Civilization of the Renaissance* (1929)
TSCHAN, FRANCIS, HAROLD J. GRIMM, AND J. DUANE SQUIRE, *Western Civilization. The Decline of Rome to 1600* (1942)

VAN DYKE, PAUL, *Age of the Renaissance* (1897 ff.)
VEDDER, HENRY, *The Reformation in Germany* (1914)

WALKER, WILLIAM, *Reformation* (in Fulton. *Ten Epochs of Church History*) (n.d.)
WALTHER, WILHELM, *Fuer Luther, wider Rom* (1906)
WATSON, PHILIP, *Let God be God* (1947)
WOLF, RICHARD, *Our Protestant Heritage* (1956)

ZANGE, FRIEDRICH, *Zeugnisse der Kirchengeschichte* (1926)

Various articles in American and German theological and historical journals.

Indexes

GENERAL INDEX TO PART ONE

BIOGRAPHICAL INDEX TO PART TWO

Acontius, James (ca. 1520-1567). Anti-Trinitarian leader of Trent. Wrote "Stratagems of Satan," 265

Adelmann, Conrad (1462-1547). Supporter of Luther at Augsburg. Returned to Roman Church, 310

Adolph of Anhalt (1458-1526). Bishop of Merseburg (1514-1526). Burned Luther's books and persecuted Lutherans, 332

Adrian VI (1459-1523). Pope (1522-1523). Professor at Louvain. Tutor of Charles V. Administrator of Spain. Last non-Italian pope, 186, 305, 308, 328, 336

Adrian of Antwerp (d. 1531). Lutheran martyr, 188

Adrian, Matthew. Taught Hebrew at Wittenberg (1520-21). Baptized Spanish Jew, 134, 153

Aepinus, John (1499-1553). Pastor at Hamburg. Superintendent (1532). D.D., Wittenberg (1533), 255

Agricola, John (1499-1566). "Magister Islebius" (from Eisleben). Table-companion of Luther. Educator. Antinomian controversy against Melanchthon (1527, 1537-40). Court chaplain of Joachim II. Helped draft Augsburg Interim (1548), 69, 85, 96, 97, 102, 108, 119, 125, 126, 140, 145, 147, 148, 157, 184

Agricola, Michael (ca. 1510-1557). Reformer of Finland. Student of Luther, 122, 177, 183, 184

Agricola, Stephen (d. 1547). Augustinian. Later pastor at Augsburg and Eisleben, 131, 140

Agrippa, Henry Cornelius (1486-1535). Occultist. First was for Luther, but later followed Erasmus, 310, 311

Ahlfeldt, Bartholomew Count von (ca. 1550). Protector of Menno, 282

Alba, Fernando Alvarez, Duke of (1508-1583?). General of Charles V and Philip II. Persecutor of Lutherans, 186, 190, 287, 301

Alber, Erasmus (ca. 1500-1553). Reformer of Hesse. Later in Brandenburg and Rothenburg-Tauber. Died in Mecklenburg, 130, 139

Alber, Matthew (1495-1570). Reformer of Swabia. Studied with Melanchthon at Tuebingen. Pastor in Reutlingen. Friend of Brenz, 133, 147, 234

Albert von Hohenzollern
See (1) Albert of Mainz; (2) Albert of Prussia

Albert of Mainz (1490-1545). Brother of Elector Joachim I. Archbishop of Magdeburg (1513), administrator of Halberstadt, archbishop of Mainz (1514). Cardinal (1518). Employed Tetzel to sell indulgences. Religiously

indifferent. On good terms with Luther until 1530, 80, 88, 103, 119, 120, 125, 126, 130, 159, 193, 198, 199, 204, 211, 213, 216, 221, 292, 293, 299, 307, 308, 312, 322, 324, 333, 334, 335
Albert of Mansfeld (1480-1560). Luther's "Beloved Count." Luther died in Eisleben on a mission of reconciliation between Albert and his family, 139, 157, 290, 310
Albert of Prussia (1490-1568). Last Grandmaster of Teutonic Knights, Duke of Prussia (1525). Introduced Reformation, 85, 120, 123, 128, 129, 292, 307, 332
Albert of Saxony (d. 1500). Father of Duke George. Divided Saxony with his brother Ernest, father of Frederick the Wise and John the Constant, 289, 290, 296
Alciati, Andrea. Teacher of Calvin at Bourges, 241
Aleander, Jerome (1480-1542). Papal nuncio at Worms (1521). Cardinal (1536). Persecuted Lutherans in the Netherlands and France, 154, 195, 297, 306, 321, 327, 329, 330
Alesius, Alexander (1500-1565). Reformer of Scotland. Studied with Barnes in Wittenberg, 246, 255
Alexander VI. Pope (1492-1503). Father of Cesare and Lucretia Borgia, 335, 337
Alveld, Augustine von (1480-1535?). Foe of Luther. Wrote "On the Apostolic See," 306, 321
Algersheimer. Lutheran of Frankfurt-Main. At Wittenberg Concord (1536), 234
Amandus, John (d. 1530). Lutheran pastor. Caused unrest in Prussia and the Hartz mountains, 128, 129
Ameaux, Pierre. Merchant of Geneva. Arrested by Calvin, 225
Amerbach, Boniface (1495-1562). Close friend of Erasmus, 154
Amsdorf, Nicholas von (1483-1565). Born at Torgau. Ph.M., Wittenberg (1504). Helped Luther translate the Old Testament. Pastor at Magdeburg (1524). Reformer of Magdeburg, Goslar, Eimbeck, Meissen. Bishop of Naumburg-Zeitz (1542-47). After Smalcald War moved to Weimar and Eisenach. Supported Flacius against Melanchthon, 80, 83, 86, 87, 88, 89, 90, 94, 104, 125, 145, 270, 333
Andersen, Jens. Catholic bishop of Viborg. Enemy of Tausen, 179
Andreae, Jacob (1528-1590). Co-author of Formula of Concord, 133
Andreae, Laurentius (1482-1552). Chancellor of Gustavus Vasa of Sweden. Helped Olavus and Laurentius Petri introduce Reformation, 175, 176, 181, 182, 183
Anhalt, Prince of. Beggar monk at Magdeburg who impressed Luther, 72, 73
Anne Boleyn, Queen of England (1533-36), 245, 246, 252, 253, 294
Anne of Brittany, Queen of France (1491-1514), 284
Anne of Cleve (1515-1557), Queen of England (1540), 254, 295
Anselm, Thomas (d. ca. 1521). Melanchthon's printer at Hagenau, 154
Apel, John (1486-1536). Canon at Wuerzburg. Married a nun. Professor at Wittenberg. Later chancellor of Albert of Prussia, 140
Aquensis, Peter. Canon at Muenster. Controversy with Luther (1520), 321
Aquila, Caspar (1488-1560). Assisted in translation of Old Testament (1523-27). Later pastor at Saalfeld. Pugnacious Lutheran, 134
Arason, John (d. 1550). Last Catholic bishop in Iceland. Lynched, 173

372 INDEXES

Holbein, Hans (The Younger) (1497-1543). Famous painter, 131, 154, 158, 159, 161
Honter, John (d. 1549). Reformer of Transylvania, 191
Hoogstraten, James (ca. 1460-1527). Inquisitor of Cologne. Enemy of Reuchlin, Erasmus and Luther, 117, 186, 193, 200, 275, 308, 310, 314, 321, 324
Horn (Roh), John (d. 1547). Leader of Bohemian Brethren. Close contacts with Luther, 258, 259
Hubmaier, Balthasar (d. 1528). Anabaptist leader. Killed by Ferdinand I, 222, 260, 261, 274, 275, 276
Hummelberg, Michael (1487-1527). Friend of Reuchlin. Humanist, 311
Huss, John (1369?-1415). Bohemian Reformer. Martyred at Constance, 185, 258, 323, 326
Hussgen, see: Oecolampadius
Hut, Hans. Anabaptist leader, 261
Huter, Jacob. Father of the Hutterites. Tyrolean Anabaptist, 263
Hutten, Ulrich von (1488-1523). Knight and humanist. Friend of Sickingen. Supported Luther. Died as fugitive in Switzerland, 99, 154, 165, 166, 210, 227, 228, 309, 330, 334

Isabella, Queen of Castile (1474-1504). Wife of Ferdinand of Aragon, 284, 286
Isolani, Isidore de'. Italian Dominican. Urged Luther to recant (1519), 321

"Jack Sausage" (Hans Worst), see: Henry, Duke of Brunswick-Wolfenbuettel
Jacobacci, Dominic. Canonist in Rome. Helped Eck draft the Bull (1520), 231
Jane Seymour (d. 1537), Queen of England (1536-1537). Third wife of Henry VIII, 294
Jensen, Jorgen, see: Sadolin
Jensen, Thøger. Parish priest at Viborg, won over by Tausen, 171, 179
Joachim I (1474-1535), Elector of Brandenburg. Brother of Albert of Mainz. Repudiated his wife. Enemy of Luther, 107, 119, 123, 126, 157, 192, 288, 293, 299, 306, 307, 333
Joachim II (1505-1571), Elector of Brandenburg (1535-1571). Reformed his country (1539). Protected Agricola, 119, 126, 138, 139, 148, 192, 293
Joan, "Black Joan," an innkeeper's daughter and Cranmer's first wife, 251
Joan "the Mad," Queen of Castile. Mother of Charles V, 284, 286
John the Constant (1468-1532), Elector of Saxony (1525-1532). Established Lutheran Church, Inaugurated visitations. Signed Protest of Speier (1529) and Augsburg Confession (1530). Organized Smalcald League, 74, 83, 85, 109, 110, 111, 114, 116, 120, 148, 155, 164, 196, 268, 269, 271, 273, 282, 288, 289, 291, 296, 298, 299, 300, 303
John VII von Schleinitz, Bishop of Meissen (1518). Enemy of Luther, 306, 307, 332
John VI von Thurzo, Bishop of Breslau. Friendly to Luther, 127, 308
John Ernest, Duke of Saxony. At Wittenberg (1533), 255
John Frederick the Magnanimous (1503-1554), Elector of Saxony (1532-1547). Deposed by Charles V and imprisoned (1547). Freed by Maurice (1552). Loyal to Luther and the Reformation, 83, 85, 88, 89, 93, 97, 98,

INDEXES 373

104, 114, 115, 116, 127, 133, 137, 148, 155, 156, 157, 158, 160, 200, 246, 255, 289, 290, 299, 300, 301, 303, 333
Jonas, Justus (Jodocus Koch) (1493-1555). Close friend of Luther. Professor at Wittenberg. Pastor at Halle. At Luther's death bed (1546), 83, 86, 94, 97, 99, 100, 101, 102, 103, 104, 111, 142, 207, 210, 217, 231, 234, 247, 272, 316, 335
Joris, David (1501?-1556). Glazier from Delft who proclaimed himself the Messiah, 263
Joy. Co-worker of Tyndale in the translation of the New Testament, 246, 250
Jud, Leo (1482-1542). Friend of Zwingli. Helped Carlstadt, 243
Julius II (1443-1513), Pope (1503-1513), 327, 328, 335

Kaiser, Leonard (d. 1527). Lutheran at Passau. Persecuted by Eck. Martyred, 194, 196, 197
Kaufmann. Citizen of Mansfeld. Married one of Luther's sisters, 71
Kaufmann, Cyriacus. Luther's nephew. At Wittenberg (1529) and at the Coburg (1530). Later, judge in Mansfeld, 71
Kayser, Leonhard, see: Kaiser
Keller. First husband of Willibrandis Rosenblatt, 237
Kern, Justus. Former monk. Followed Muenzer in Alstedt, 141
Kessler, John (1502-1574). Reformer of St. Gall. Met Luther in the "Black Bear" of Jena (1522), 71, 121, 224, 243
Khummer. Table-companion of Luther. Wrote "Table Talk," 84, 122, 138
Koch, Jodocus, see: Justus Jonas
Koepfel, Wolfgang Fabricius (1478-1541). At Ingolstadt (1512) and Mainz (1520). Joined Reformation (1523) and lived in Strassburg, 204
Knipperdolling, Bernard. Mayor during Muenster Madness (1533-1534), 262
Knox, John (1505?-1574). Reformer of Scotland. Friend of Calvin, 226
Kohlhase, Hans ("Michael Kohlhaas") (d. 1540). Outlaw from Brandenburg who raided Wittenberg. Luther gave him absolution before he was executed, 85
Kolb, Francis (1465-1535). Reformer of Berne, 243
Kraft, Ulrich, see: Crafft
Kram, Asa von (d. 1528). Distinguished soldier. Luther dedicated to him the book "Whether Soldiers Too Can Be Saved," 154
Krapp, Catherine. Melanchthon's wife, 106
Krause. Councillor of Albert of Mainz. Committed suicide after the murder of Pastor Winkler (1528), 199
Krautwald, Valentine. Friend of Melanchthon. Later, Schwenkfeldian, 239
Kronberg, Hartmut von (d. 1549). Franconian knight. Persecuted by Albert of Mainz, but remained faithful Lutheran to the end, 154, 165, 193, 335

Lambert, Francis (1486-1530). Franciscan from Avignon. Translated Luther's works into French while at Strassburg. Later at Marburg, 121, 130, 202, 204, 250
Lang, John (ca. 1480-1548). Friend of Luther in monastery (1505). Reformer of Erfurt, 76, 80, 99, 112, 113, 125, 139, 142, 143, 321
Lang, Matthew Cardinal (1468-1540), Archbishop of Salzburg (1519-1540). Friend of Staupitz. Later persecuted Lutherans, 121, 194, 308, 318

374 Indexes

Lange, Paul (d. ca. 1536). Chronicler. Early admirer of Luther, later his enemy, 80, 309, 310, 319

Langenmantel, Christopher. Canon at Freiburg. Supported Luther at Augsburg (1518), 310

Lantschad, John von (d. 1531). Swabian knight. Helped Reformation (1525), 154

Latomus, James Masson (ca. 1475-1544). Theologian of Louvain. Ablest opponent of Luther and Erasmus in the Netherlands. Persecuted Tyndale, 311

Laurensen, Peder. Former Carmelite monk of Copenhagen. Wrote Reformation writings, 171

Lauterbach. Table-companion of Luther. Wrote "Table-Talk," 84, 122, 138

Lee, Edward (1482-1544). Archbishop of York (1531), Opposed Greek New Testament, 245, 249

Lefevre d'Etaples, Jacques (1450?-1536). "The Little Luther of France." Translated Bible (1530). Taught Justification by Faith. Influenced Calvin, 189, 203, 242

Leiffer, George. Augustinian in Erfurt. Reader at Meals (ca. 1510), 78

Leo X (1475-1521), Pope (1513-1521). Excommunicated Luther, 85, 115, 162, 166, 244, 285, 305, 306, 308, 326, 327, 328, 329, 333, 335, 336

Leonora of Portugal, Empress of Frederick III. Mother of Maximilian I, 284

Lichtenstein, Lord of. Bohemian protector of Hubmaier (1527), 275

Liegnitz, Duke of. Protector of Schwenkfeld, later expelled him, 277

Liere, Nicholas van. "Marquis of Antwerp." Persecutor of Lutherans (1520's), 249

Linck (Link), Wenceslas (1483-1547). Friend of Luther. Last Vicar-General of Augustinian Order. Married (1523) and served as pastor in Altenburg and Nuremberg, 80, 116, 124, 132, 139, 143, 144, 146, 149, 270, 318, 320

Loeser, John. Hereditary marshal of Saxony. Supported Luther, 154

Lohmueller, John. Riga city councillor. Wrote to Luther (1522) about introducing Reformation in Baltic States, 120, 129, 154

Lohr, Andrew. Prior of Augustinian monastery in Erfurt, 78

Longland, John (1473-1569), Bishop of Lincoln. Staunch Catholic, 245

Lonicer, John (1499-1569). Fellow-monk with Luther in Wittenberg. Later taught Hebrew in Freiburg. Professor at Marburg (1527), 141

Lotther, Melchior (Sr.) (d. 1528). Leipzig printer. Host to Luther (1519), 154, 161, 310, 327

Lotther, Melchior (Jr.) (d. 1542). Moved to Wittenberg (1519), but left again (1525) to work with his father in Leipzig, 84, 85, 123, 154, 160, 161, 162, 310

Lotther, Michael (d. 1555). With Melchior, Jr., in Wittenberg. Moved to Magdeburg (1529). Supporter of Flacius after Smalcald War, 84, 85, 123, 154, 160, 161, 162, 310

Lucas. Senior of the Bohemian Brethren (1520's). Friendly to Luther, 258

Lufft, Hans (1495-1584). "The Bible Printer." Mayor of Wittenberg, 85, 123, 153, 154, 160, 161, 162, 163

Lupetino (Lupetinus), Baldo. Uncle of Flacius. Martyred, 144, 190

Lupinus (Wolf), Peter (d. 1521). Professor at Wittenberg and friend of Luther, 152

Luther, Catherine, see: Bora

Praepositus, James (Probst) (1486-1562). Pastor in Bremen, 129, 140, 188, 200
Prierias, Sylvester (Mazzolini) (1456-1523). Wrote against Luther, 306, 327, 328
Probst (Propst), see: Praepositus

Quercu, William a (de Chesne). Inquisitor of Paris. Enemy of Luther, 321
Quintana, Juan de. Father-confessor of Charles V. Protected Servetus, 283

Rabe. Table-companion of Luther. Wrote "Table-Talk," 84, 122, 138
Rantzau, Johan von. Minister of Frederick I of Denmark-Norway. Protected Tausen, 170, 171
Ratzeberger, Matthew (1501-1559). Physician of Frederick the Wise and Elizabeth of Brandenburg. Wrote biography of Luther, 74, 134, 136, 156, 157, 158
Redwitz, Weigand von, Bishop of Bamberg (1522-26). Opposed papal collections, 308
Reifenstein, William (d. 1538). Baptized Jew. Tax collector. Friend of Luther, 153
Reinecke (Reinicke), John (d. 1538). Attended Magdeburg school with Luther (1497), 71, 72, 151
Reinecke (Reinicke), Peter. Mansfeld bailiff. Father of John, 71, 72
Reinhard, Anna. Zwingli's wife, 229
Reinhard, Martin. Sent to Denmark to help Christian II introduce Reformation (1520-21). Pastor at Jena. At Nuremberg (1524), 169
Reissenbusch, Wolfgang. At Wittenberg (1502). Teacher at Lichtenberg (1526), 141
Renata, Duches of Ferrara. Protected Lutherans (1530's), 190, 242
Renato, Camillo. Italian Anti-Trinitarian, 265
Rennebecher. Pastor at Eisleben. Baptized Luther (1483), 71
Reuchlin, John (1455-1522). Hebrew scholar. Great-uncle of Melanchthon. Controversy with Hoogstraten. Withdrew from Luther (1520), 105, 117, 135, 186, 200, 214, 307, 311, 314, 315, 316, 321
Rhau, George (1488-1548). Wittenberg printer and composer, 154, 164
Rhegius, Urbanus (Rieger) (1489-1541). Lutheran at Augsburg (1524). Fought against Anabaptists. Superintendent of Lueneburg (1534), 131, 280, 316
Rhenanus (Bild), Beatus (1485-1547). Co-worker of Froben (1511-1526), 204, 205, 209, 311, 315
Richard von Greifenklau, Archbishop of Trier, Elector (1511-1531). First friendly to Luther, later persecuted Lutherans, 165, 187, 192, 206, 308, 324
Rodzalowski. Provost of Prague. Hussite leader, 258
Roerer, George (1492-1557). Table-companion of Luther and his secretary. Edited Luther's works. After Smalcald War in Denmark, later in Jena, 84, 94, 122, 125, 137, 138, 211, 234
Roeubli, William. One of the first Anabapitsts of Zurich (1524), 260
Rosenblatt, Willibrandis. Wife of Keller, Oecolampadius, Capito, Bucer, 214, 237, 280